Fruits Basket

Volume 4

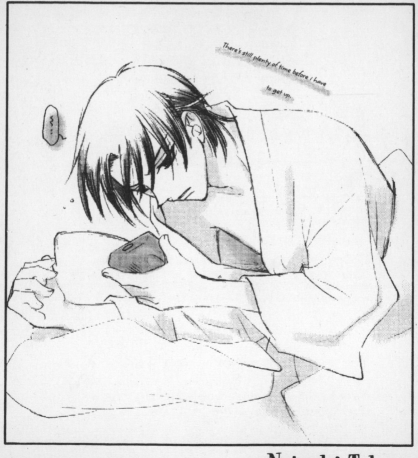

There's still plenty of time before I have to get up.

Natsuki Takaya

Translators - Alethea Nibley and Athena Nibley
Associate Editor - Kelly Sue DeConnick
Additional Translation - Alexis Kirsch
Contributing Writer - Adam Arnold
Copy Editor - Carol Fox
Retouch and Lettering - Deron Bennett
Cover Designer - Gary Shum
Graphic Designer - John Lo

Editor - Jake Forbes
Digital Imaging Manager - Chris Buford
Pre-Press Manager - Antonio DePietro
Production Managers - Jennifer Miller, Mutsumi Miyazaki
Art Director - Matt Alford
Managing Editor - Jill Freshney
VP of Production - Ron Klamert
President & C.O.O. - John Parker
Publisher & C.E.O. - Stuart Levy

E-mail: info@TOKYOPOP.com
Come visit us online at www.TOKYOPOP.com

A  Manga

TOKYOPOP Inc.
5900 Wilshire Blvd. Suite 2000
Los Angeles, CA 90036

Fruits Basket Vol. 4

ISBN: 1-59182-606-3

First TOKYOPOP printing: August 2004

20 19 18 17 16 15 14 13

Printed in the USA

Fruits Basket™

Volume 4

By
Natsuki Takaya

HAMBURG // LONDON // LOS ANGELES // TOKYO

Fruits Basket™

Table of Contents

STORY SO FAR...

Hello, I'm Tohru Honda, and I have come to know a terrible secret. After the death of my mother, I was living by myself in a tent when the Sohma family took me in. I soon learned that the Sohma family lives with a curse! Each family member is possessed by the vengeful spirit of an animal from the Chinese Zodiac. Whenever one of them becomes weak or is hugged by a member of the opposite sex, they change into their Zodiac animal!

TODAY YUKI-KUN, KYO-KUN AND I START OUR SECOND YEAR OF HIGH SCHOOL.
MOMIJI-KUN AND HATSUKASU-SAN WILL BE ATTENDING OUR SCHOOL, TOO. LIFE IS SURE TO GET EXCITING!
I WONDER WHICH MEMBERS OF THE ZODIAC I'LL ENCOUNTER THIS TIME...?

Tohru Honda

The ever-optimistic hero of our story. Recently orphaned, Tohru has taken up residence in Shigure Sohma's house, along with Yuki and Kyo. She's the only person outside of the Sohma family who knows about their Zodiac curse.

Yuki Sohma

At school he's known as Prince Charming. Polite and soft-spoken, he's the polar opposite of Kyo. Yuki is possessed by the spirit of the Rat.

Kyo Sohma

Just as the Cat of legend (whose spirit possesses him) was left out of the Zodiac, Kyo is ostracized by the Sohma family. His greatest wish in life is to defeat Yuki in battle and win his rightful place in the Zodiac.

Shigure Sohma

The enigmatic Shigure keeps a house outside of the Sohma estate where he lives with Yuki, Kyo and Tohru. He may act perverted at times, but he has a good heart. His Zodiac spirit is the Dog.

Hatori Sohma

The family doctor of the Sohma clan and one of the Juunichi (his symbol is the Dragon, which manifests as a seahorse). When Akito wills it, he erases the memories of those who stumble upon the family's secret. Hatori once had to erase the memories of the woman he loved, and ever since has been firmly against letting anyone else know the secret--even Tohru.

Fruits Basket Characters

Kagura Sohma

Stubborn and jealous as her Zodiac symbol, the Boar, Kagura is determined to marry Kyo... even if she kills him in the process.

Momiji Sohma

Playful and carefree as the Rabbit he turns into, Momiji is the youngest member of the Sohma family that Tohru has met. He's half German and half Japanese, and switches casually between the two languages. His father owns the building where Tohru works.

Hatsuharu Sohma

Usually cool, calm and collected, like a cow, Haru turns into a raging bull when his "Black" personality comes out. He's a rival to Kyo and a friend to Yuki (after years of unfounded animosity). Believe it or not, Haru and Momiji are in the same grade!

Akito Sohma

The mysterious leader of the Sohma clan, the other family members treat him with equal measures of fear and reverence. Tohru hasn't met him...yet.

Hanajima & Arisa

"A psychic freak and a yankee thug." The two best friends a girl could hope for. They always look out for Tohru; they've become friends with Yuki and Kyo as well.

Chapter 19

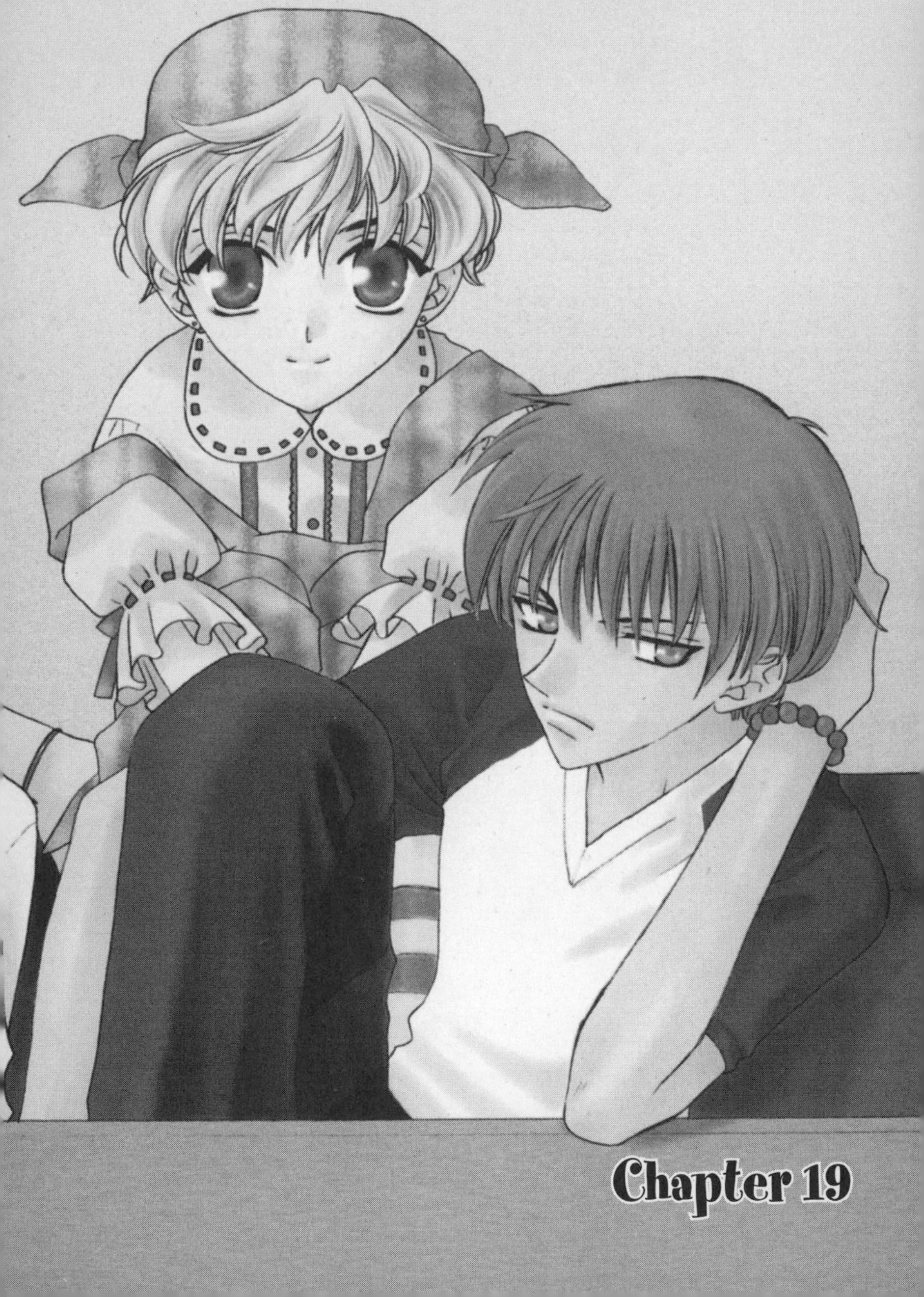

Fruits Basket™

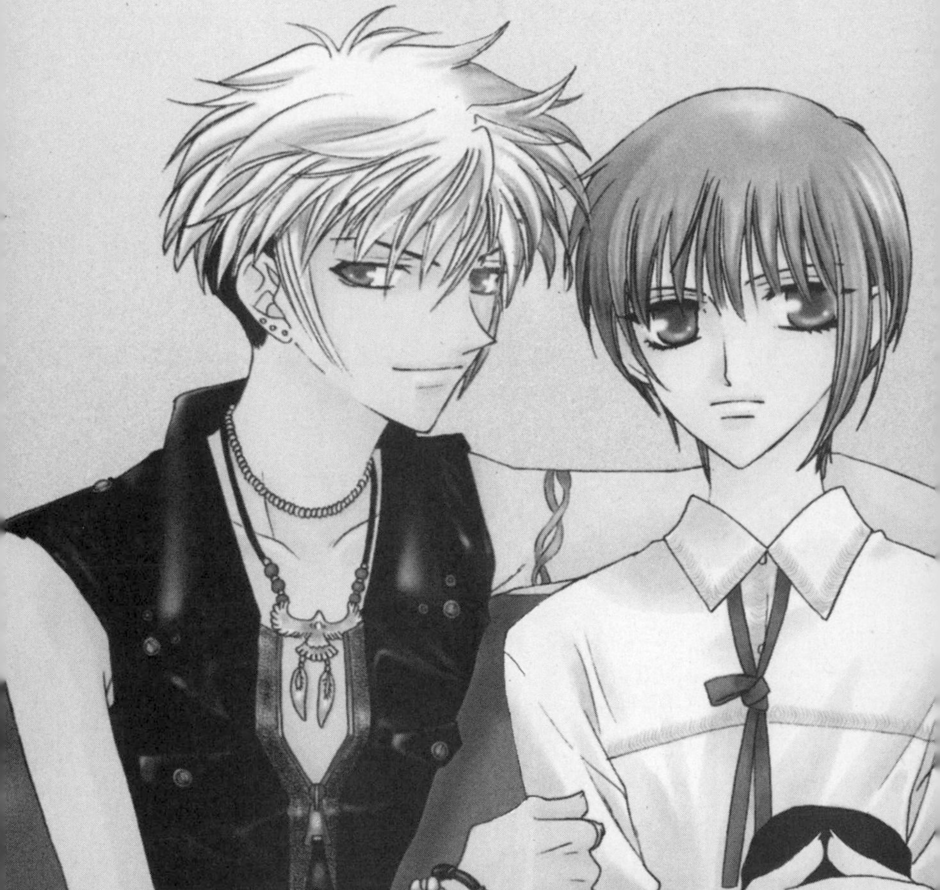

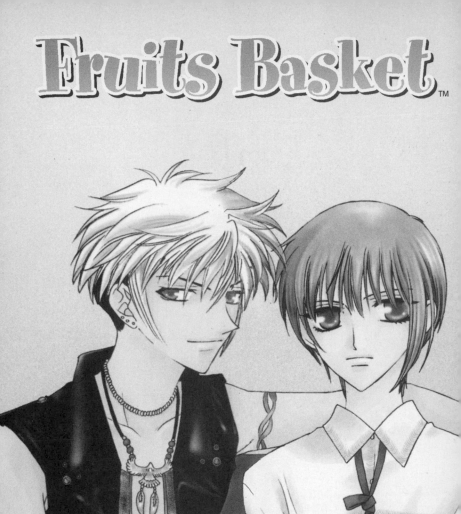

A story that's near and dear to my heart.

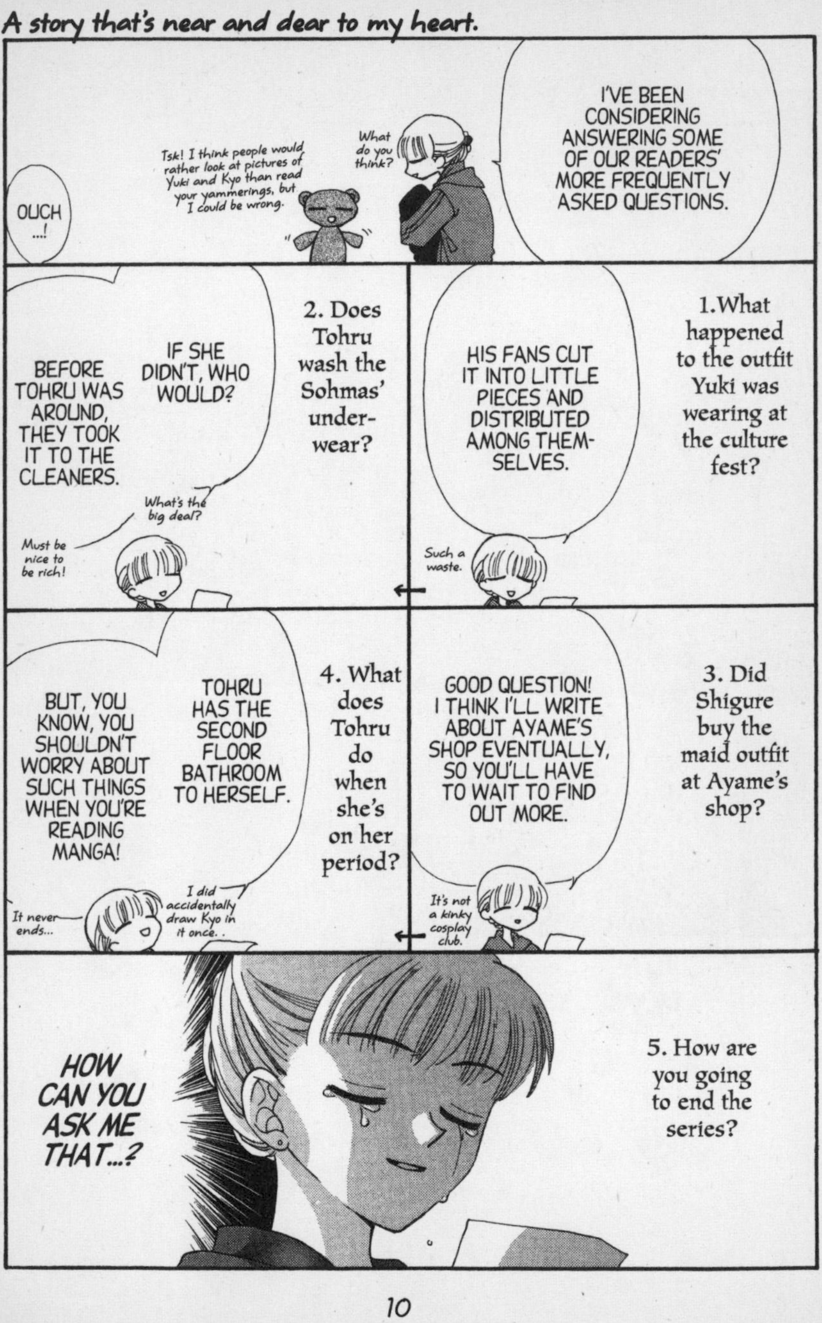

I'VE BEEN CONSIDERING ANSWERING SOME OF OUR READERS' MORE FREQUENTLY ASKED QUESTIONS.
What do you think?
Tsk! I think people would rather look at pictures of Yuki and Kyo than read your yammerings, but I could be wrong.
OUCH ...!
1.What happened to the outfit Yuki was wearing at the culture fest?
HIS FANS CUT IT INTO LITTLE PIECES AND DISTRIBUTED AMONG THEMSELVES.
Such a waste.
2. Does Tohru wash the Sohmas' underwear?
IF SHE DIDN'T, WHO WOULD?
BEFORE TOHRU WAS AROUND, THEY TOOK IT TO THE CLEANERS.
What's the big deal?
Must be nice to be rich!
3. Did Shigure buy the maid outfit at Ayame's shop?
GOOD QUESTION! I THINK I'LL WRITE ABOUT AYAME'S SHOP EVENTUALLY, SO YOU'LL HAVE TO WAIT TO FIND OUT MORE.
It's not a kinky cosplay club.
4. What does Tohru do when she's on her period?
TOHRU HAS THE SECOND FLOOR BATHROOM TO HERSELF.
BUT, YOU KNOW, YOU SHOULDN'T WORRY ABOUT SUCH THINGS WHEN YOU'RE READING MANGA!
I did accidentally draw Kyo in it once. .
It never ends...
5. How are you going to end the series?
HOW CAN YOU ASK ME THAT...?

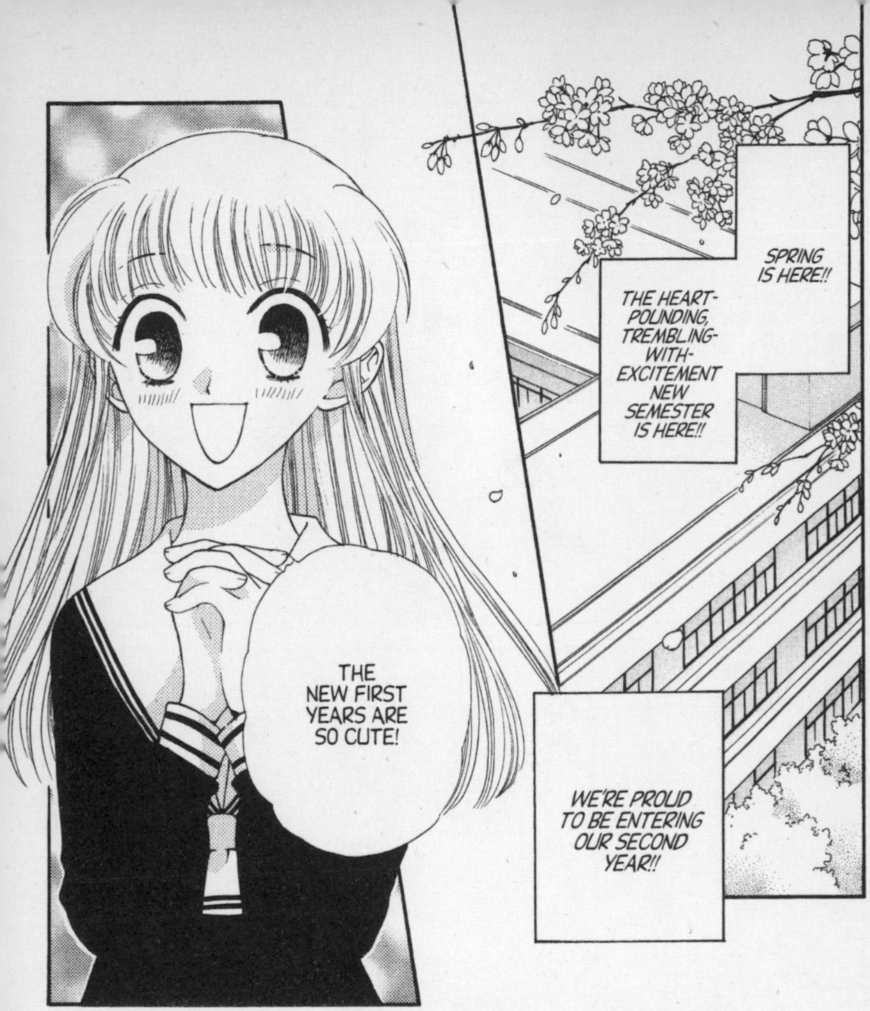
SPRING IS HERE!!
THE HEART-POUNDING, TREMBLING-WITH-EXCITEMENT NEW SEMESTER IS HERE!!
WE'RE PROUD TO BE ENTERING OUR SECOND YEAR!!
THE NEW FIRST YEARS ARE SO CUTE!

ULTRA SPECIAL BLAH BLAH BLAH 1

I forgot to mention it last time, but starting with volume 3, there will be character introductions and summaries at the beginning of each volume. I mean, there already are! I meant to do it earlier, but I just didn't have the time. At last, another Takaya dream is realized! (ha ha!)

NOTE: These features were added in Vol. 2 of the English edition.

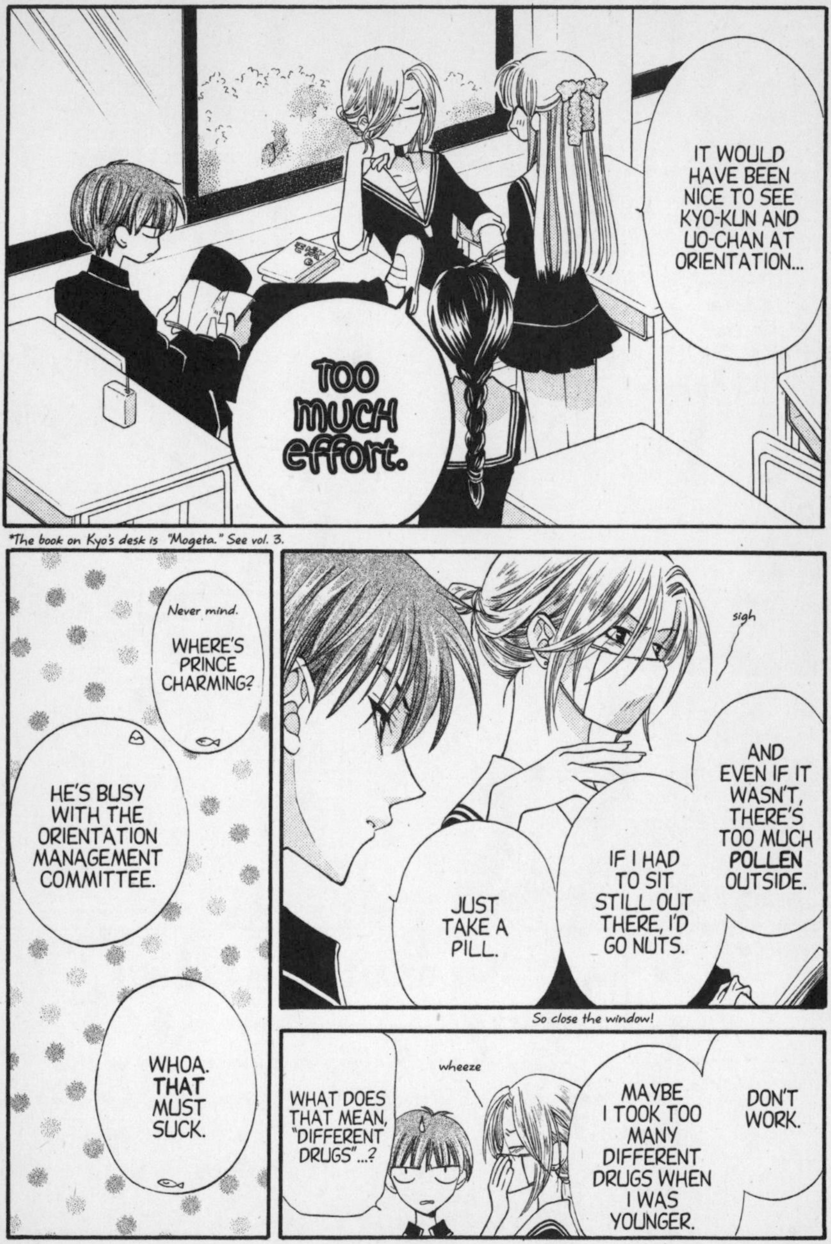
IT WOULD HAVE BEEN NICE TO SEE KYO-KUN AND UO-CHAN AT ORIENTATION...
TOO MUCH effort.
sigh
AND EVEN IF IT WASN'T, THERE'S TOO MUCH POLLEN OUTSIDE.
IF I HAD TO SIT STILL OUT THERE, I'D GO NUTS.
JUST TAKE A PILL.
So close the window!
DON'T WORK.
MAYBE I TOOK TOO MANY DIFFERENT DRUGS WHEN I WAS YOUNGER.
wheeze
WHAT DOES THAT MEAN, "DIFFERENT DRUGS"...?
Never mind.
WHERE'S PRINCE CHARMING?
HE'S BUSY WITH THE ORIENTATION MANAGEMENT COMMITTEE.
WHOA. THAT MUST SUCK.

*The book on Kyo's desk is "Mogeta." See vol. 3.

Fruits Basket 4 Part 1:

Hajimemashite! (That's Japanese for "how do you do.") Takaya here. Furuba has made it to volume 4! As each volume is released, the big picture starts to reveal itself. Until now, I've had to keep my gloating to myself! It feels so much better to let it out! (Ha!) But "Guretchi." Guretchi the jellyfish: I keep getting letters begging, "please say he isn't over 25!" Sorry. Shigure is 27. Don't worry--a man's stock only goes up as he gets older! Oh yeah, Shigure's name is pronounced without an accent--the intonation doesn't go up **or** down. So now you know. Okay, as usual I'm exhausted, but Furuba is raring to go--so let's get on with it!

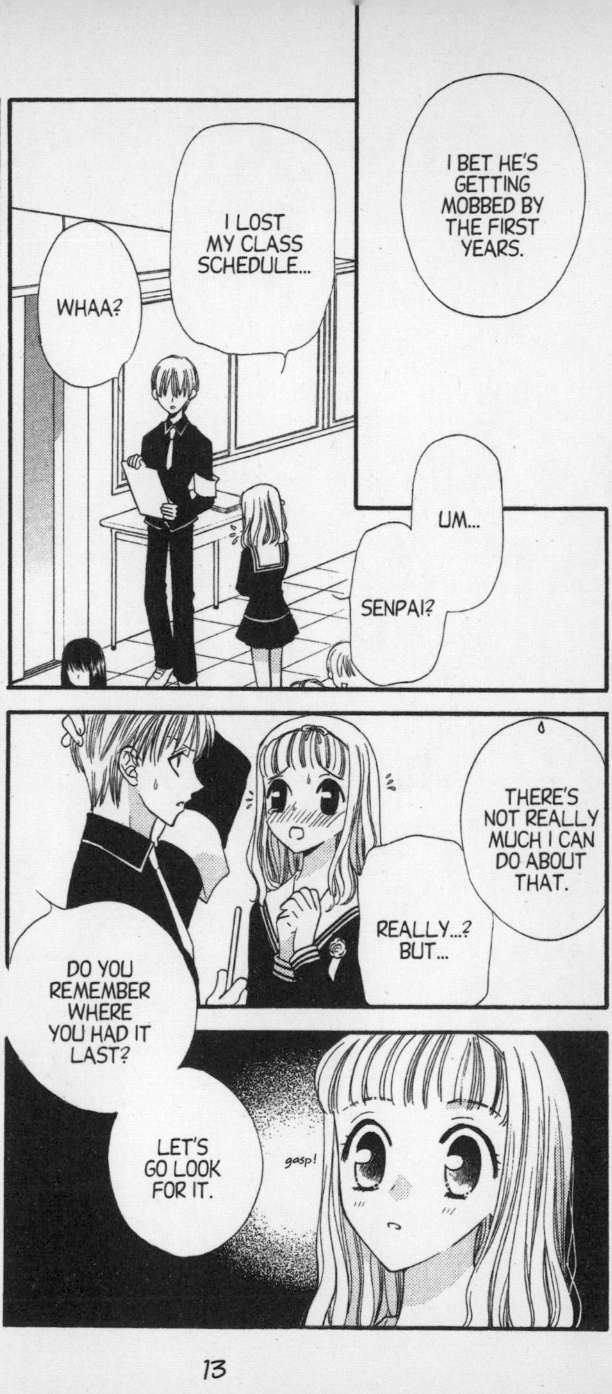
I BET HE'S GETTING MOBBED BY THE FIRST YEARS.
I LOST MY CLASS SCHEDULE...
WHAA?
UM... SENPAI?
THERE'S NOT REALLY MUCH I CAN DO ABOUT THAT.
REALLY...? BUT...
DO YOU REMEMBER WHERE YOU HAD IT LAST?
LET'S GO LOOK FOR IT.
gasp!

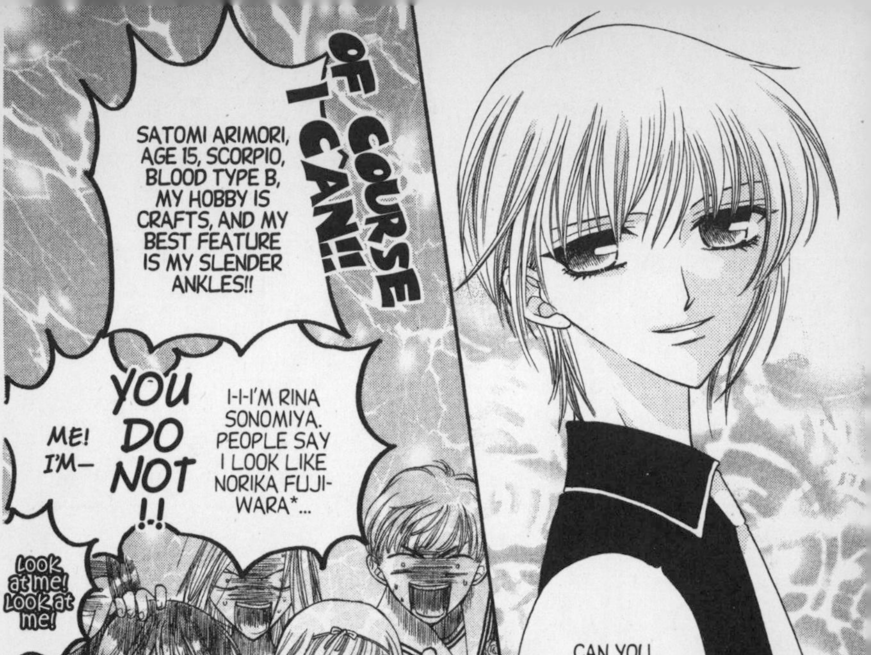
CAN YOU TELL ME YOUR NAME AND WHICH CLASS YOU'RE IN?
OF COURSE I-CAN!!
SATOMI ARIMORI, AGE 15, SCORPIO, BLOOD TYPE B, MY HOBBY IS CRAFTS, AND MY BEST FEATURE IS MY SLENDER ANKLES!!
I-I-I'M RINA SONOMIYA. PEOPLE SAY I LOOK LIKE NORIKA FUJIWARA*...
YOU DO NOT!!
ME! I'M—
Look at me! Look at me!
I'M TOO FREAKED OUT TO BE JEALOUS, SOHMA...

* A famous actress who starred in the GTO drama, she's also a model. Her official web site is: www.norikanesque.com

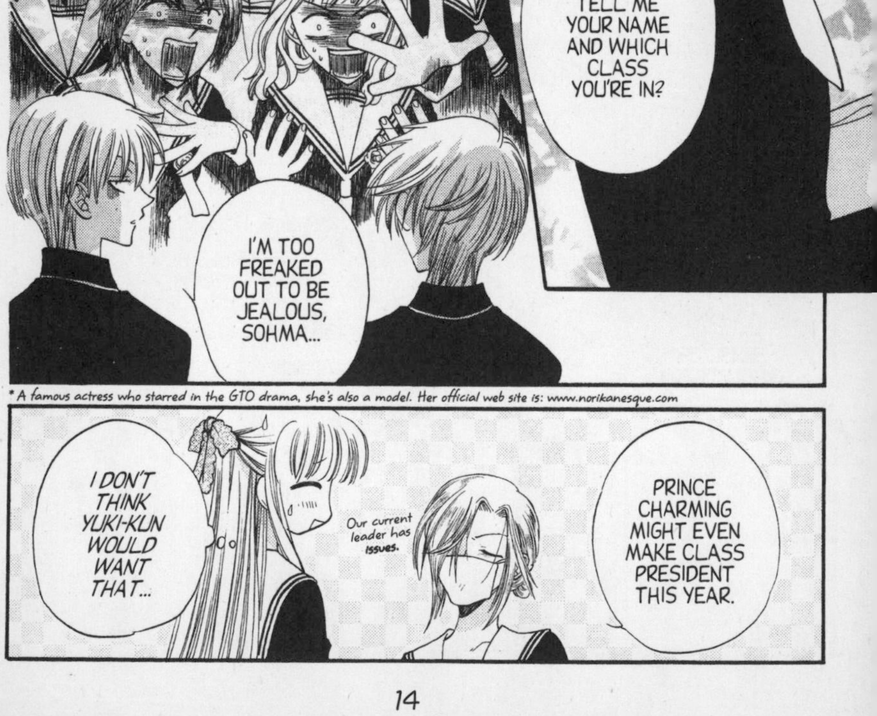
PRINCE CHARMING MIGHT EVEN MAKE CLASS PRESIDENT THIS YEAR.
Our current leader has issues.
I DON'T THINK YUKI-KUN WOULD WANT THAT...

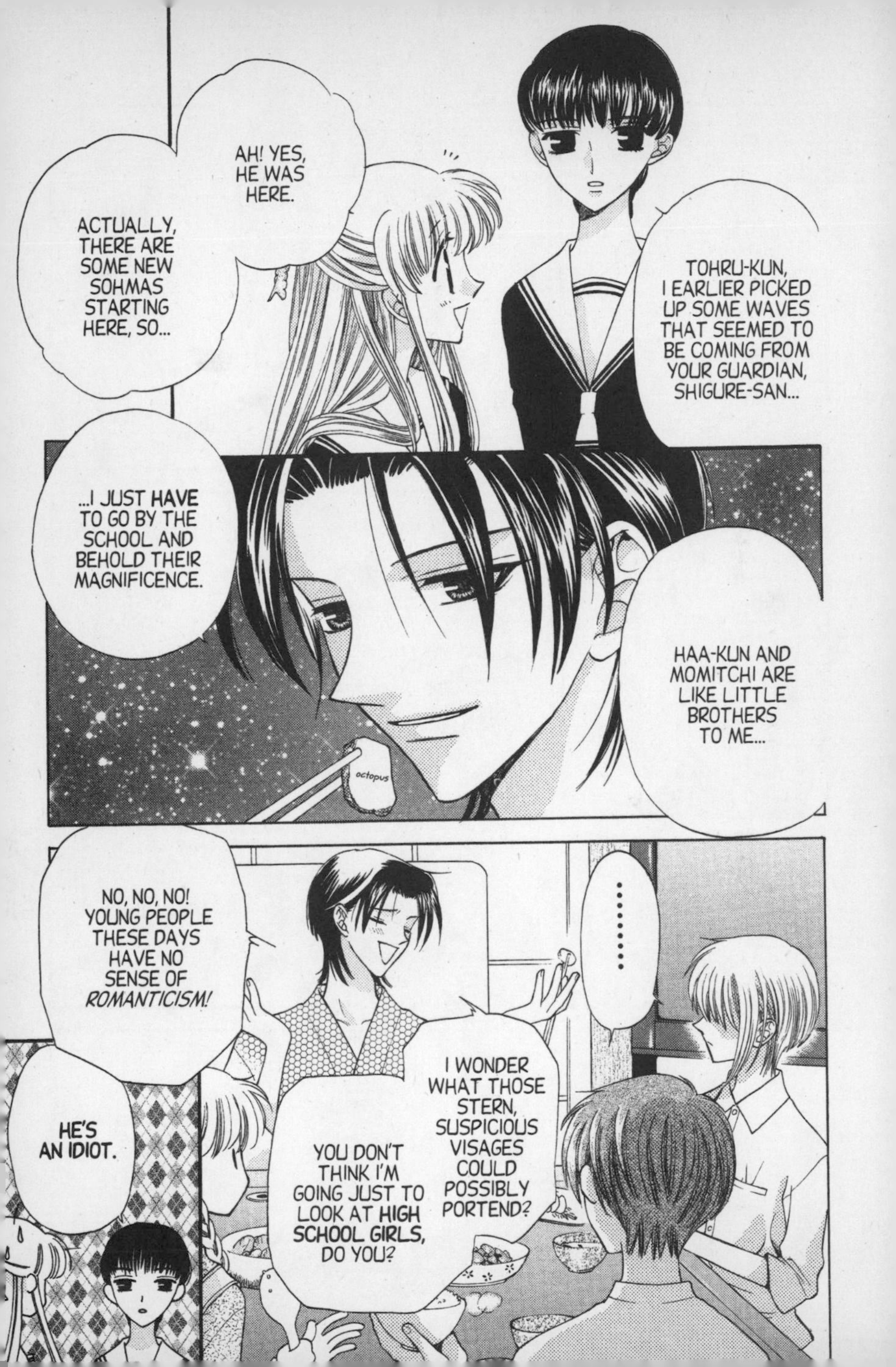

TOHRU-KUN, I EARLIER PICKED UP SOME WAVES THAT SEEMED TO BE COMING FROM YOUR GUARDIAN, SHIGURE-SAN...
AH! YES, HE WAS HERE.
ACTUALLY, THERE ARE SOME NEW SOHMAS STARTING HERE, SO...
HAA-KUN AND MOMITCHI ARE LIKE LITTLE BROTHERS TO ME...
...I JUST HAVE TO GO BY THE SCHOOL AND BEHOLD THEIR MAGNIFICENCE.
octopus
......
YOU DON'T THINK I'M GOING JUST TO LOOK AT HIGH SCHOOL GIRLS, DO YOU?
I WONDER WHAT THOSE STERN, SUSPICIOUS VISAGES COULD POSSIBLY PORTEND?
NO, NO, NO! YOUNG PEOPLE THESE DAYS HAVE NO SENSE OF *ROMANTICISM!*
HE'S AN IDIOT.

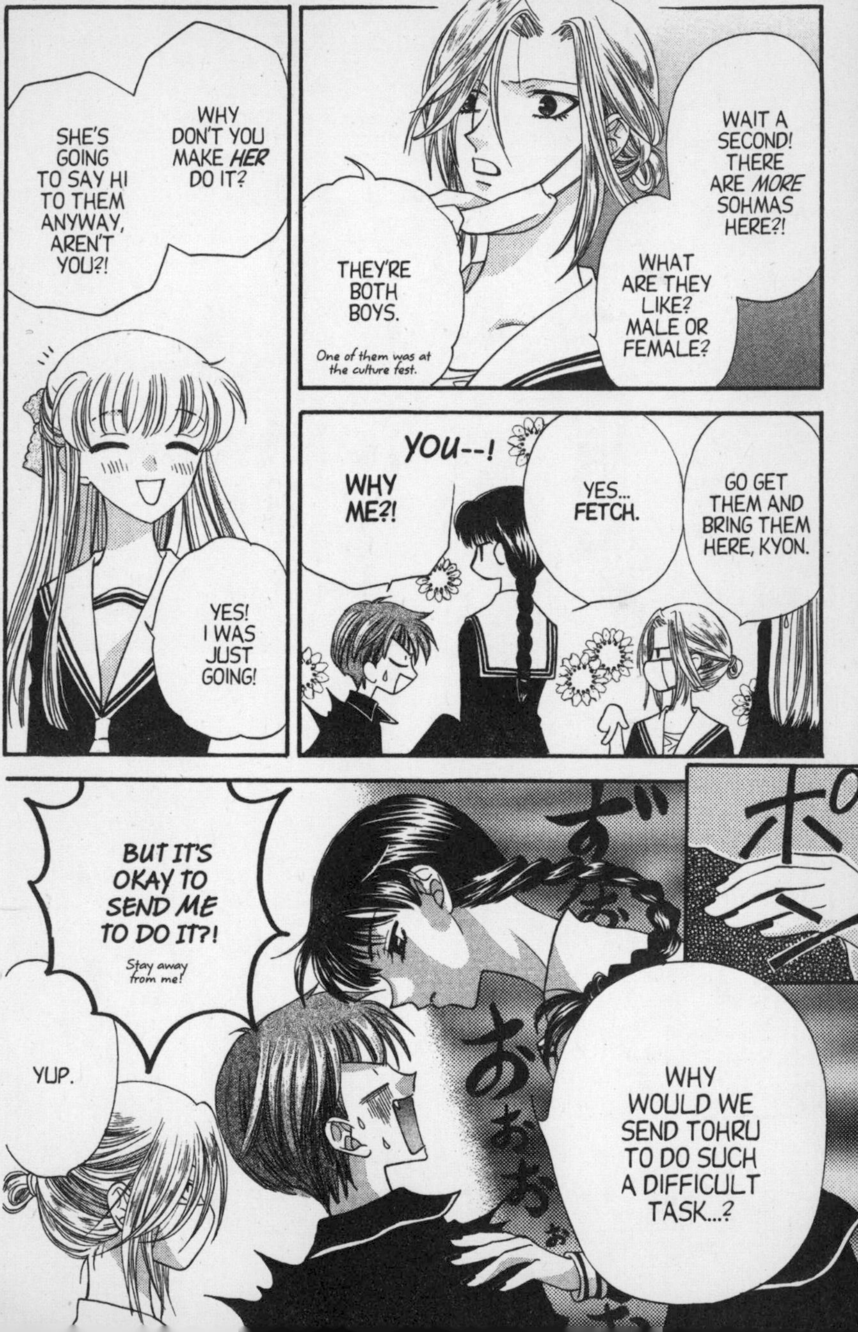
WAIT A SECOND! THERE ARE *MORE* SOHMAS HERE?!
WHAT ARE THEY LIKE? MALE OR FEMALE?
THEY'RE BOTH BOYS.
One of them was at the culture fest.
GO GET THEM AND BRING THEM HERE, KYON.
YES... FETCH.
YOU--!
WHY ME?!
WHY DON'T YOU MAKE *HER* DO IT?
SHE'S GOING TO SAY HI TO THEM ANYWAY, AREN'T YOU?!
YES! I WAS JUST GOING!
ポ
ずおおおおお
WHY WOULD WE SEND TOHRU TO DO SUCH A DIFFICULT TASK...?
BUT IT'S OKAY TO SEND ME TO DO IT?!
Stay away from me!
YUP.

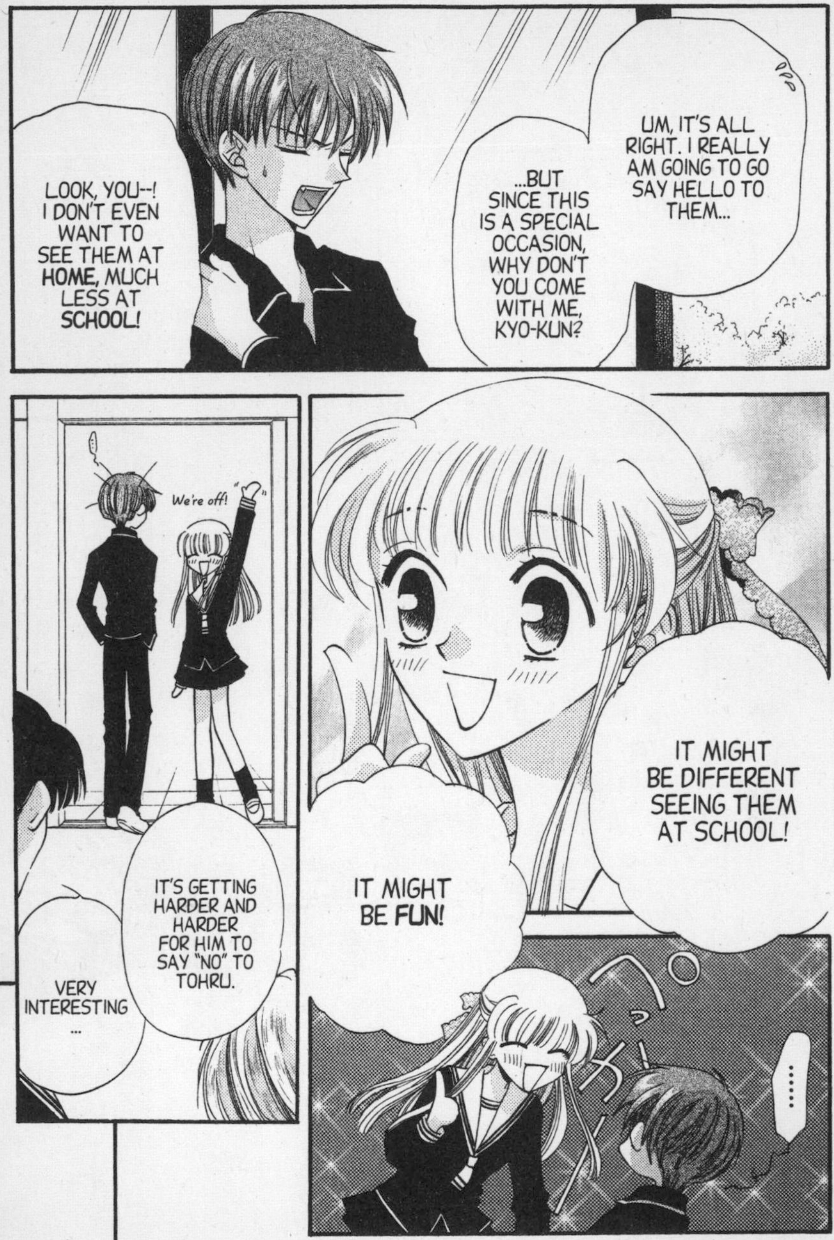
UM, IT'S ALL RIGHT. I REALLY AM GOING TO GO SAY HELLO TO THEM...
...BUT SINCE THIS IS A SPECIAL OCCASION, WHY DON'T YOU COME WITH ME, KYO-KUN?
LOOK, YOU--! I DON'T EVEN WANT TO SEE THEM AT **HOME**, MUCH LESS AT **SCHOOL**!
IT MIGHT BE DIFFERENT SEEING THEM AT SCHOOL!
IT MIGHT BE **FUN**!
......
We're off!
IT'S GETTING HARDER AND HARDER FOR HIM TO SAY "NO" TO TOHRU.
VERY INTERESTING ...

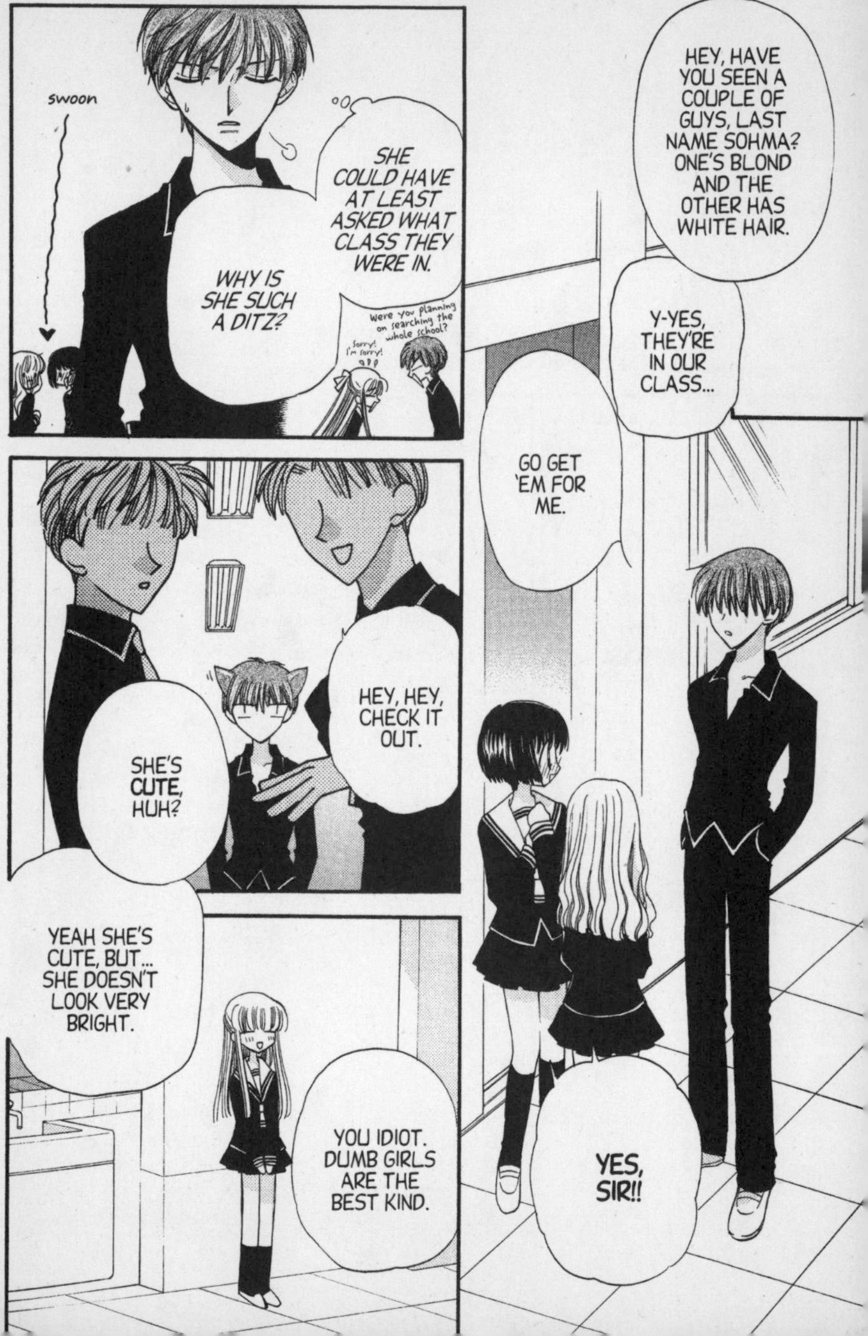
HEY, HAVE YOU SEEN A COUPLE OF GUYS, LAST NAME SOHMA? ONE'S BLOND AND THE OTHER HAS WHITE HAIR.
Y-YES, THEY'RE IN OUR CLASS...
GO GET 'EM FOR ME.
YES, SIR!!
SHE COULD HAVE AT LEAST ASKED WHAT CLASS THEY WERE IN.
WHY IS SHE SUCH A DITZ?
Were you planning on searching the whole school?
Sorry! I'm sorry!
swoon
HEY, HEY, CHECK IT OUT.
SHE'S CUTE, HUH?
YEAH SHE'S CUTE, BUT... SHE DOESN'T LOOK VERY BRIGHT.
YOU IDIOT. DUMB GIRLS ARE THE BEST KIND.

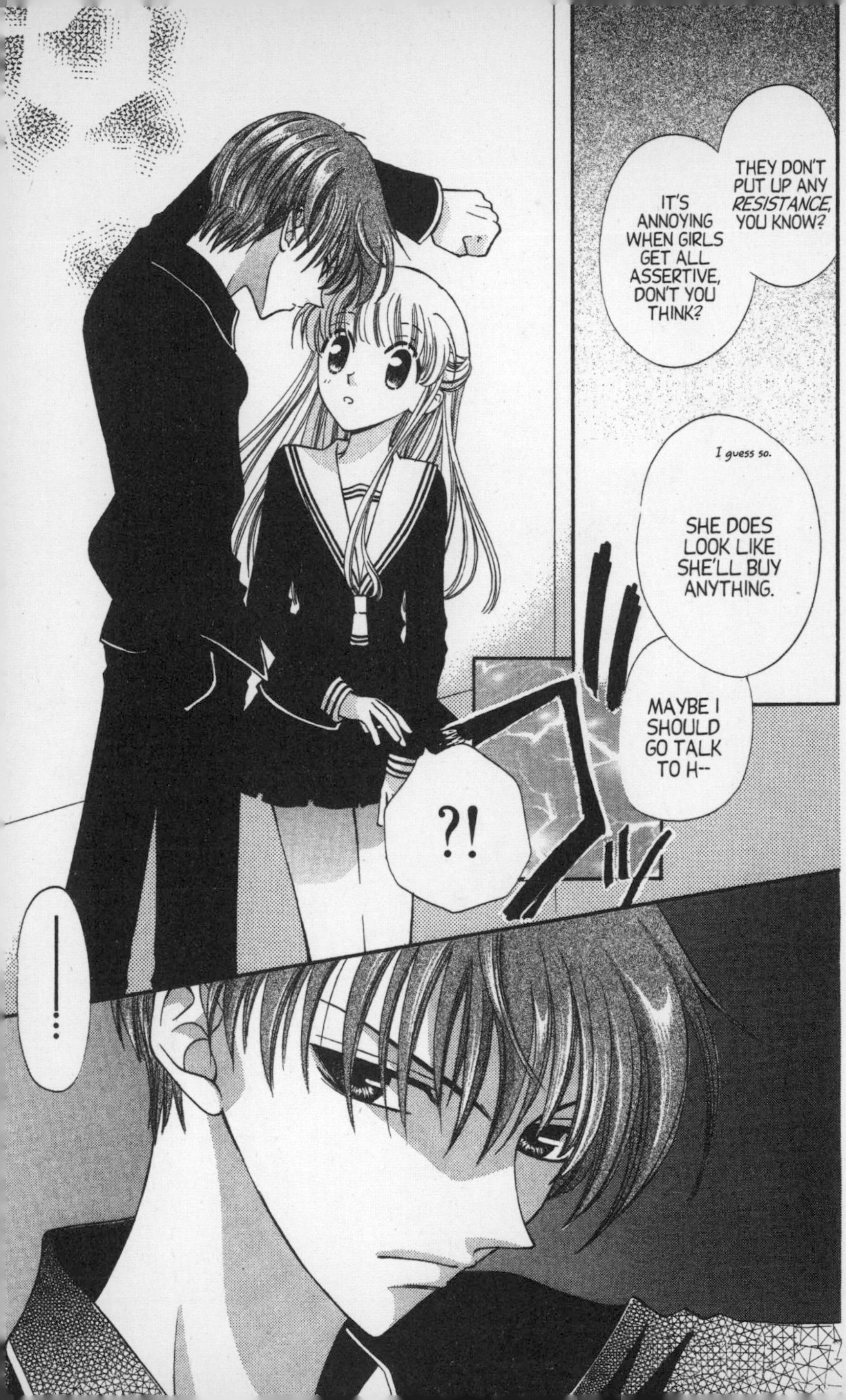
THEY DON'T PUT UP ANY *RESISTANCE*, YOU KNOW?
IT'S ANNOYING WHEN GIRLS GET ALL ASSERTIVE, DON'T YOU THINK?
I guess so.
SHE DOES LOOK LIKE SHE'LL BUY ANYTHING.
MAYBE I SHOULD GO TALK TO H--
?!
—!...

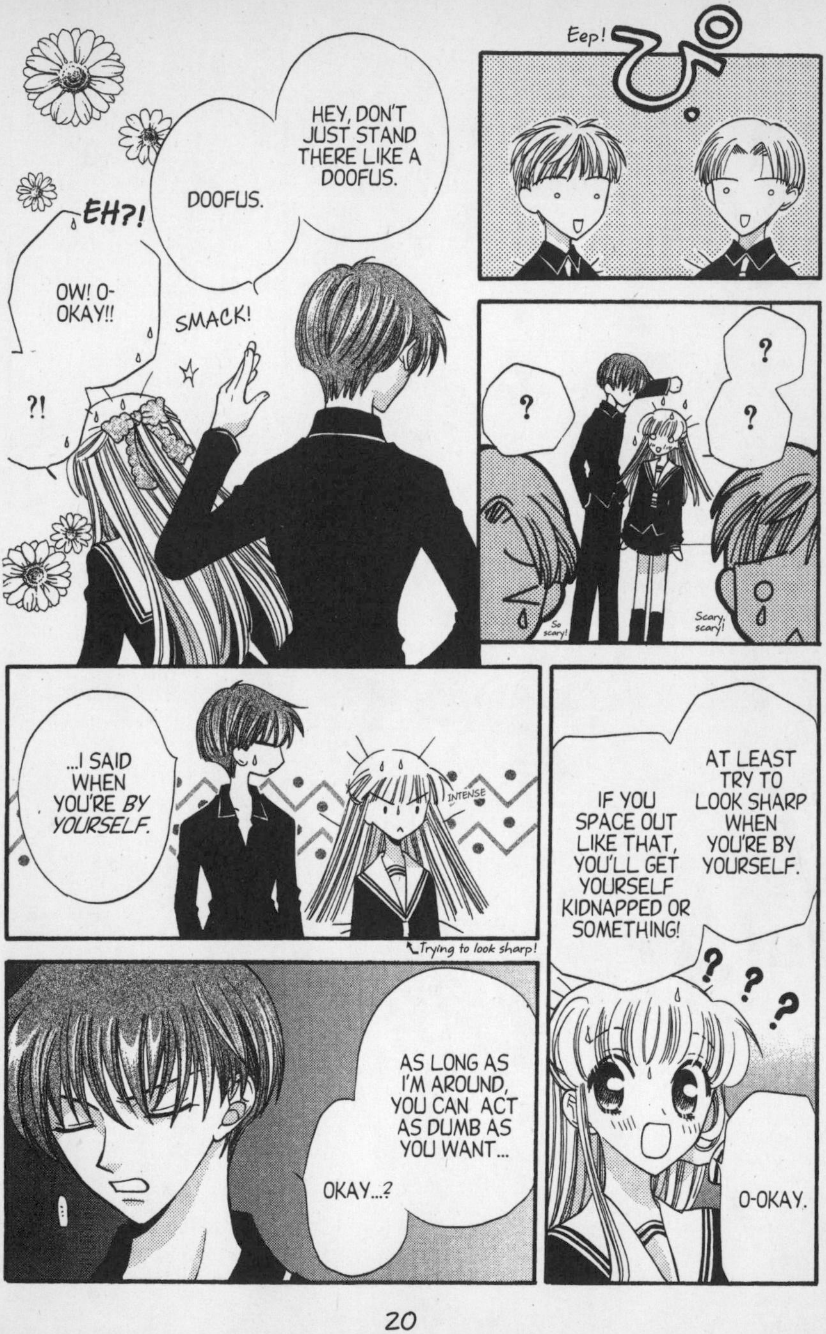
Eep!
?
?
?
So scary!
Scary, scary!
HEY, DON'T JUST STAND THERE LIKE A DOOFUS.
DOOFUS.
EH?!
OW! O-OKAY!!
SMACK!
?!
AT LEAST TRY TO LOOK SHARP WHEN YOU'RE BY YOURSELF.
IF YOU SPACE OUT LIKE THAT, YOU'LL GET YOURSELF KIDNAPPED OR SOMETHING!
O-OKAY.
...I SAID WHEN YOU'RE *BY YOURSELF*.
INTENSE
Trying to look sharp!
AS LONG AS I'M AROUND, YOU CAN ACT AS DUMB AS YOU WANT...
OKAY...?
...

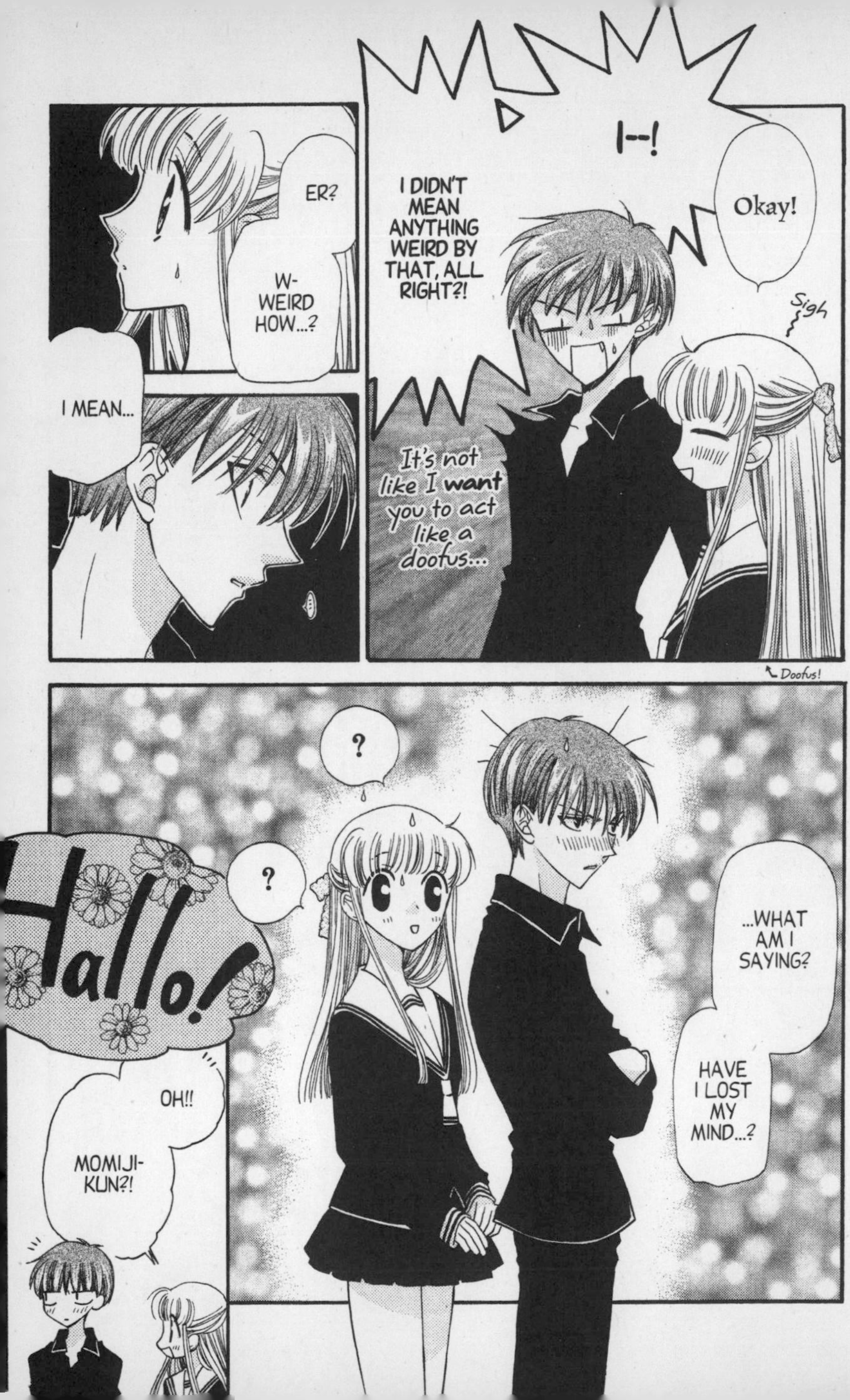
Okay!
I--!
I DIDN'T MEAN ANYTHING WEIRD BY THAT, ALL RIGHT?!
Sigh
It's not like I want you to act like a doofus...
Doofus!
ER?
W-WEIRD HOW...?
I MEAN...
?
?
...WHAT AM I SAYING?
HAVE I LOST MY MIND...?
Hallo!
OH!!
MOMIJI-KUN?!

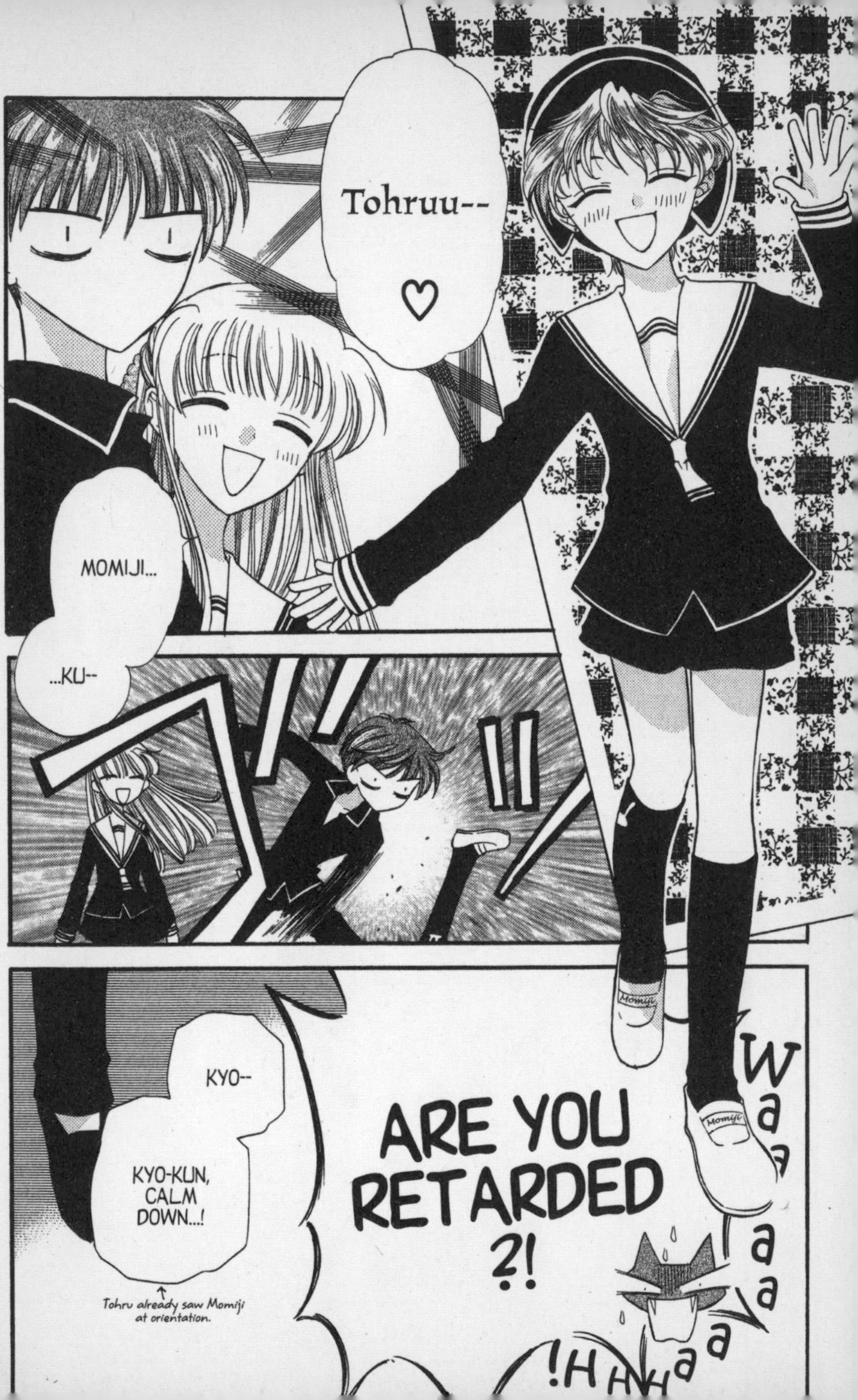
Tohruu-- ♡
MOMIJI...
...KU--
ARE YOU RETARDED ?!
Waaaaaaaaaaaaa HHHH!
KYO--
KYO-KUN, CALM DOWN...!
Tohru already saw Momiji at orientation.

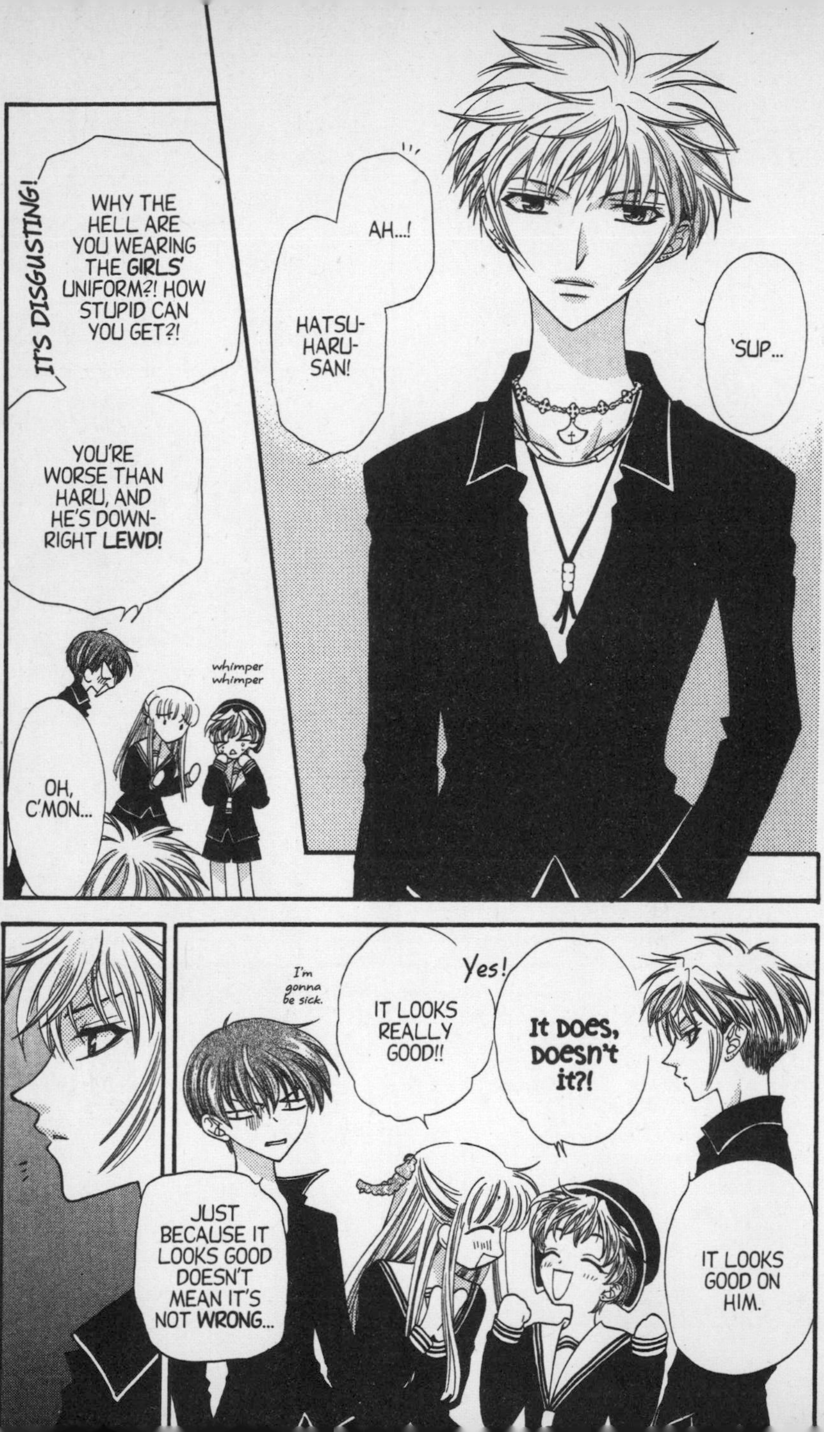
AH...! HATSU-HARU-SAN!
'SUP...
WHY THE HELL ARE YOU WEARING THE GIRLS' UNIFORM?! HOW STUPID CAN YOU GET?!
IT'S DISGUSTING!
YOU'RE WORSE THAN HARU, AND HE'S DOWN-RIGHT LEWD!
whimper whimper
OH, C'MON...
IT LOOKS GOOD ON HIM.
It does, doesn't it?!
Yes!
IT LOOKS REALLY GOOD!!
I'm gonna be sick.
JUST BECAUSE IT LOOKS GOOD DOESN'T MEAN IT'S NOT WRONG...

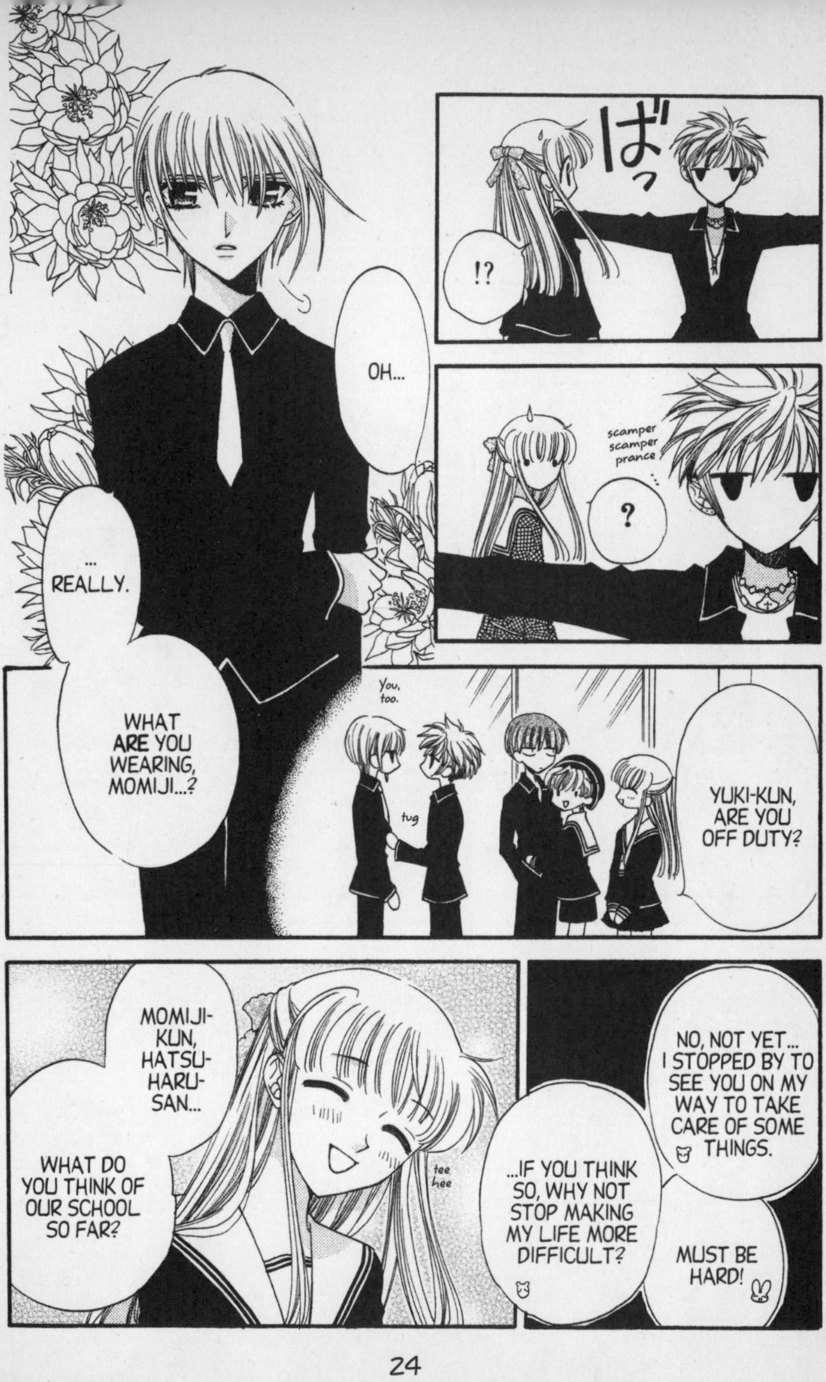
ばっ
!?
scamper scamper prance
?
OH...
...REALLY.
WHAT ARE YOU WEARING, MOMIJI...?
YUKI-KUN, ARE YOU OFF DUTY?
You, too.
tug
NO, NOT YET... I STOPPED BY TO SEE YOU ON MY WAY TO TAKE CARE OF SOME THINGS.
MUST BE HARD!
...IF YOU THINK SO, WHY NOT STOP MAKING MY LIFE MORE DIFFICULT?
MOMIJI-KUN, HATSUHARU-SAN...
WHAT DO YOU THINK OF OUR SCHOOL SO FAR?
tee hee

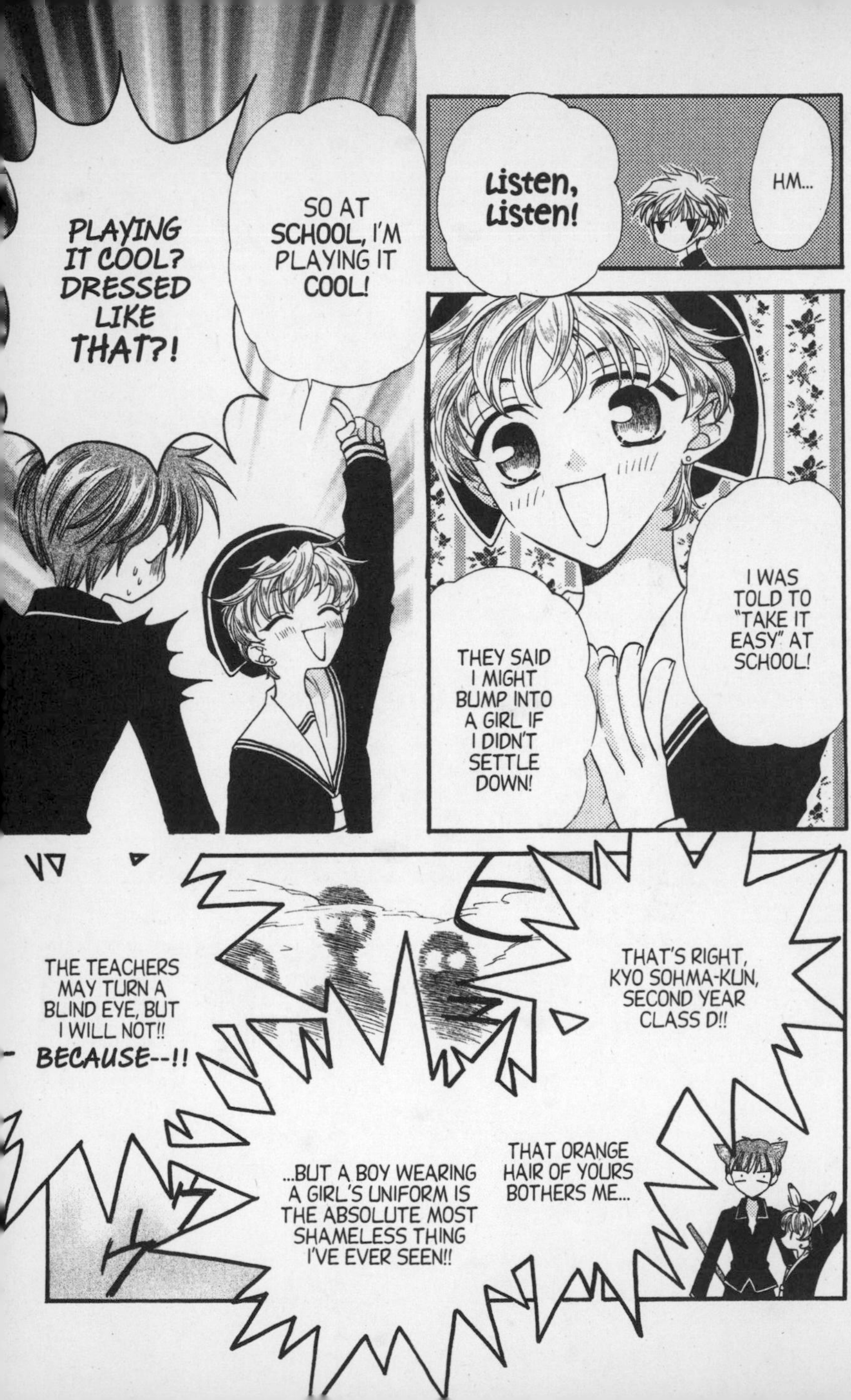
HM...
Listen, Listen!
I WAS TOLD TO "TAKE IT EASY" AT SCHOOL!
THEY SAID I MIGHT BUMP INTO A GIRL IF I DIDN'T SETTLE DOWN!
SO AT SCHOOL, I'M PLAYING IT COOL!
PLAYING IT COOL? DRESSED LIKE THAT?!
THAT'S RIGHT, KYO SOHMA-KUN, SECOND YEAR CLASS D!!
THE TEACHERS MAY TURN A BLIND EYE, BUT I WILL NOT!!
BECAUSE--!!
THAT ORANGE HAIR OF YOURS BOTHERS ME...
...BUT A BOY WEARING A GIRL'S UNIFORM IS THE ABSOLUTE MOST SHAMELESS THING I'VE EVER SEEN!!

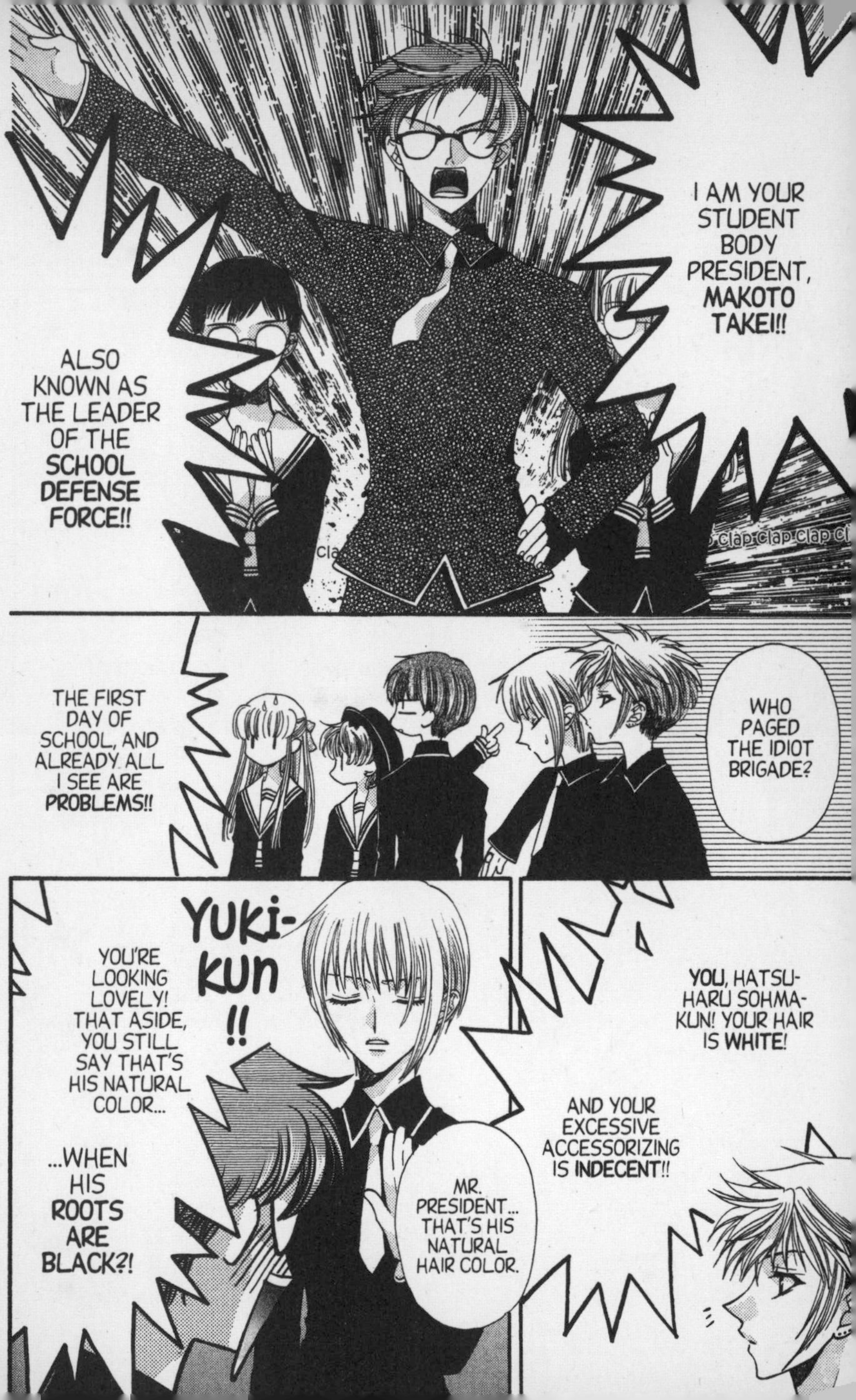
I AM YOUR STUDENT BODY PRESIDENT, MAKOTO TAKEI!!
ALSO KNOWN AS THE LEADER OF THE SCHOOL DEFENSE FORCE!!
clap clap clap
WHO PAGED THE IDIOT BRIGADE?
THE FIRST DAY OF SCHOOL, AND ALREADY ALL I SEE ARE PROBLEMS!!
YOU, HATSUHARU SOHMA-KUN! YOUR HAIR IS WHITE!
AND YOUR EXCESSIVE ACCESSORIZING IS INDECENT!!
YUKI-KUN!!
YOU'RE LOOKING LOVELY! THAT ASIDE, YOU STILL SAY THAT'S HIS NATURAL COLOR...
...WHEN HIS ROOTS ARE BLACK?!
MR. PRESIDENT... THAT'S HIS NATURAL HAIR COLOR.

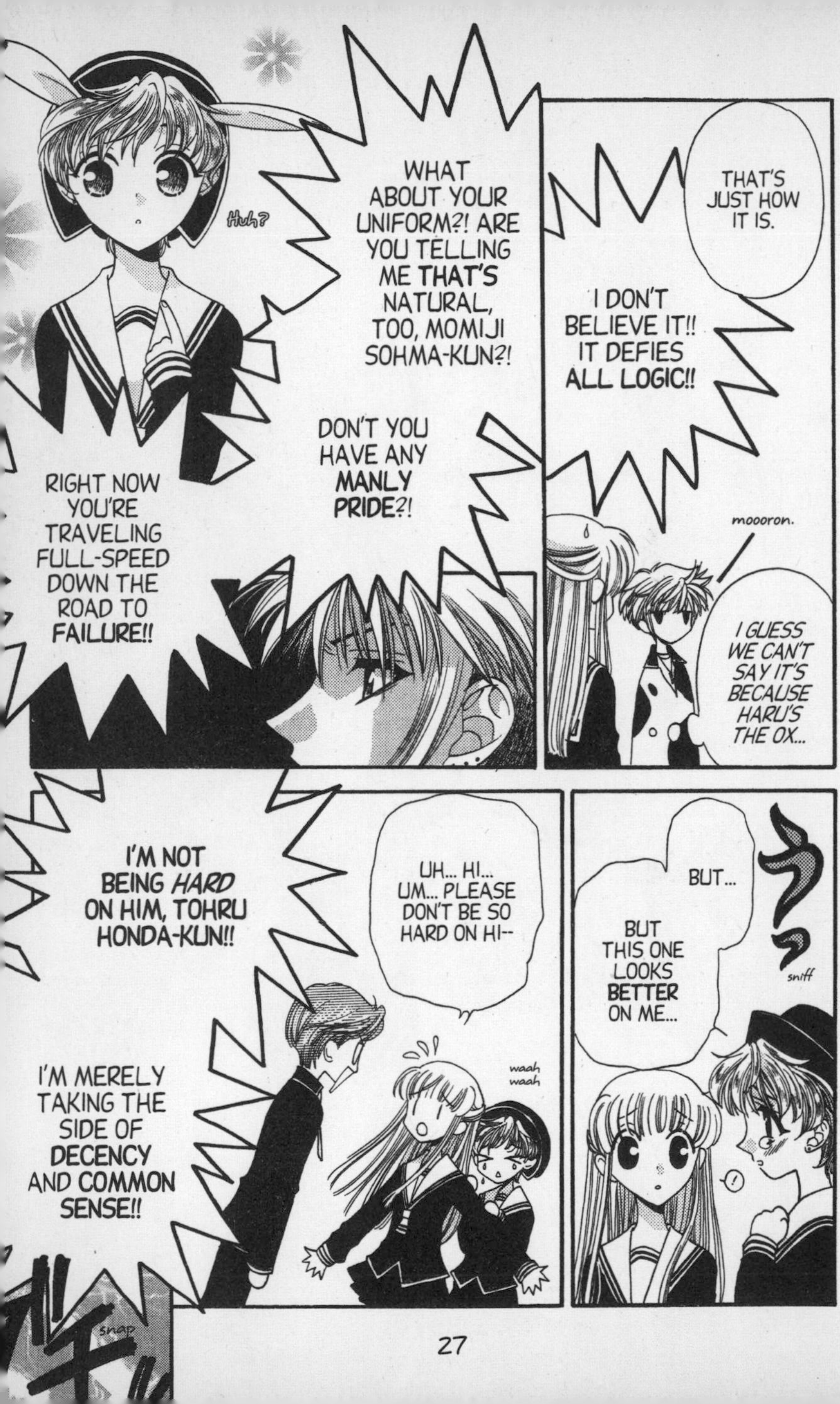
THAT'S JUST HOW IT IS.
I DON'T BELIEVE IT!! IT DEFIES ALL LOGIC!!
mooooron.
I GUESS WE CAN'T SAY IT'S BECAUSE HARU'S THE OX...
Huh?
WHAT ABOUT YOUR UNIFORM?! ARE YOU TELLING ME THAT'S NATURAL, TOO, MOMIJI SOHMA-KUN?!
DON'T YOU HAVE ANY MANLY PRIDE?!
RIGHT NOW YOU'RE TRAVELING FULL-SPEED DOWN THE ROAD TO FAILURE!!
BUT...
BUT THIS ONE LOOKS BETTER ON ME...
sniff
UH... HI... UM... PLEASE DON'T BE SO HARD ON HI--
waah waah
I'M NOT BEING HARD ON HIM, TOHRU HONDA-KUN!!
I'M MERELY TAKING THE SIDE OF DECENCY AND COMMON SENSE!!
snap

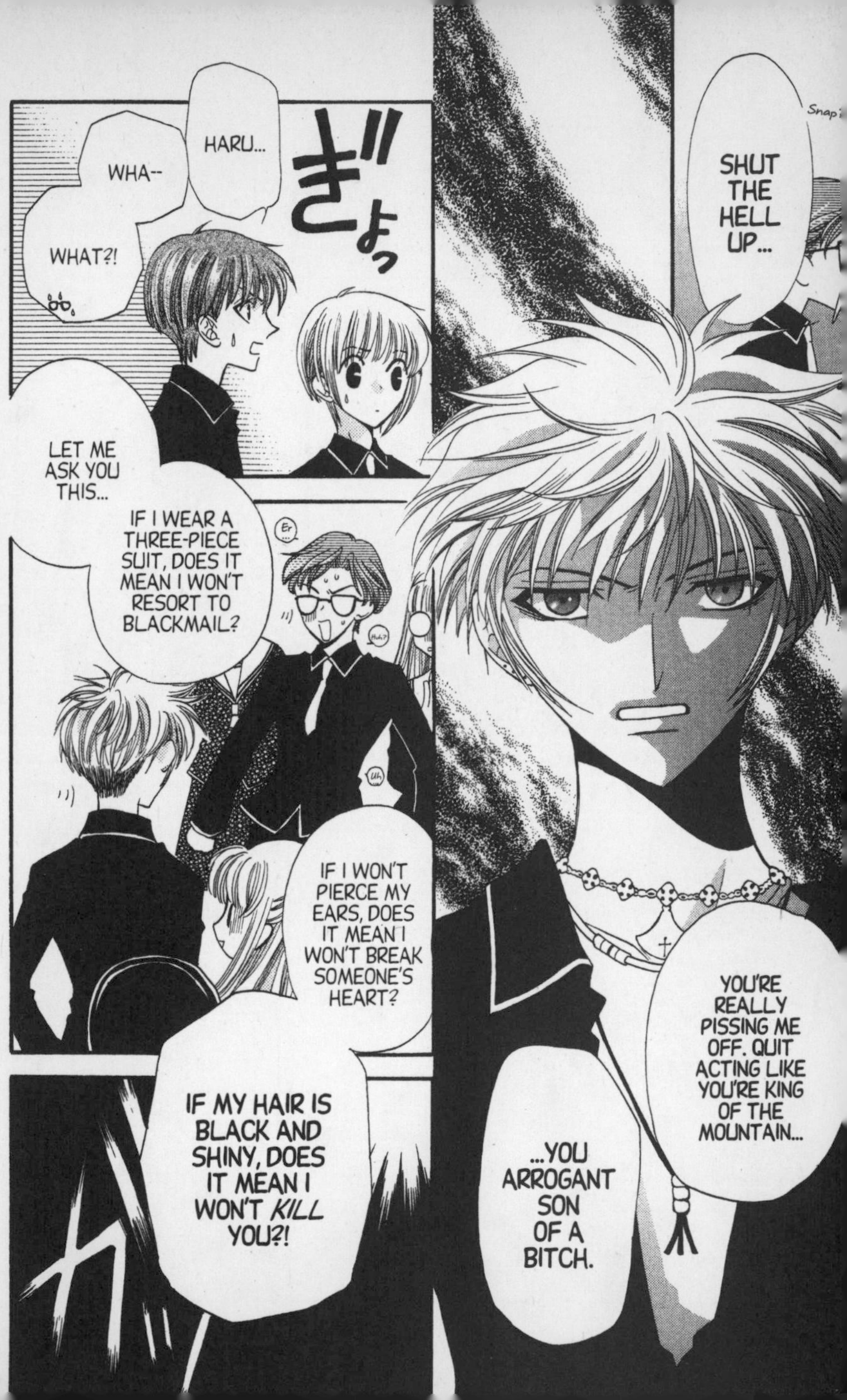
Snap
SHUT THE HELL UP...
YOU'RE REALLY PISSING ME OFF. QUIT ACTING LIKE YOU'RE KING OF THE MOUNTAIN...
...YOU ARROGANT SON OF A BITCH.
ぎょっ
HARU...
WHA--
WHAT?!
LET ME ASK YOU THIS...
IF I WEAR A THREE-PIECE SUIT, DOES IT MEAN I WON'T RESORT TO BLACKMAIL?
Er...
Huh?
Uh
IF I WON'T PIERCE MY EARS, DOES IT MEAN I WON'T BREAK SOMEONE'S HEART?
IF MY HAIR IS BLACK AND SHINY, DOES IT MEAN I WON'T *KILL* YOU?!

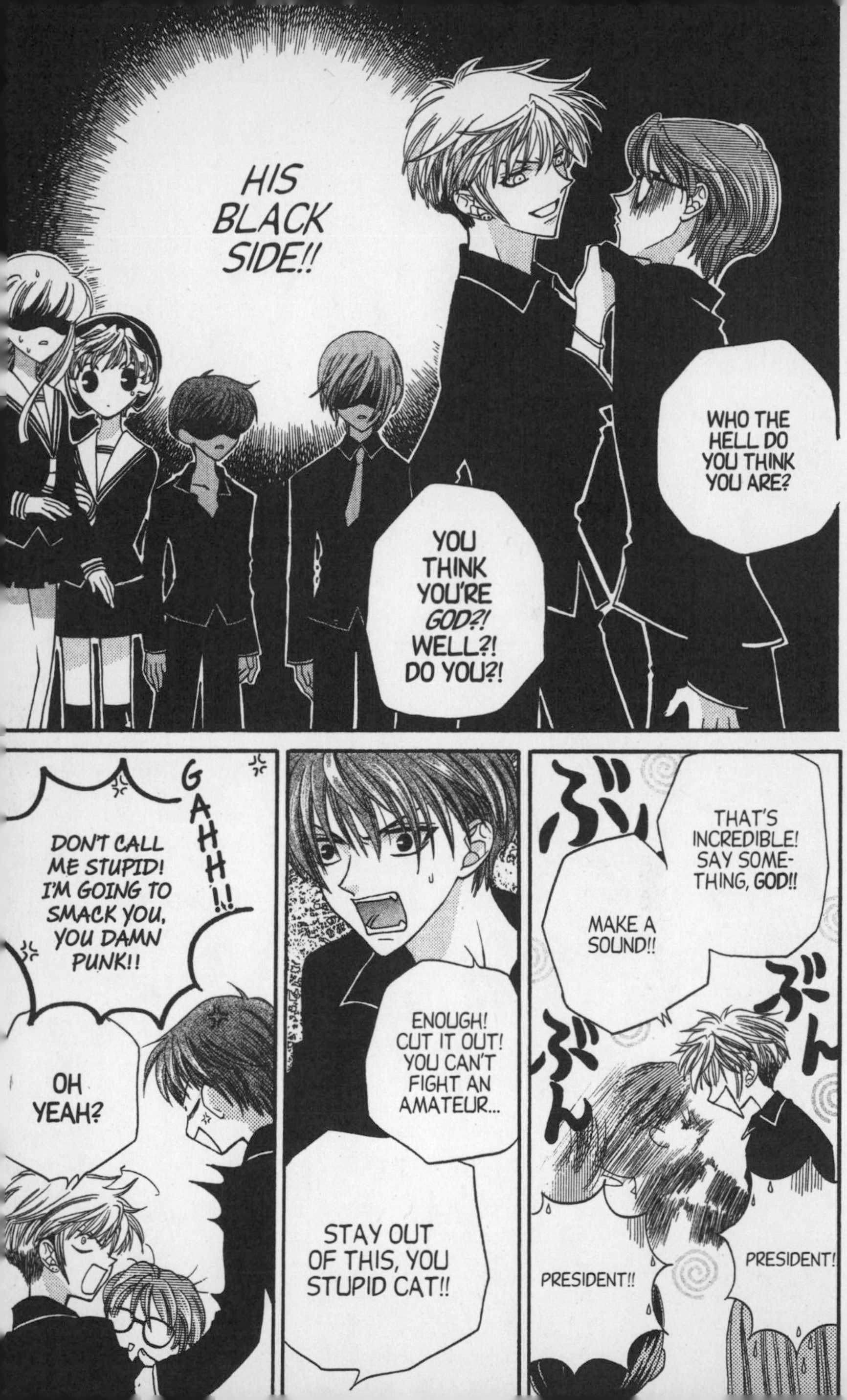
WHO THE HELL DO YOU THINK YOU ARE?
YOU THINK YOU'RE GOD?! WELL?! DO YOU?!
HIS BLACK SIDE!!
ぶん
THAT'S INCREDIBLE! SAY SOME-THING, GOD!!
MAKE A SOUND!!
ぶん
ぶん
PRESIDENT!
PRESIDENT!!
ENOUGH! CUT IT OUT! YOU CAN'T FIGHT AN AMATEUR...
STAY OUT OF THIS, YOU STUPID CAT!!
GAHHH!!
DON'T CALL ME STUPID! I'M GOING TO SMACK YOU, YOU DAMN PUNK!!
OH YEAH?

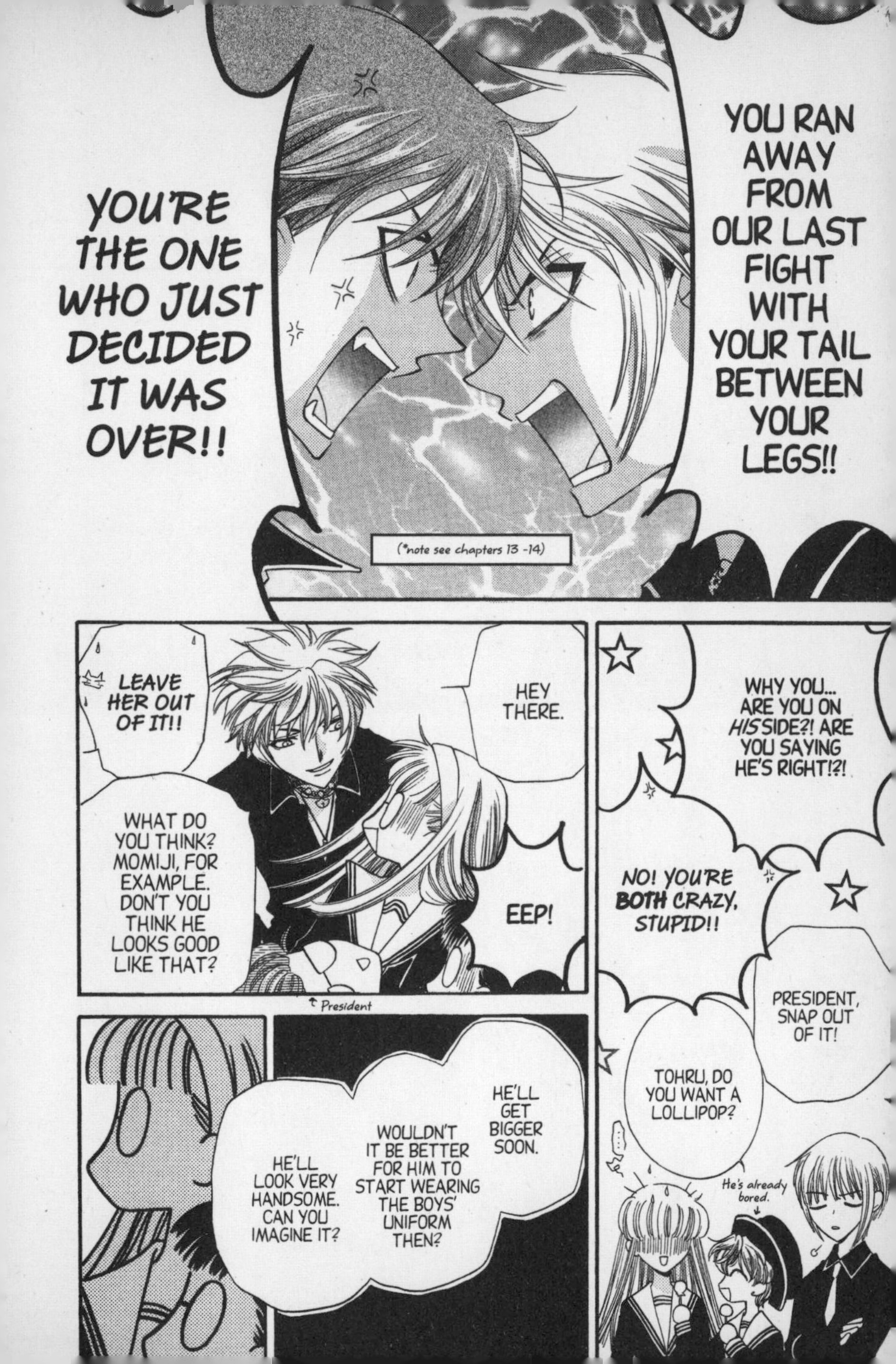
YOU RAN AWAY FROM OUR LAST FIGHT WITH YOUR TAIL BETWEEN YOUR LEGS!!
YOU'RE THE ONE WHO JUST DECIDED IT WAS OVER!!
(*note see chapters 13 -14)
WHY YOU... ARE YOU ON *HIS* SIDE?! ARE YOU SAYING HE'S RIGHT!?!
NO! YOU'RE **BOTH** CRAZY, STUPID!!
PRESIDENT, SNAP OUT OF IT!
TOHRU, DO YOU WANT A LOLLIPOP?
...
He's already bored.
HEY THERE.
EEP!
LEAVE HER OUT OF IT!!
WHAT DO YOU THINK? MOMIJI, FOR EXAMPLE. DON'T YOU THINK HE LOOKS GOOD LIKE THAT?
President
HE'LL GET BIGGER SOON.
WOULDN'T IT BE BETTER FOR HIM TO START WEARING THE BOYS' UNIFORM THEN?
HE'LL LOOK VERY HANDSOME. CAN YOU IMAGINE IT?

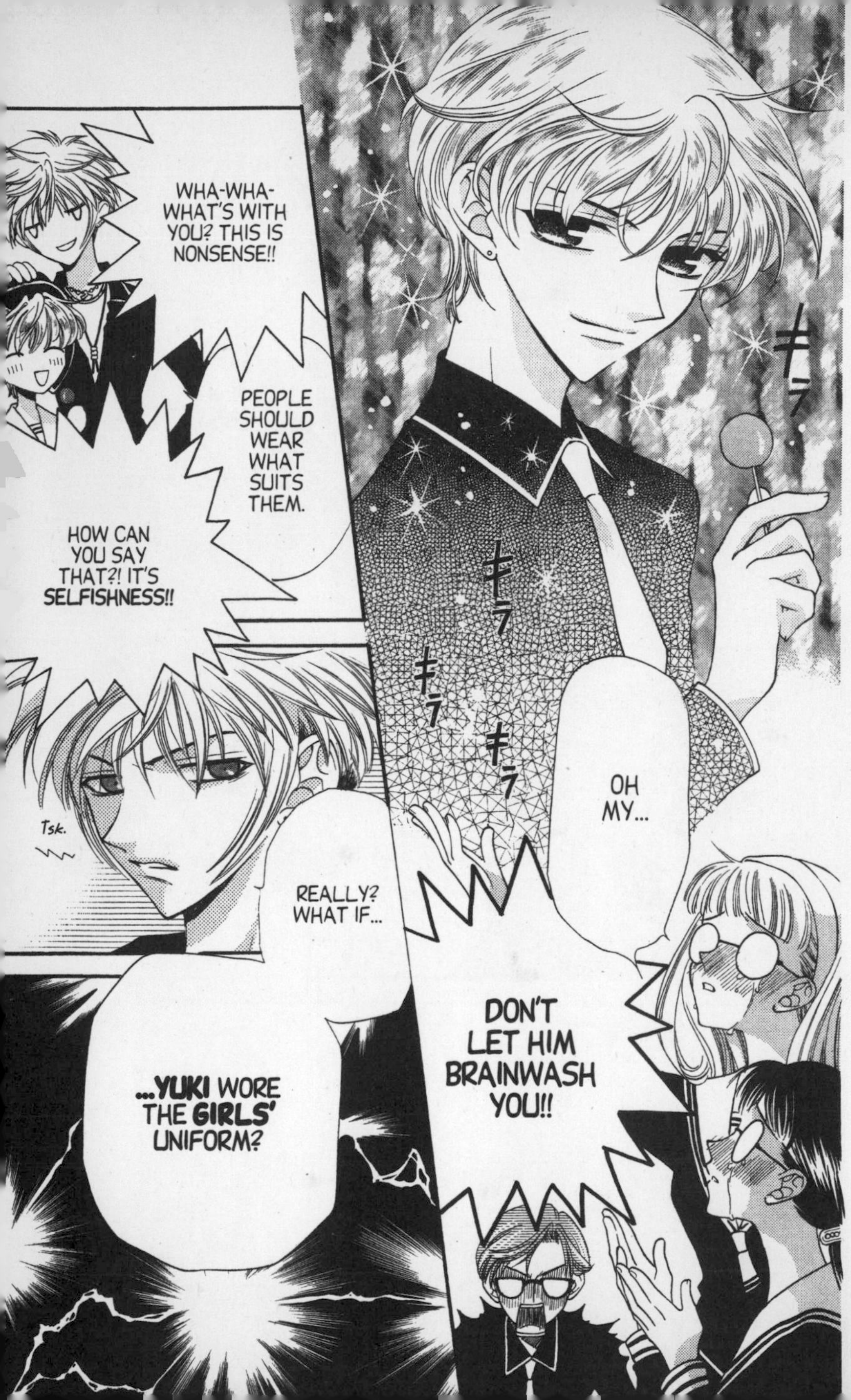

OH MY...
DON'T LET HIM BRAINWASH YOU!!
WHA-WHA-WHAT'S WITH YOU? THIS IS NONSENSE!!
PEOPLE SHOULD WEAR WHAT SUITS THEM.
HOW CAN YOU SAY THAT?! IT'S SELFISHNESS!!
Tsk.
REALLY? WHAT IF...
...YUKI WORE THE GIRLS' UNIFORM?

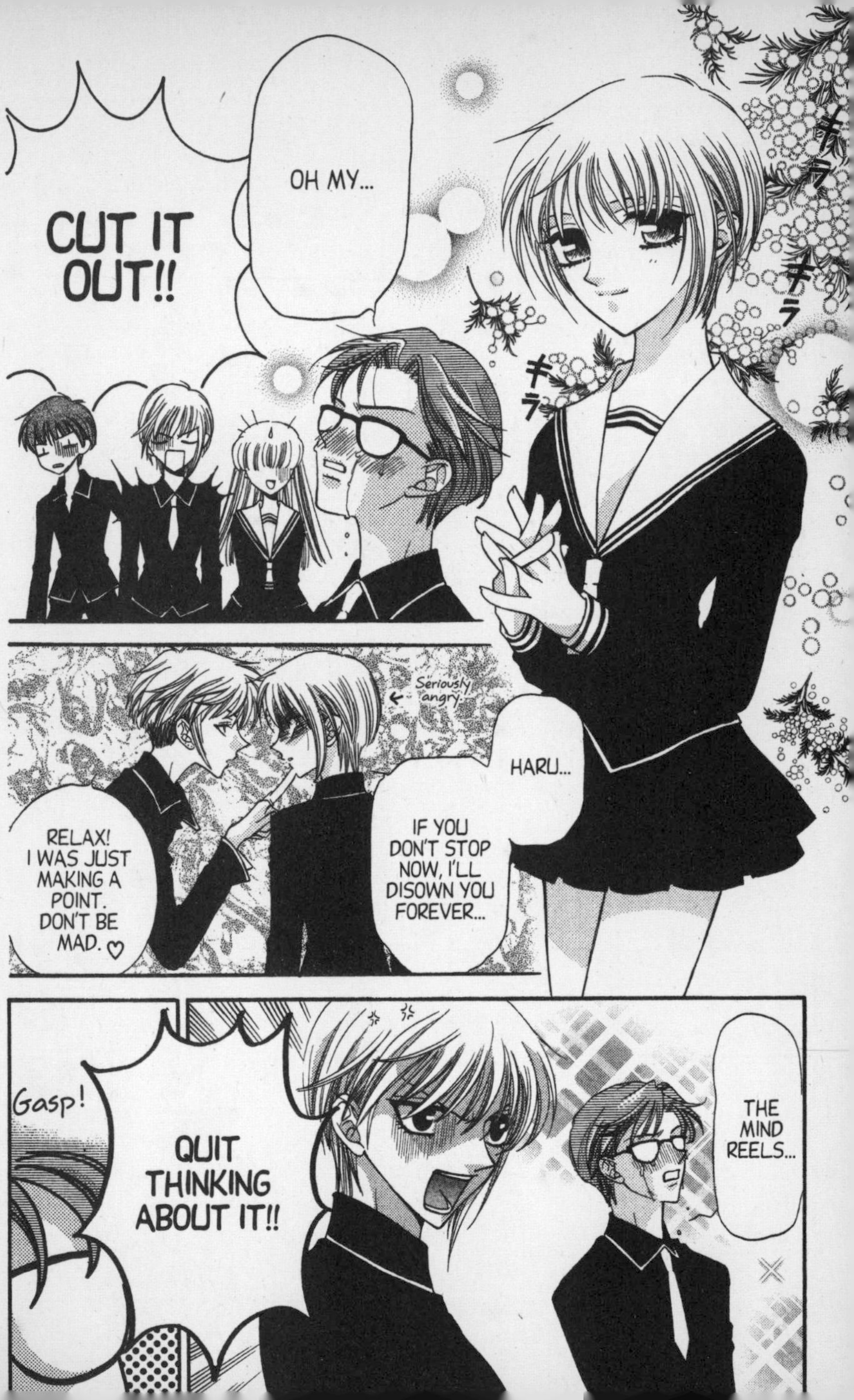
キラ
キラ
キラ
OH MY...
CUT IT OUT!!
HARU...
IF YOU DON'T STOP NOW, I'LL DISOWN YOU FOREVER...
Seriously angry.
RELAX! I WAS JUST MAKING A POINT. DON'T BE MAD. ♡
THE MIND REELS...
QUIT THINKING ABOUT IT!!
Gasp!

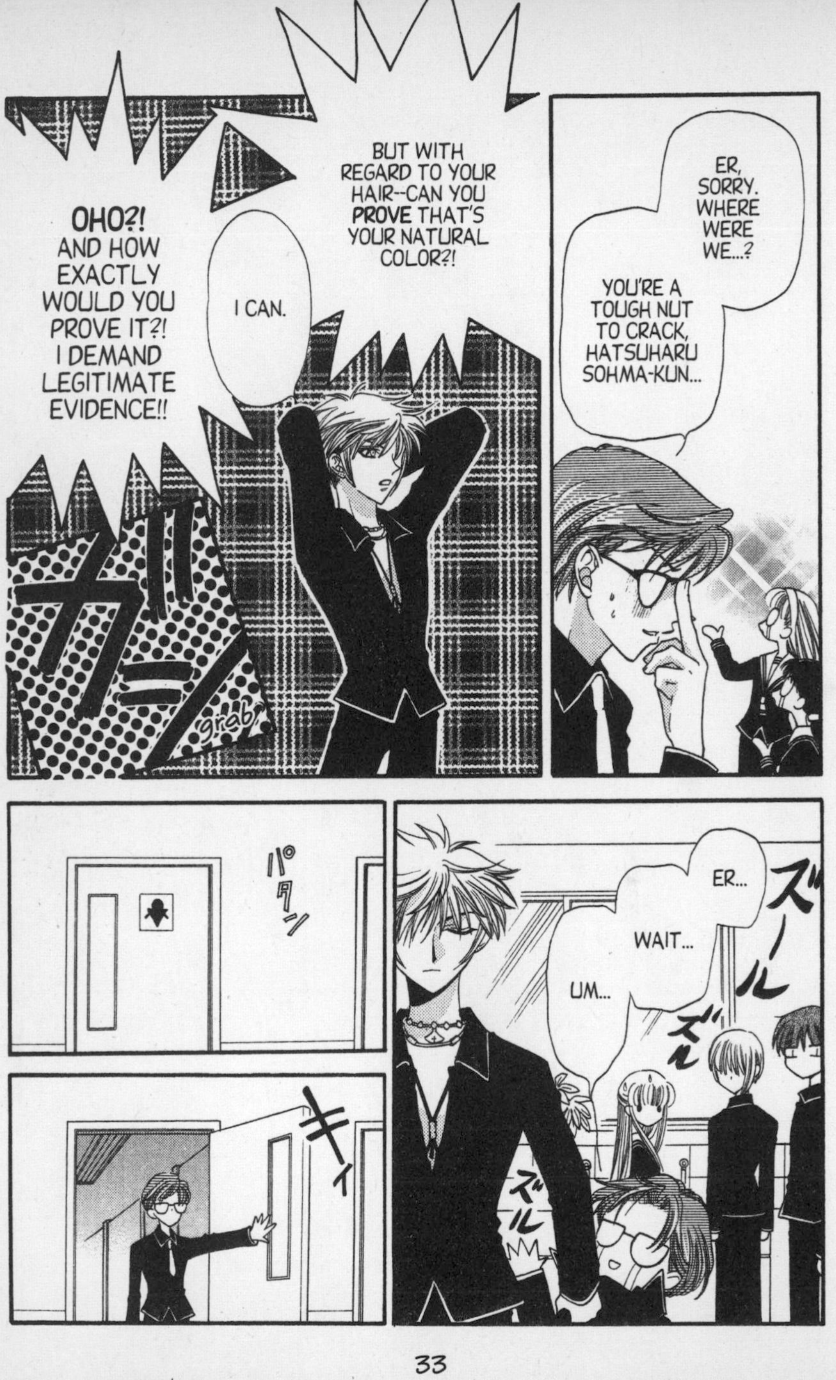
ER, SORRY. WHERE WERE WE...?
YOU'RE A TOUGH NUT TO CRACK, HATSUHARU SOHMA-KUN...
BUT WITH REGARD TO YOUR HAIR--CAN YOU **PROVE** THAT'S YOUR NATURAL COLOR?!
I CAN.
OHO?! AND HOW EXACTLY WOULD YOU PROVE IT?! I DEMAND LEGITIMATE EVIDENCE!!
grab
ER...
WAIT...
UM...

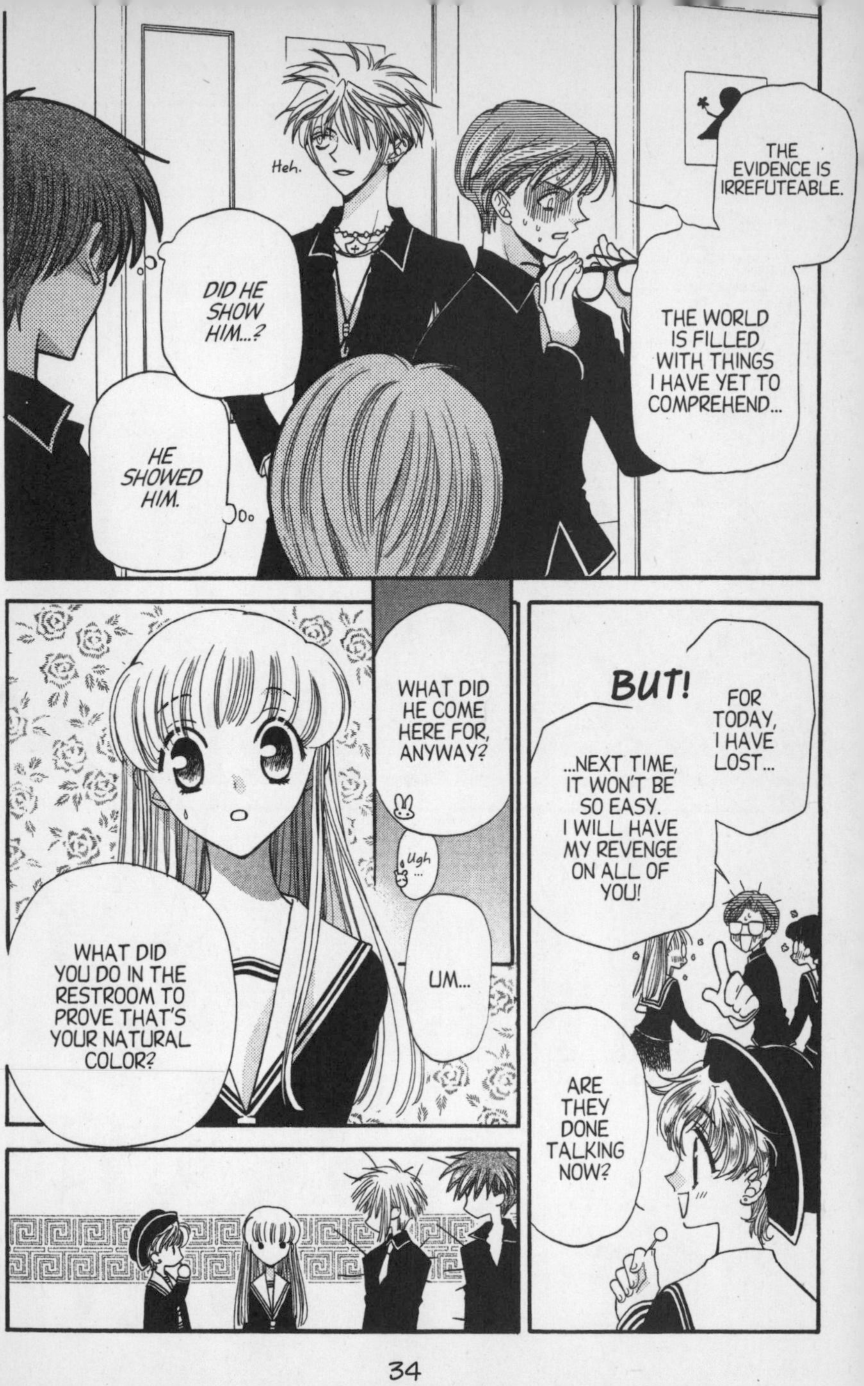
THE EVIDENCE IS IRREFUTEABLE.
THE WORLD IS FILLED WITH THINGS I HAVE YET TO COMPREHEND...
Heh.
DID HE SHOW HIM...?
HE SHOWED HIM.
BUT!
FOR TODAY, I HAVE LOST...
...NEXT TIME, IT WON'T BE SO EASY. I WILL HAVE MY REVENGE ON ALL OF YOU!
ARE THEY DONE TALKING NOW?
WHAT DID HE COME HERE FOR, ANYWAY?
Ugh...
UM...
WHAT DID YOU DO IN THE RESTROOM TO PROVE THAT'S YOUR NATURAL COLOR?

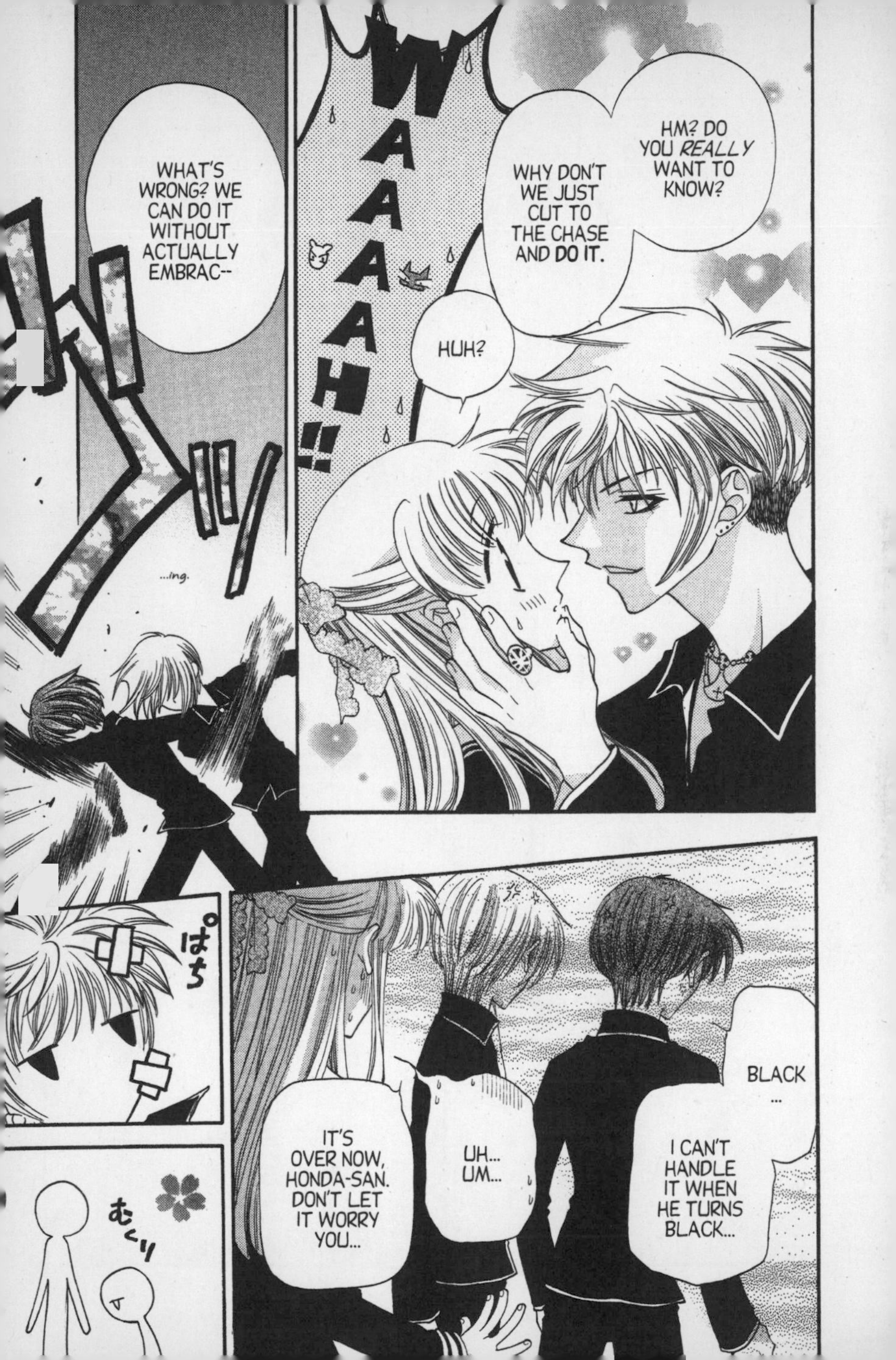
HM? DO YOU *REALLY* WANT TO KNOW?
WHY DON'T WE JUST CUT TO THE CHASE AND **DO IT**.
HUH?
WAAAAAH!!
WHAT'S WRONG? WE CAN DO IT WITHOUT ACTUALLY EMBRAC--
...ing.
BLACK ...
I CAN'T HANDLE IT WHEN HE TURNS BLACK...
UH... UM...
IT'S OVER NOW, HONDA-SAN. DON'T LET IT WORRY YOU...
ぱち
むくり

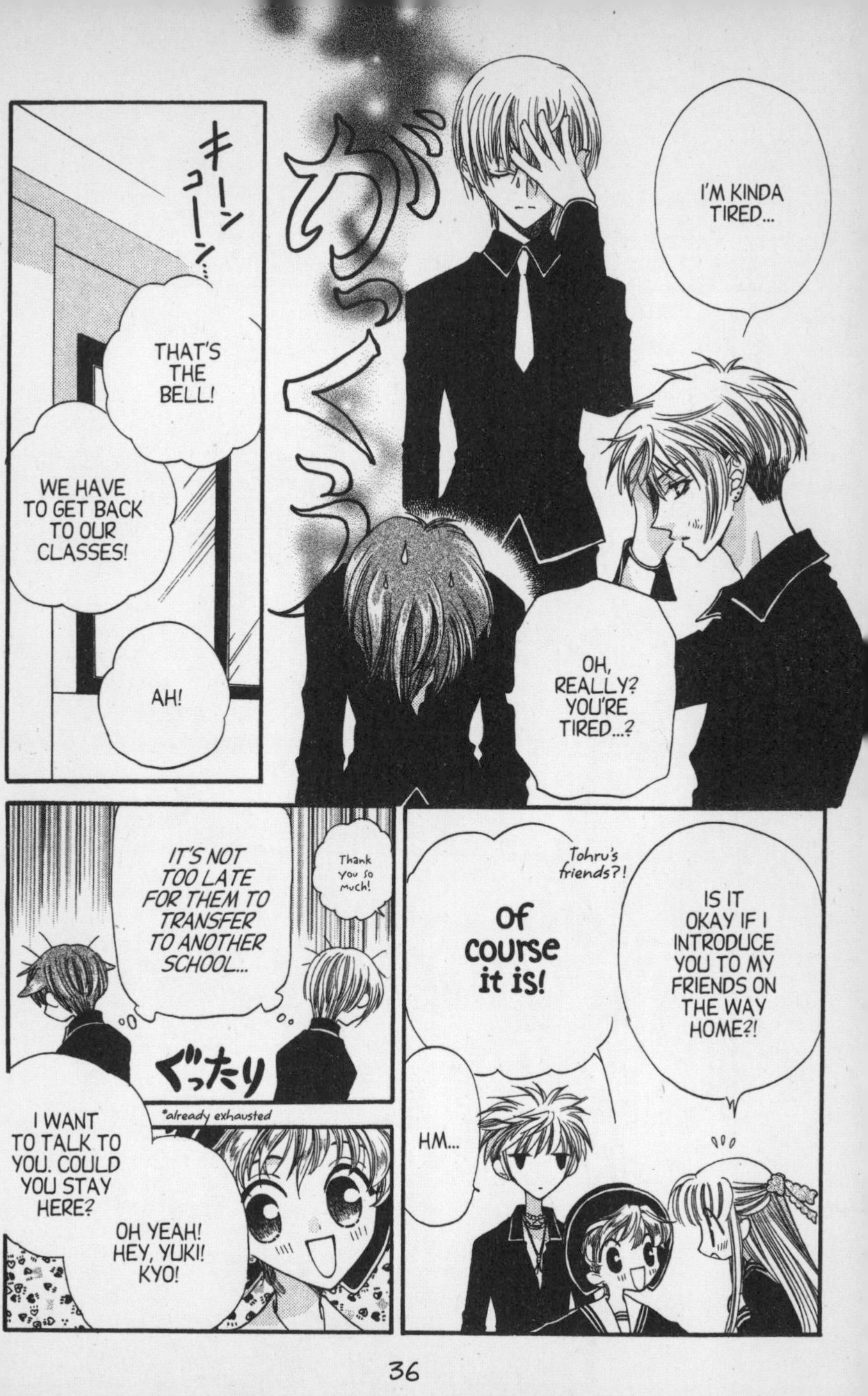
I'M KINDA TIRED...
OH, REALLY? YOU'RE TIRED...?
キーンコーン…
THAT'S THE BELL!
WE HAVE TO GET BACK TO OUR CLASSES!
AH!
IS IT OKAY IF I INTRODUCE YOU TO MY FRIENDS ON THE WAY HOME?!
Tohru's friends?!
Of course it is!
HM...
IT'S NOT TOO LATE FOR THEM TO TRANSFER TO ANOTHER SCHOOL...
Thank you so much!
ぐったり
*already exhausted
I WANT TO TALK TO YOU. COULD YOU STAY HERE?
OH YEAH! HEY, YUKI! KYO!

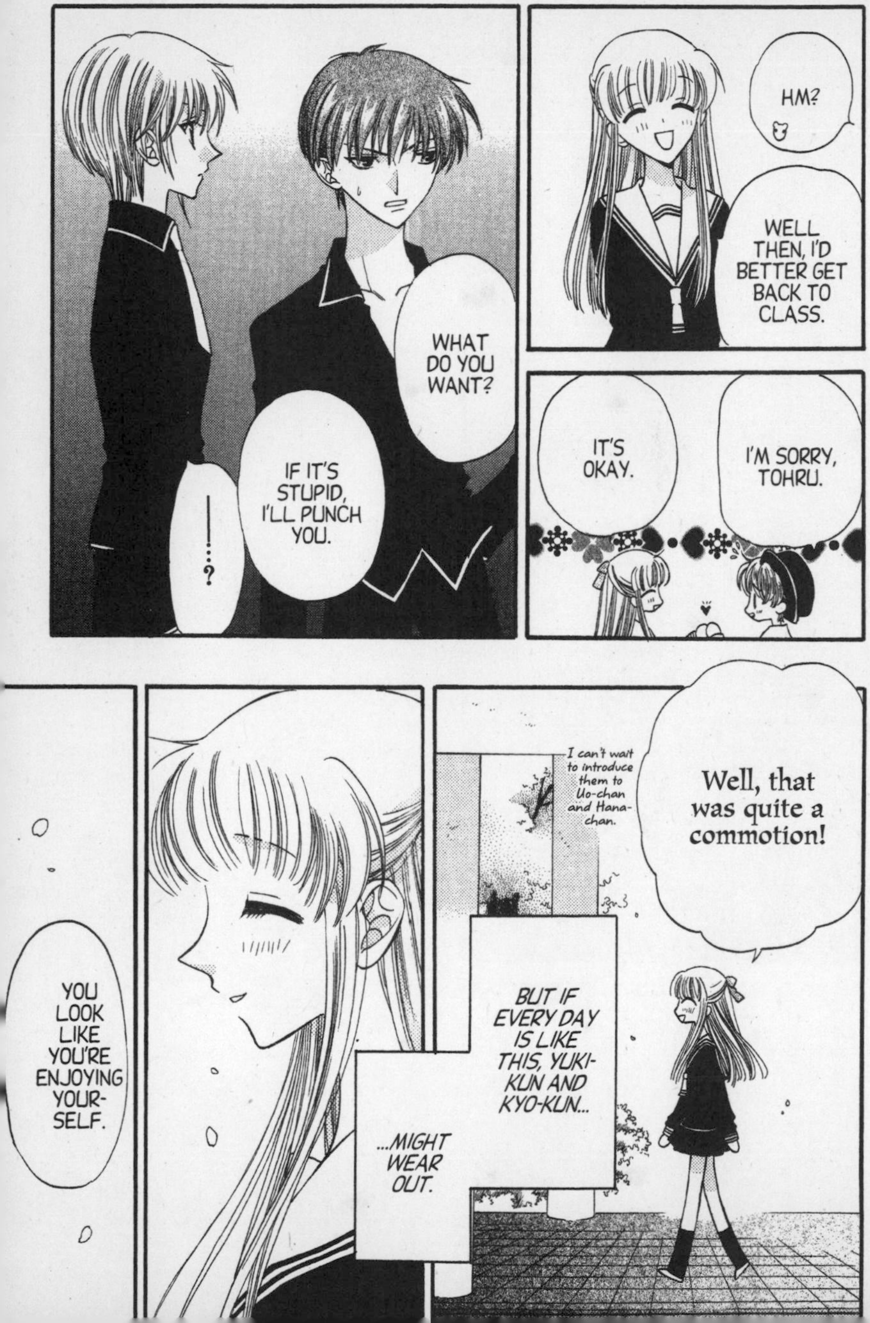
HM?
WELL THEN, I'D BETTER GET BACK TO CLASS.
I'M SORRY, TOHRU.
IT'S OKAY.
WHAT DO YOU WANT?
IF IT'S STUPID, I'LL PUNCH YOU.
—...?
Well, that was quite a commotion!
I can't wait to introduce them to Uo-chan and Hana-chan.
BUT IF EVERY DAY IS LIKE THIS, YUKI-KUN AND KYO-KUN...
...MIGHT WEAR OUT.
YOU LOOK LIKE YOU'RE ENJOYING YOUR-SELF.

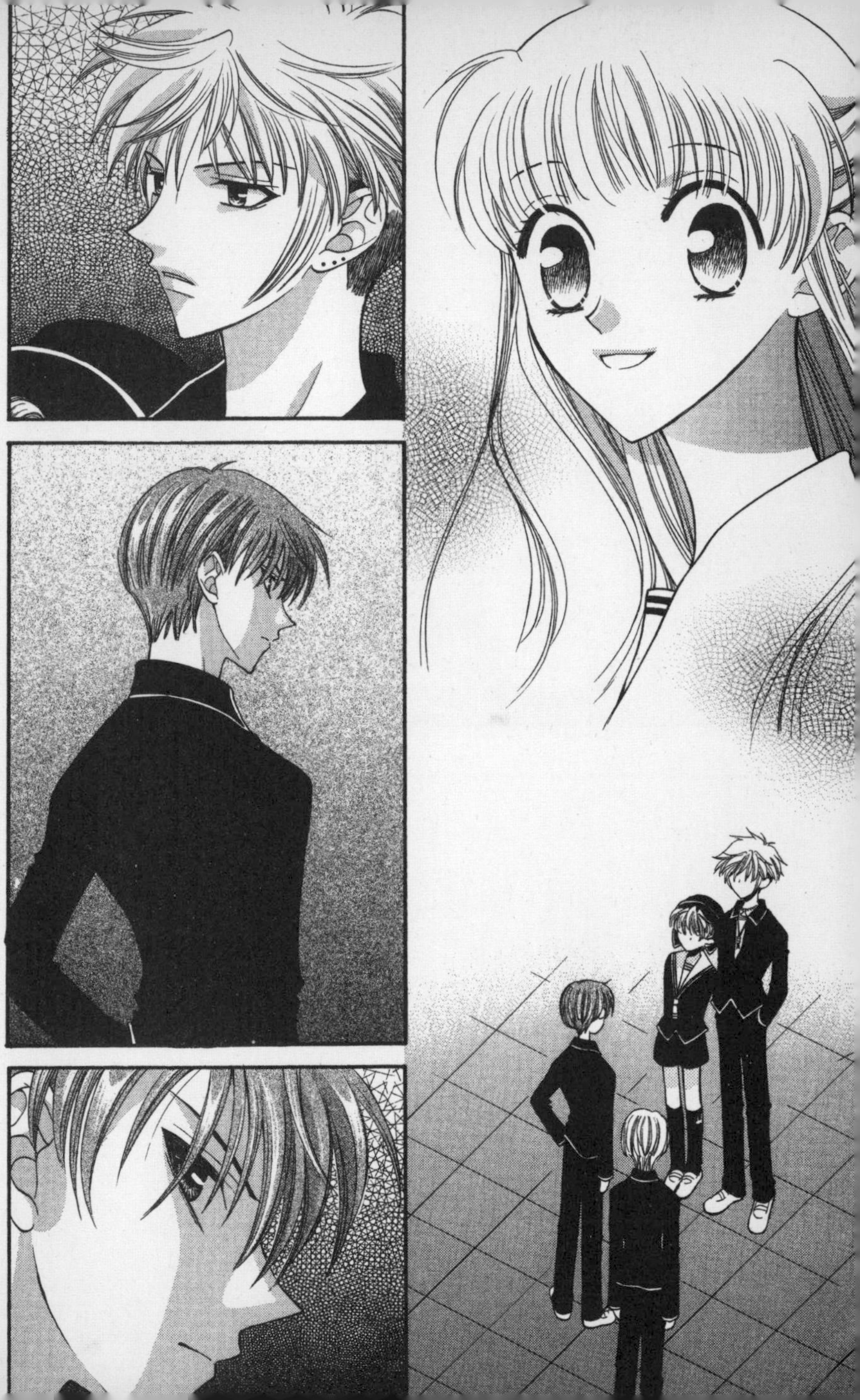

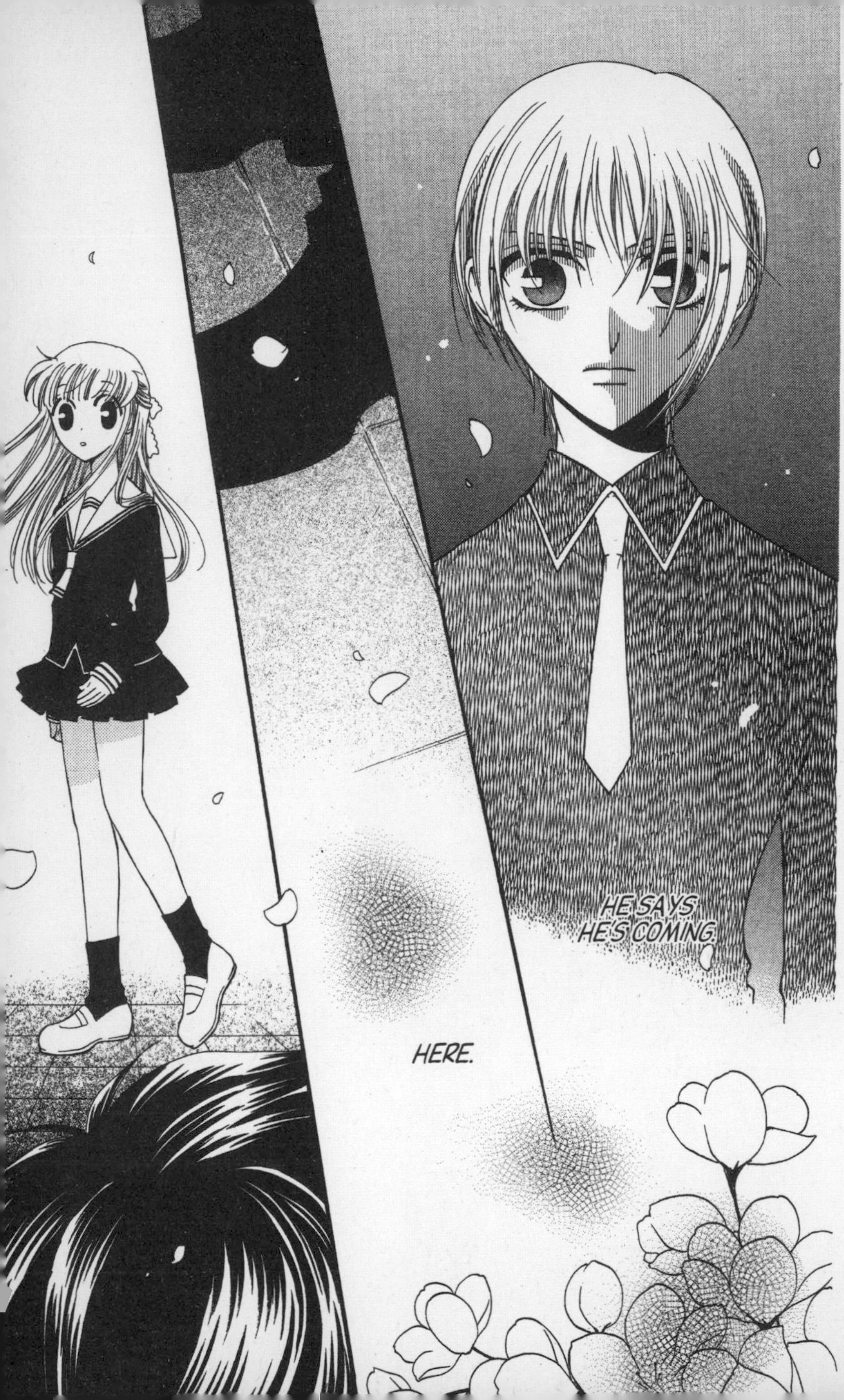
HE SAYS HE'S COMING
HERE.

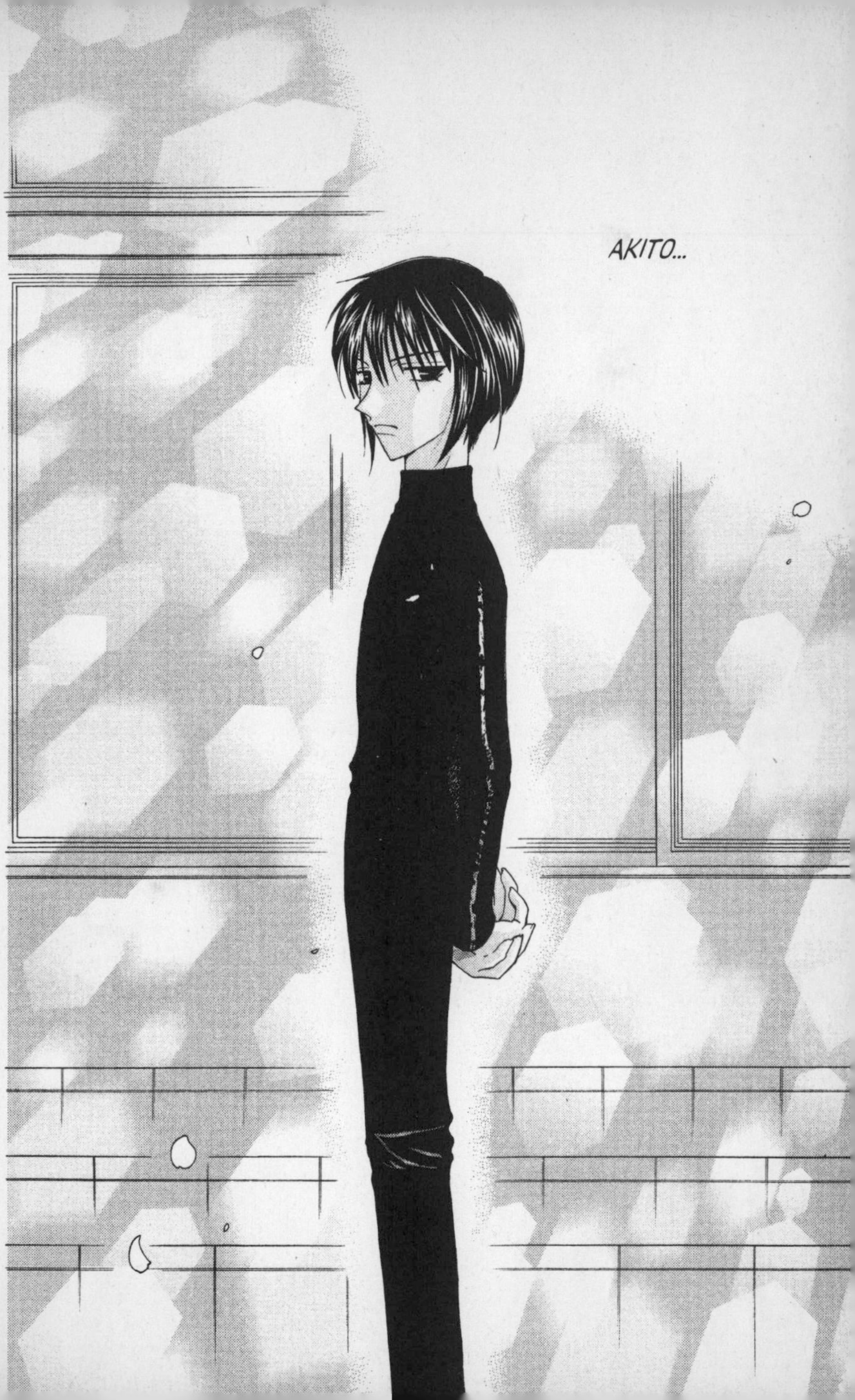
AKITO...

Chapter 20

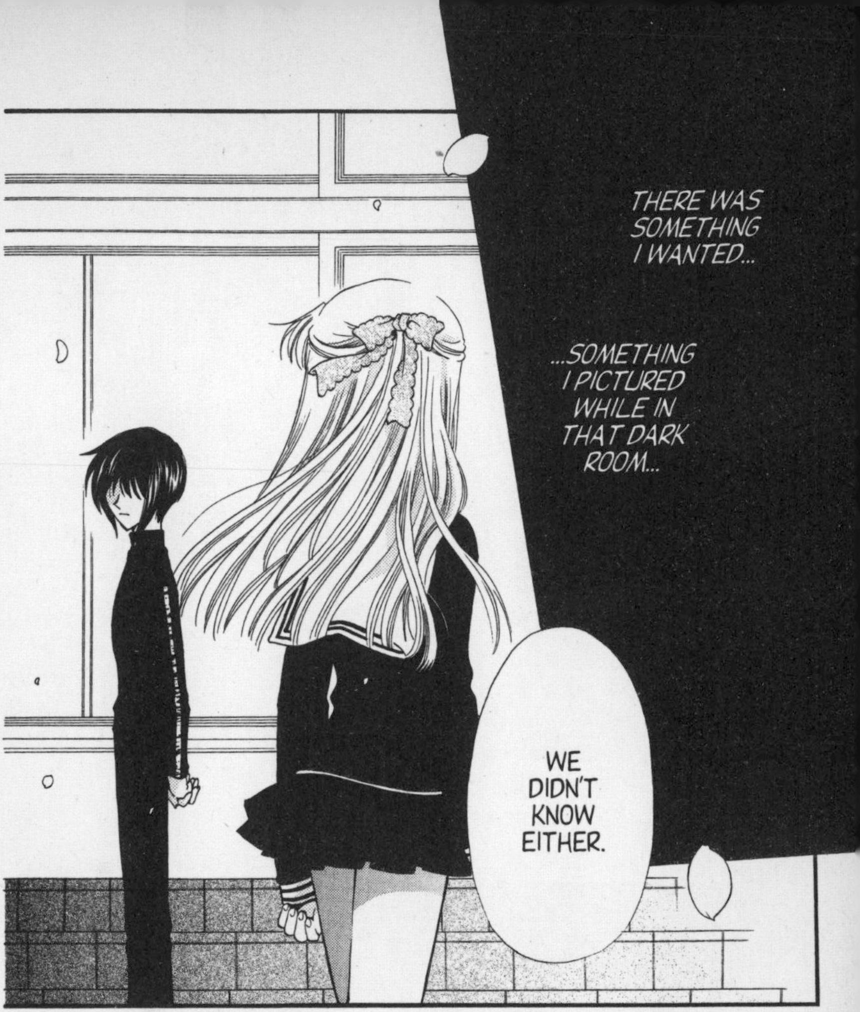
THERE WAS SOMETHING I WANTED...
...SOMETHING I PICTURED WHILE IN THAT DARK ROOM...
WE DIDN'T KNOW EITHER.

ULTRA SPECIAL BLAH BLAH BLAH 2

Akkii, Akkii, poisonous Akkii... My Mabudachi Akkii! Ha ha! (Er...sorry, inside joke.) I'm sure he slaps a cynical smile on the faces of the people who like him and the people who hate him. Mmm, poison. I actually meant to have him show up in the first volume, but looking back at it now, I'm glad I didn't. Better to draw things out...

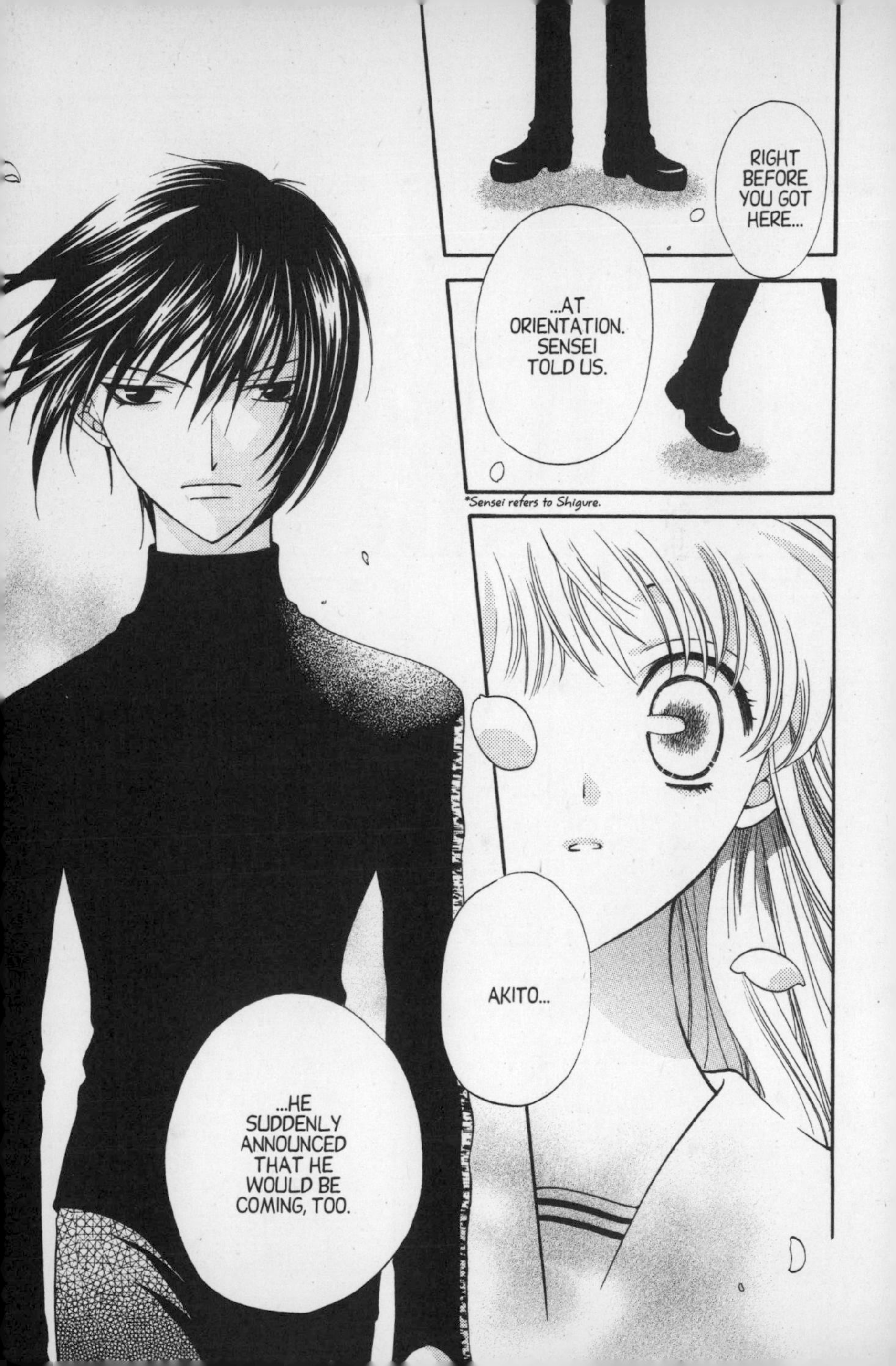
RIGHT BEFORE YOU GOT HERE...
...AT ORIENTATION. SENSEI TOLD US.
*Sensei refers to Shigure.
AKITO...
...HE SUDDENLY ANNOUNCED THAT HE WOULD BE COMING, TOO.

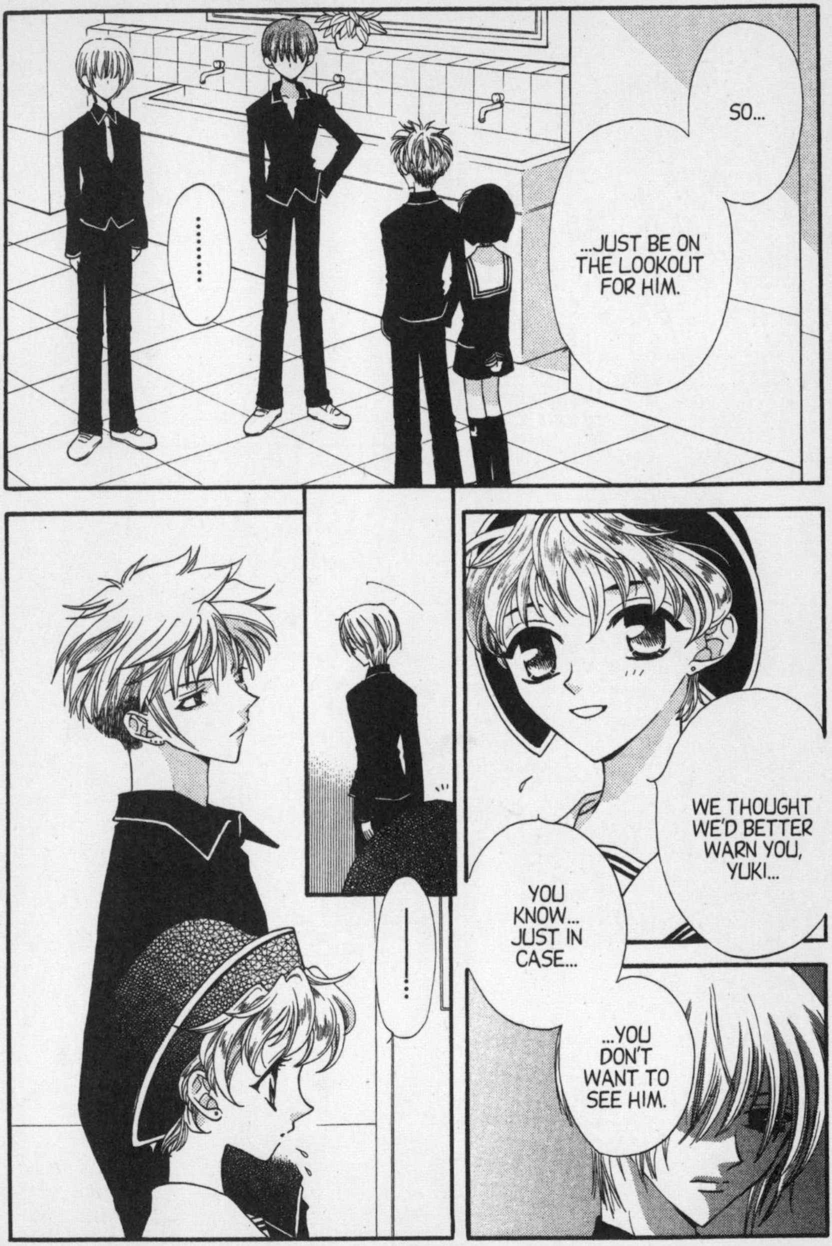
SO...
...JUST BE ON THE LOOKOUT FOR HIM.
....
WE THOUGHT WE'D BETTER WARN YOU, YUKI...
YOU KNOW... JUST IN CASE...
...YOU DON'T WANT TO SEE HIM.
—...

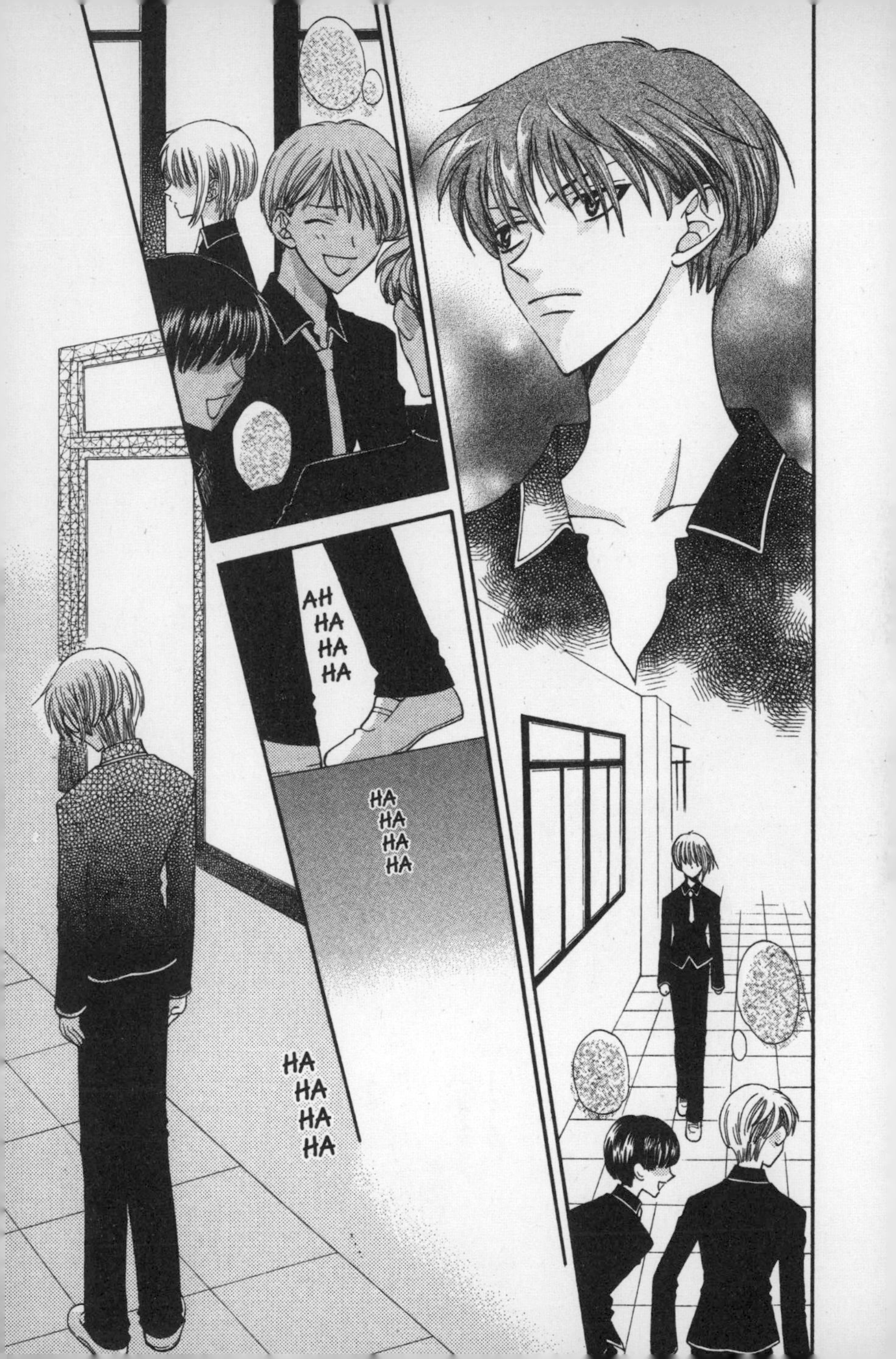
AH HA HA HA
HA HA HA HA
HA HA HA HA

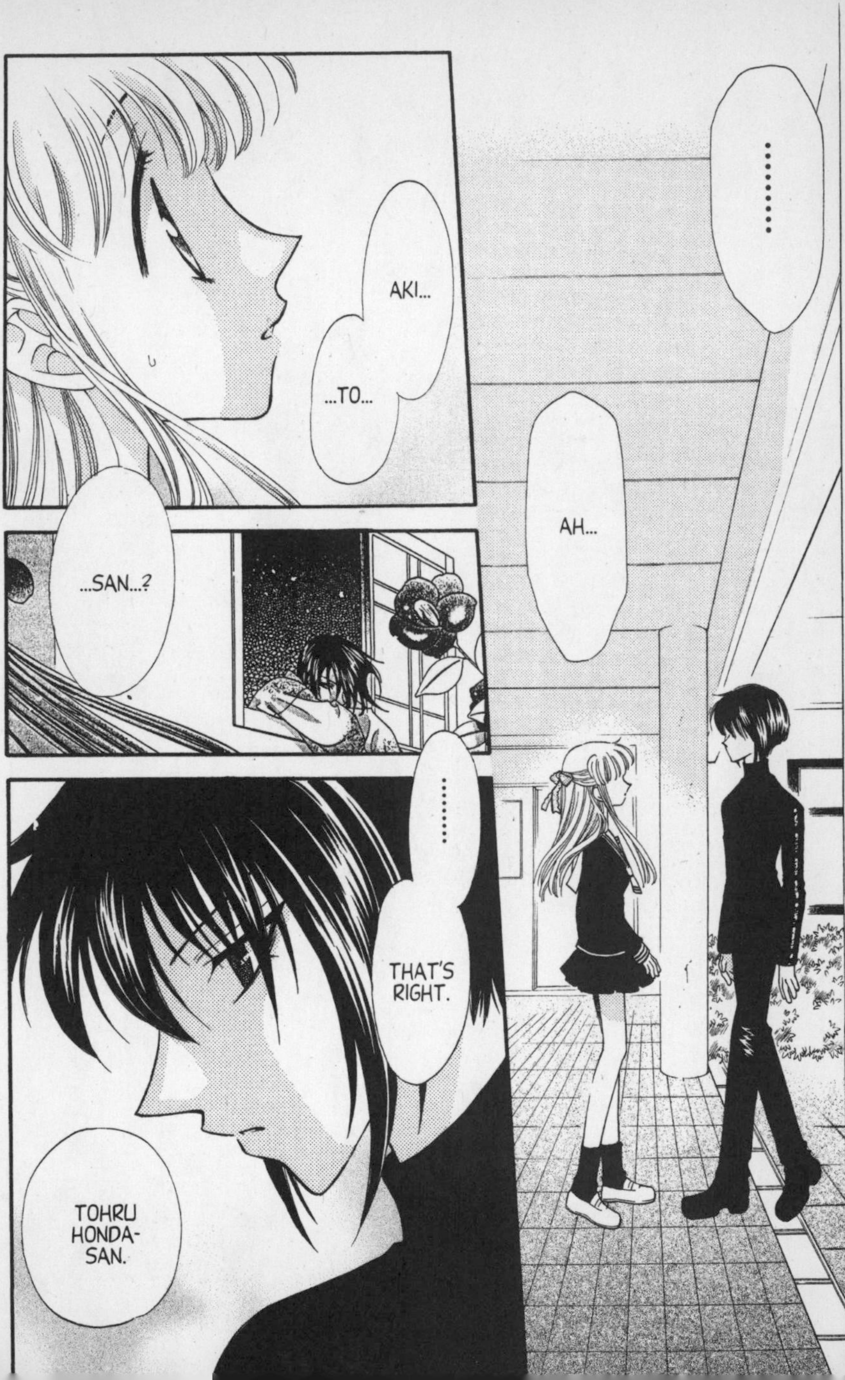
……
AH…
AKI…
…TO…
…SAN…?
……
THAT'S RIGHT.
TOHRU HONDA-SAN.

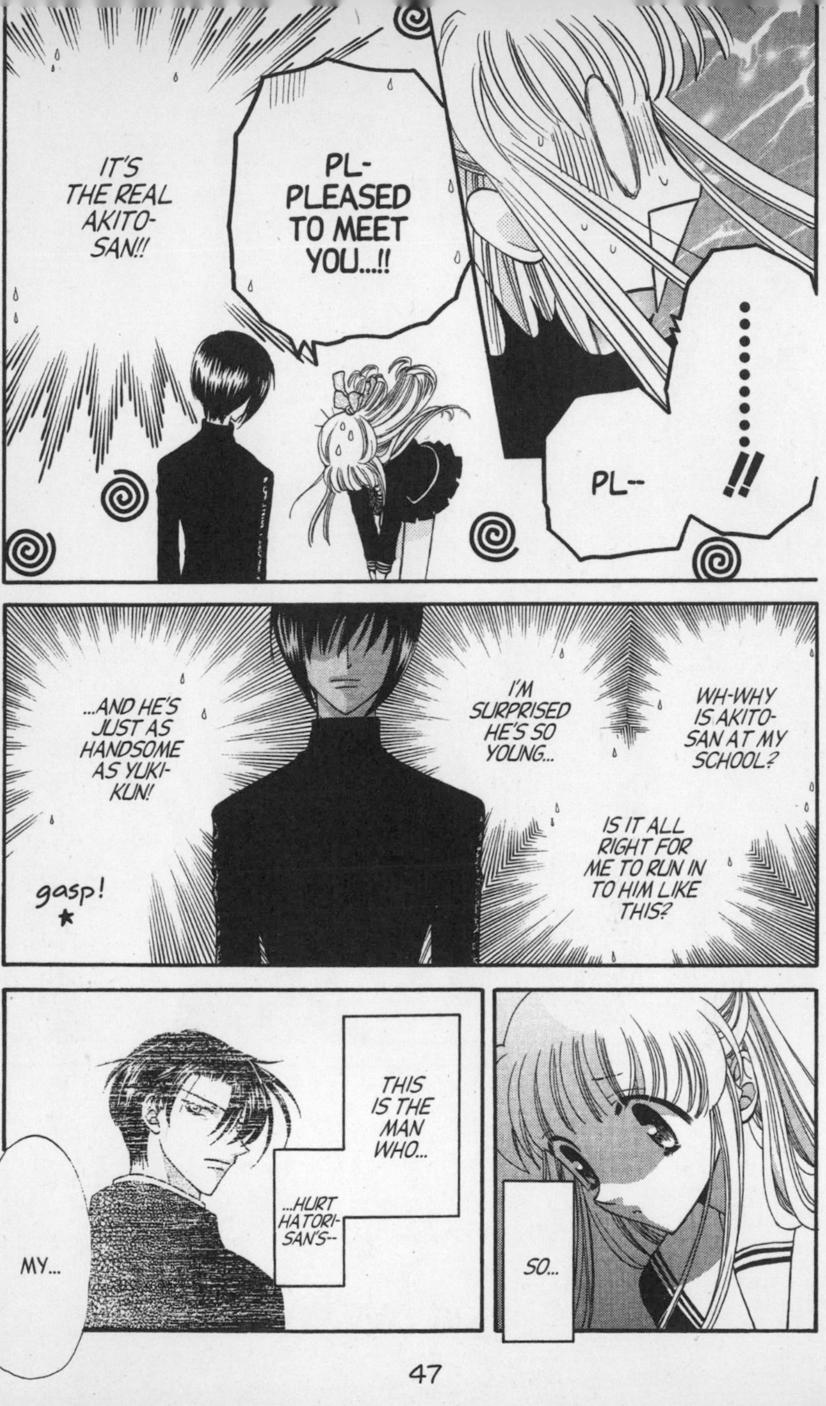
......!! PL--
PL- PLEASED TO MEET YOU...!!
IT'S THE REAL AKITO-SAN!!
WH-WHY IS AKITO-SAN AT MY SCHOOL?
IS IT ALL RIGHT FOR ME TO RUN IN TO HIM LIKE THIS?
I'M SURPRISED HE'S SO YOUNG...
...AND HE'S JUST AS HANDSOME AS YUKI-KUN!
gasp!
SO...
THIS IS THE MAN WHO...
...HURT HATORI-SAN'S--
MY...

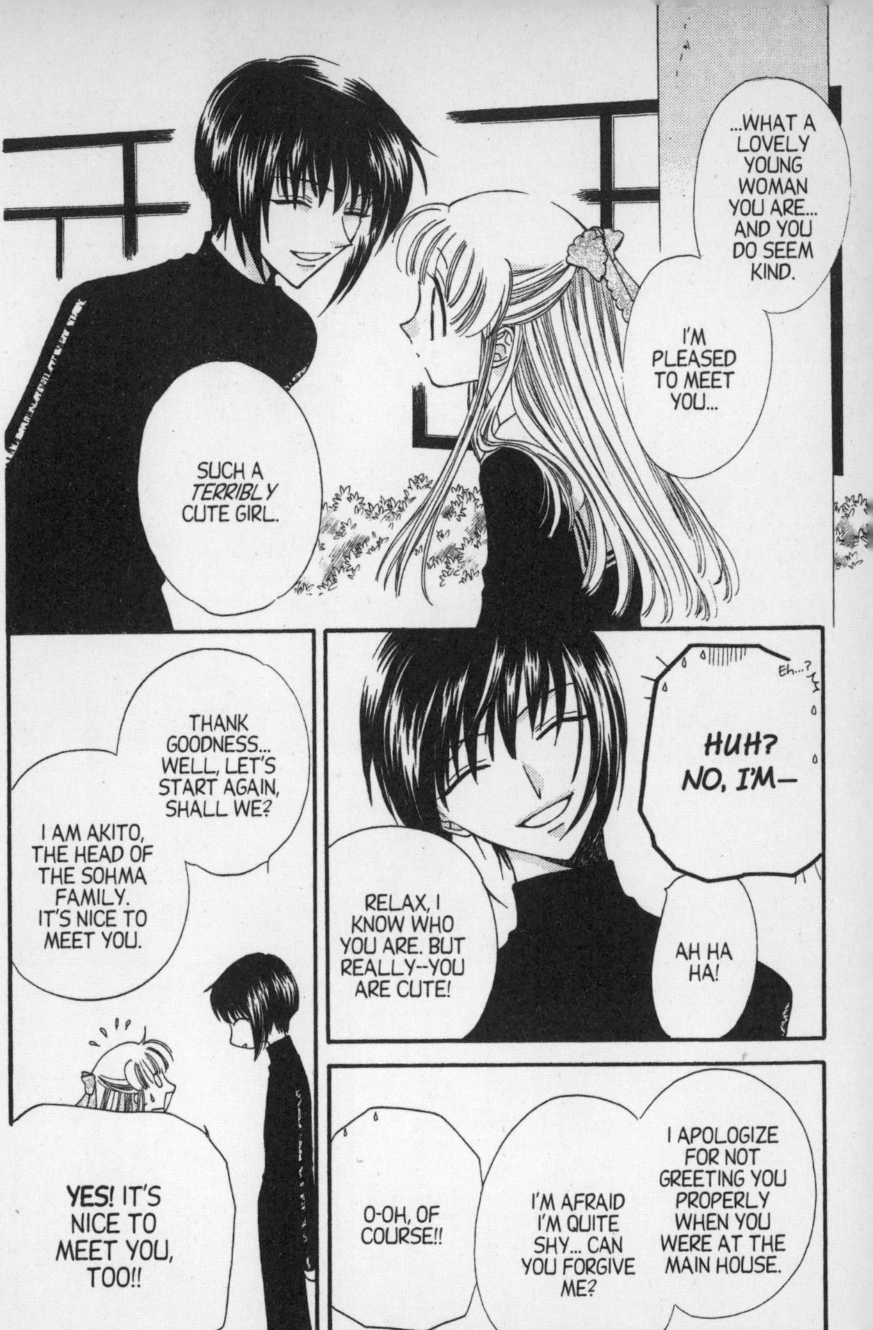

...WHAT A LOVELY YOUNG WOMAN YOU ARE... AND YOU DO SEEM KIND.
I'M PLEASED TO MEET YOU...
SUCH A *TERRIBLY* CUTE GIRL.
Eh...?
HUH? NO, I'M—
AH HA HA!
RELAX, I KNOW WHO YOU ARE. BUT REALLY--YOU ARE CUTE!
I APOLOGIZE FOR NOT GREETING YOU PROPERLY WHEN YOU WERE AT THE MAIN HOUSE.
I'M AFRAID I'M QUITE SHY... CAN YOU FORGIVE ME?
O-OH, OF COURSE!!
THANK GOODNESS... WELL, LET'S START AGAIN, SHALL WE?
I AM AKITO, THE HEAD OF THE SOHMA FAMILY. IT'S NICE TO MEET YOU.
YES! IT'S NICE TO MEET YOU, TOO!!

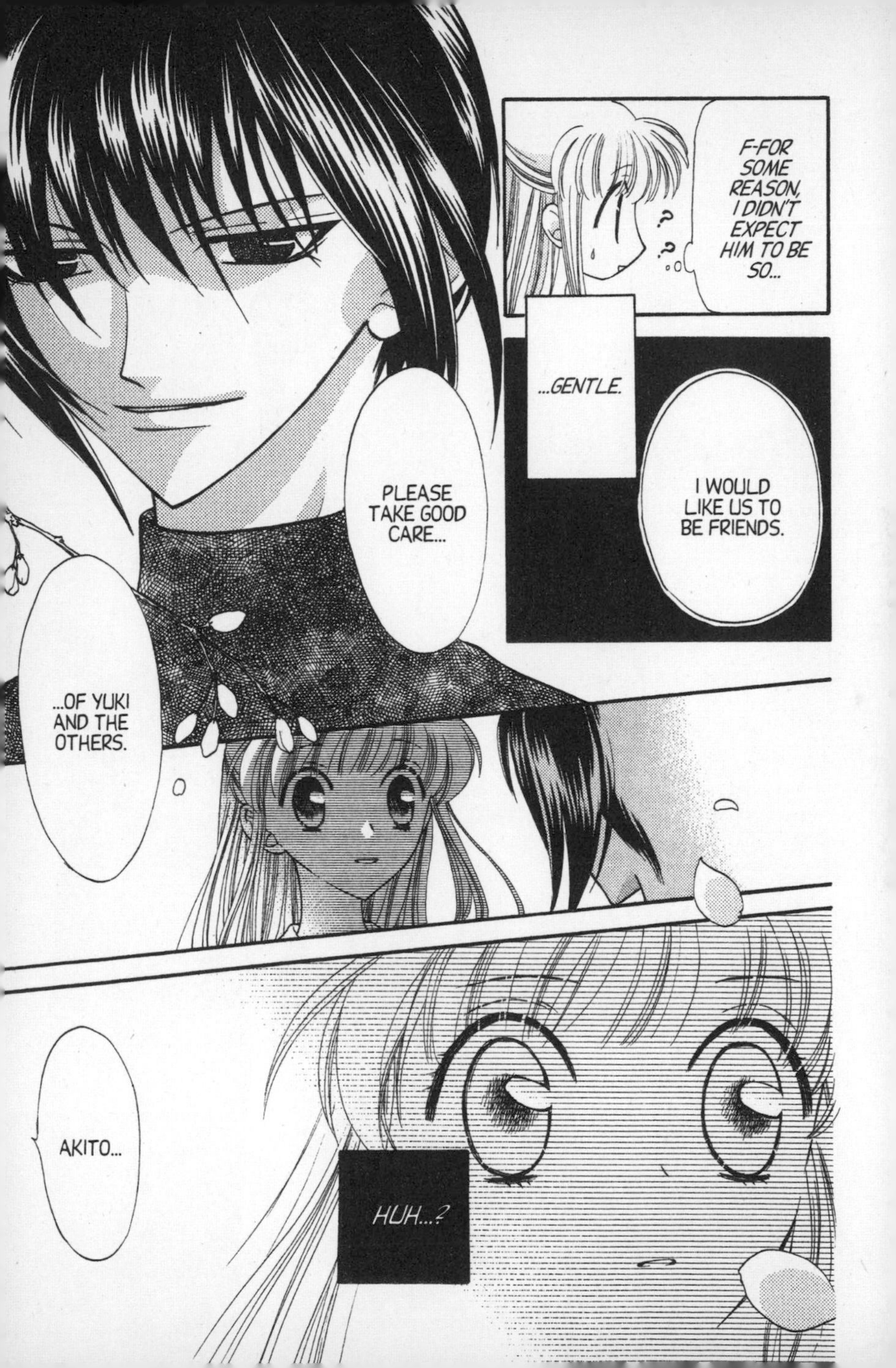
F-FOR SOME REASON, I DIDN'T EXPECT HIM TO BE SO...
...GENTLE.
I WOULD LIKE US TO BE FRIENDS.
PLEASE TAKE GOOD CARE...
...OF YUKI AND THE OTHERS.
AKITO...
HUH...?

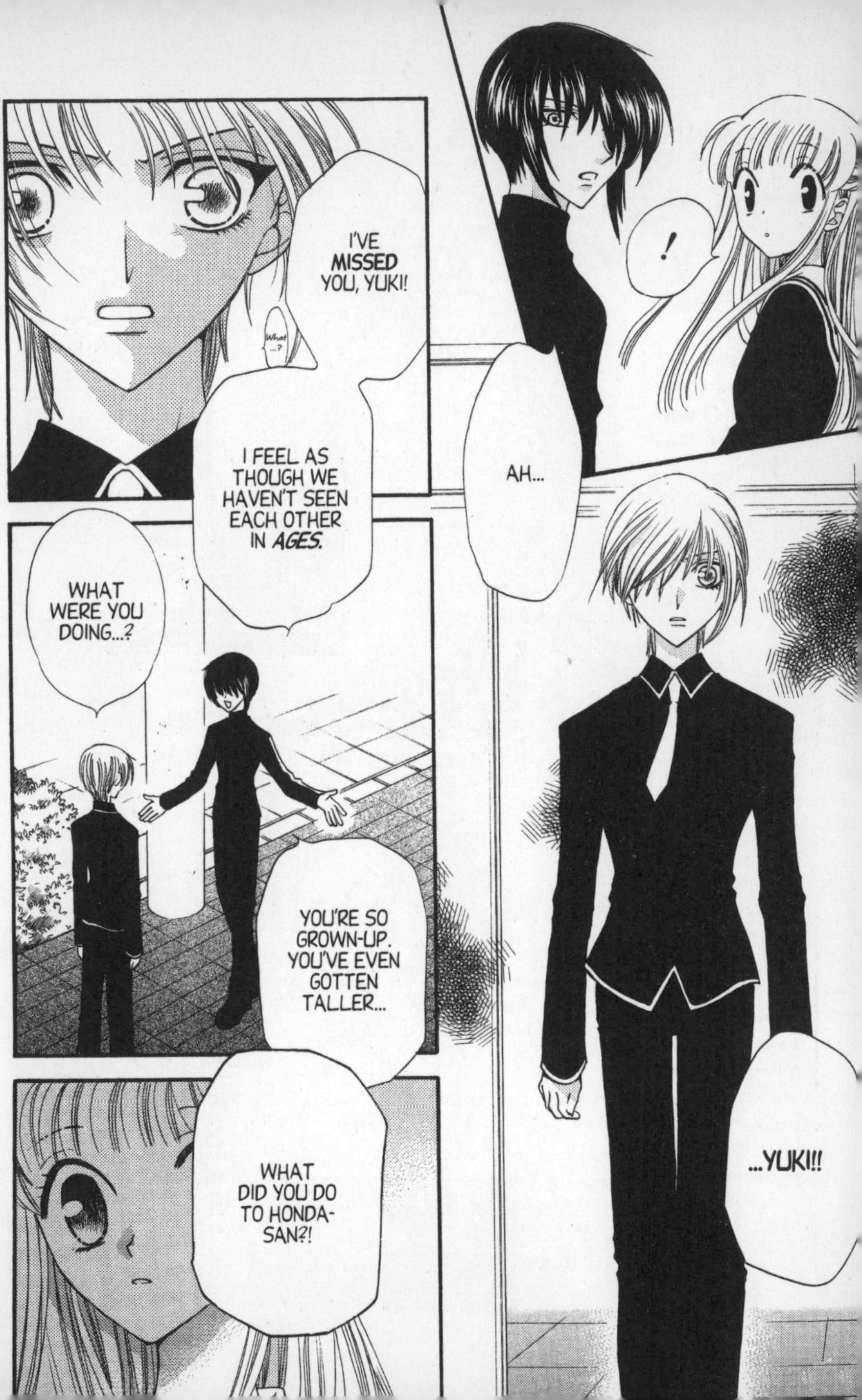
!
AH...
...YUKI!!
I'VE MISSED YOU, YUKI!
What ...?
I FEEL AS THOUGH WE HAVEN'T SEEN EACH OTHER IN AGES.
YOU'RE SO GROWN-UP. YOU'VE EVEN GOTTEN TALLER...
WHAT WERE YOU DOING...?
WHAT DID YOU DO TO HONDA-SAN?!

Fruits Basket 4 Part 2:

At the end of this book, I inserted a manga advertising the CD drama. It's a special offer, so it won't be on sale to the general public. And it's past the deadline to apply! Ha ha! Thank you very much for sending so many applications. I'll say clearly that I am in **love** with the Furuba CD. It's such a fun CD! I can't thank the voice actors who performed in it enough. I've shed so many tears of gratitude that my eyes have just about gone dry. What I find interesting is that even while listening to the lines, I split them into panels. I wonder if this is what they call an occupational hazard. I even break things into panels when I'm watching TV!

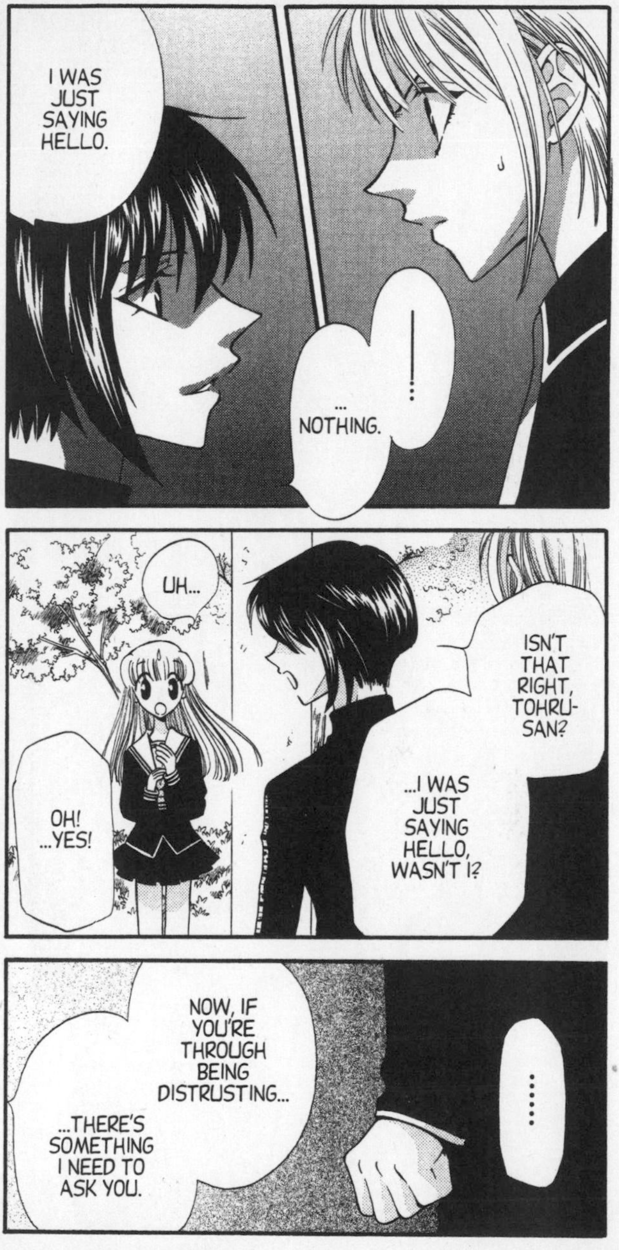
!
... NOTHING.
I WAS JUST SAYING HELLO.
ISN'T THAT RIGHT, TOHRU-SAN?
...I WAS JUST SAYING HELLO, WASN'T I?
UH...
OH! ...YES!
......
NOW, IF YOU'RE THROUGH BEING DISTRUSTING...
...THERE'S SOMETHING I NEED TO ASK YOU.

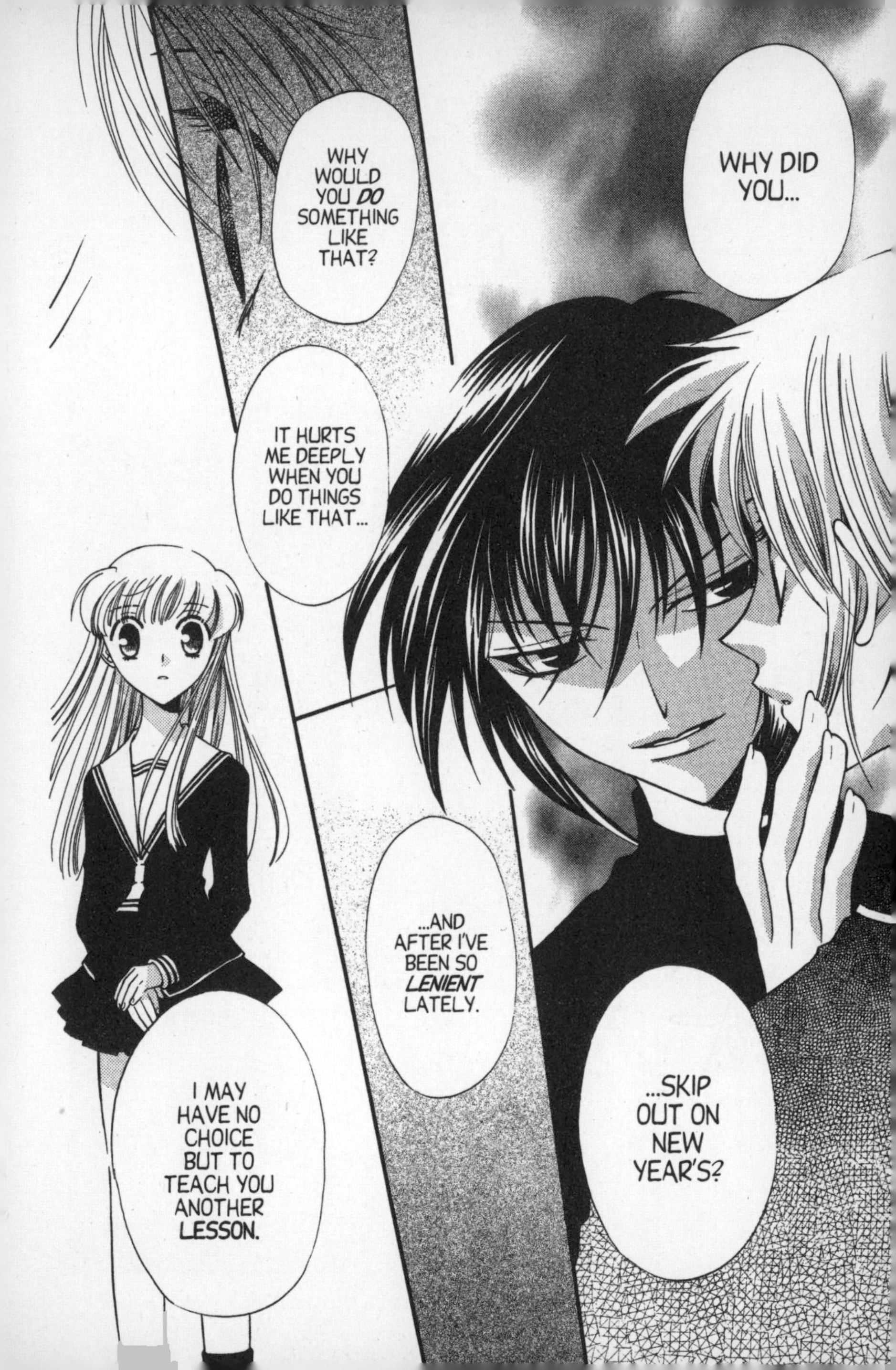
WHY DID YOU...
...SKIP OUT ON NEW YEAR'S?
...AND AFTER I'VE BEEN SO *LENIENT* LATELY.
WHY WOULD YOU *DO* SOMETHING LIKE THAT?
IT HURTS ME DEEPLY WHEN YOU DO THINGS LIKE THAT...
I MAY HAVE NO CHOICE BUT TO TEACH YOU ANOTHER **LESSON.**

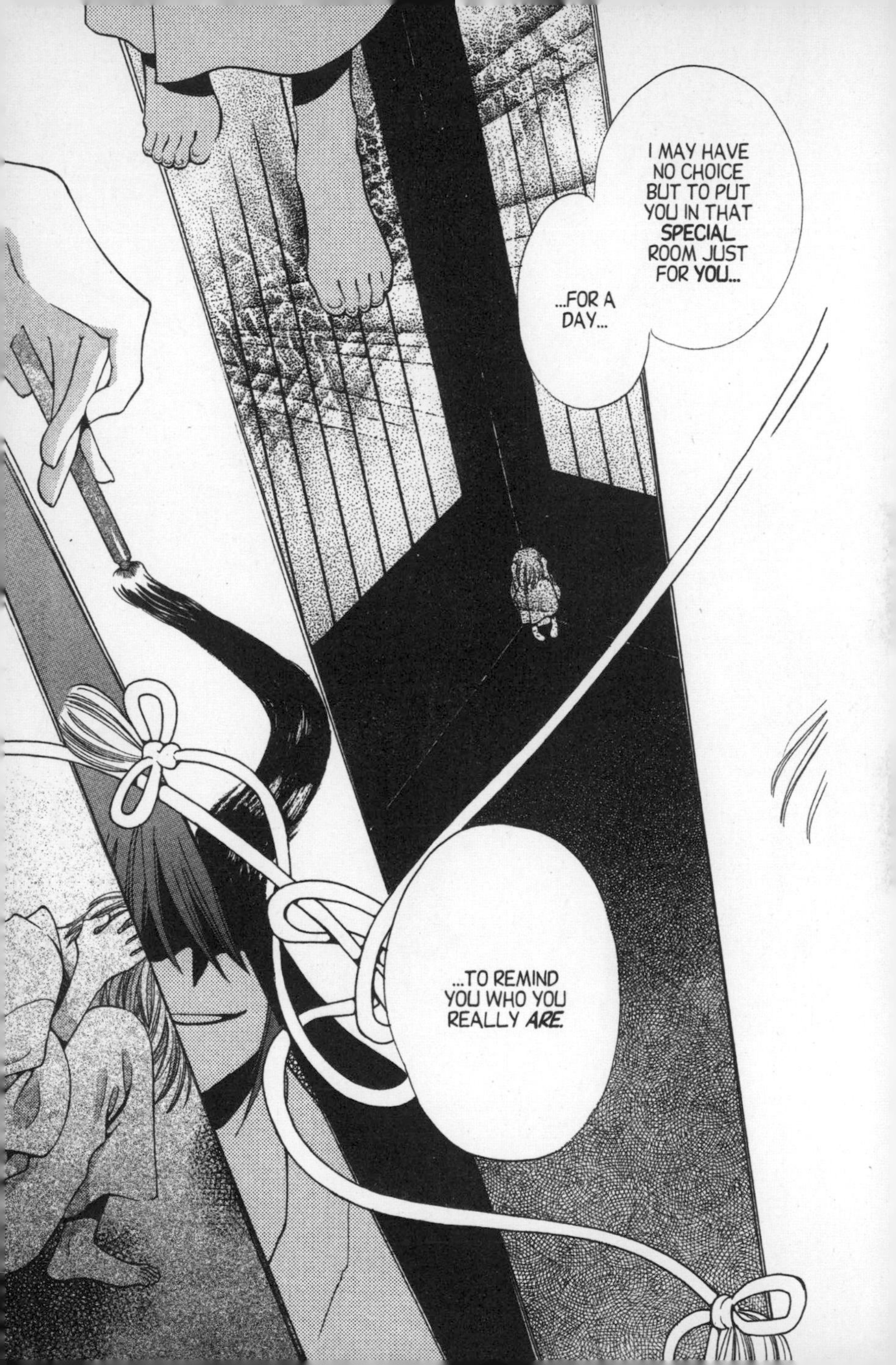
I MAY HAVE NO CHOICE BUT TO PUT YOU IN THAT SPECIAL ROOM JUST FOR YOU...
...FOR A DAY...
...TO REMIND YOU WHO YOU REALLY ARE.

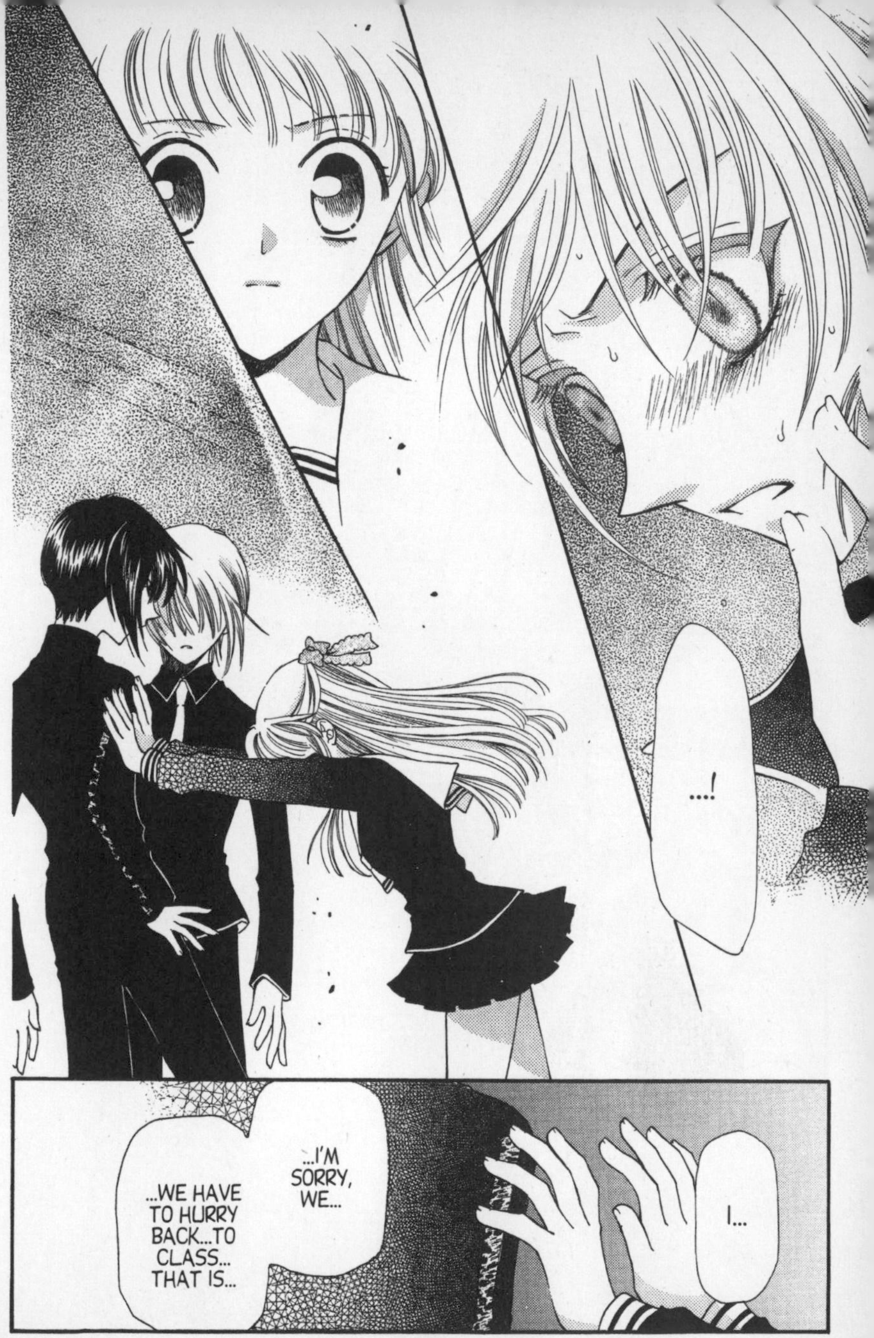
...!
I...
...I'M SORRY, WE...
...WE HAVE TO HURRY BACK...TO CLASS... THAT IS...

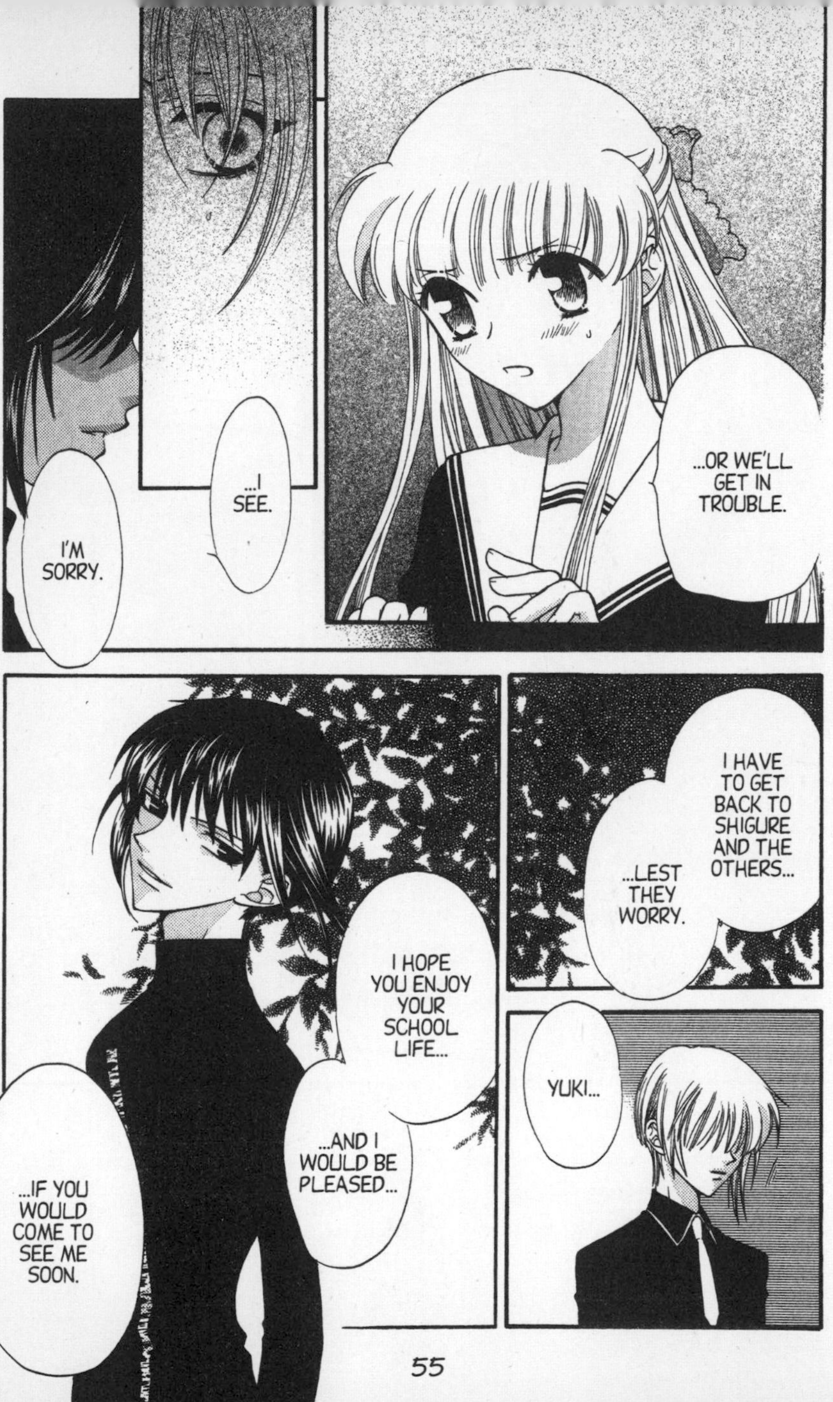
...OR WE'LL GET IN TROUBLE.
...I SEE.
I'M SORRY.
I HAVE TO GET BACK TO SHIGURE AND THE OTHERS...
...LEST THEY WORRY.
YUKI...
I HOPE YOU ENJOY YOUR SCHOOL LIFE...
...AND I WOULD BE PLEASED...
...IF YOU WOULD COME TO SEE ME SOON.

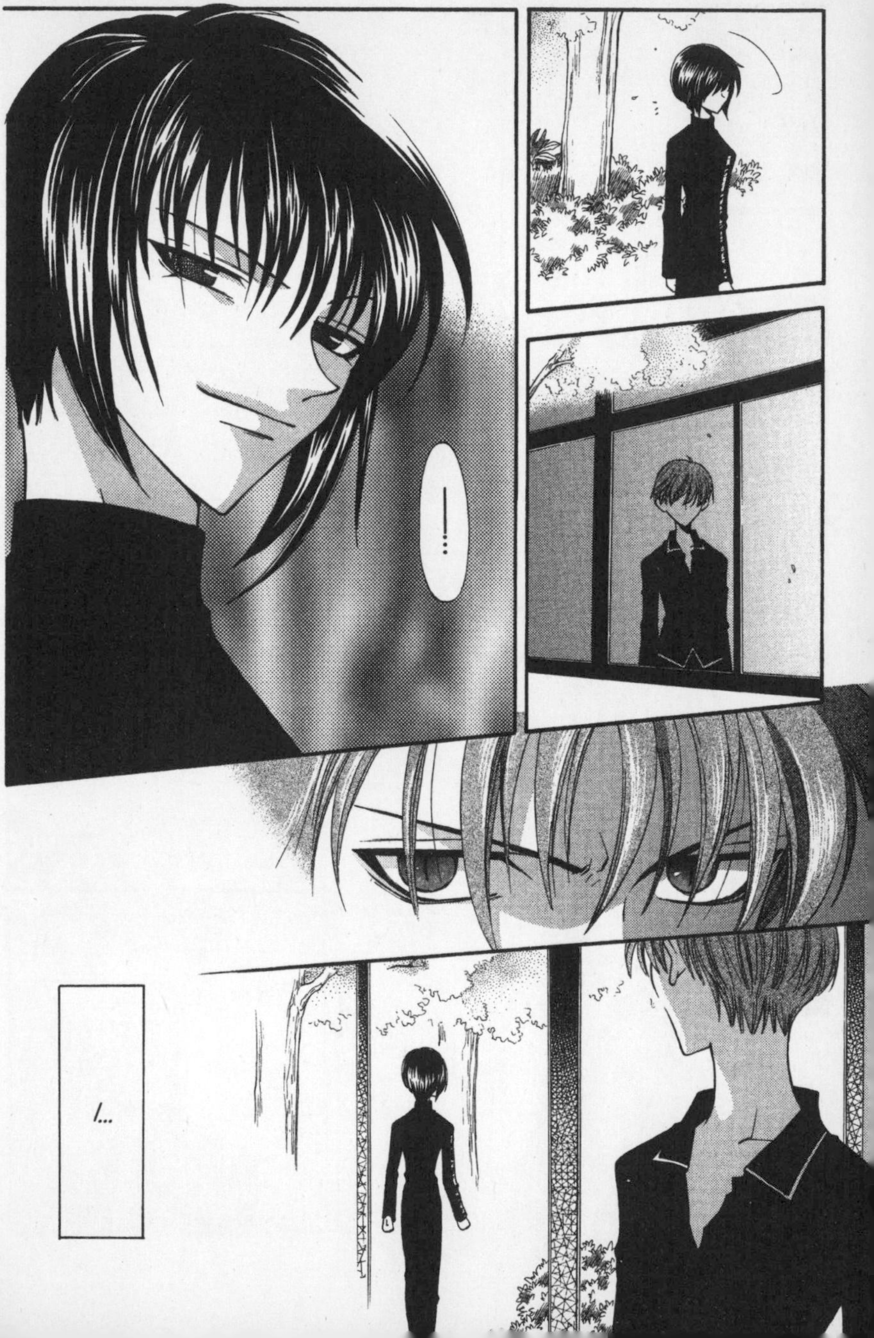

...!
I...

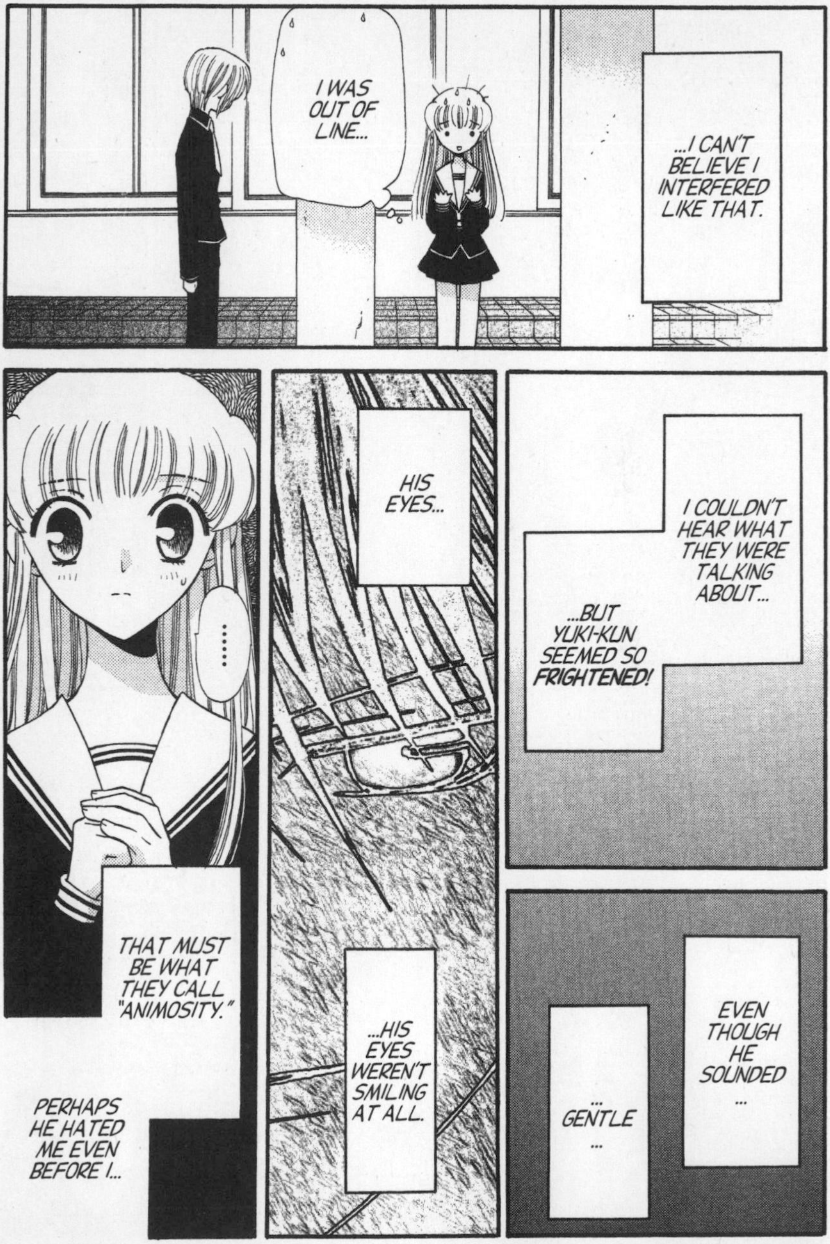
...I CAN'T BELIEVE I INTERFERED LIKE THAT.
I WAS OUT OF LINE...
I COULDN'T HEAR WHAT THEY WERE TALKING ABOUT...
...BUT YUKI-KUN SEEMED SO FRIGHTENED!
EVEN THOUGH HE SOUNDED...
...GENTLE...
HIS EYES...
...HIS EYES WEREN'T SMILING AT ALL.
......
THAT MUST BE WHAT THEY CALL "ANIMOSITY."
PERHAPS HE HATED ME EVEN BEFORE I...

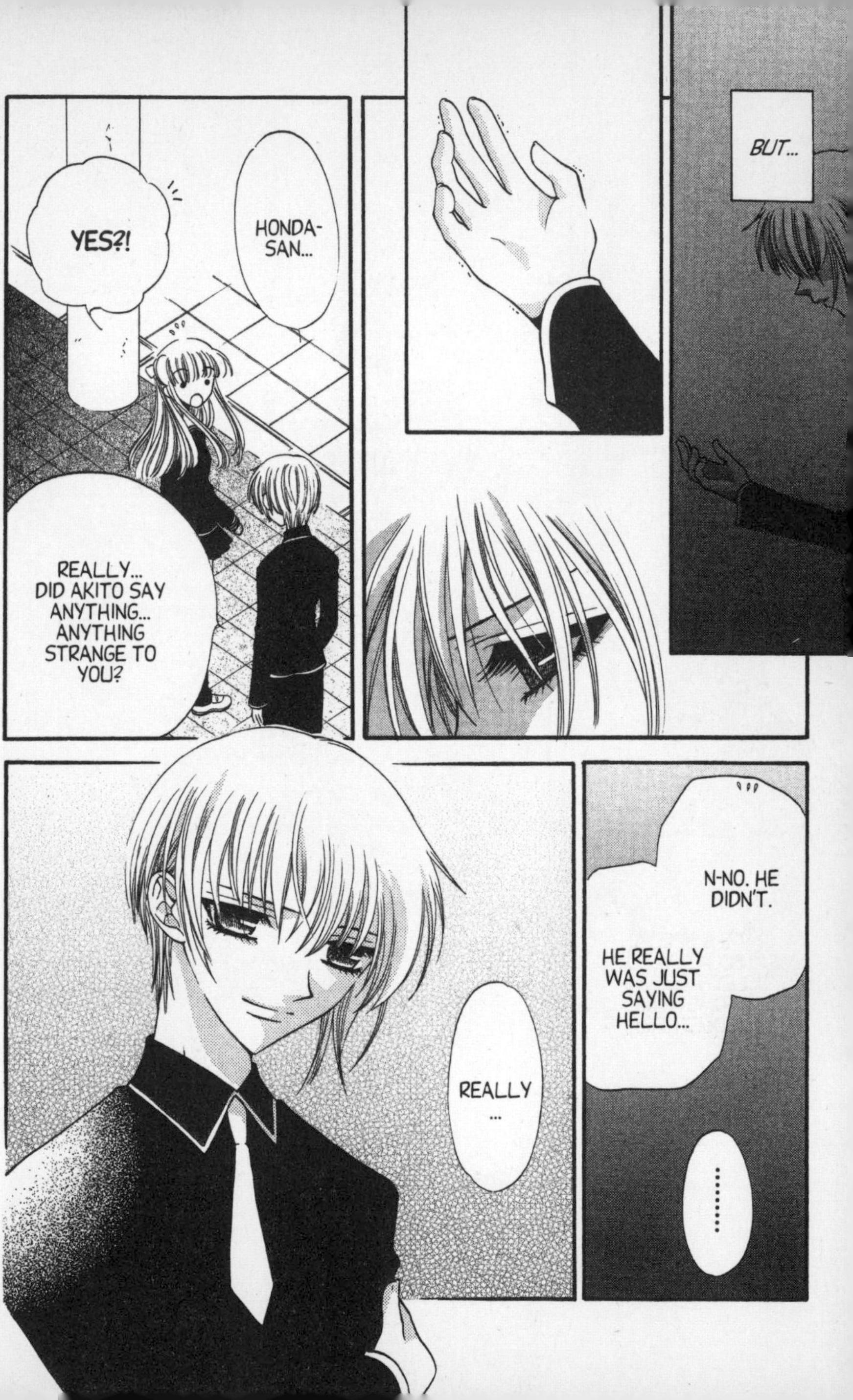
BUT...
HONDA-SAN...
YES?!
REALLY... DID AKITO SAY ANYTHING... ANYTHING STRANGE TO YOU?
N-NO. HE DIDN'T.
HE REALLY WAS JUST SAYING HELLO...
......
REALLY...

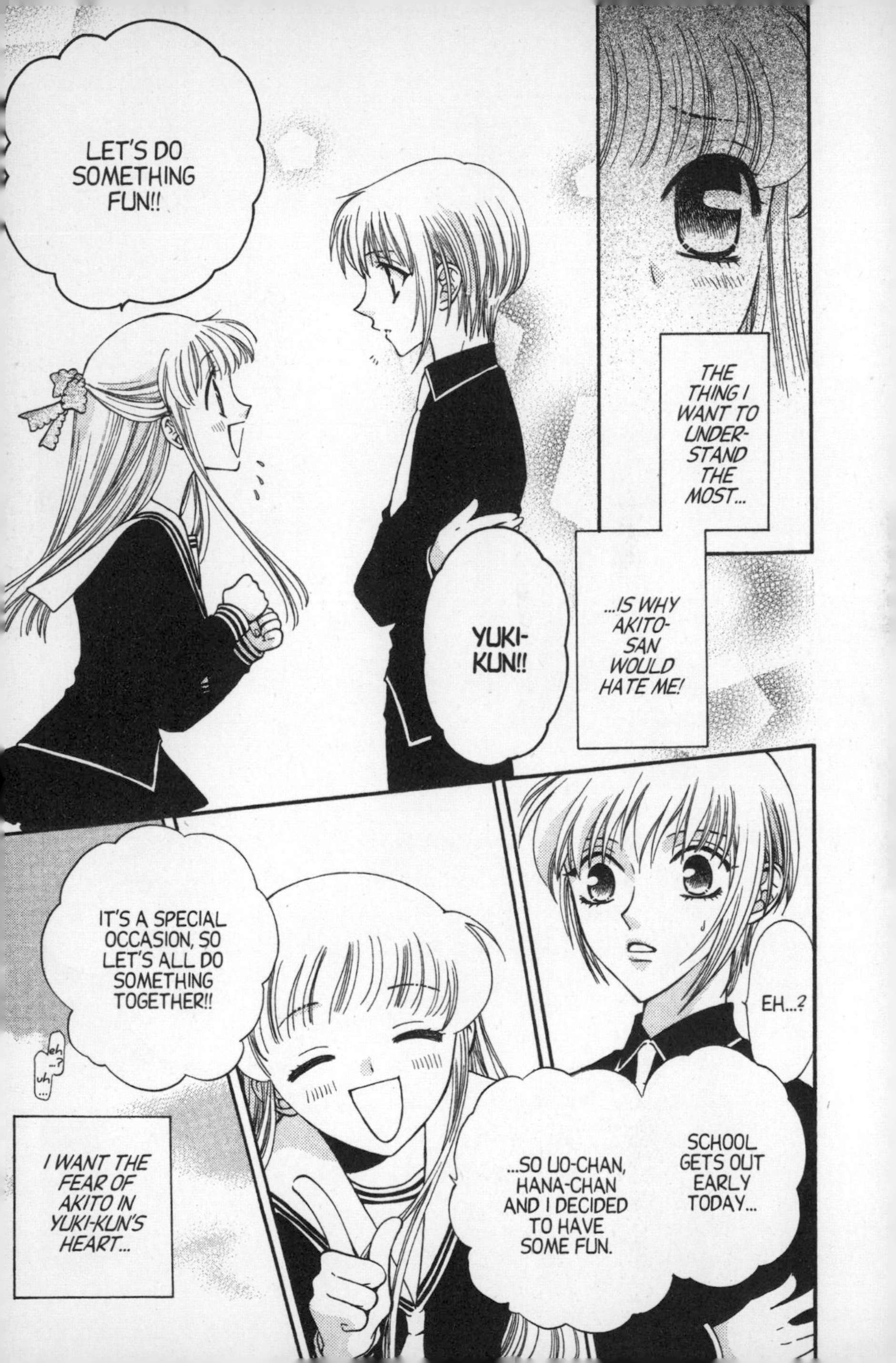
THE THING I WANT TO UNDER-STAND THE MOST...
...IS WHY AKITO-SAN WOULD HATE ME!
YUKI-KUN!!
LET'S DO SOMETHING FUN!!
EH...?
SCHOOL GETS OUT EARLY TODAY...
...SO UO-CHAN, HANA-CHAN AND I DECIDED TO HAVE SOME FUN.
IT'S A SPECIAL OCCASION, SO LET'S ALL DO SOMETHING TOGETHER!!
eh ...? uh ...
I WANT THE FEAR OF AKITO IN YUKI-KUN'S HEART...

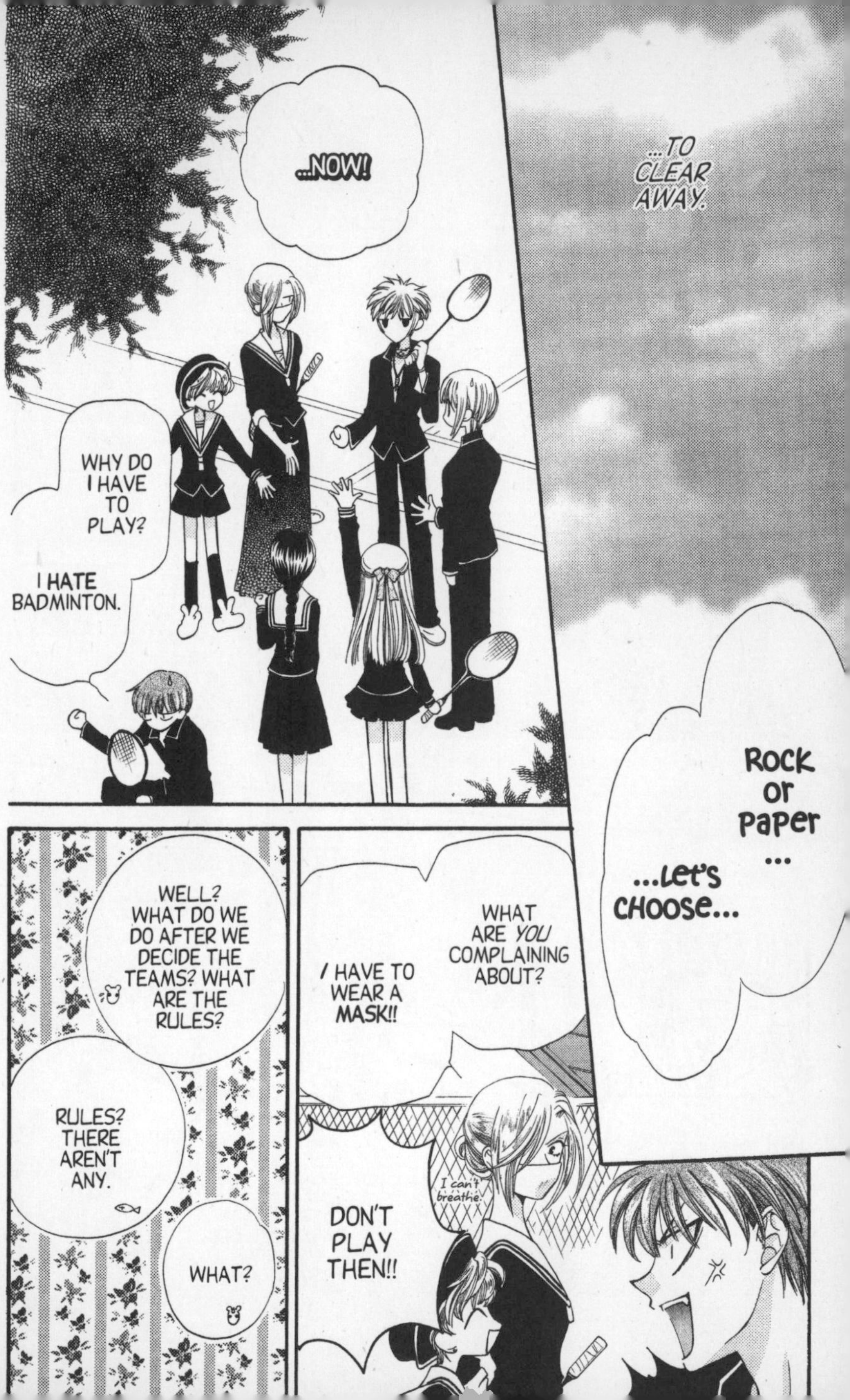
...TO CLEAR AWAY.
Rock or Paper ...
...let's choose...
...NOW!
WHY DO I HAVE TO PLAY?
I HATE BADMINTON.
WHAT ARE YOU COMPLAINING ABOUT?
I HAVE TO WEAR A MASK!!
I can't breathe.
DON'T PLAY THEN!!
WELL? WHAT DO WE DO AFTER WE DECIDE THE TEAMS? WHAT ARE THE RULES?
RULES? THERE AREN'T ANY.
WHAT?

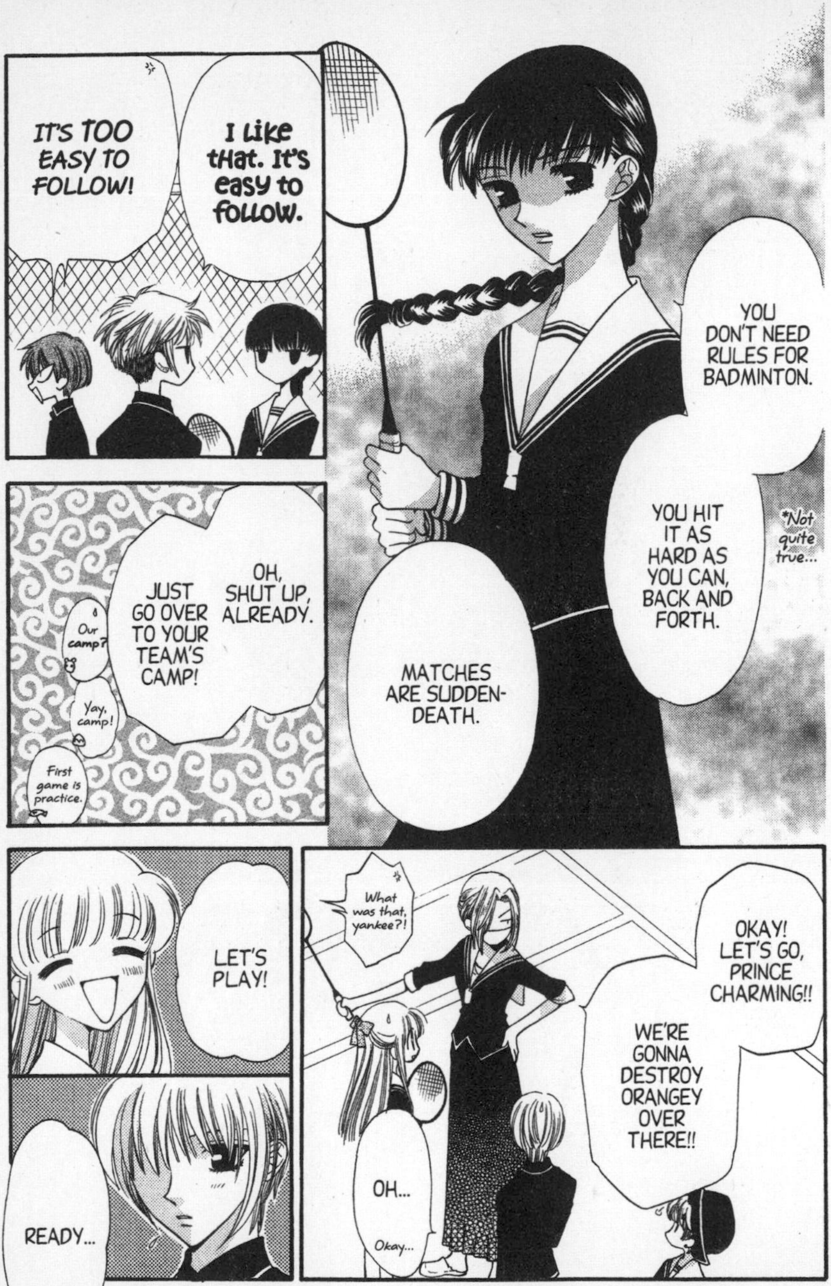
YOU DON'T NEED RULES FOR BADMINTON.
YOU HIT IT AS HARD AS YOU CAN, BACK AND FORTH.
*Not quite true...
MATCHES ARE SUDDEN-DEATH.
I like that. It's easy to follow.
IT'S TOO EASY TO FOLLOW!
OH, SHUT UP, ALREADY.
JUST GO OVER TO YOUR TEAM'S CAMP!
Our camp?
Yay, camp!
First game is practice.
OKAY! LET'S GO, PRINCE CHARMING!!
WE'RE GONNA DESTROY ORANGEY OVER THERE!!
What was that, yankee?!
OH...
Okay...
LET'S PLAY!
READY...

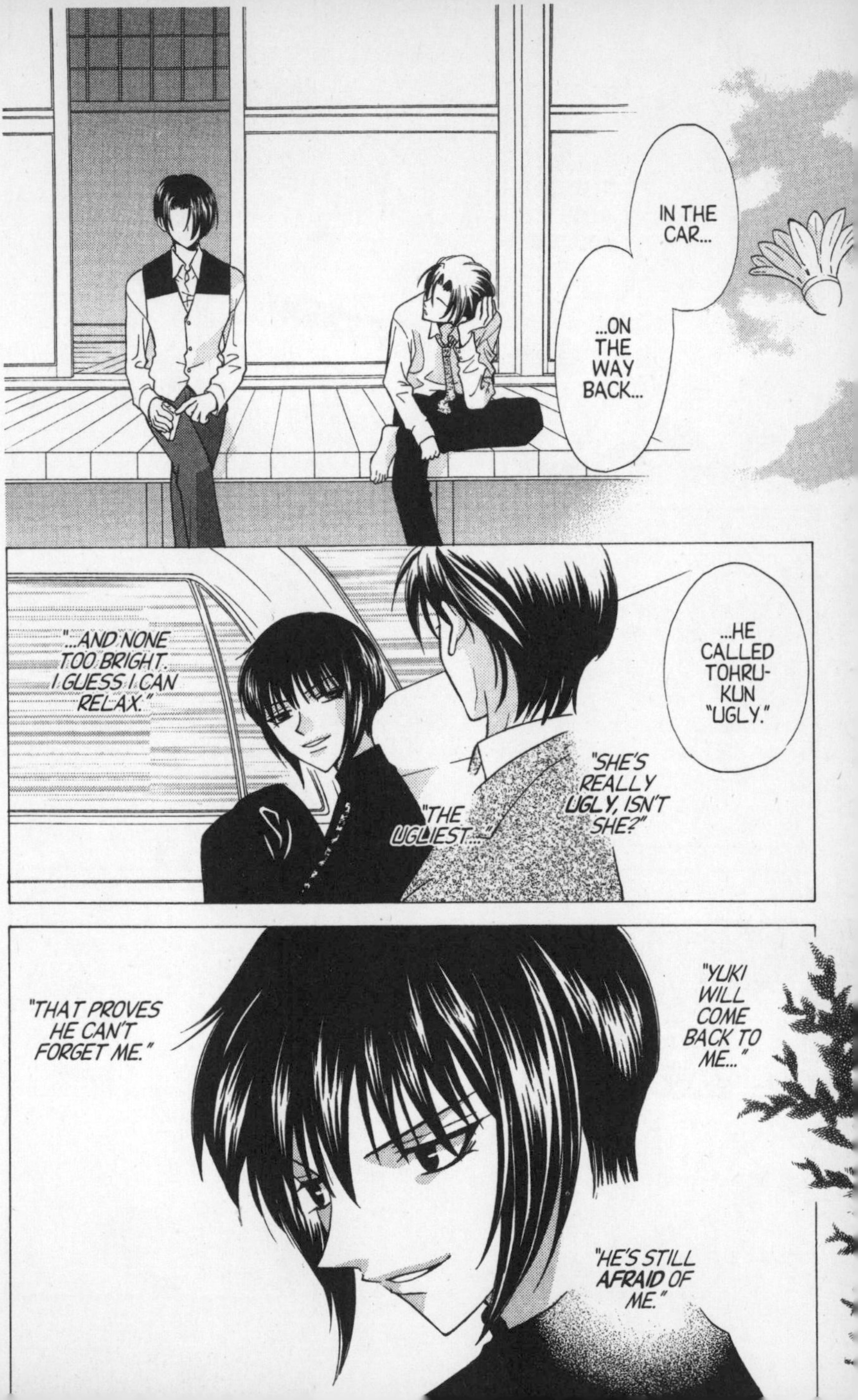
IN THE CAR...
...ON THE WAY BACK...
...HE CALLED TOHRU-KUN "UGLY."
"SHE'S REALLY UGLY, ISN'T SHE?"
"THE UGLIEST..."
"...AND NONE TOO BRIGHT. I GUESS I CAN RELAX."
"YUKI WILL COME BACK TO ME..."
"THAT PROVES HE CAN'T FORGET ME."
"HE'S STILL AFRAID OF ME."

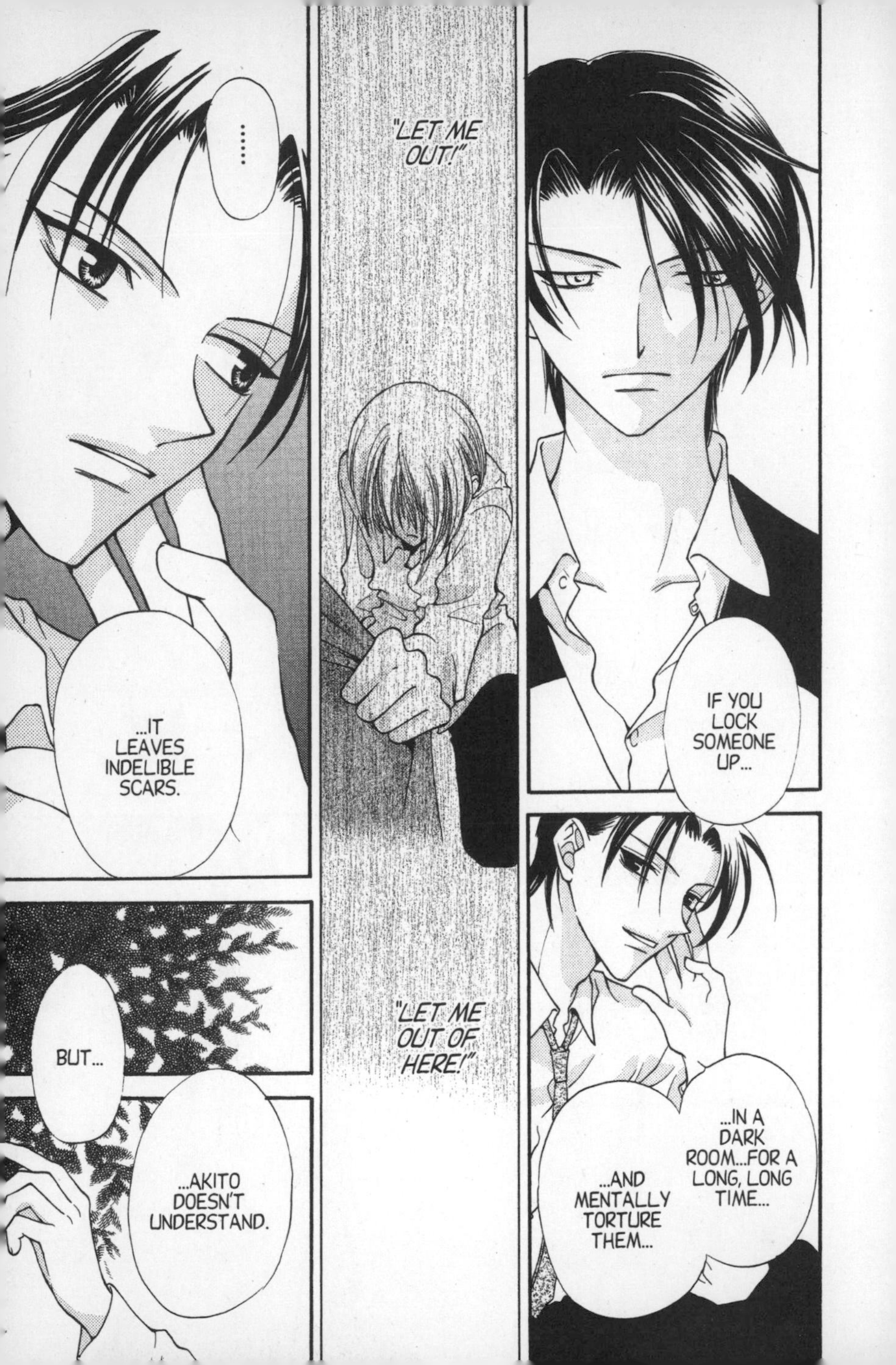

IF YOU LOCK SOMEONE UP...
...IN A DARK ROOM...FOR A LONG, LONG TIME...
...AND MENTALLY TORTURE THEM...
"LET ME OUT!"
"LET ME OUT OF HERE!"
......
...IT LEAVES INDELIBLE SCARS.
BUT...
...AKITO DOESN'T UNDERSTAND.

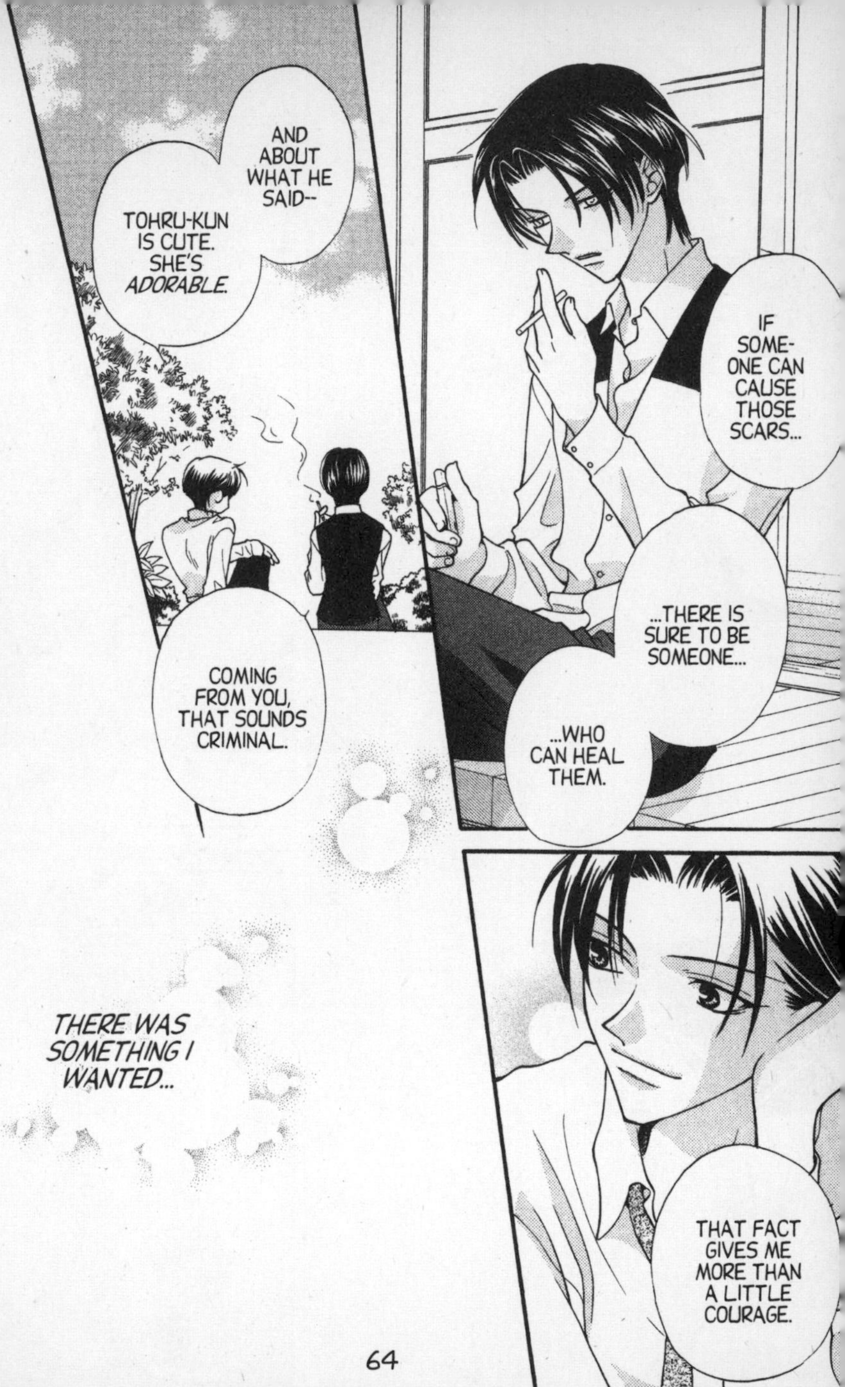
IF SOMEONE CAN CAUSE THOSE SCARS...
...THERE IS SURE TO BE SOMEONE...
...WHO CAN HEAL THEM.
AND ABOUT WHAT HE SAID--
TOHRU-KUN IS CUTE. SHE'S *ADORABLE.*
COMING FROM YOU, THAT SOUNDS CRIMINAL.
THAT FACT GIVES ME MORE THAN A LITTLE COURAGE.
THERE WAS SOMETHING I WANTED...

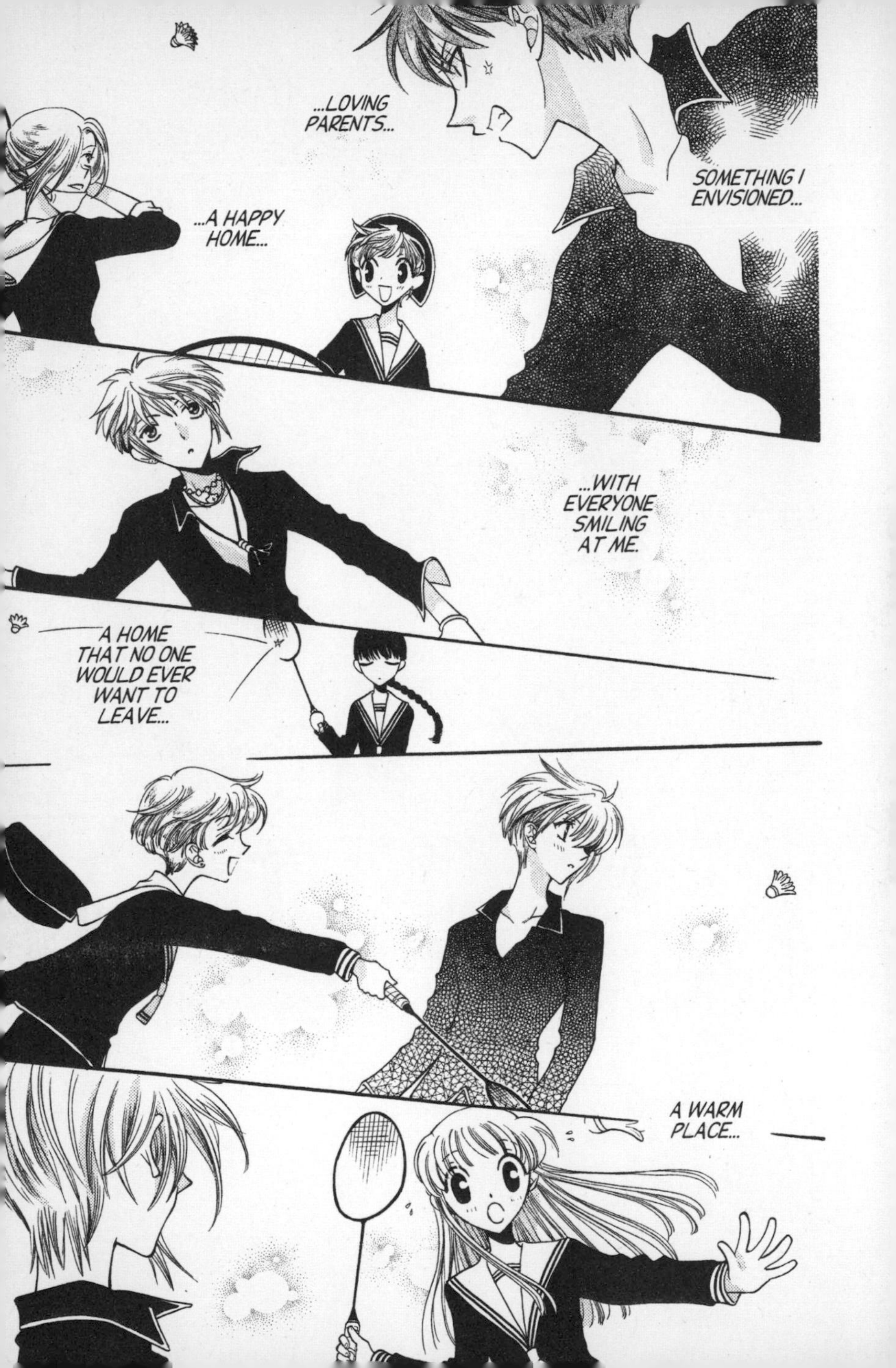
SOMETHING I ENVISIONED...
...LOVING PARENTS...
...A HAPPY HOME...
...WITH EVERYONE SMILING AT ME.
A HOME THAT NO ONE WOULD EVER WANT TO LEAVE...
A WARM PLACE...

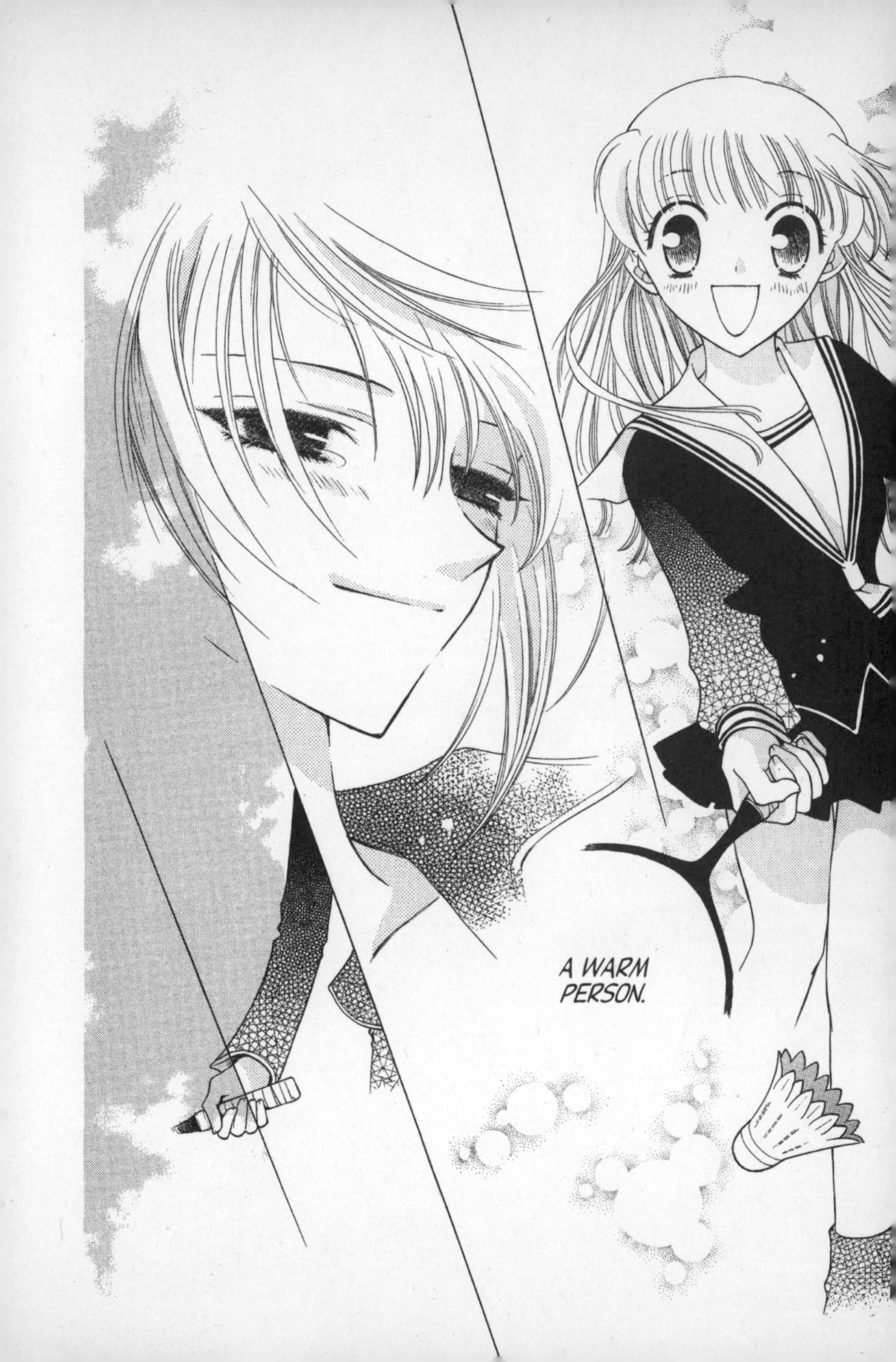
A WARM PERSON.

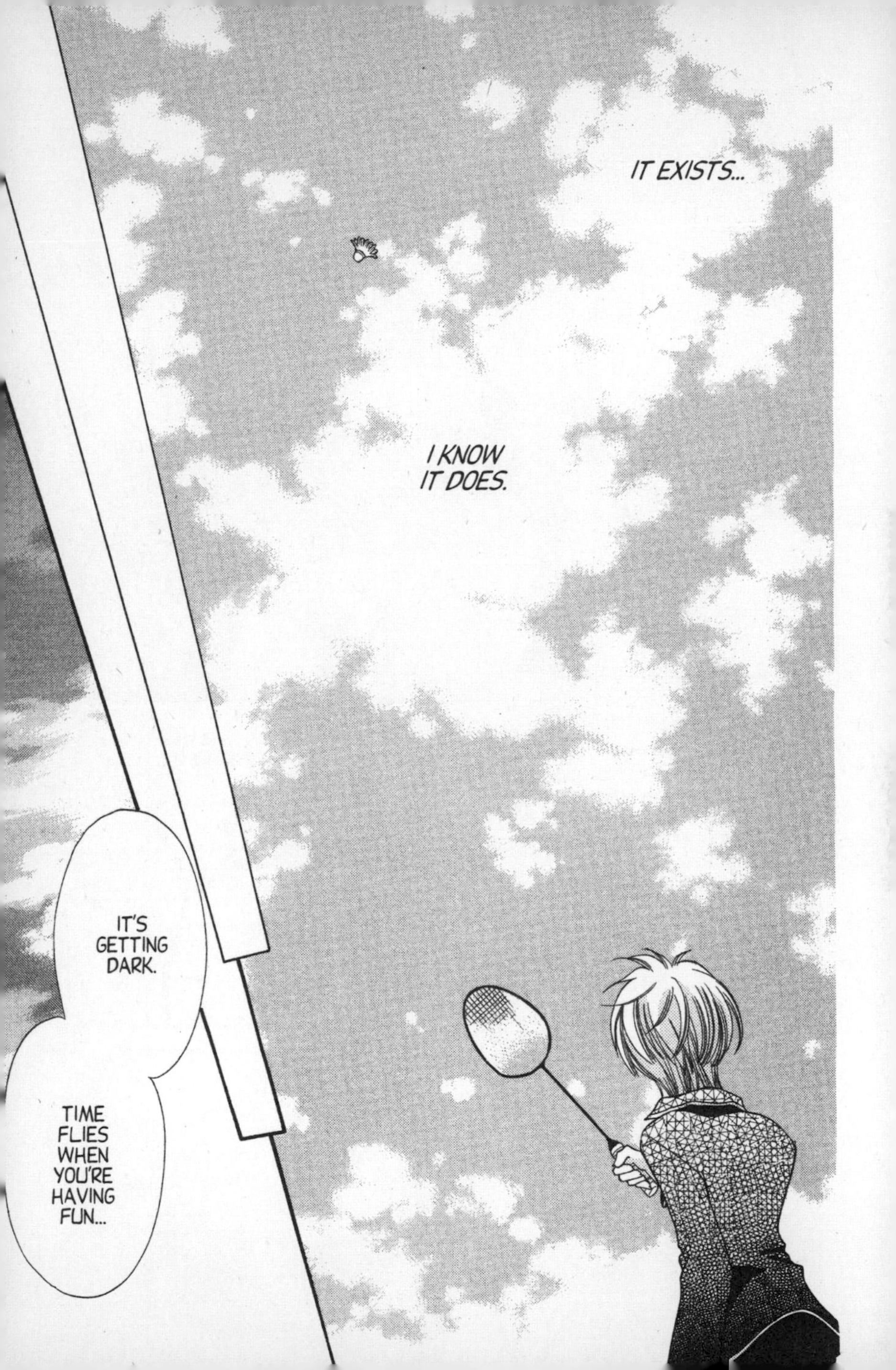
IT EXISTS...
I KNOW IT DOES.
IT'S GETTING DARK.
TIME FLIES WHEN YOU'RE HAVING FUN...

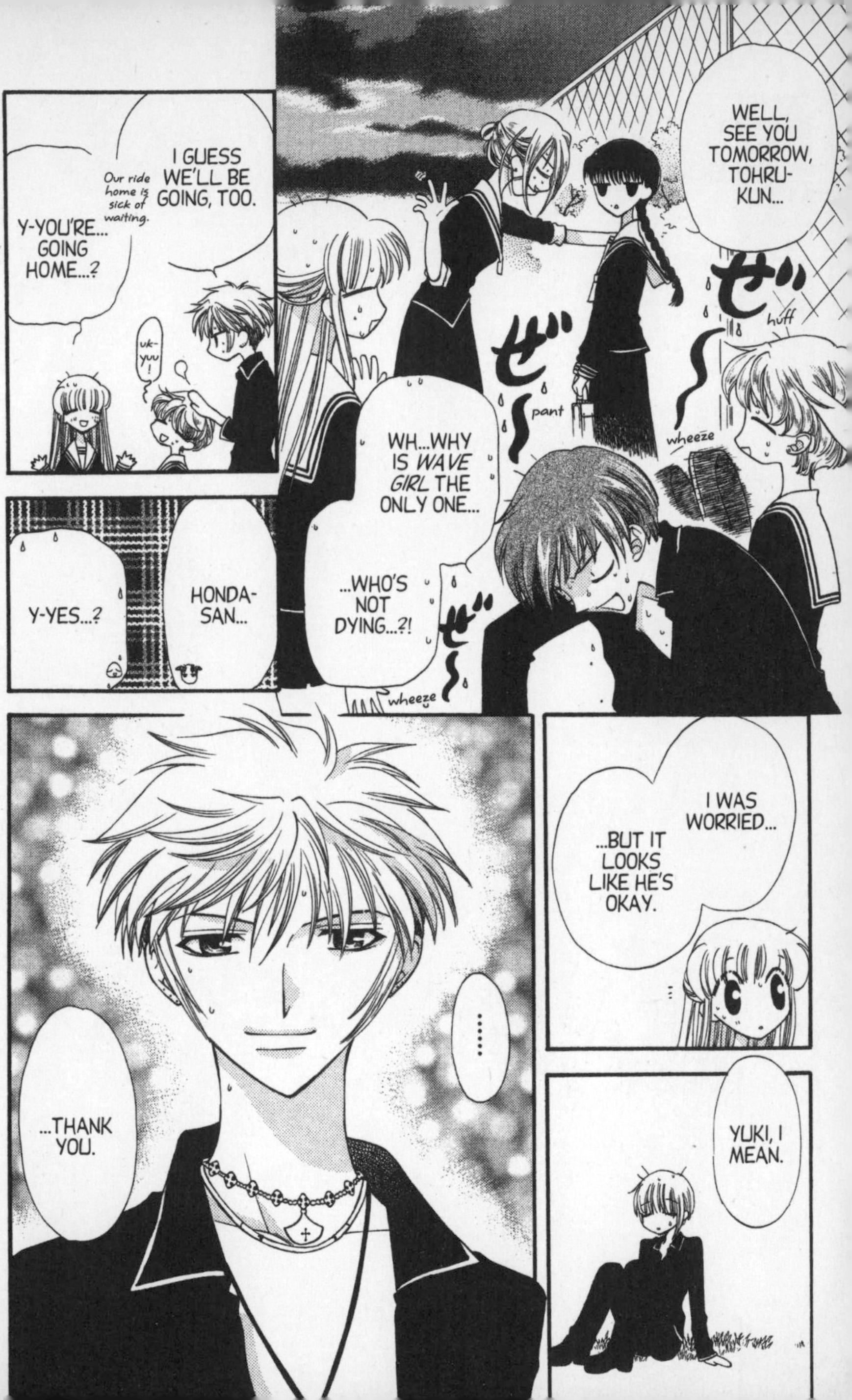
WELL, SEE YOU TOMORROW, TOHRU-KUN...
huff
wheeze
pant
WH...WHY IS *WAVE GIRL* THE ONLY ONE...
...WHO'S NOT DYING...?!
wheeze
I GUESS WE'LL BE GOING, TOO.
Our ride home is sick of waiting.
Y-YOU'RE... GOING HOME...?
uk-yuu!
HONDA-SAN...
Y-YES...?
I WAS WORRIED...
...BUT IT LOOKS LIKE HE'S OKAY.
YUKI, I MEAN.
......
...THANK YOU.

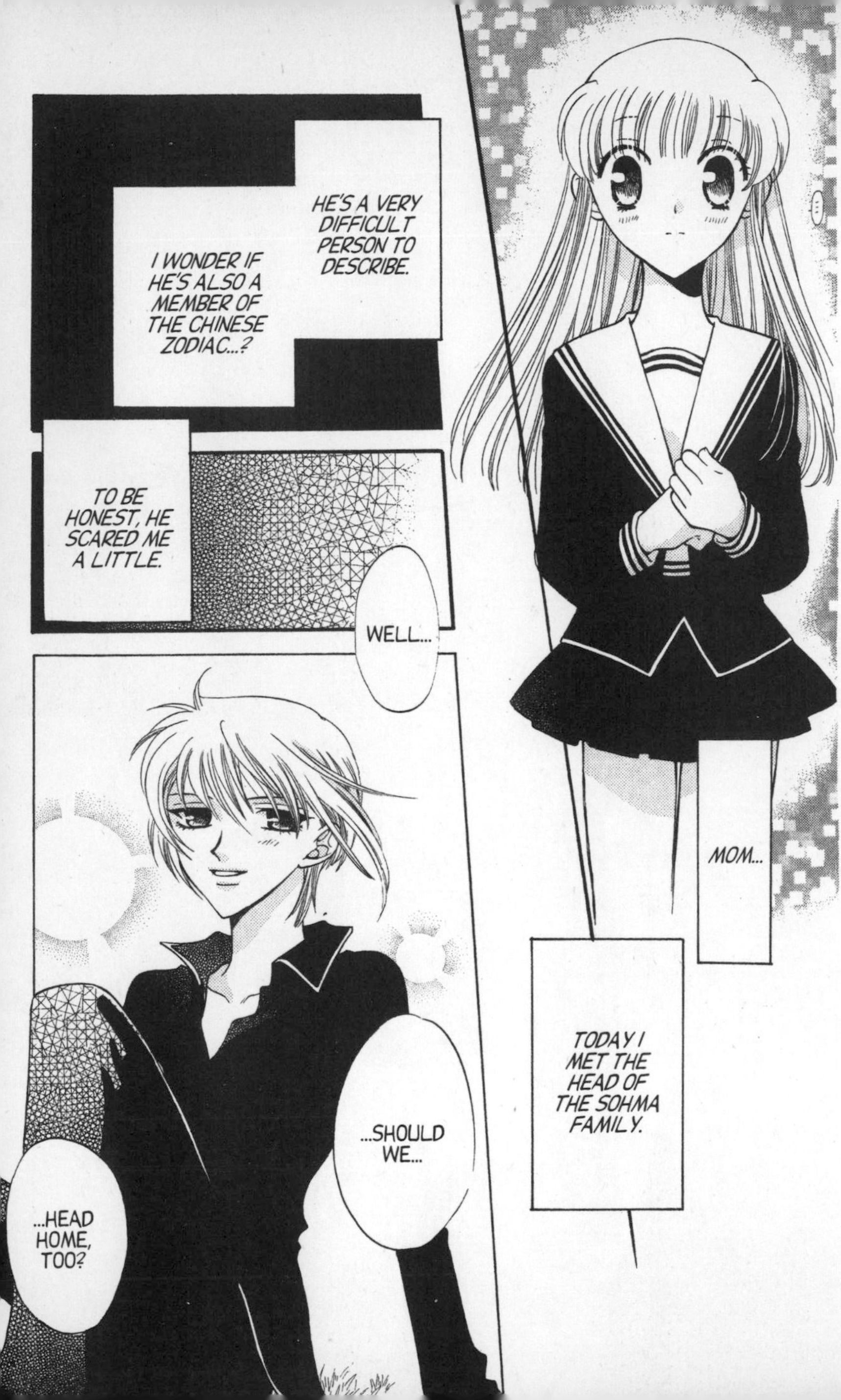
MOM...
TODAY I MET THE HEAD OF THE SOHMA FAMILY.
HE'S A VERY DIFFICULT PERSON TO DESCRIBE.
I WONDER IF HE'S ALSO A MEMBER OF THE CHINESE ZODIAC...?
TO BE HONEST, HE SCARED ME A LITTLE.
WELL...
...SHOULD WE...
...HEAD HOME, TOO?

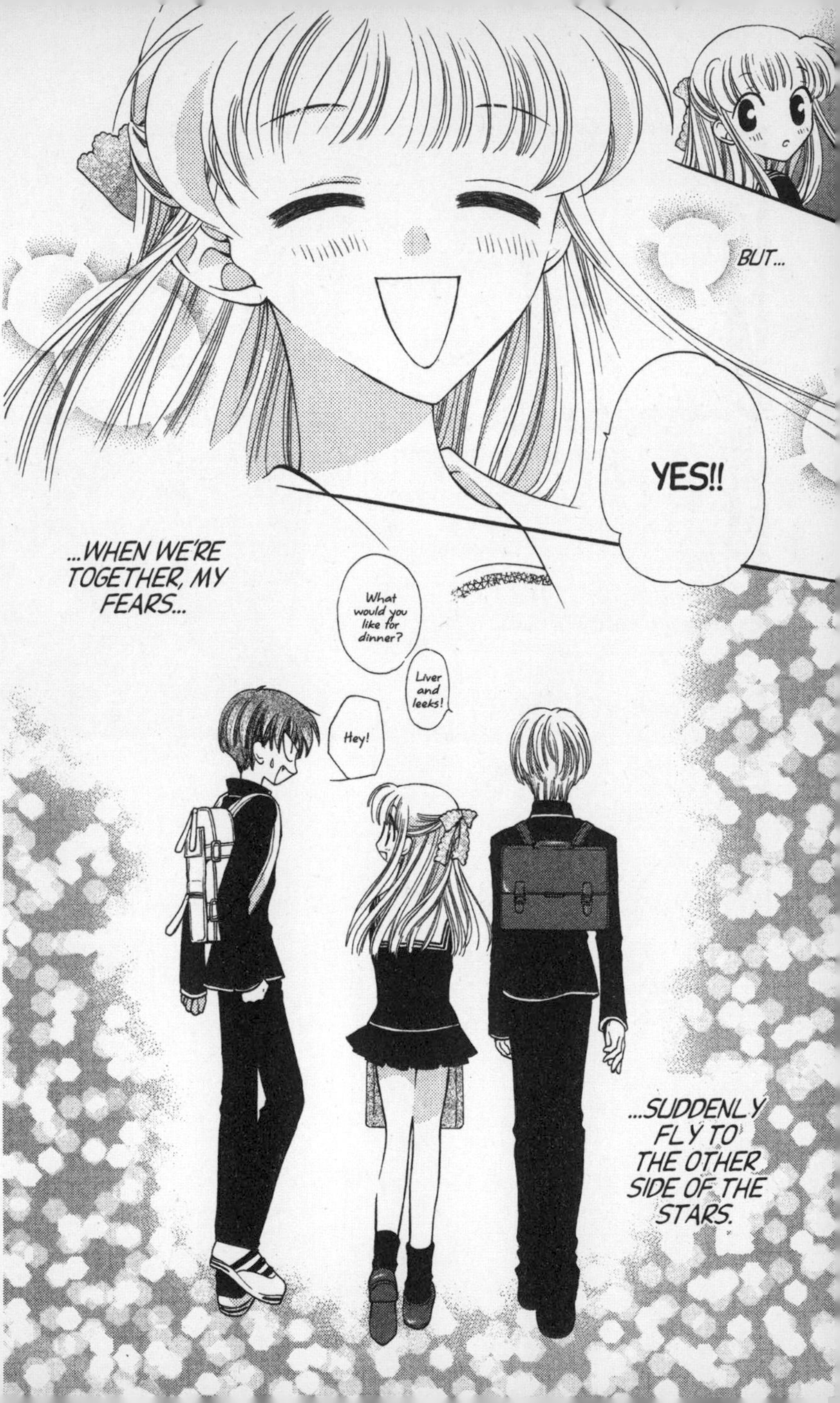

BUT...
YES!!
...WHEN WE'RE TOGETHER, MY FEARS...
What would you like for dinner?
Liver and leeks!
Hey!
...SUDDENLY FLY TO THE OTHER SIDE OF THE STARS.

Chapter 21

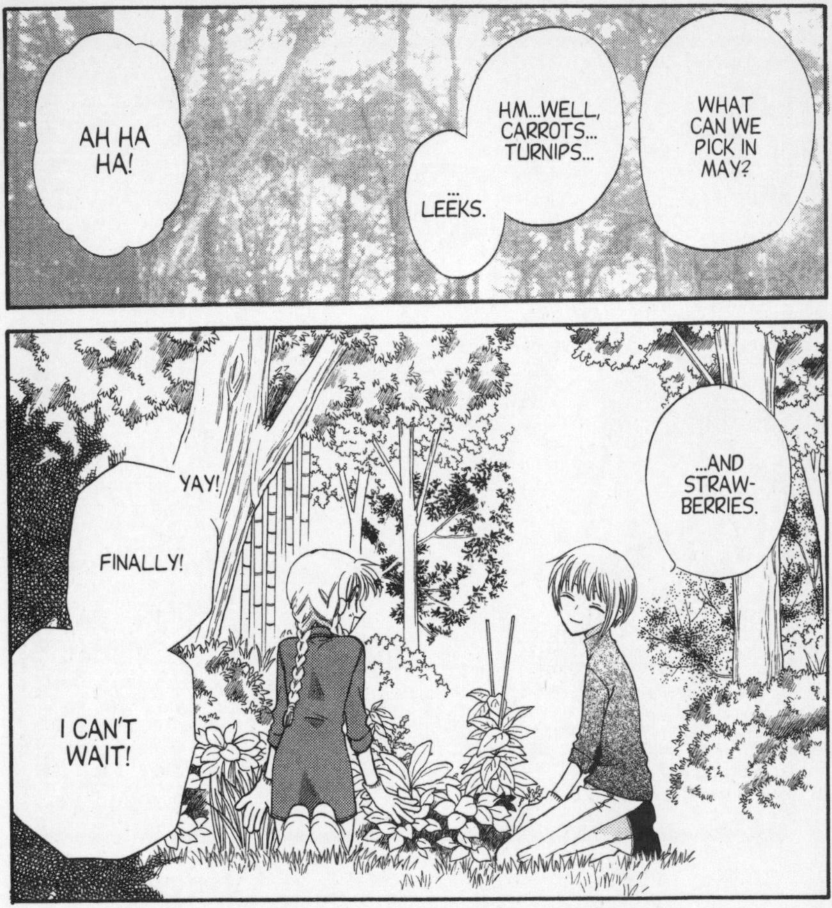
WHAT CAN WE PICK IN MAY?
HM...WELL, CARROTS... TURNIPS...
...LEEKS.
AH HA HA!
...AND STRAW-BERRIES.
YAY!
FINALLY!
I CAN'T WAIT!

ULTRA SPECIAL BLAH BLAH BLAH 3

Enter the moron...er, I mean--the older brother! He was dragged into the story pretty late, huh? He's very popular, though not as popular as the Mabudachi Trio! Sometimes people tell me that a character of mine looks like some famous person and it kind of hurts my feelings because I work so hard to create original characters! For some reason, it doesn't bother me if people compare my characters to each other, though.

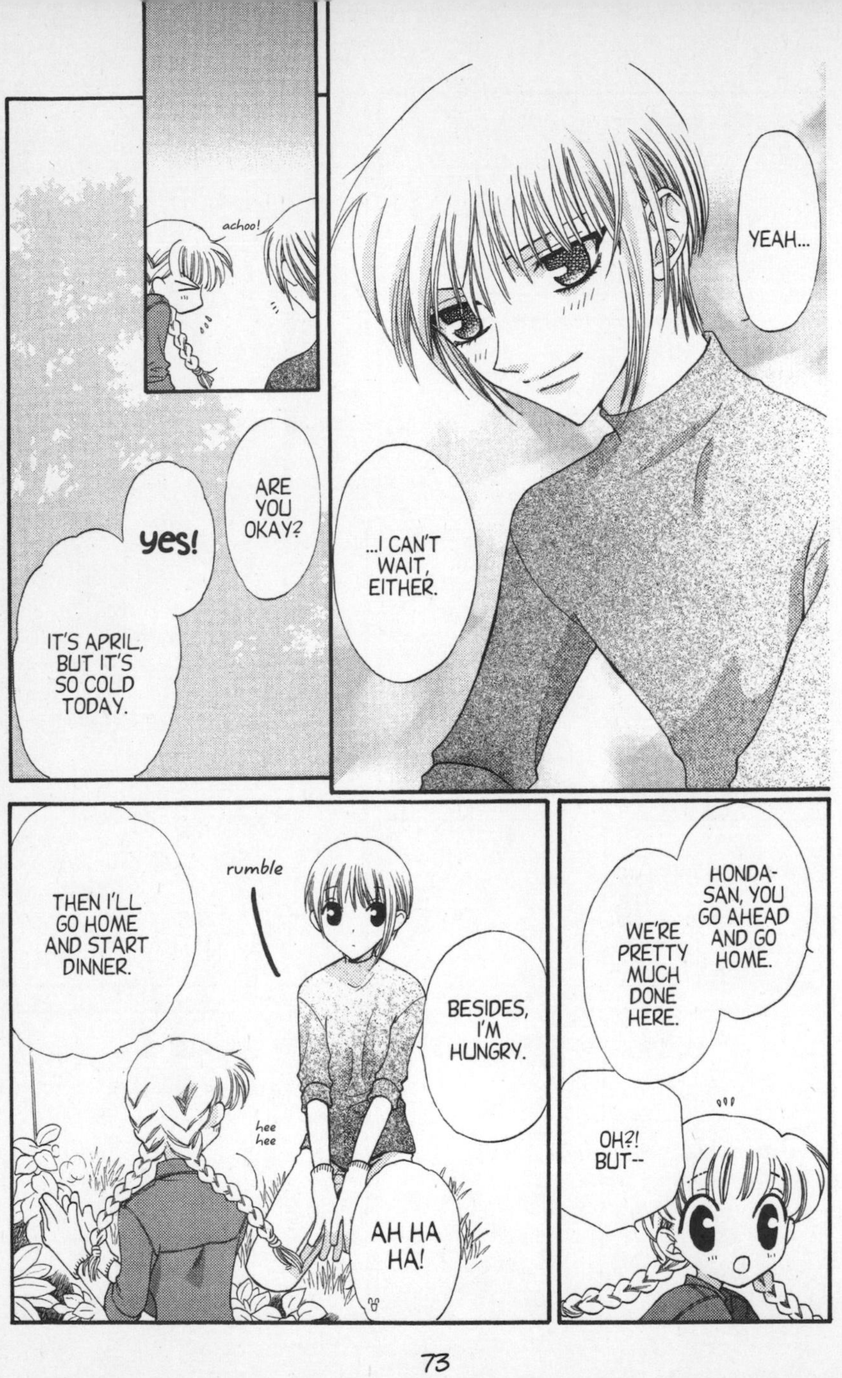
YEAH...
...I CAN'T WAIT, EITHER.
achoo!
ARE YOU OKAY?
yes!
IT'S APRIL, BUT IT'S SO COLD TODAY.
HONDA-SAN, YOU GO AHEAD AND GO HOME.
WE'RE PRETTY MUCH DONE HERE.
OH?! BUT--
BESIDES, I'M HUNGRY.
rumble
AH HA HA!
hee hee
THEN I'LL GO HOME AND START DINNER.

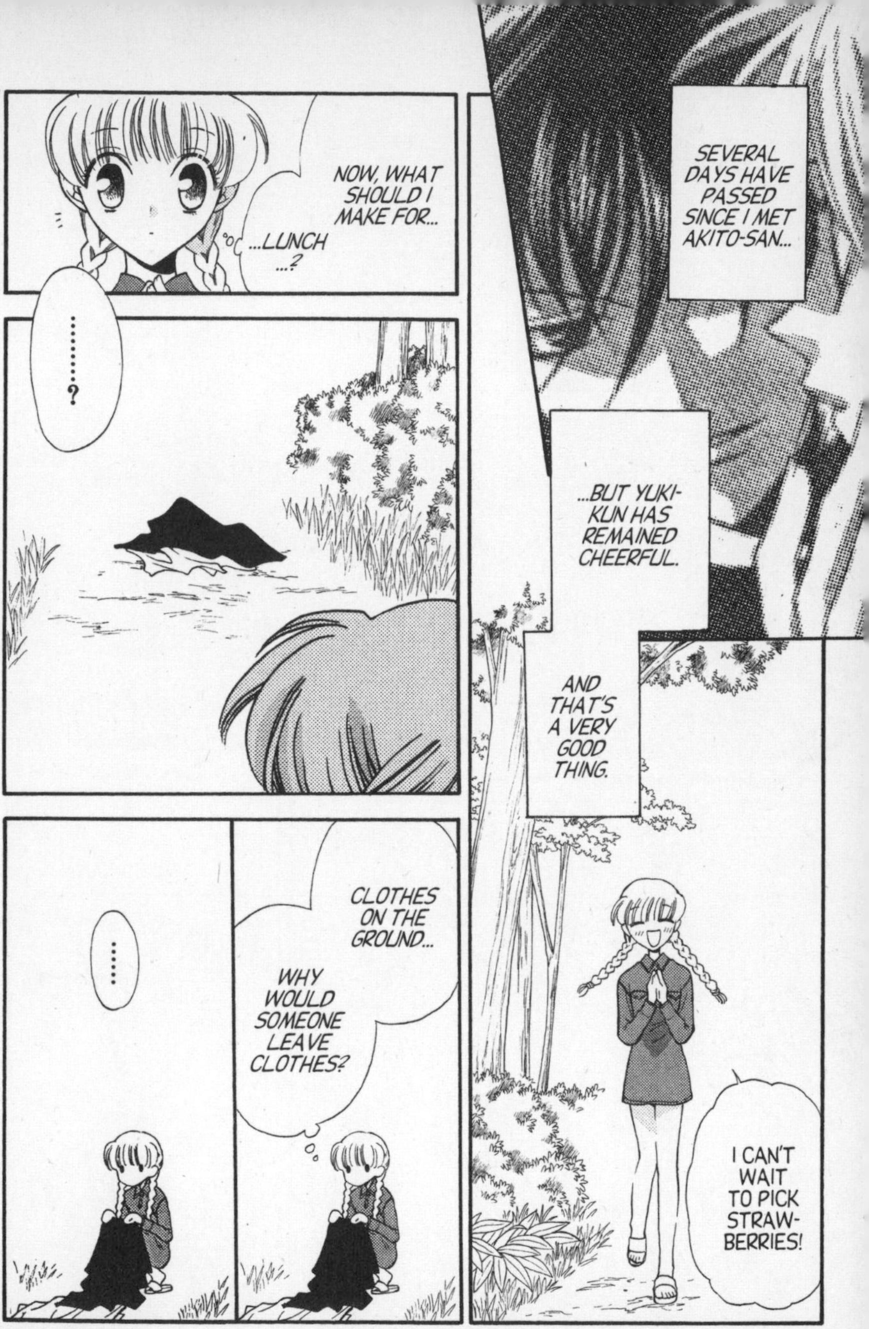
SEVERAL DAYS HAVE PASSED SINCE I MET AKITO-SAN...
...BUT YUKI-KUN HAS REMAINED CHEERFUL.
AND THAT'S A VERY GOOD THING.
I CAN'T WAIT TO PICK STRAW-BERRIES!
NOW, WHAT SHOULD I MAKE FOR...
...LUNCH ...?
......?
CLOTHES ON THE GROUND...
WHY WOULD SOMEONE LEAVE CLOTHES?
......

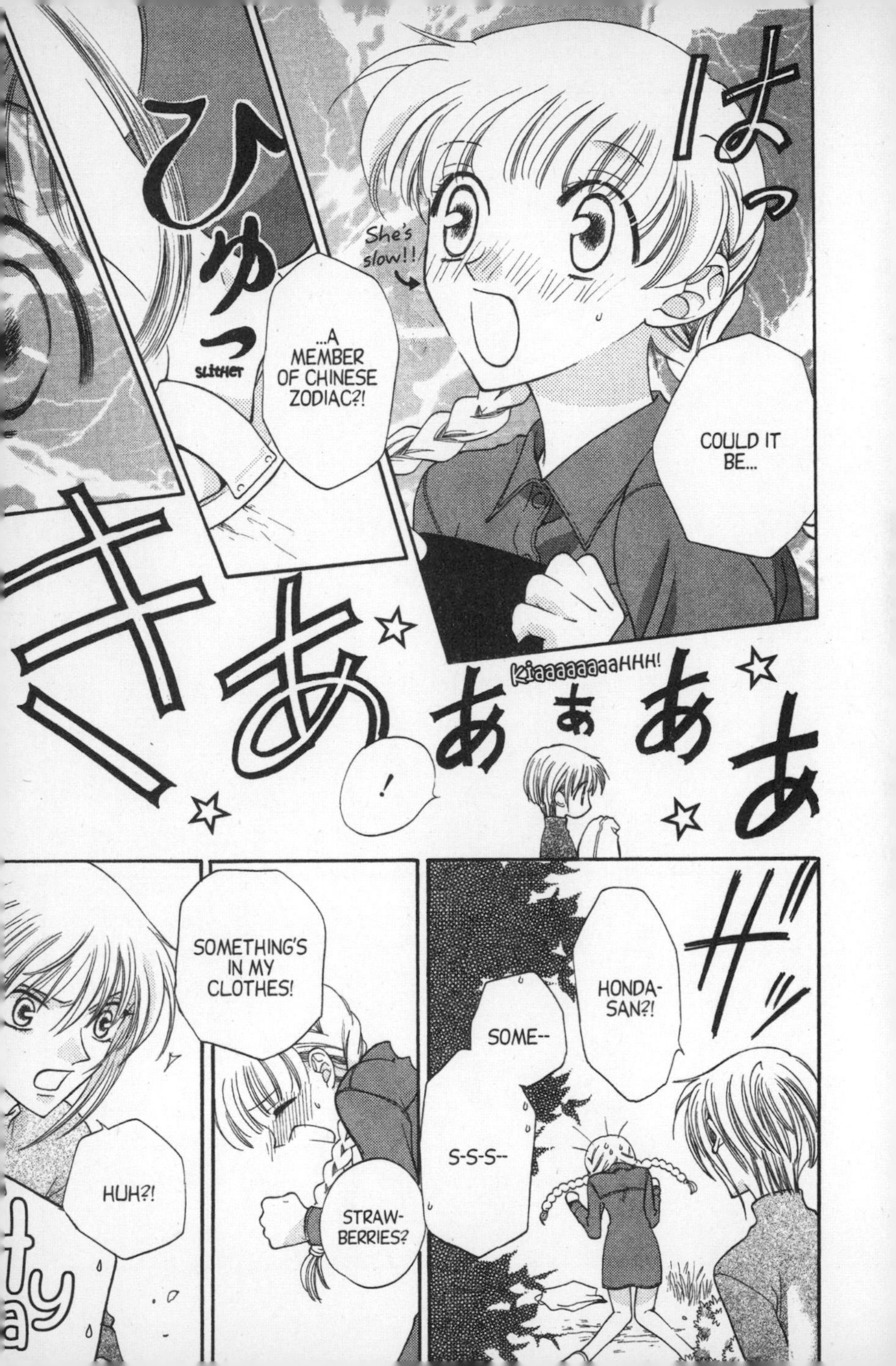

はっ
COULD IT BE...
She's slow!!
...A MEMBER OF CHINESE ZODIAC?!
ひゅっ
slither
キああぁああ
Kiaaaaaaaahhh!
!
ザッ
HONDA-SAN?!
SOME--
S-S-S--
SOMETHING'S IN MY CLOTHES!
STRAW-BERRIES?
HUH?!

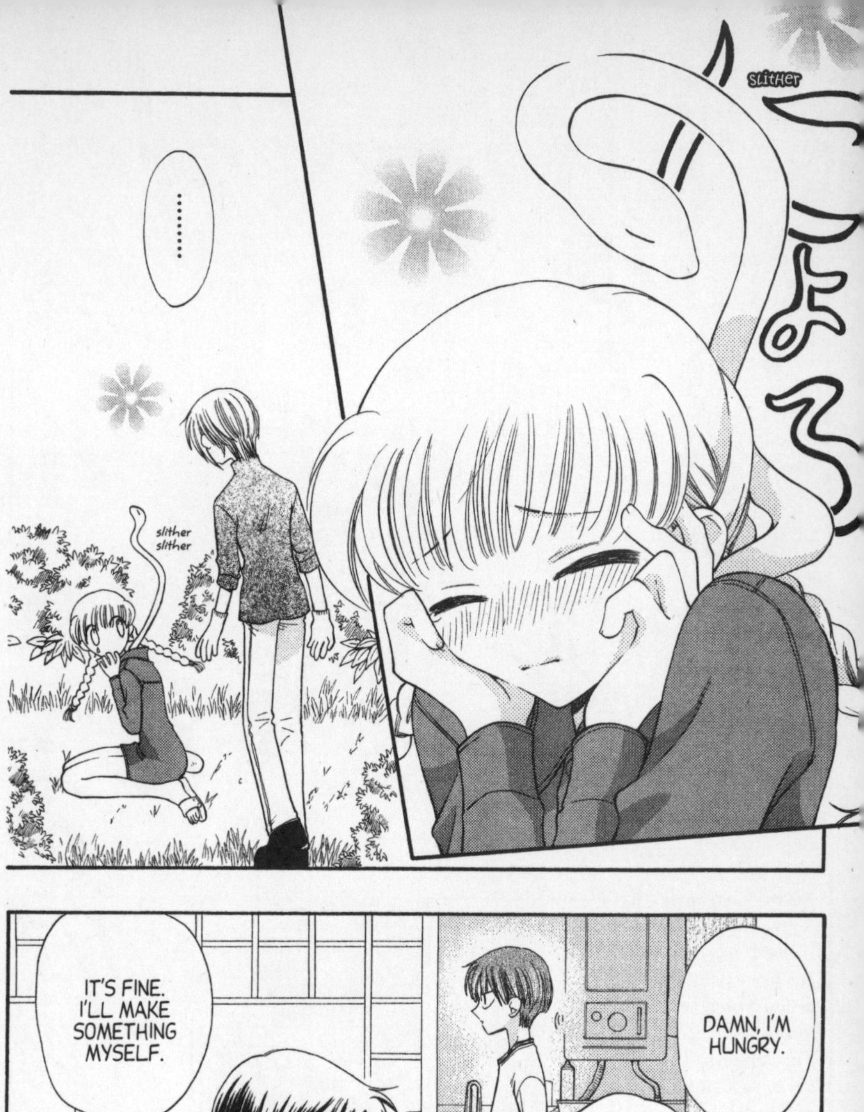
slither
……
slither slither
DAMN, I'M HUNGRY.
TOHRU-KUN SHOULD BE HOME SOON.
IT'S FINE. I'LL MAKE SOMETHING MYSELF.

HERE, KYO-KUN...
...HAVE SOME OF THIS.
IT'LL HOLD YOU OVER UNTIL DINNER.
Your miso
Onions, leeks and miso
DAMMIT, QUIT MAKING FUN OF ME!!
Oh my!
YOU MUSTN'T MISTREAT FOOD LIKE THAT, KYO-CHAN!!
slam
stomp stomp stomp
AT LAST!
IT LOOKS LIKE THEY'RE BA...

Fruits Basket 4 Part 3:

I went to my first autograph session—at the HanaYume festival. There were so many people, I got nervous! I wanted to say, "I'm not that great," you know? (I'm really not.) I even got presents. Thank you.
I thought of getting a Furuba print club, too, but the line was so long I gave up. (By the way, I've never taken a print club picture. There actually are people who haven't.) But I was very happy to have people thank me so sincerely. I really felt they meant it.
Anyway, did you enjoy the Hana-Yume festival? I'm very happy because I got a Hanya* plush toy! (Ha ha!)

*A character from the Hana to Yume comic, "Uchuu no Hate kara Konnichi wa"

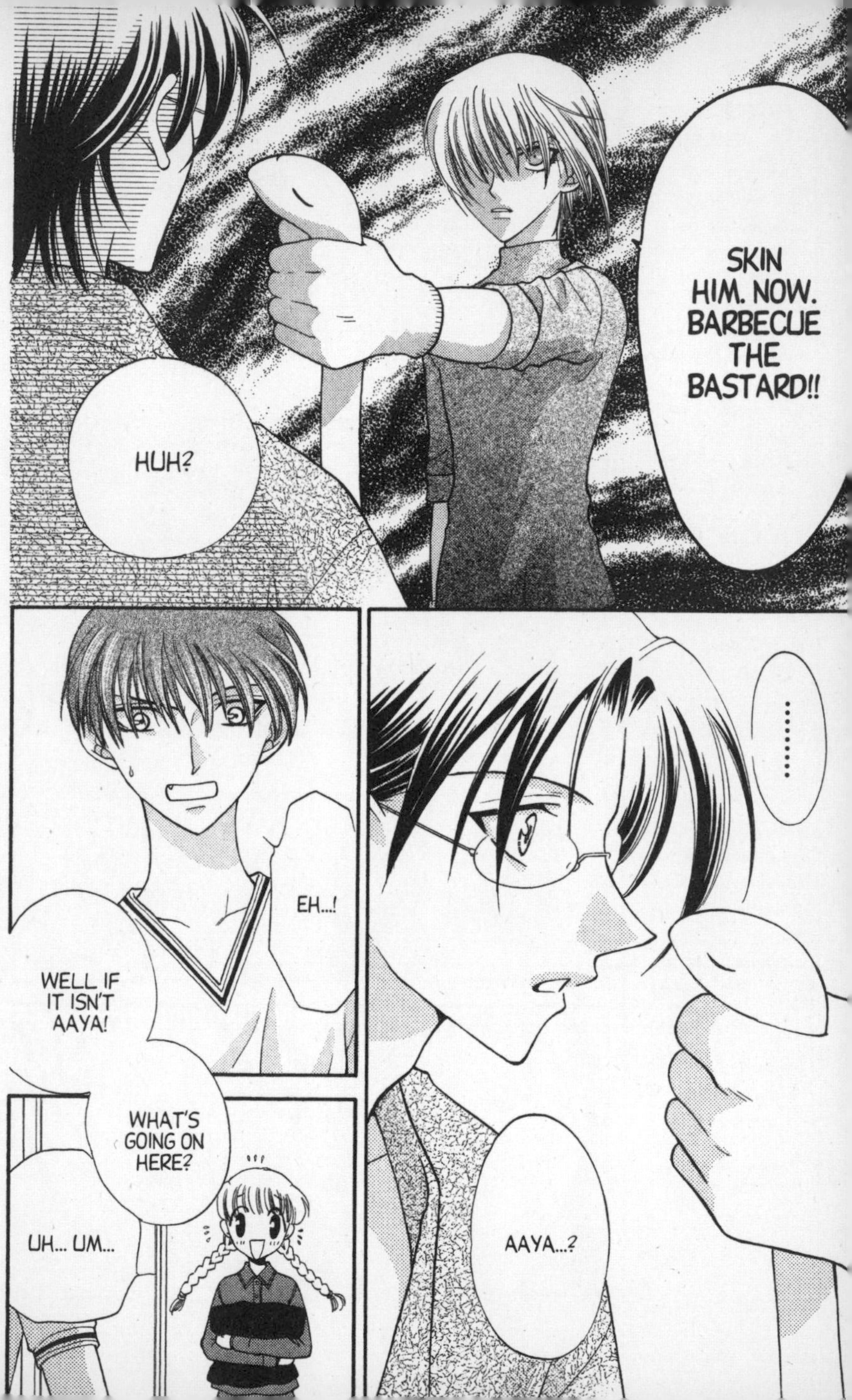
SKIN HIM. NOW. BARBECUE THE BASTARD!!
HUH?
......
AAYA...?
EH...!
WELL IF IT ISN'T AAYA!
WHAT'S GOING ON HERE?
UH... UM...

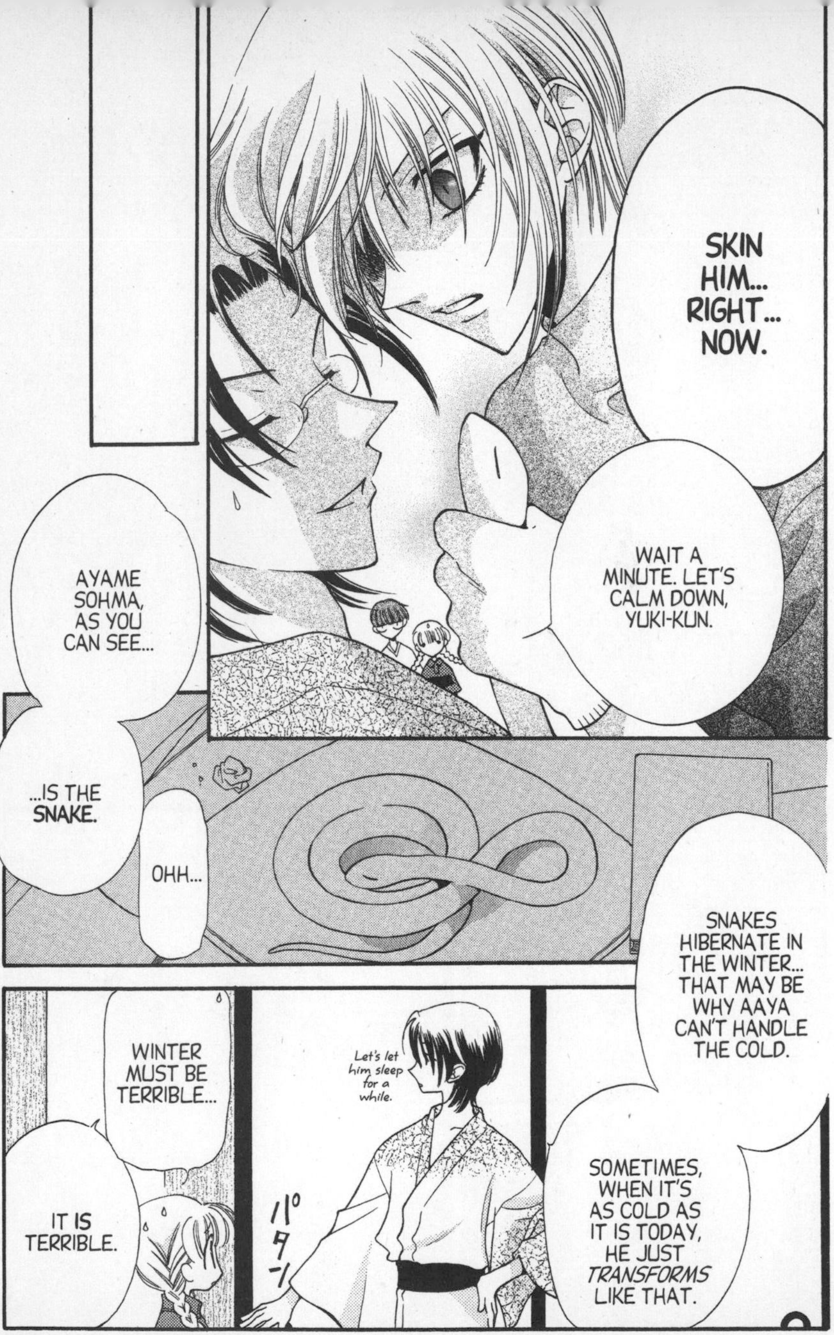
SKIN HIM... RIGHT... NOW.
WAIT A MINUTE. LET'S CALM DOWN, YUKI-KUN.
AYAME SOHMA, AS YOU CAN SEE...
...IS THE SNAKE.
OHH...
SNAKES HIBERNATE IN THE WINTER... THAT MAY BE WHY AAYA CAN'T HANDLE THE COLD.
SOMETIMES, WHEN IT'S AS COLD AS IT IS TODAY, HE JUST *TRANSFORMS* LIKE THAT.
Let's let him sleep for a while.
パタン
WINTER MUST BE TERRIBLE...
IT IS TERRIBLE.

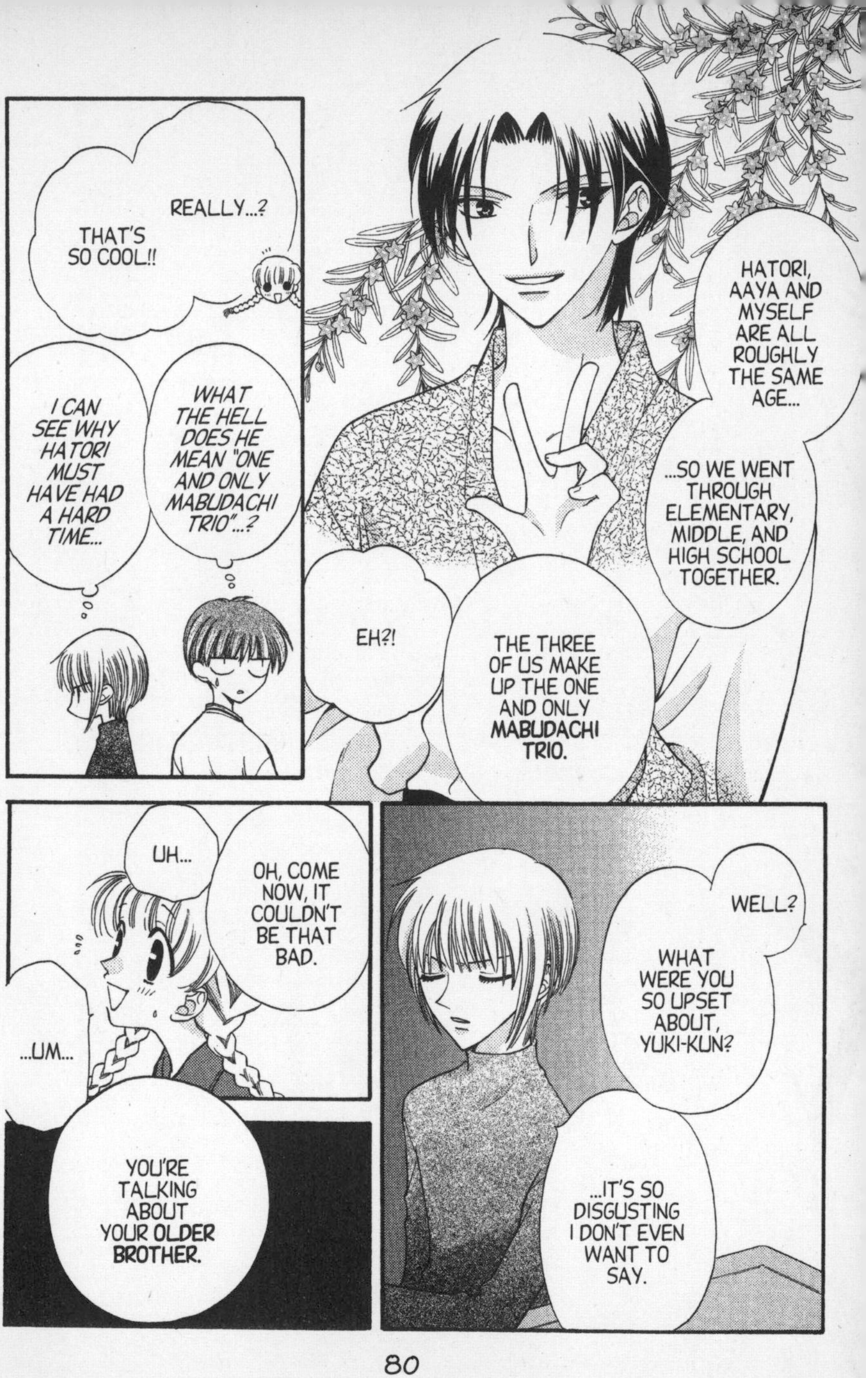
HATORI, AAYA AND MYSELF ARE ALL ROUGHLY THE SAME AGE...
...SO WE WENT THROUGH ELEMENTARY, MIDDLE, AND HIGH SCHOOL TOGETHER.
THE THREE OF US MAKE UP THE ONE AND ONLY **MABUDACHI TRIO.**
EH?!
REALLY...? THAT'S SO COOL!!
WHAT THE HELL DOES HE MEAN "ONE AND ONLY MABUDACHI TRIO"...?
I CAN SEE WHY HATORI MUST HAVE HAD A HARD TIME...
WELL?
WHAT WERE YOU SO UPSET ABOUT, YUKI-KUN?
...IT'S SO DISGUSTING I DON'T EVEN WANT TO SAY.
OH, COME NOW, IT COULDN'T BE THAT BAD.
UH...
...UM...
YOU'RE TALKING ABOUT YOUR **OLDER BROTHER.**

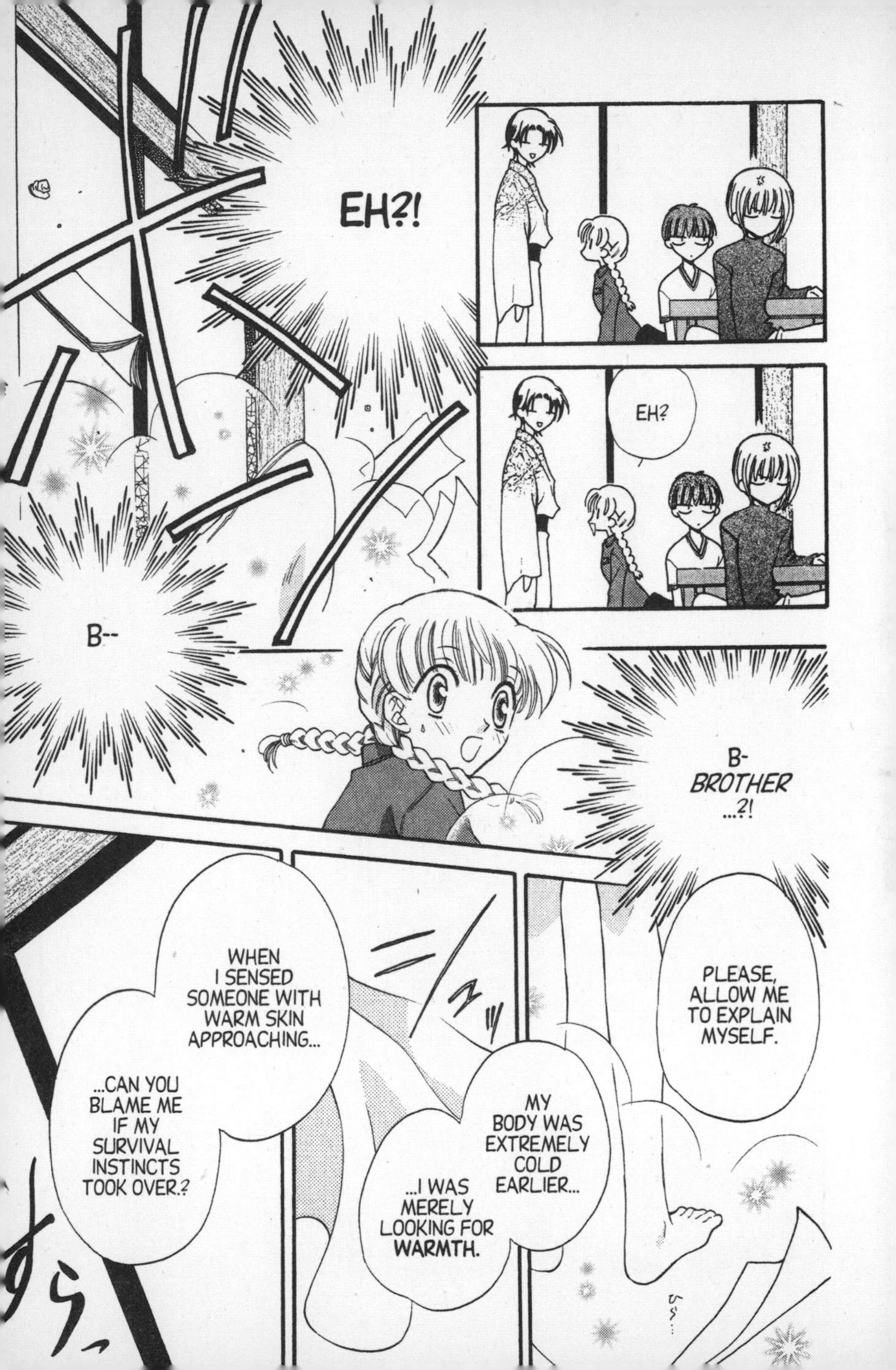
EH?
EH?!
B--
B-BROTHER ...?!
PLEASE, ALLOW ME TO EXPLAIN MYSELF.
MY BODY WAS EXTREMELY COLD EARLIER...
...I WAS MERELY LOOKING FOR WARMTH.
WHEN I SENSED SOMEONE WITH WARM SKIN APPROACHING...
...CAN YOU BLAME ME IF MY SURVIVAL INSTINCTS TOOK OVER.?

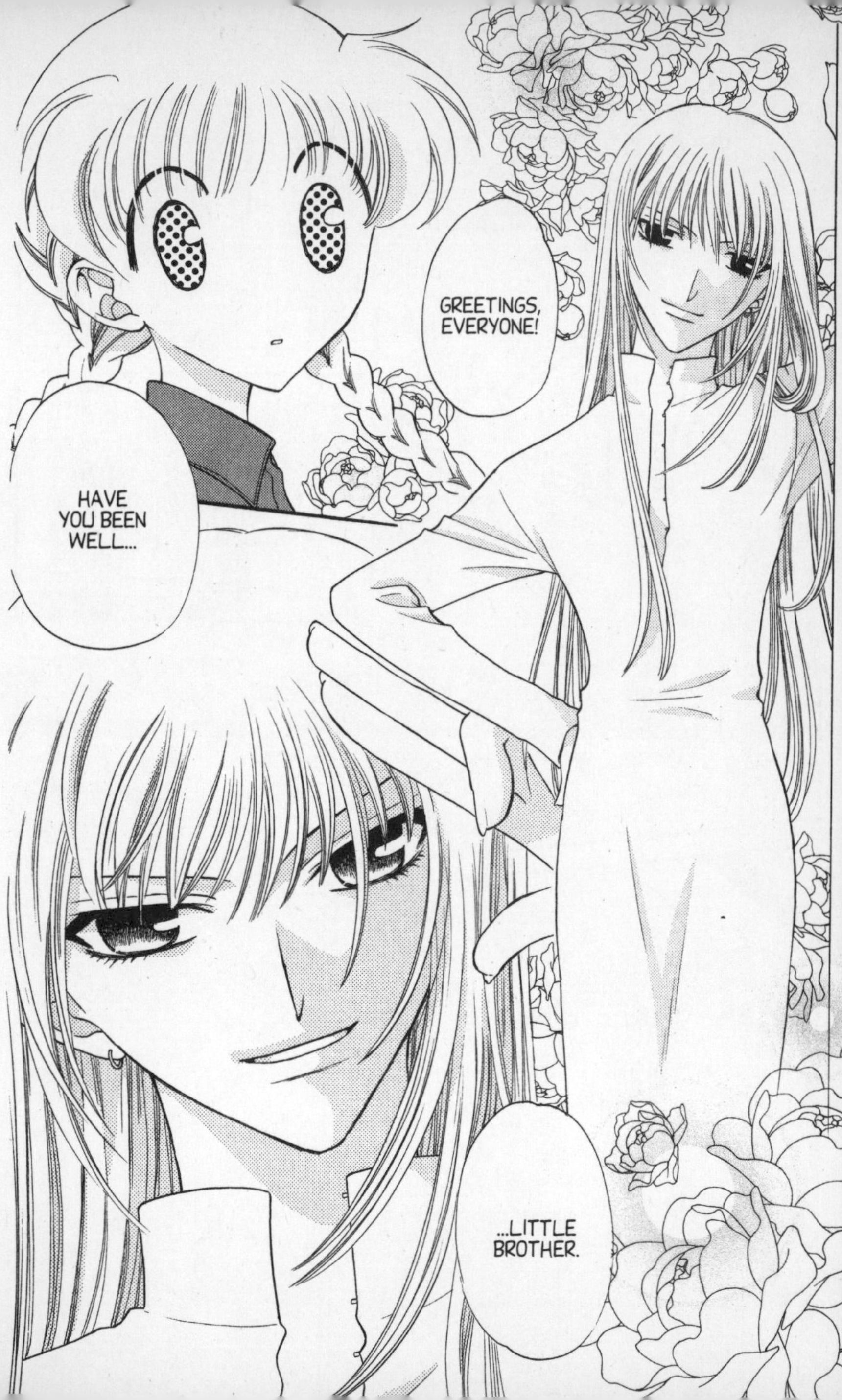
GREETINGS, EVERYONE!
HAVE YOU BEEN WELL...
...LITTLE BROTHER.

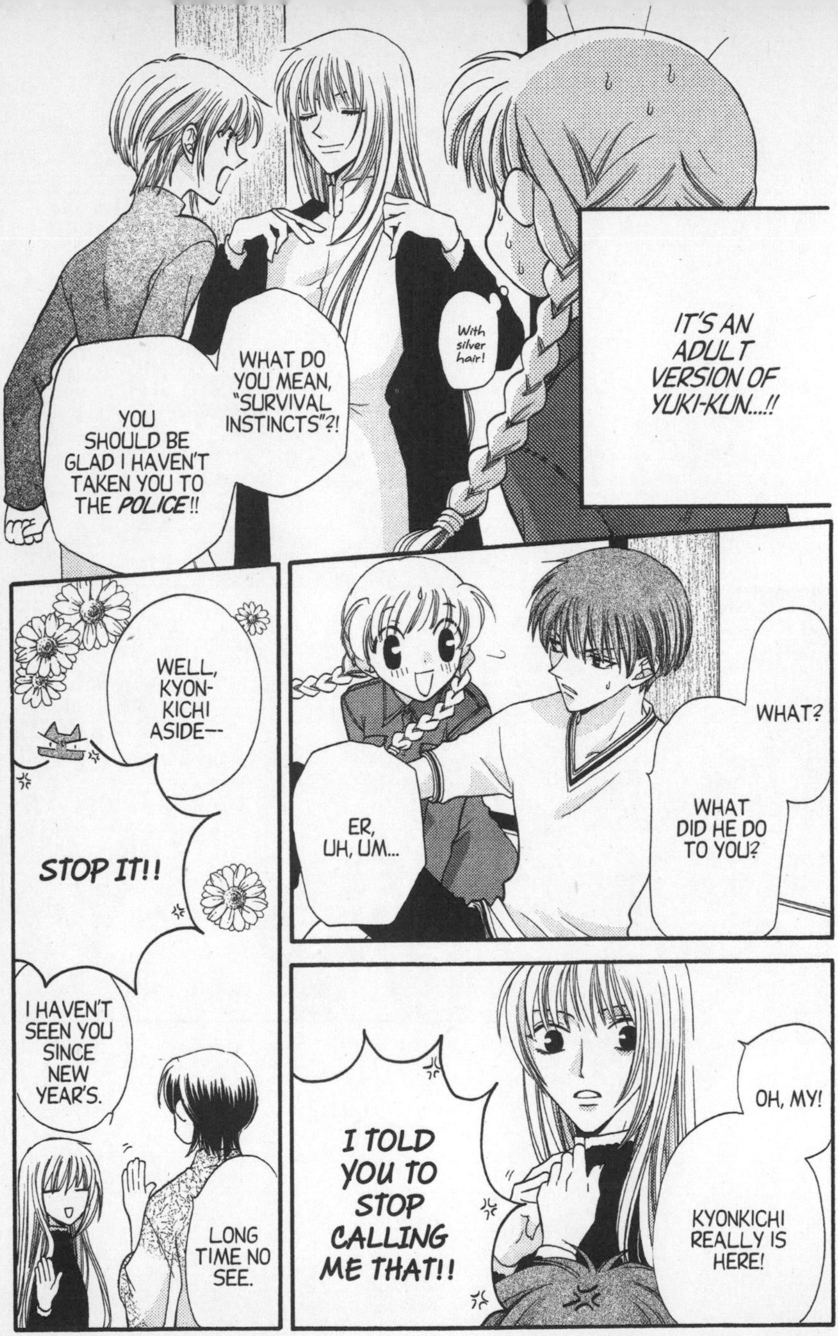
IT'S AN ADULT VERSION OF YUKI-KUN...!!
With silver hair!
WHAT DO YOU MEAN, "SURVIVAL INSTINCTS"?!
YOU SHOULD BE GLAD I HAVEN'T TAKEN YOU TO THE POLICE!!
WHAT?
WHAT DID HE DO TO YOU?
ER, UH, UM...
OH, MY!
KYONKICHI REALLY IS HERE!
I TOLD YOU TO STOP CALLING ME THAT!!
WELL, KYON-KICHI ASIDE--
STOP IT!!
I HAVEN'T SEEN YOU SINCE NEW YEAR'S.
LONG TIME NO SEE.

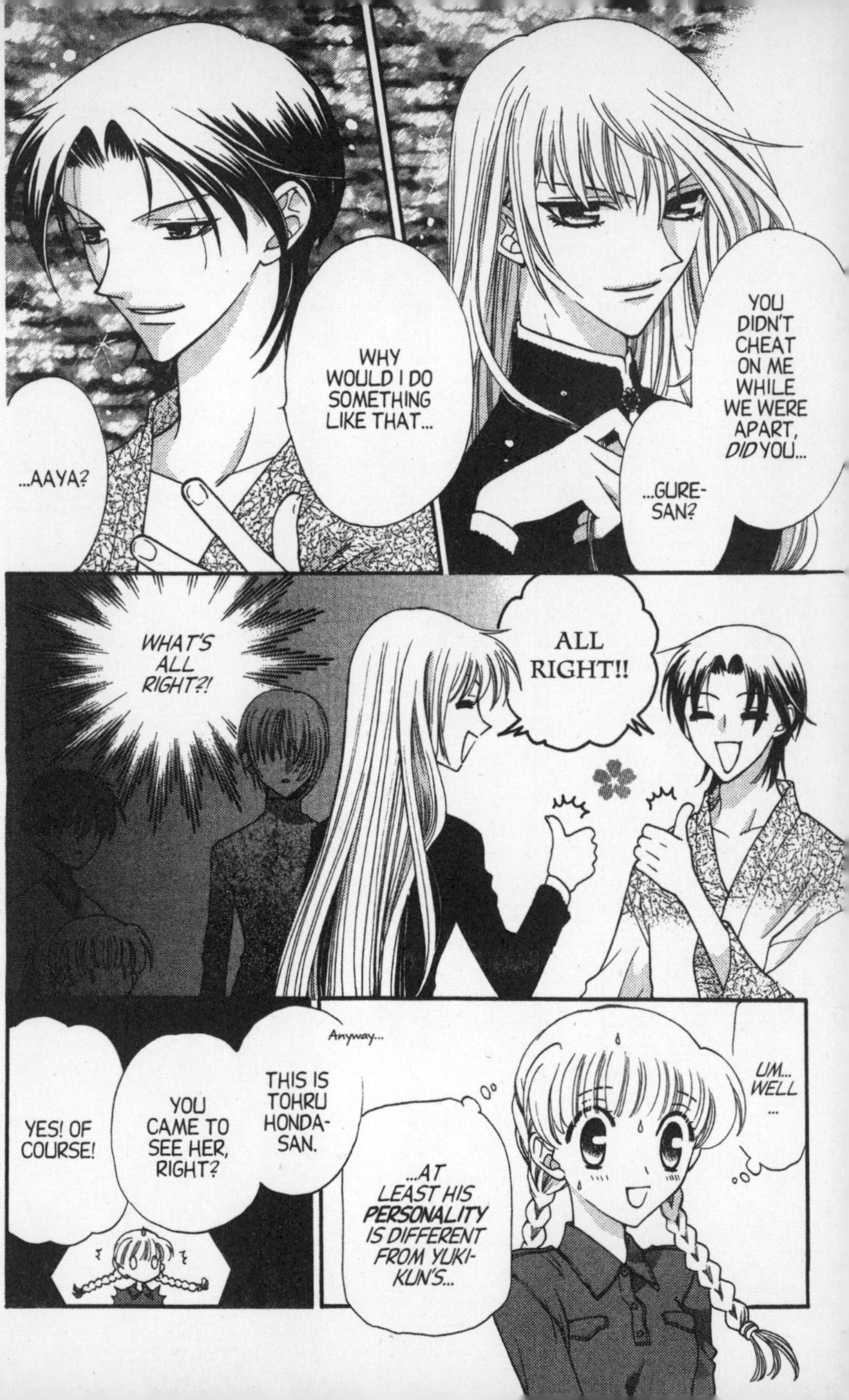

YOU DIDN'T CHEAT ON ME WHILE WE WERE APART, DID YOU...
...GURE-SAN?
WHY WOULD I DO SOMETHING LIKE THAT...
...AAYA?
ALL RIGHT!!
WHAT'S ALL RIGHT?!
UM... WELL ...
...AT LEAST HIS PERSONALITY IS DIFFERENT FROM YUKI-KUN'S...
Anyway...
THIS IS TOHRU HONDA-SAN.
YOU CAME TO SEE HER, RIGHT?
YES! OF COURSE!

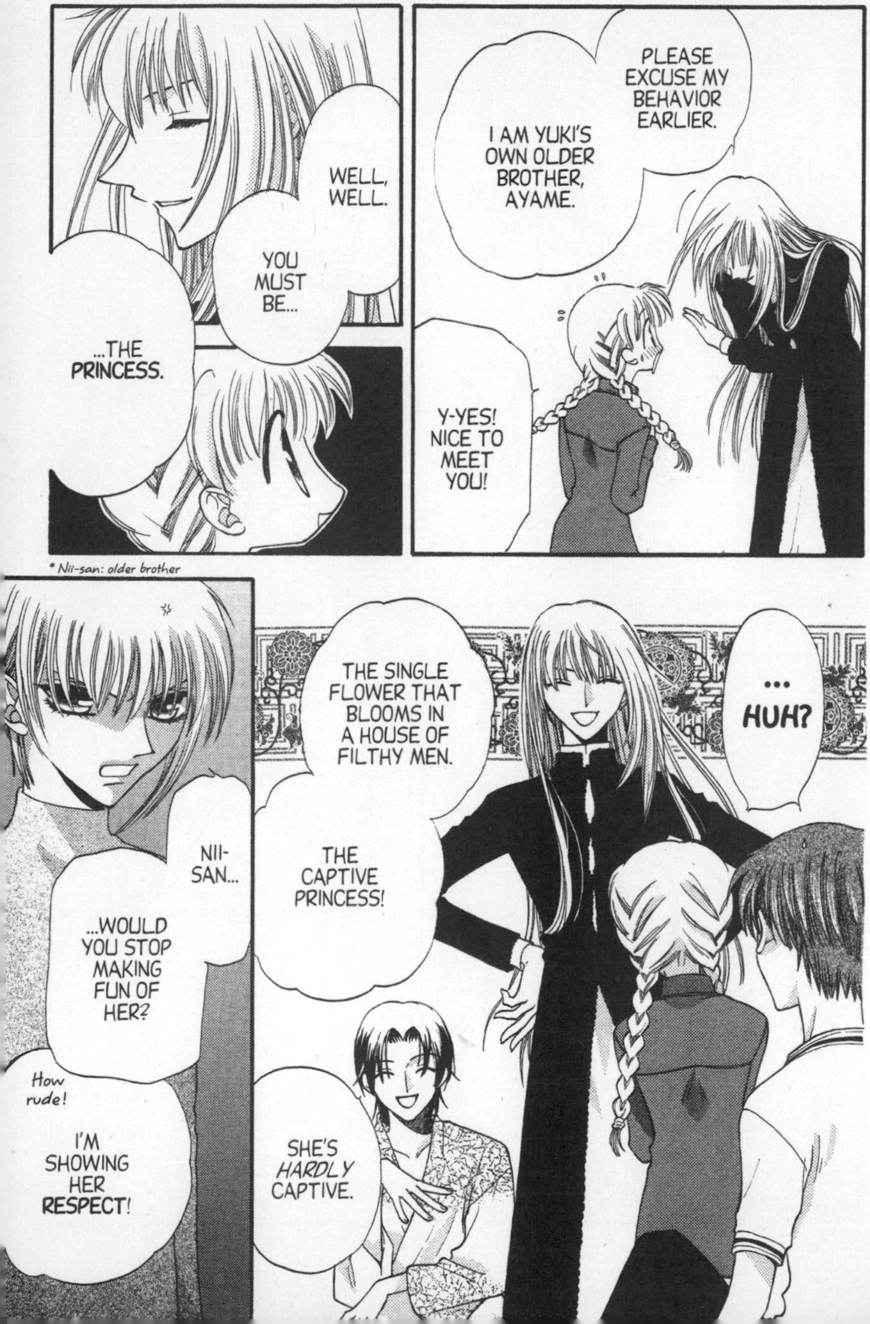
PLEASE EXCUSE MY BEHAVIOR EARLIER.
I AM YUKI'S OWN OLDER BROTHER, AYAME.
Y-YES! NICE TO MEET YOU!
WELL, WELL.
YOU MUST BE...
...THE PRINCESS.
... HUH?
THE SINGLE FLOWER THAT BLOOMS IN A HOUSE OF FILTHY MEN.
THE CAPTIVE PRINCESS!
SHE'S HARDLY CAPTIVE.
NII-SAN...
...WOULD YOU STOP MAKING FUN OF HER?
How rude!
I'M SHOWING HER RESPECT!

* Nii-san: older brother

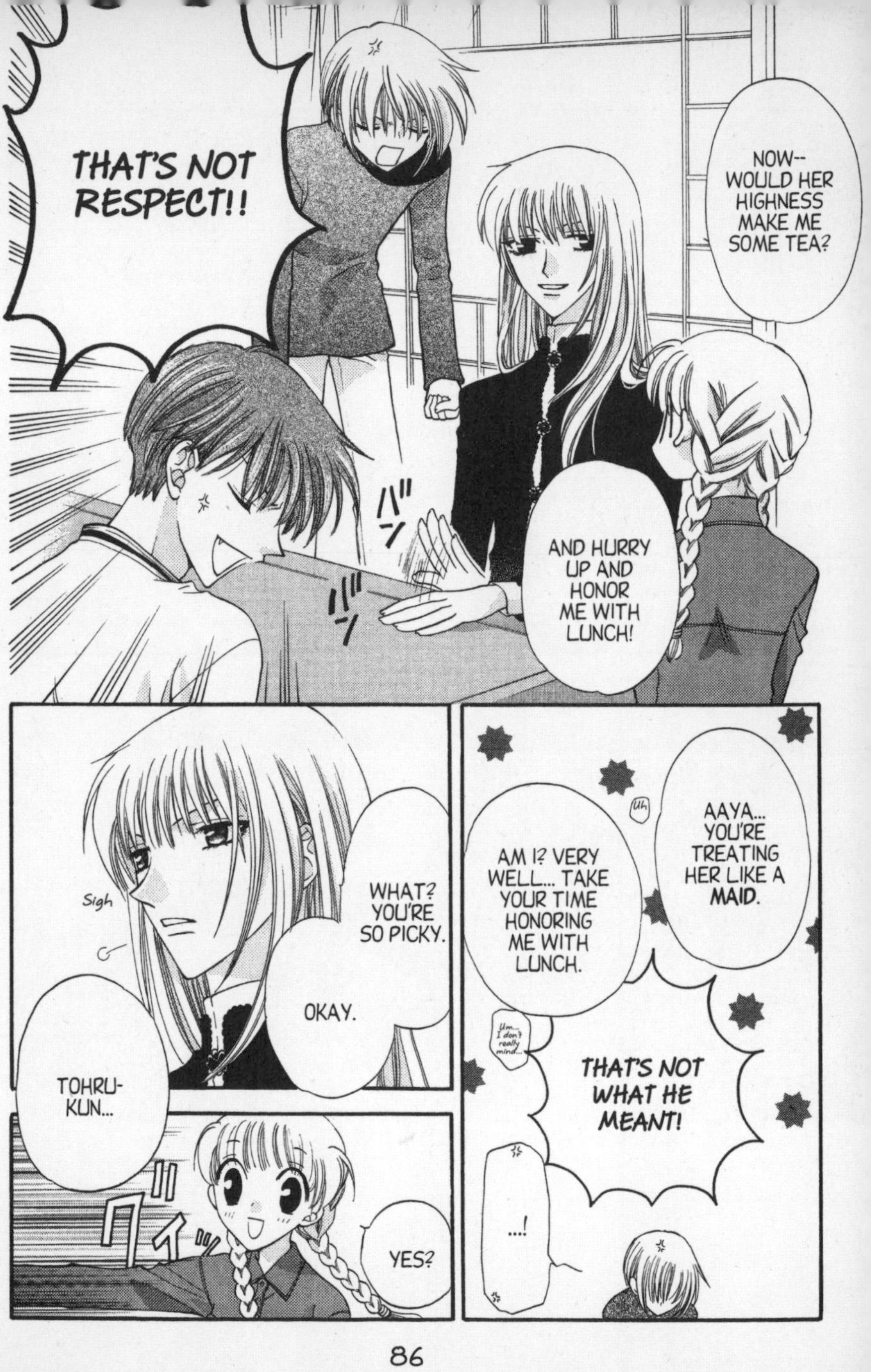
NOW-- WOULD HER HIGHNESS MAKE ME SOME TEA?
AND HURRY UP AND HONOR ME WITH LUNCH!
バン
バン
THAT'S NOT RESPECT!!
AAYA... YOU'RE TREATING HER LIKE A MAID.
Uh
AM I? VERY WELL... TAKE YOUR TIME HONORING ME WITH LUNCH.
THAT'S NOT WHAT HE MEANT!
Um... I don't really mind...
...!
WHAT? YOU'RE SO PICKY.
OKAY.
Sigh
TOHRU-KUN...
YES?

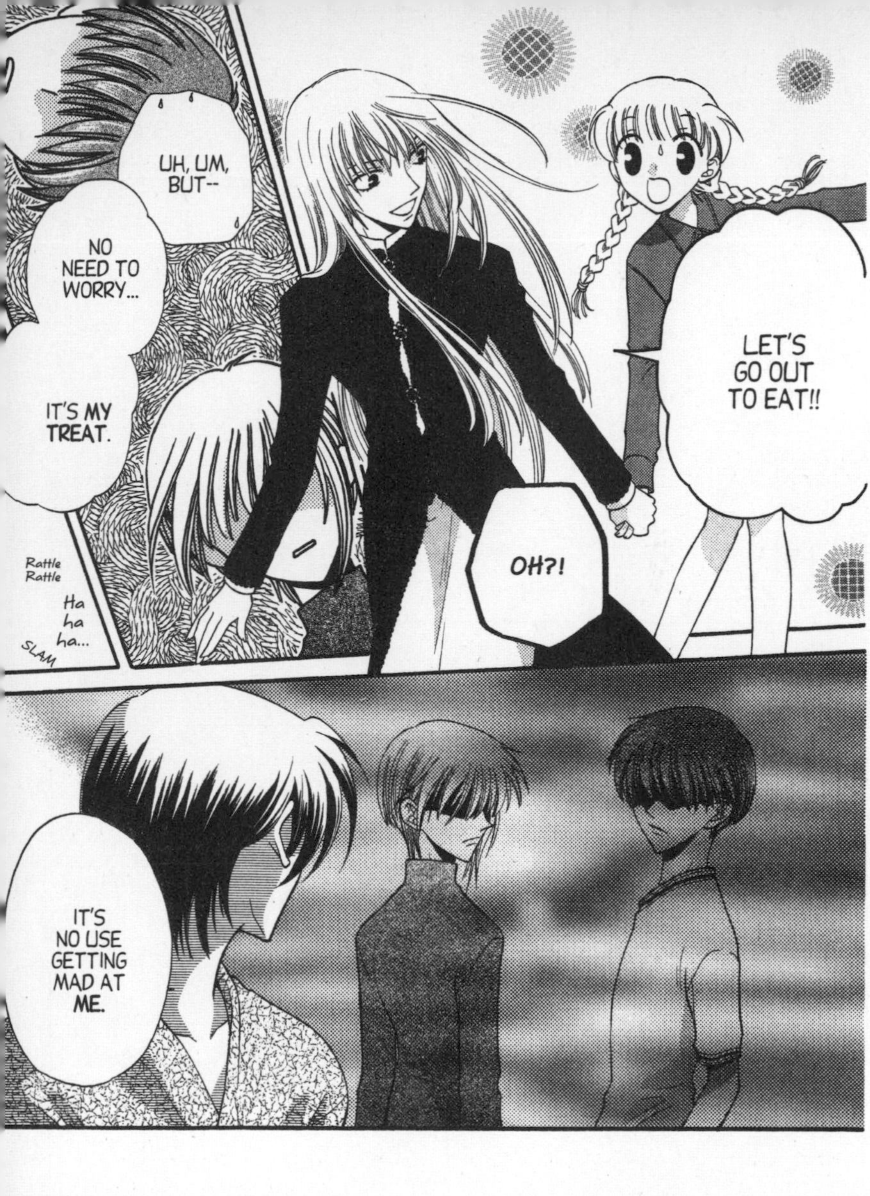

LET'S GO OUT TO EAT!!
OH?!
UH, UM, BUT--
NO NEED TO WORRY...
IT'S MY TREAT.
Rattle Rattle
Ha ha ha...
SLAM
IT'S NO USE GETTING MAD AT ME.

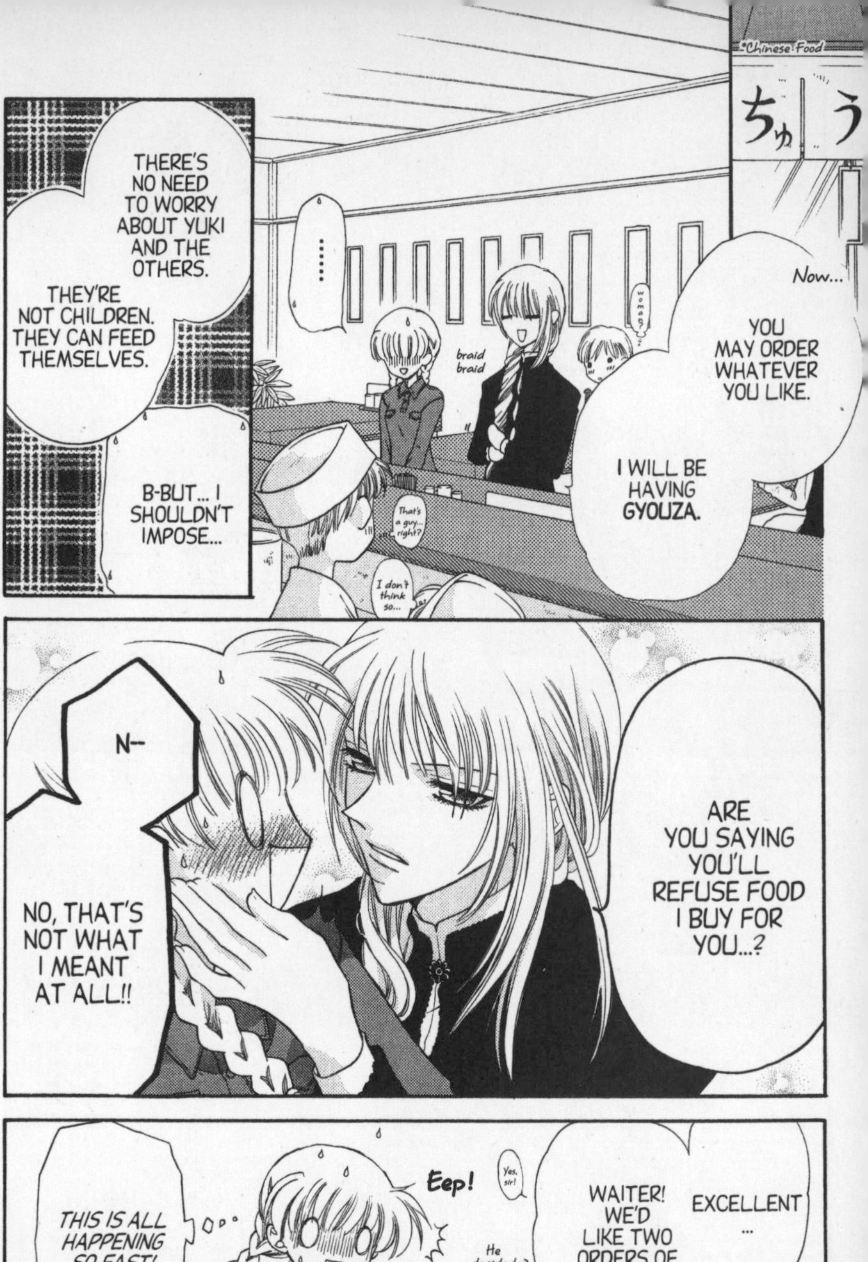
*Chinese Food
ちゅう
Now...
YOU MAY ORDER WHATEVER YOU LIKE.
I WILL BE HAVING GYOUZA.
woman?
braid braid
That's a guy... right?
I don't think so...
......
THERE'S NO NEED TO WORRY ABOUT YUKI AND THE OTHERS.
THEY'RE NOT CHILDREN. THEY CAN FEED THEMSELVES.
B-BUT... I SHOULDN'T IMPOSE...
ARE YOU SAYING YOU'LL REFUSE FOOD I BUY FOR YOU...?
N-
NO, THAT'S NOT WHAT I MEANT AT ALL!!
EXCELLENT...
WAITER! WE'D LIKE TWO ORDERS OF GYOUZA!
Yes, sir!
Eep!
He decided for her.
THIS IS ALL HAPPENING SO FAST!

*Gyouza: dumpling

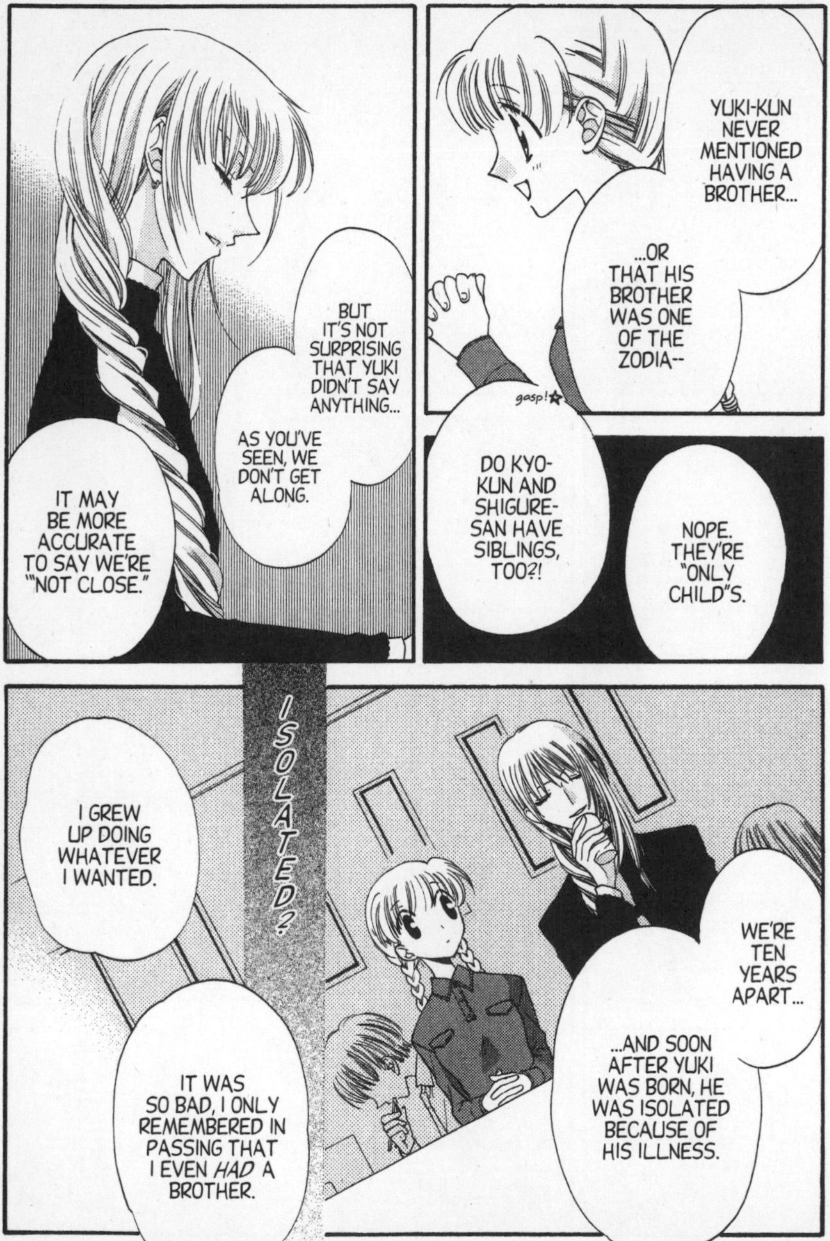

YUKI-KUN NEVER MENTIONED HAVING A BROTHER...
...OR THAT HIS BROTHER WAS ONE OF THE ZODIA--
gasp!
DO KYO-KUN AND SHIGURE-SAN HAVE SIBLINGS, TOO?!
NOPE. THEY'RE "ONLY CHILD"S.
BUT IT'S NOT SURPRISING THAT YUKI DIDN'T SAY ANYTHING...
AS YOU'VE SEEN, WE DON'T GET ALONG.
IT MAY BE MORE ACCURATE TO SAY WE'RE "NOT CLOSE."
WE'RE TEN YEARS APART...
...AND SOON AFTER YUKI WAS BORN, HE WAS ISOLATED BECAUSE OF HIS ILLNESS.
ISOLATED?
I GREW UP DOING WHATEVER I WANTED.
IT WAS SO BAD, I ONLY REMEMBERED IN PASSING THAT I EVEN *HAD* A BROTHER.

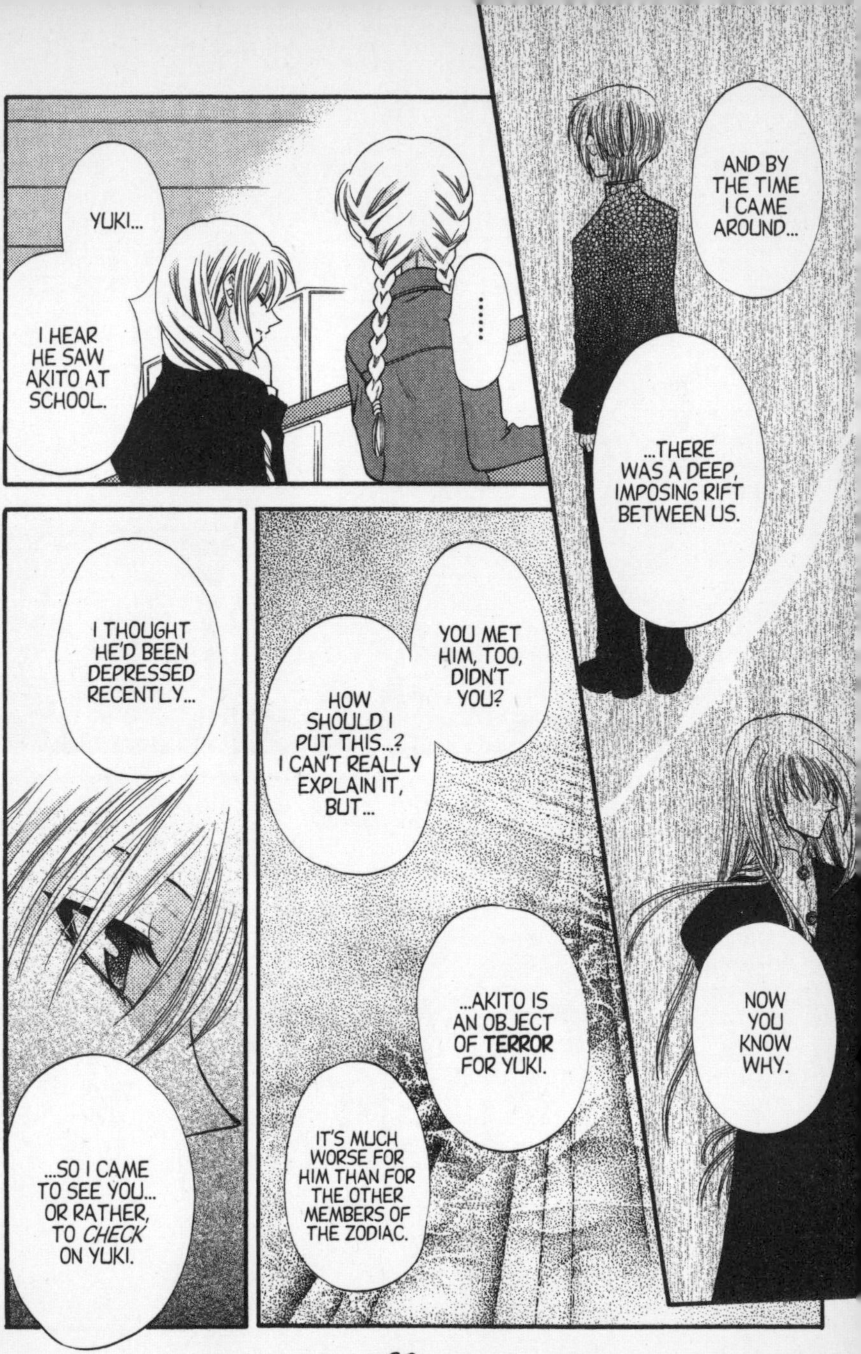
AND BY THE TIME I CAME AROUND...
...THERE WAS A DEEP, IMPOSING RIFT BETWEEN US.
NOW YOU KNOW WHY.
YUKI...
I HEAR HE SAW AKITO AT SCHOOL.
......
YOU MET HIM, TOO, DIDN'T YOU?
HOW SHOULD I PUT THIS...? I CAN'T REALLY EXPLAIN IT, BUT...
...AKITO IS AN OBJECT OF **TERROR** FOR YUKI.
IT'S MUCH WORSE FOR HIM THAN FOR THE OTHER MEMBERS OF THE ZODIAC.
I THOUGHT HE'D BEEN DEPRESSED RECENTLY...
...SO I CAME TO SEE YOU... OR RATHER, TO *CHECK* ON YUKI.

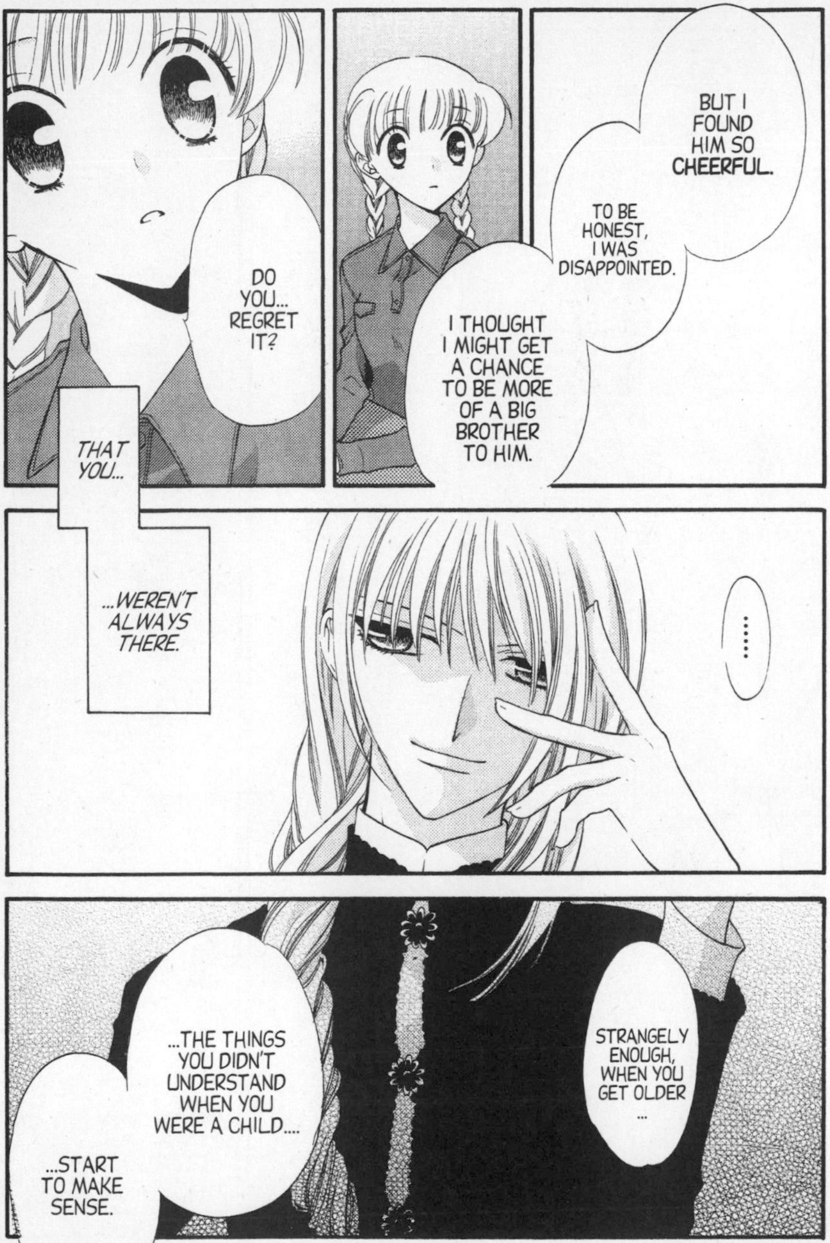
BUT I FOUND HIM SO CHEERFUL.
TO BE HONEST, I WAS DISAPPOINTED.
I THOUGHT I MIGHT GET A CHANCE TO BE MORE OF A BIG BROTHER TO HIM.
DO YOU... REGRET IT?
THAT YOU...
...WEREN'T ALWAYS THERE.
......
STRANGELY ENOUGH, WHEN YOU GET OLDER ...
...THE THINGS YOU DIDN'T UNDERSTAND WHEN YOU WERE A CHILD....
...START TO MAKE SENSE.

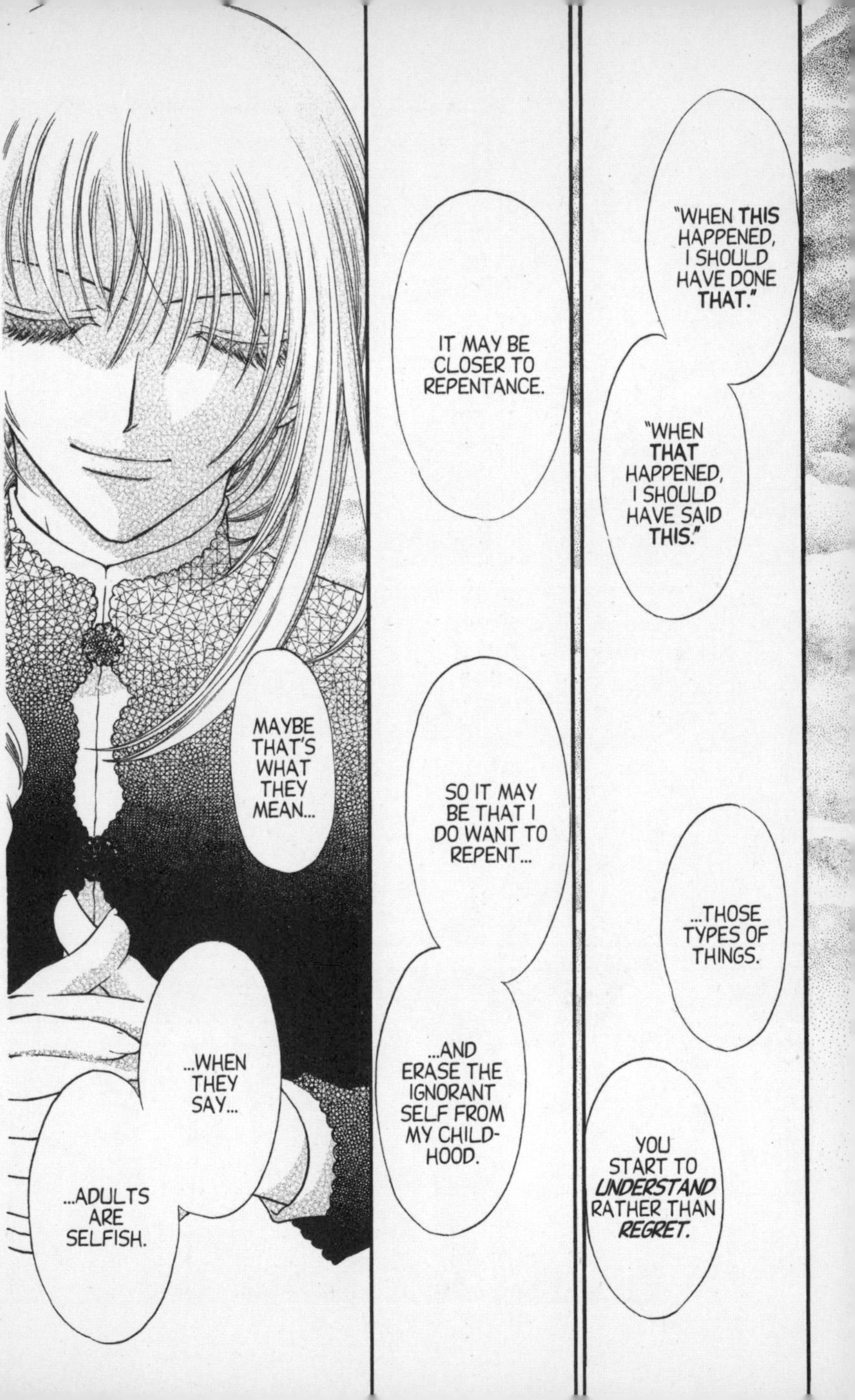
"WHEN THIS HAPPENED, I SHOULD HAVE DONE THAT."
"WHEN THAT HAPPENED, I SHOULD HAVE SAID THIS."
...THOSE TYPES OF THINGS.
YOU START TO UNDERSTAND RATHER THAN REGRET.
IT MAY BE CLOSER TO REPENTANCE.
SO IT MAY BE THAT I DO WANT TO REPENT...
...AND ERASE THE IGNORANT SELF FROM MY CHILD-HOOD.
MAYBE THAT'S WHAT THEY MEAN...
...WHEN THEY SAY...
...ADULTS ARE SELFISH.

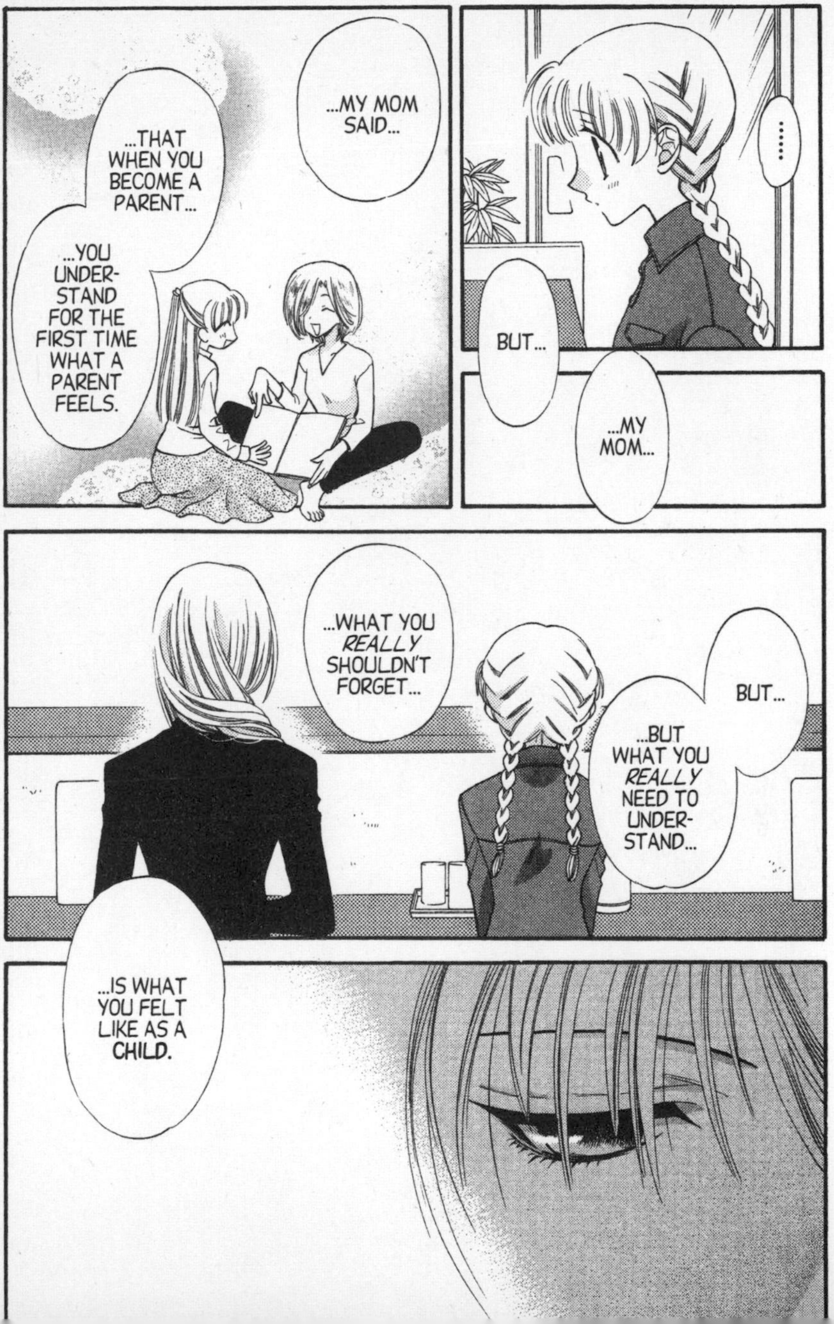
......
BUT...
...MY MOM...
...MY MOM SAID...
...THAT WHEN YOU BECOME A PARENT...
...YOU UNDER-STAND FOR THE FIRST TIME WHAT A PARENT FEELS.
BUT...
...BUT WHAT YOU *REALLY* NEED TO UNDER-STAND...
...WHAT YOU *REALLY* SHOULDN'T FORGET...
...IS WHAT YOU FELT LIKE AS A CHILD.

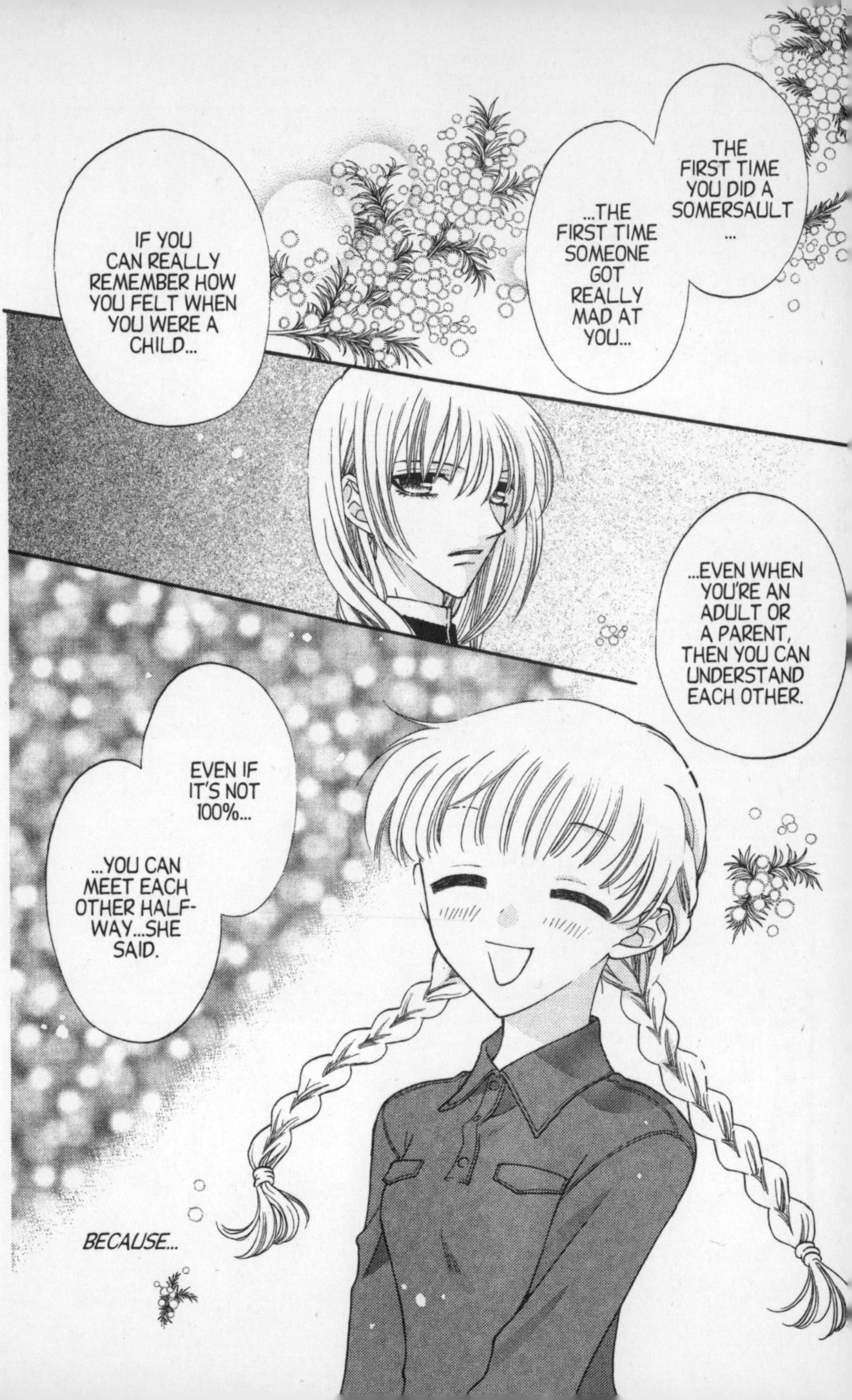
THE FIRST TIME YOU DID A SOMERSAULT ...
...THE FIRST TIME SOMEONE GOT REALLY MAD AT YOU...
IF YOU CAN REALLY REMEMBER HOW YOU FELT WHEN YOU WERE A CHILD...
...EVEN WHEN YOU'RE AN ADULT OR A PARENT, THEN YOU CAN UNDERSTAND EACH OTHER.
EVEN IF IT'S NOT 100%...
...YOU CAN MEET EACH OTHER HALF-WAY...SHE SAID.
BECAUSE...

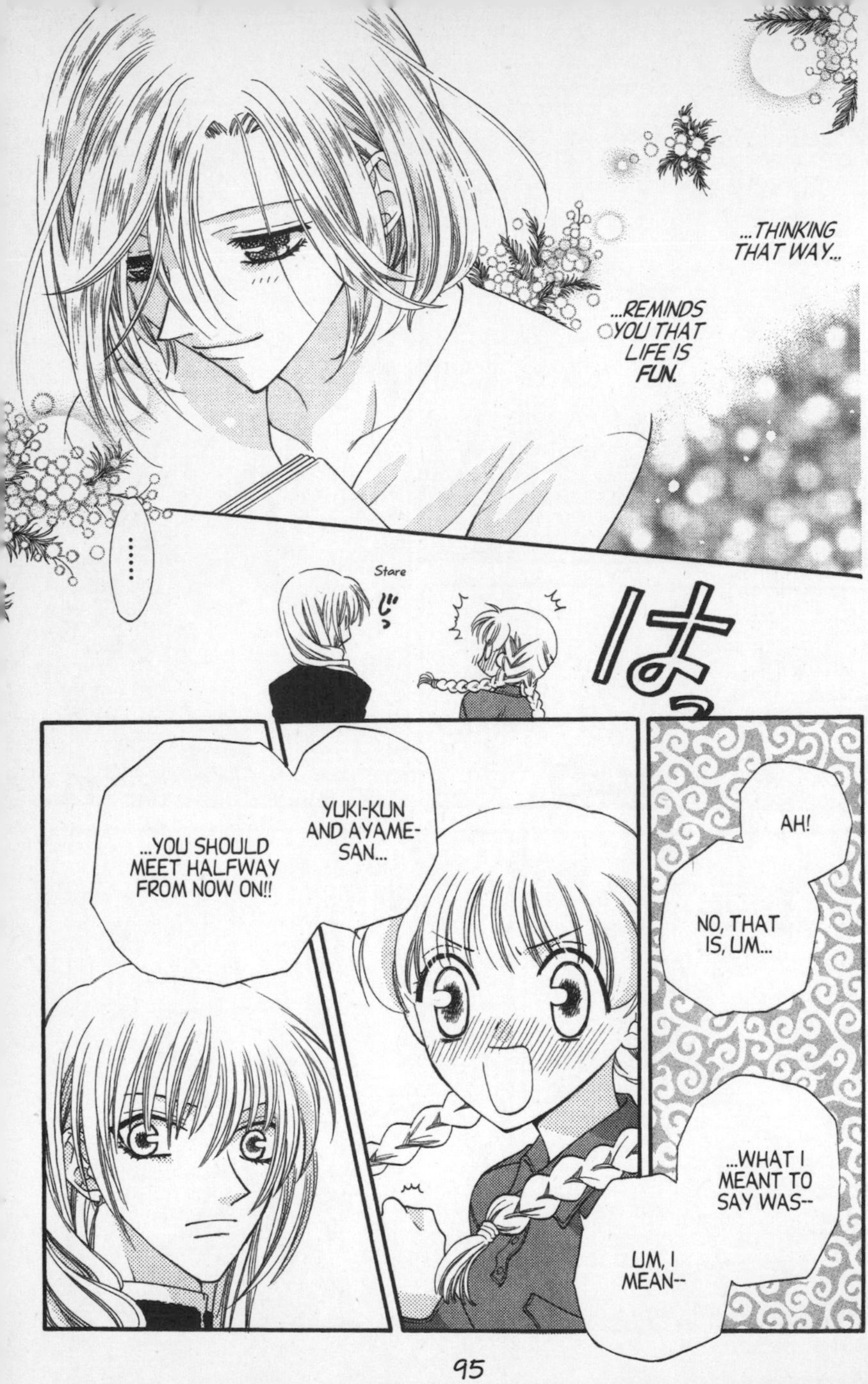
...THINKING THAT WAY...
...REMINDS YOU THAT LIFE IS FUN.
......
はっ
Stare
じっ
AH!
NO, THAT IS, UM...
...WHAT I MEANT TO SAY WAS--
UM, I MEAN--
YUKI-KUN AND AYAME-SAN...
...YOU SHOULD MEET HALFWAY FROM NOW ON!!

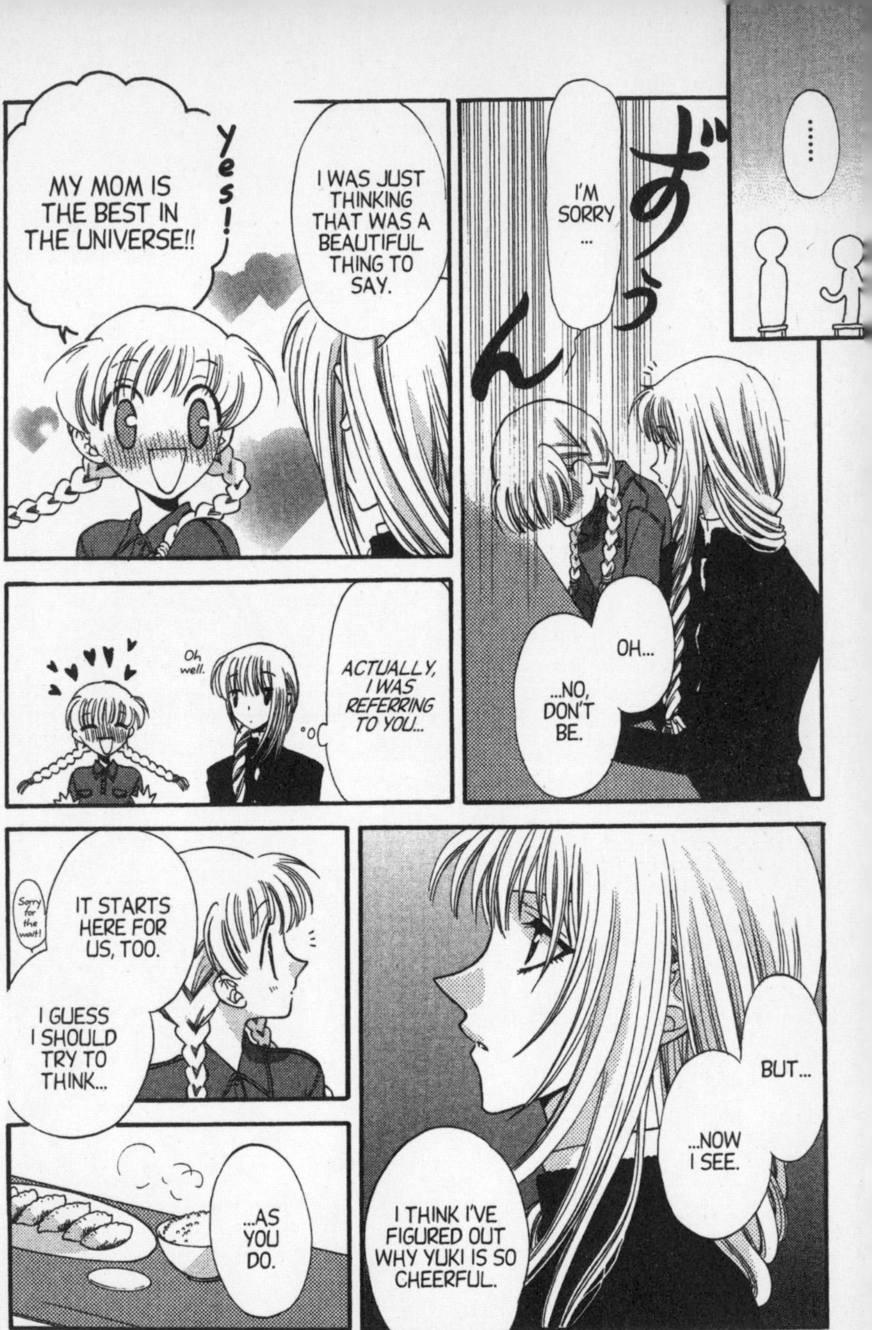
......
I'M SORRY ...
ずうん
OH...
...NO, DON'T BE.
I WAS JUST THINKING THAT WAS A BEAUTIFUL THING TO SAY.
Yes!
MY MOM IS THE BEST IN THE UNIVERSE!!
ACTUALLY, I WAS REFERRING TO YOU...
Oh well.
BUT...
...NOW I SEE.
I THINK I'VE FIGURED OUT WHY YUKI IS SO CHEERFUL.
Sorry for the wait!
IT STARTS HERE FOR US, TOO.
I GUESS I SHOULD TRY TO THINK...
...AS YOU DO.

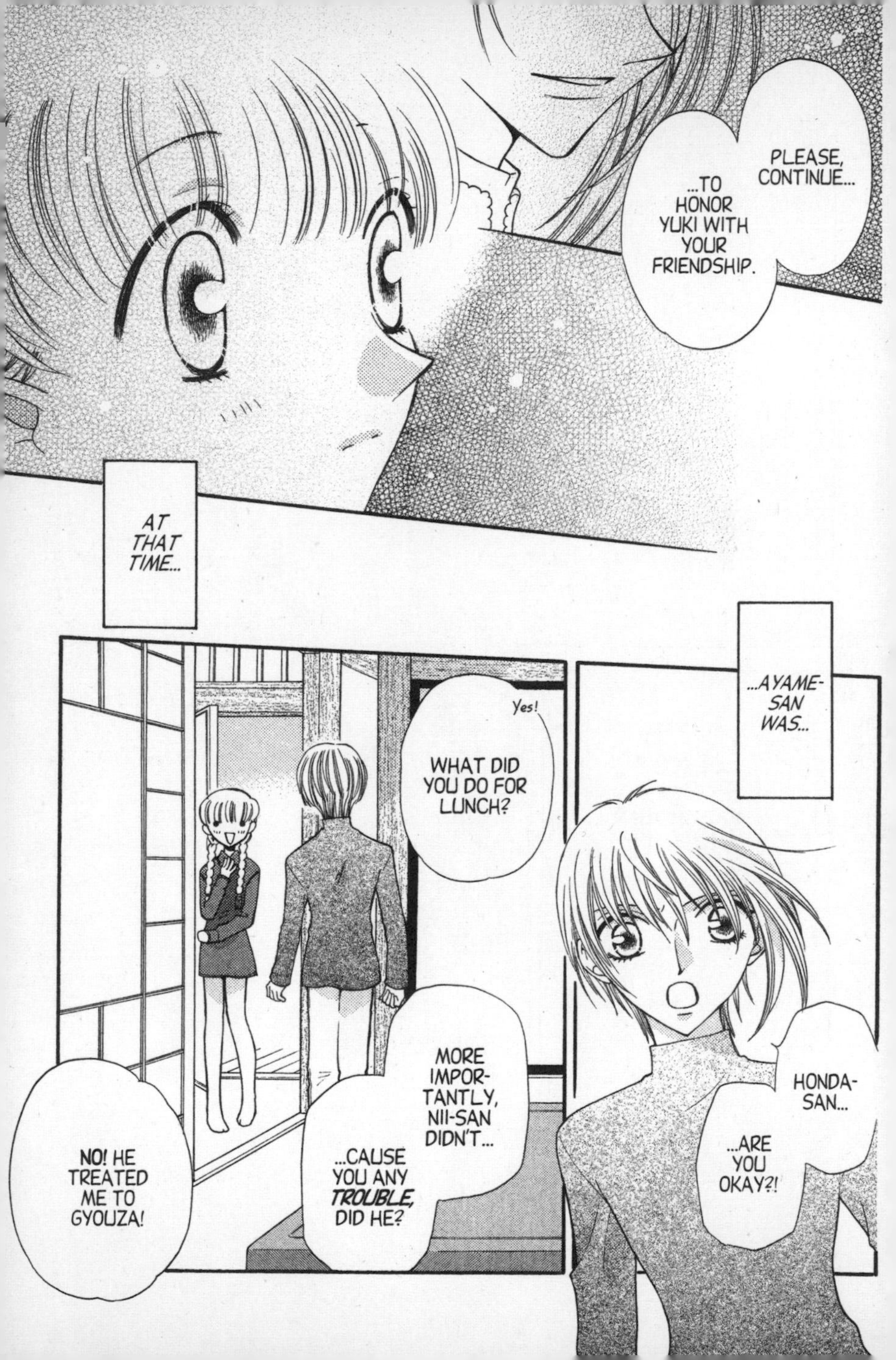
PLEASE, CONTINUE...
...TO HONOR YUKI WITH YOUR FRIENDSHIP.
AT THAT TIME...
...AYAME-SAN WAS...
HONDA-SAN...
...ARE YOU OKAY?!
Yes!
WHAT DID YOU DO FOR LUNCH?
MORE IMPORTANTLY, NII-SAN DIDN'T...
...CAUSE YOU ANY *TROUBLE*, DID HE?
NO! HE TREATED ME TO GYOUZA!

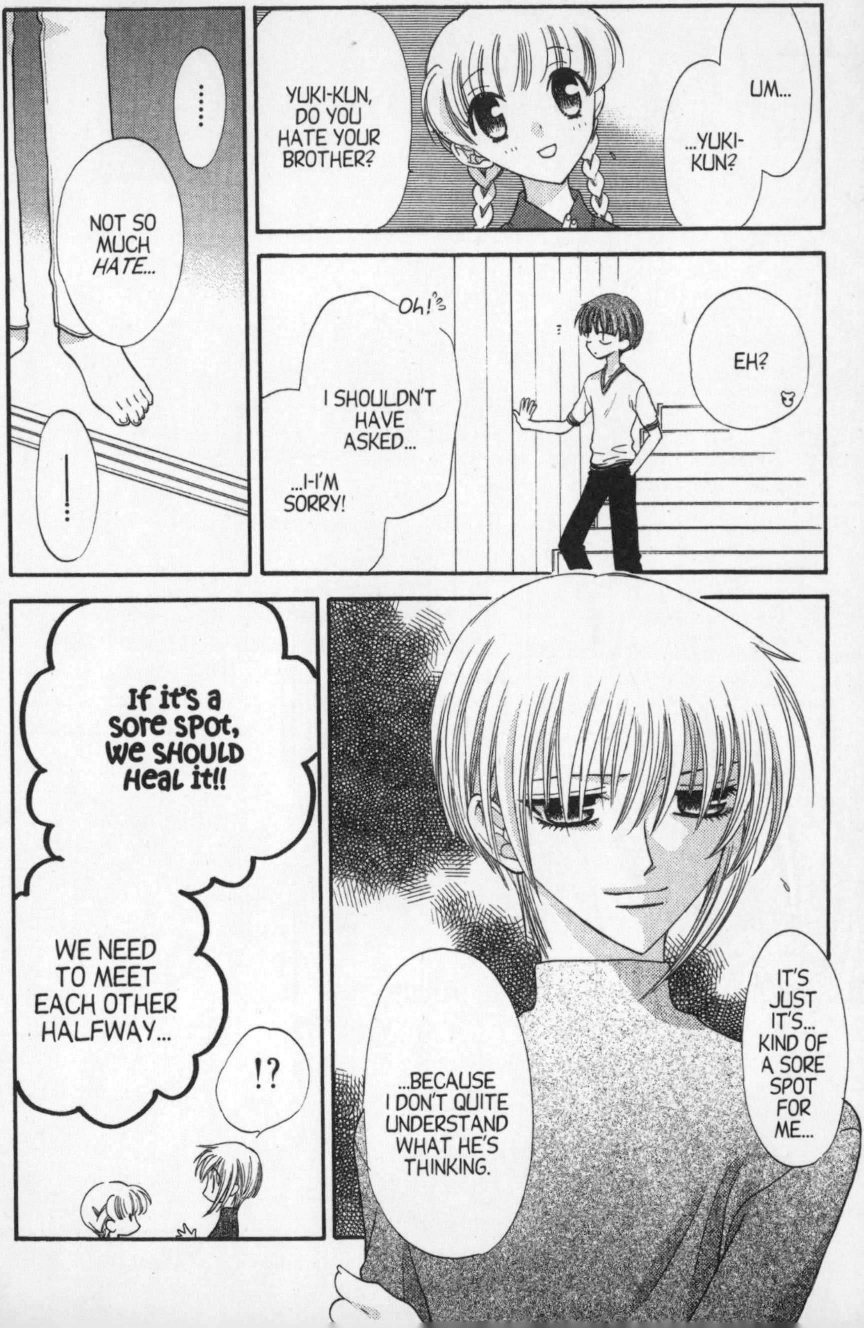
UM...
...YUKI-KUN?
YUKI-KUN, DO YOU HATE YOUR BROTHER?
EH?
Oh!
I SHOULDN'T HAVE ASKED...
...I-I'M SORRY!
......
NOT SO MUCH *HATE*...
......!
IT'S JUST IT'S... KIND OF A SORE SPOT FOR ME...
...BECAUSE I DON'T QUITE UNDERSTAND WHAT HE'S THINKING.
If it's a sore spot, we SHOULD Heal it!!
WE NEED TO MEET EACH OTHER HALFWAY...
!?

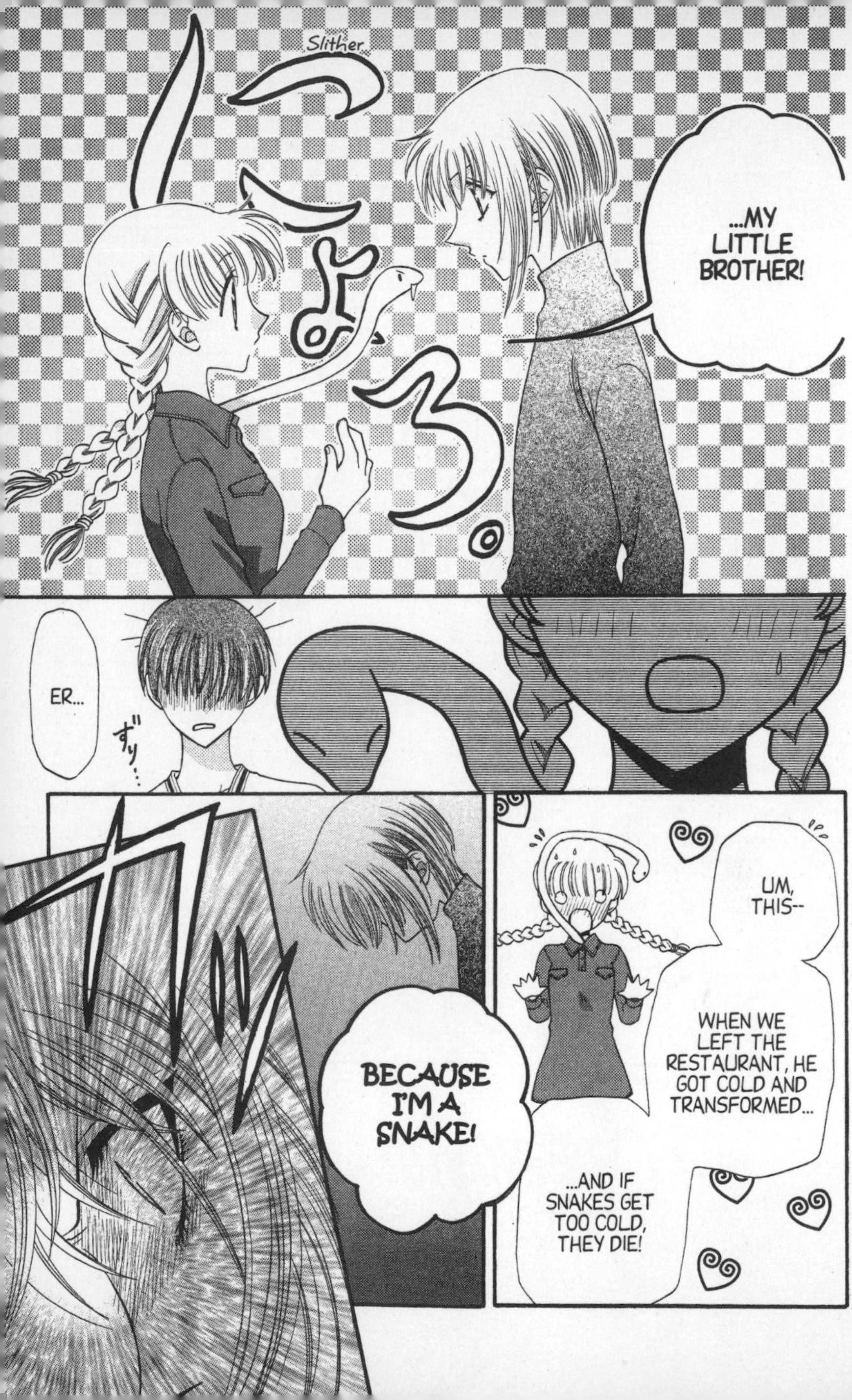
...MY LITTLE BROTHER!
Slither
にょろ。
ER...
ずり...
UM, THIS--
WHEN WE LEFT THE RESTAURANT, HE GOT COLD AND TRANSFORMED...
...AND IF SNAKES GET TOO COLD, THEY DIE!
BECAUSE I'M A SNAKE!

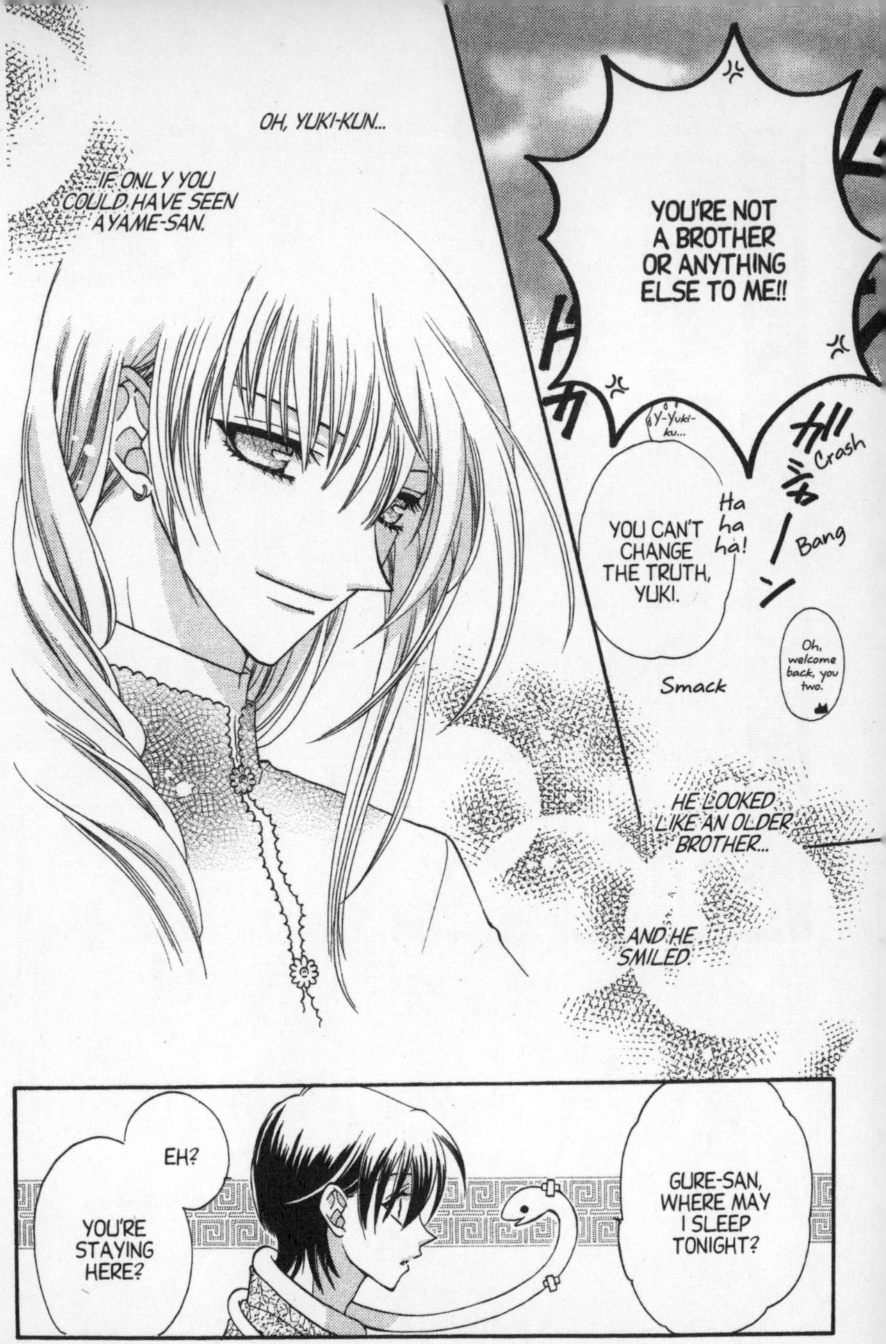
YOU'RE NOT A BROTHER OR ANYTHING ELSE TO ME!!
Y-Yuki-ku...
Crash
Bang
Ha ha ha!
YOU CAN'T CHANGE THE TRUTH, YUKI.
Oh, welcome back, you two.
Smack
OH, YUKI-KUN...
...IF ONLY YOU COULD HAVE SEEN AYAME-SAN.
HE LOOKED LIKE AN OLDER BROTHER...
AND HE SMILED.
GURE-SAN, WHERE MAY I SLEEP TONIGHT?
EH?
YOU'RE STAYING HERE?

Chapter 22

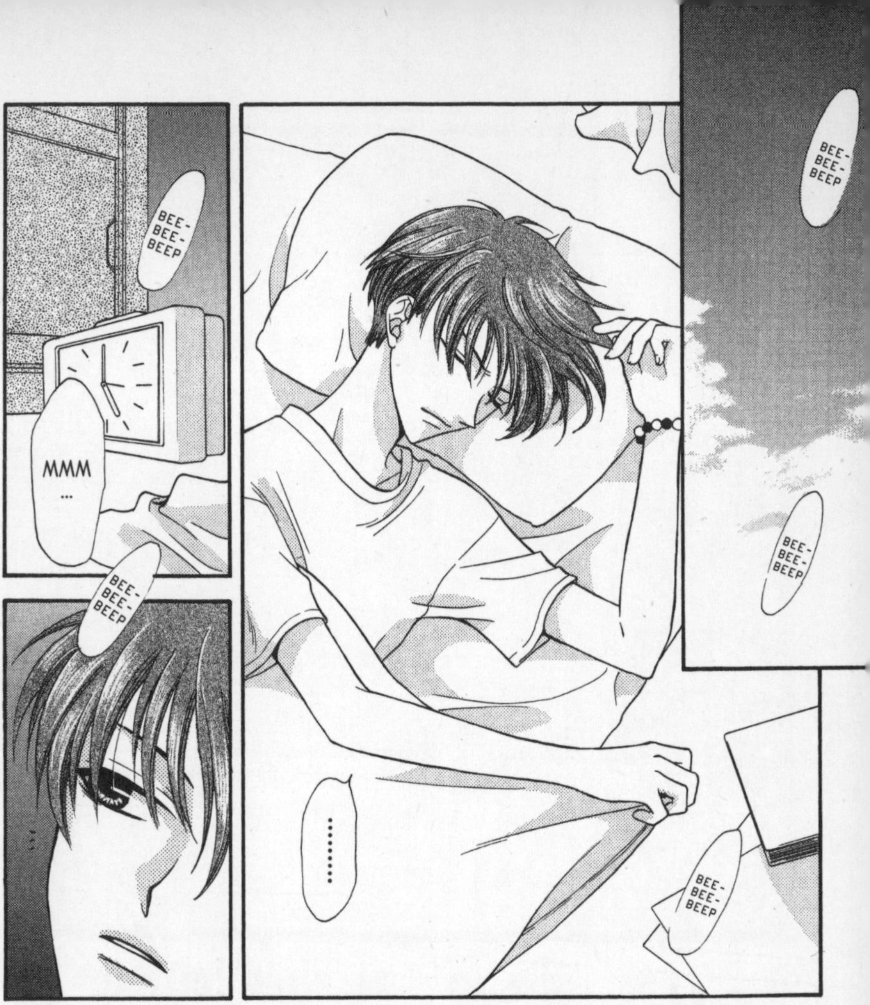
BEE-BEE-BEEP
BEE-BEE-BEEP
BEE-BEE-BEEP
....
BEE-BEE-BEEP
MMM...
BEE-BEE-BEEP
...

ULTRA SPECIAL BLAH BLAH BLAH 4

People who like stuff like that, *really* like it. But I'd like it if they'd stop getting my manga involved...^-^-- I'm kidding! The Mabudachi trio's years in high school are actually pretty muddled. They were still kids. They're probably the way they are now because of their "flower," but it wasn't always fun.

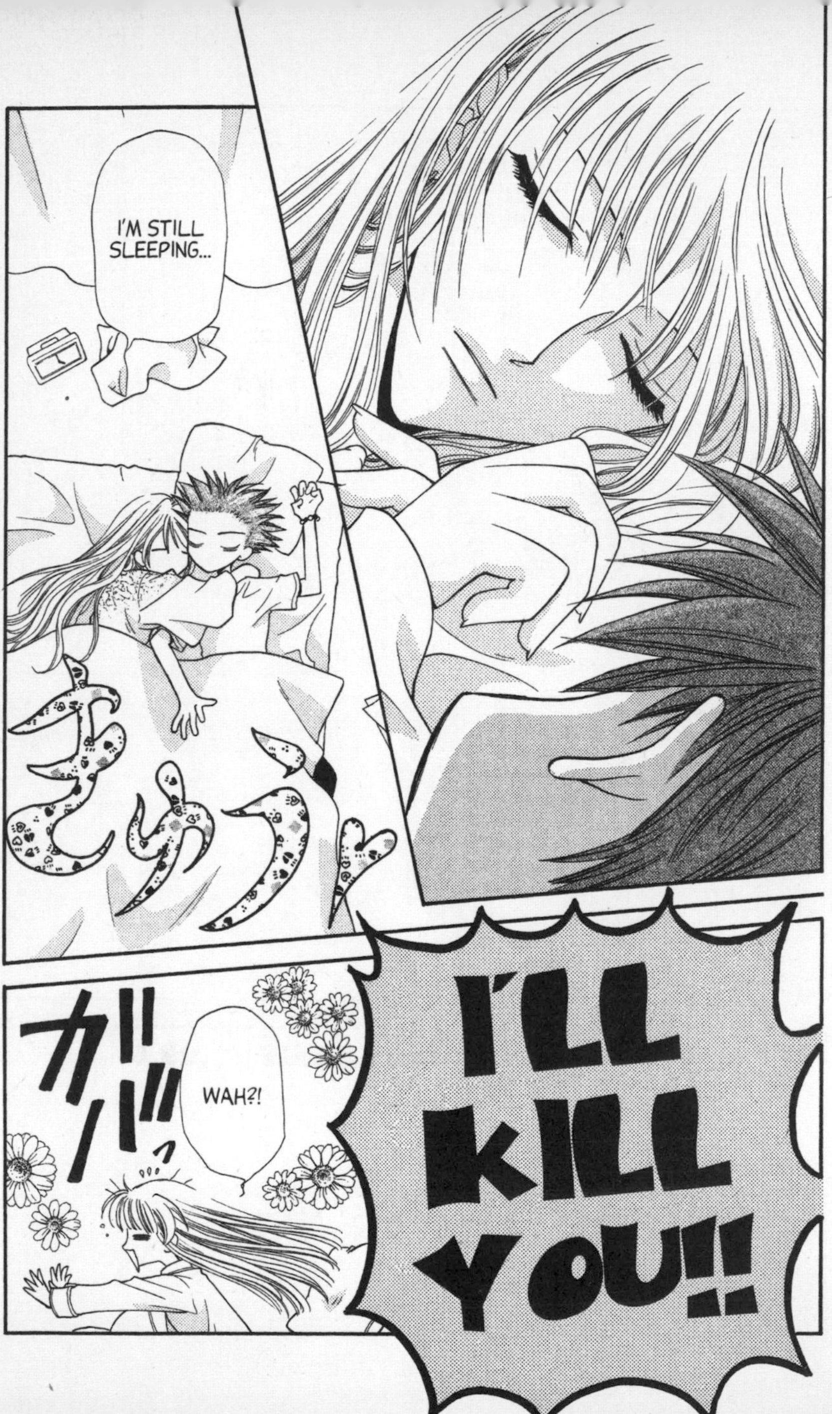
I'M STILL SLEEPING...
I'LL KILL YOU!!
ガバッ
WAH?!

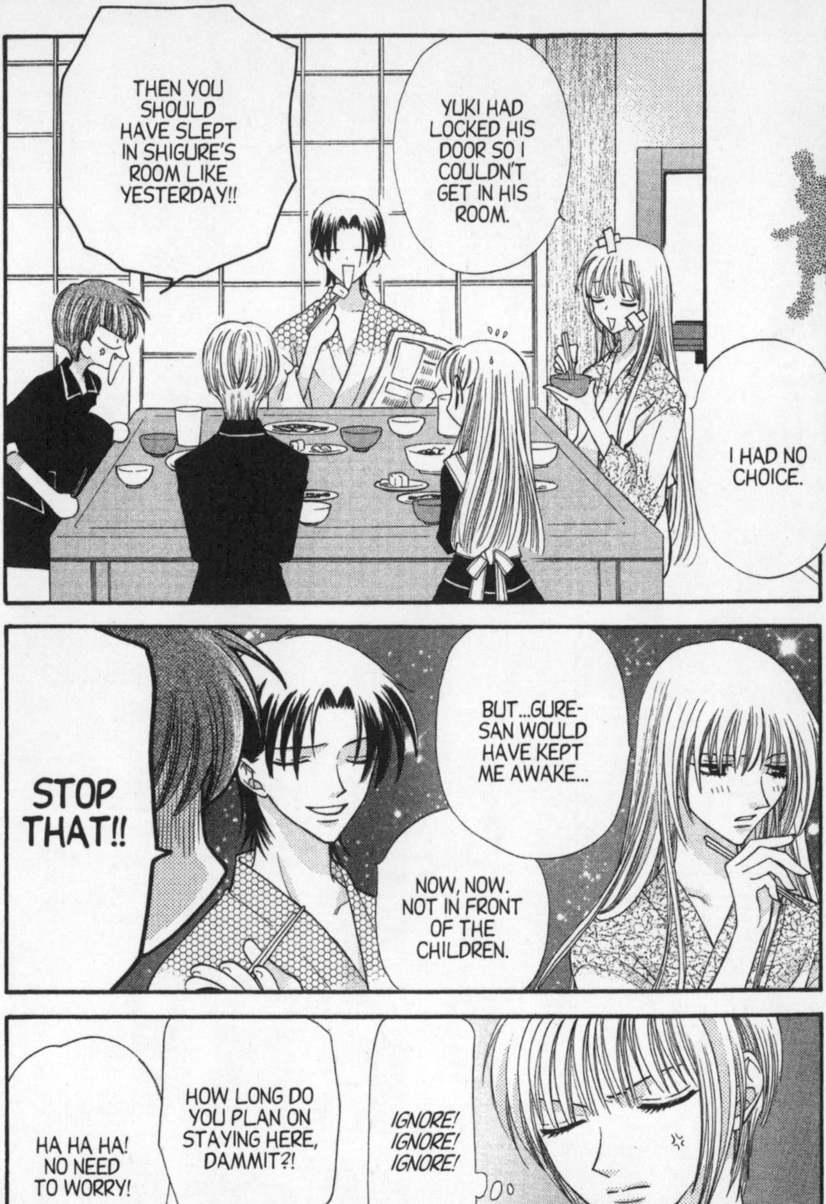
I HAD NO CHOICE.
YUKI HAD LOCKED HIS DOOR SO I COULDN'T GET IN HIS ROOM.
THEN YOU SHOULD HAVE SLEPT IN SHIGURE'S ROOM LIKE YESTERDAY!!
BUT...GURE-SAN WOULD HAVE KEPT ME AWAKE...
NOW, NOW. NOT IN FRONT OF THE CHILDREN.
STOP THAT!!
IGNORE! IGNORE! IGNORE!
HOW LONG DO YOU PLAN ON STAYING HERE, DAMMIT?!
HA HA HA! NO NEED TO WORRY!

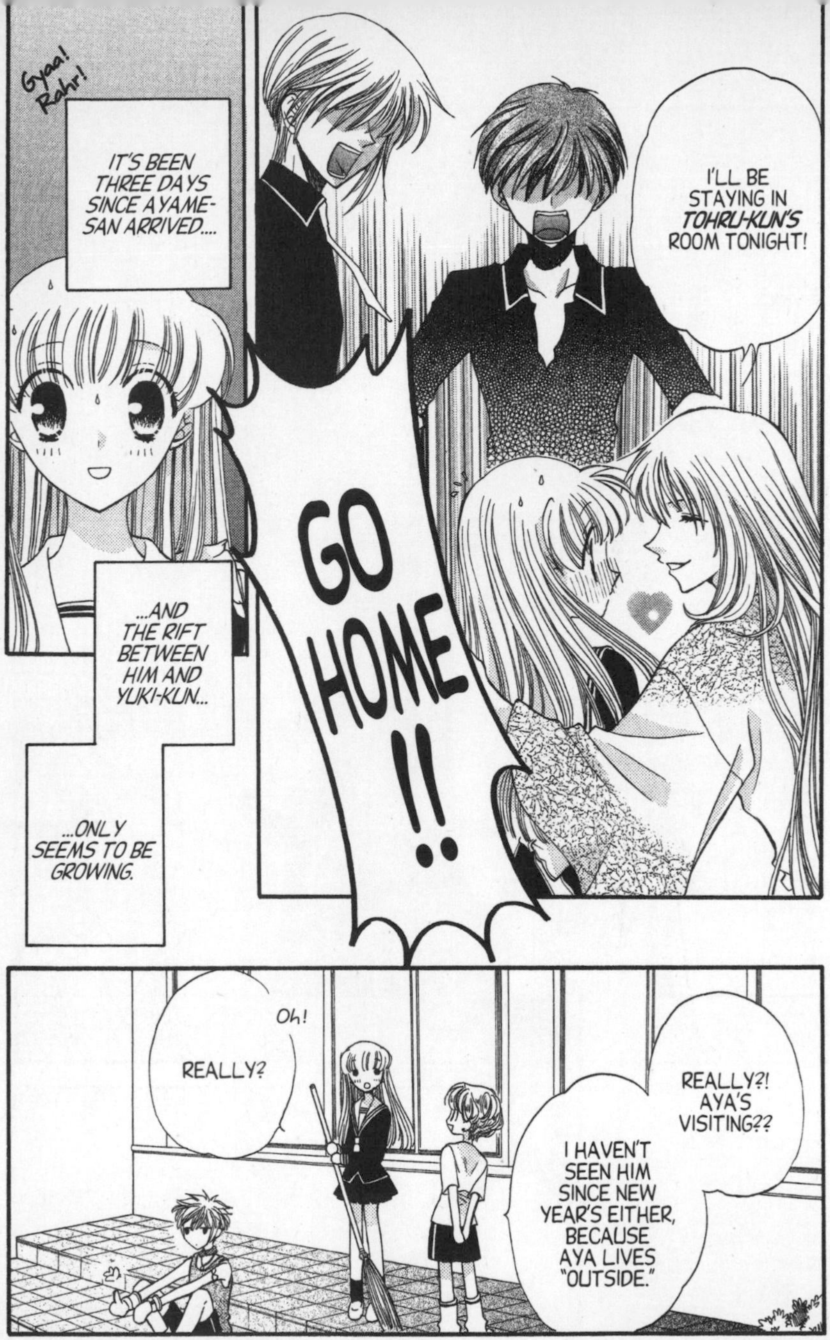
I'LL BE STAYING IN *TOHRU-KUN'S* ROOM TONIGHT!
GO HOME!!
Gyaa! Rahr!
IT'S BEEN THREE DAYS SINCE AYAME-SAN ARRIVED....
...AND THE RIFT BETWEEN HIM AND YUKI-KUN...
...ONLY SEEMS TO BE GROWING.
REALLY?! AYA'S VISITING??
I HAVEN'T SEEN HIM SINCE NEW YEAR'S EITHER, BECAUSE AYA LIVES "OUTSIDE."
Oh!
REALLY?

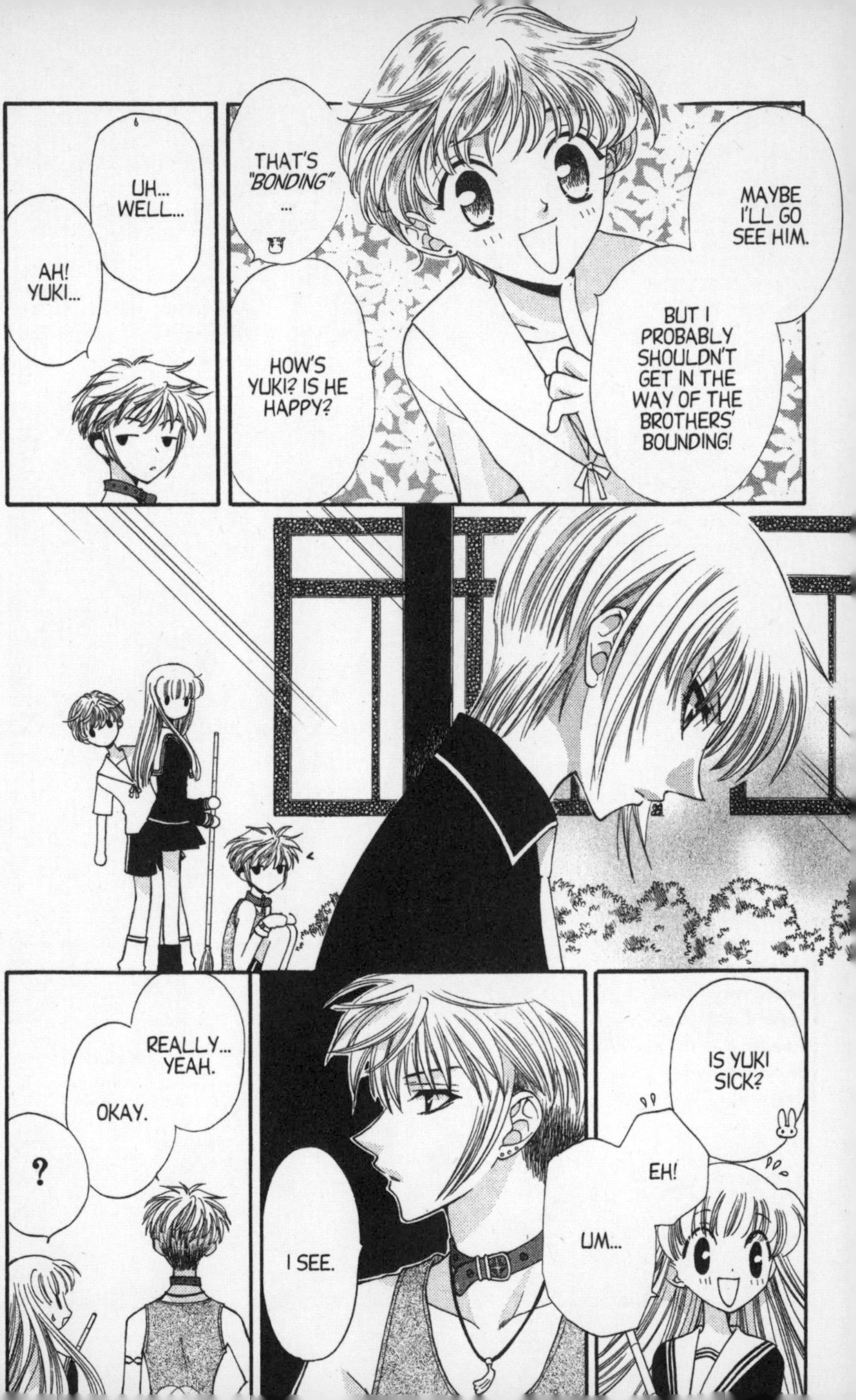
MAYBE I'LL GO SEE HIM.
BUT I PROBABLY SHOULDN'T GET IN THE WAY OF THE BROTHERS' BOUNDING!
THAT'S *"BONDING"* ...
HOW'S YUKI? IS HE HAPPY?
UH... WELL...
AH! YUKI...
IS YUKI SICK?
EH!
UM...
I SEE.
REALLY... YEAH.
OKAY.
?

IS IT OKAY FOR AYA TO LEAVE HIS SHOP FOR SO LONG?
Hm?
HE'S THE MANAGER.
AYAME-SAN HAS A SHOP?!
YES. HE SELLS...
...OUTFITS FOR NURSES, STEWARDESSES, MAIDS...
...AND STUFF.

Fruits Basket 4 Part 4:

As usual, I'm playing video games. I play so many that I can't list them all. I'm stuck on the last boss in Persona 2....With the Megami Tensei series, I'm the type who, once stopped, takes a while to get back to it. I stopped playing Persona 1 for several months before I finally beat it. I'm also stopped in the middle of "Ore-Shika" (Ed: short for "Ore no Shikabane o Koete Yuke." Not published in the U.S.). It looks like I just can't go on. It's interesting. I wonder why I can't go on...? Actually, I bet I know why--the older I get, the harder it is for me to concentrate. It's scary. I think there are a bunch of other games I'm playing too much. This has nothing to do with it, but my handwriting is really bad.

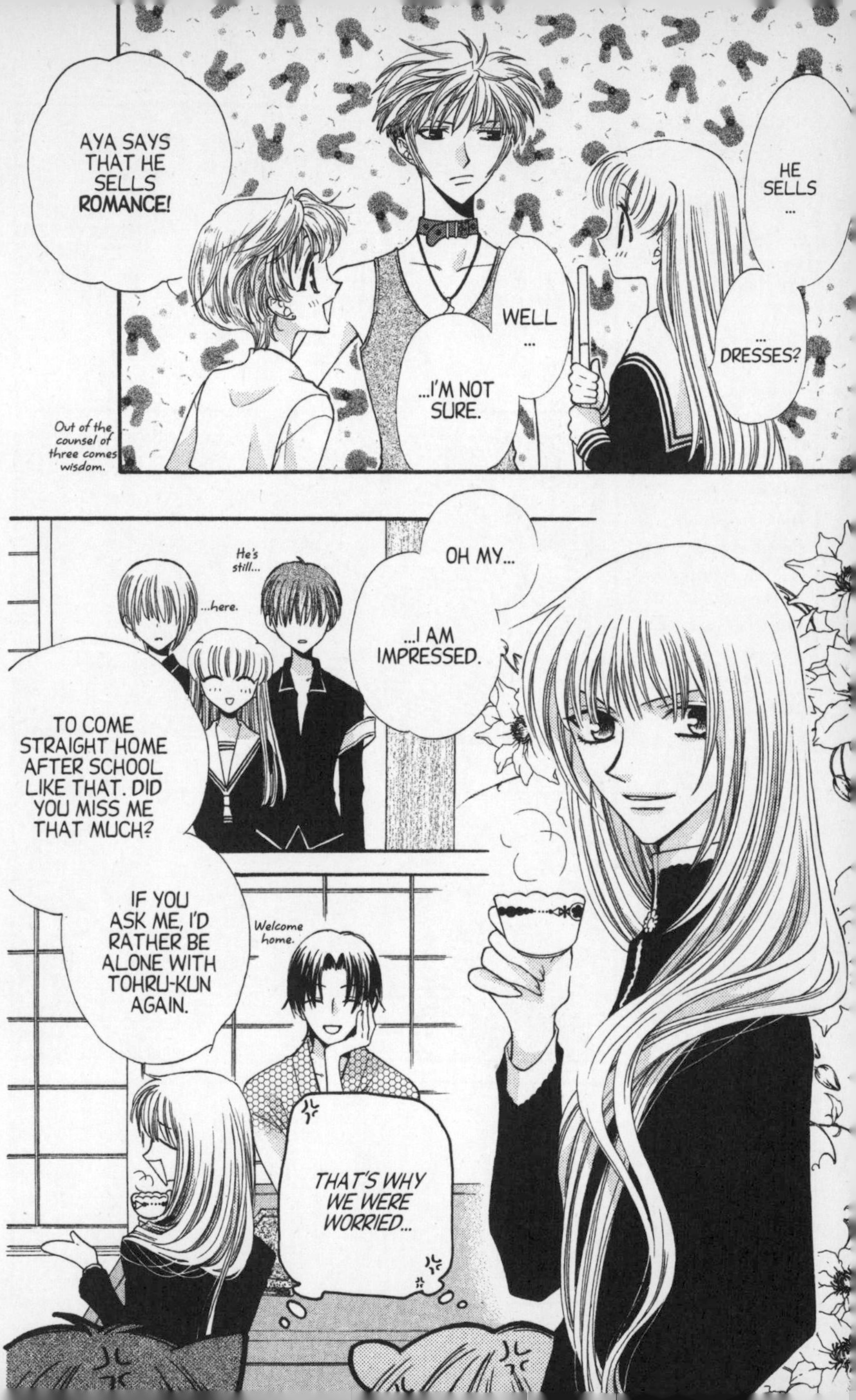
HE SELLS ...
... DRESSES?
WELL ...
...I'M NOT SURE.
AYA SAYS THAT HE SELLS ROMANCE!
Out of the counsel of three comes wisdom.
OH MY...
...I AM IMPRESSED.
He's still...
...here.
TO COME STRAIGHT HOME AFTER SCHOOL LIKE THAT. DID YOU MISS ME THAT MUCH?
IF YOU ASK ME, I'D RATHER BE ALONE WITH TOHRU-KUN AGAIN.
Welcome home.
THAT'S WHY WE WERE WORRIED...

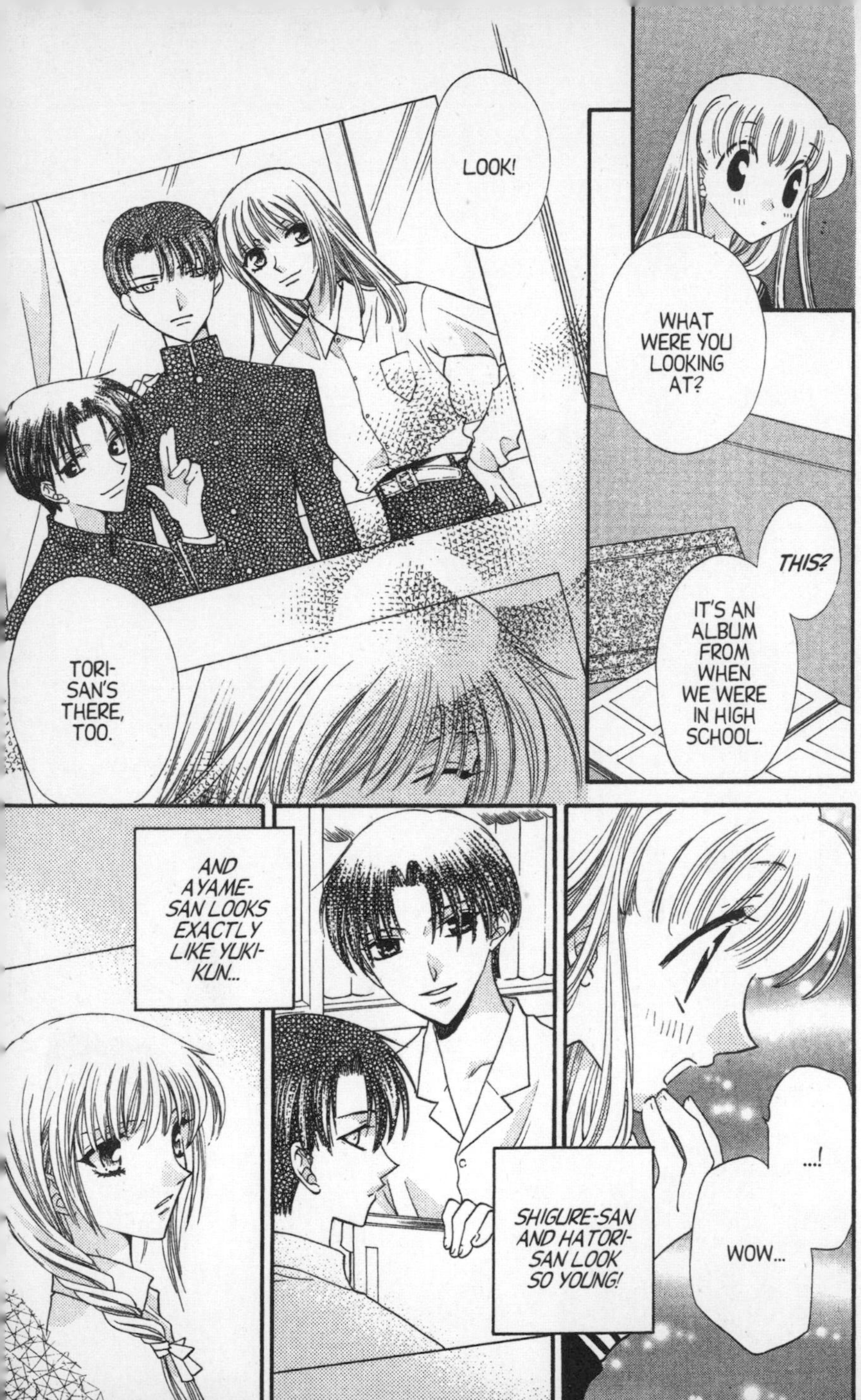
WHAT WERE YOU LOOKING AT?
THIS?
IT'S AN ALBUM FROM WHEN WE WERE IN HIGH SCHOOL.
LOOK!
TORI-SAN'S THERE, TOO.
...!
WOW...
SHIGURE-SAN AND HATORI-SAN LOOK SO YOUNG!
AND AYAME-SAN LOOKS EXACTLY LIKE YUKI-KUN...

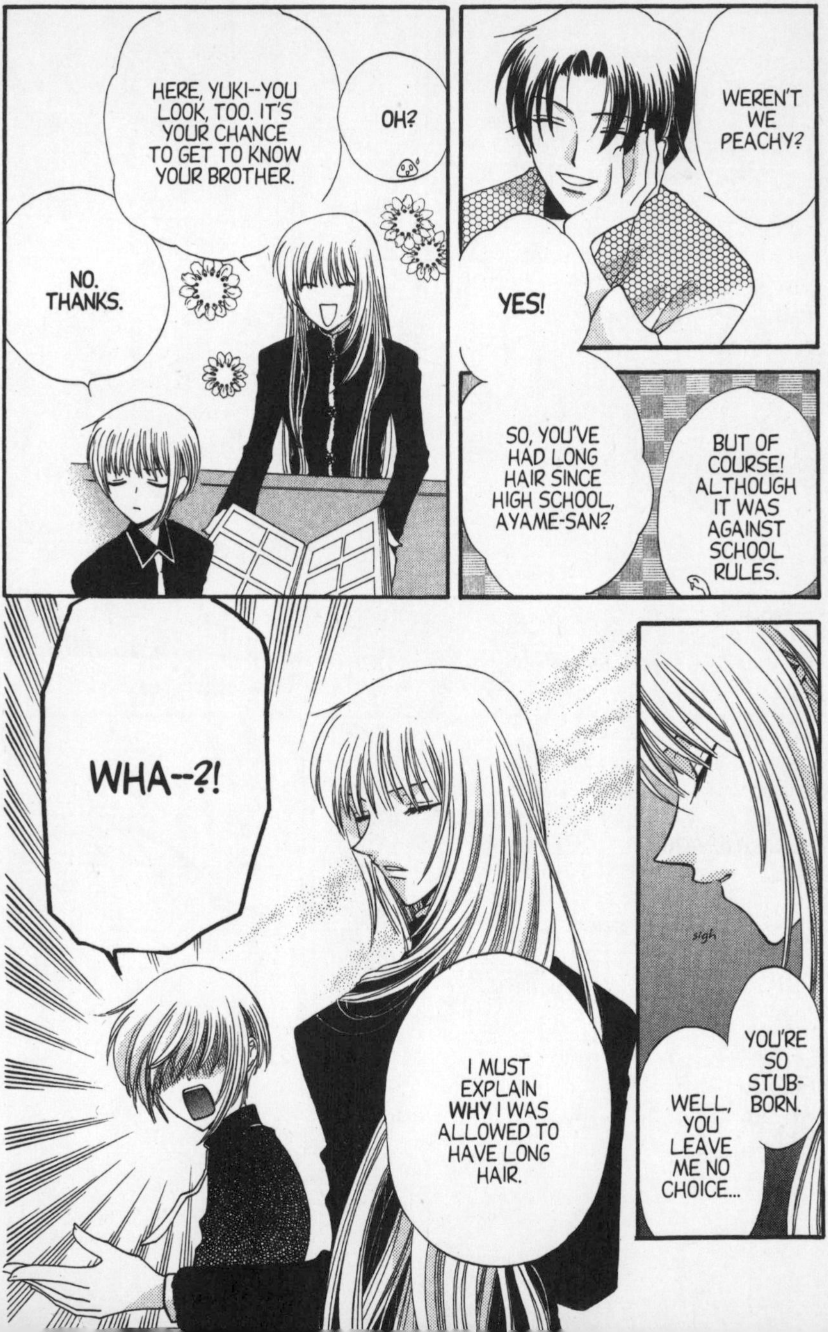
WEREN'T WE PEACHY?
YES!
SO, YOU'VE HAD LONG HAIR SINCE HIGH SCHOOL, AYAME-SAN?
BUT OF COURSE! ALTHOUGH IT WAS AGAINST SCHOOL RULES.
OH?
HERE, YUKI--YOU LOOK, TOO. IT'S YOUR CHANCE TO GET TO KNOW YOUR BROTHER.
NO. THANKS.
YOU'RE SO STUB-BORN.
sigh
WELL, YOU LEAVE ME NO CHOICE...
I MUST EXPLAIN WHY I WAS ALLOWED TO HAVE LONG HAIR.
WHA--?!

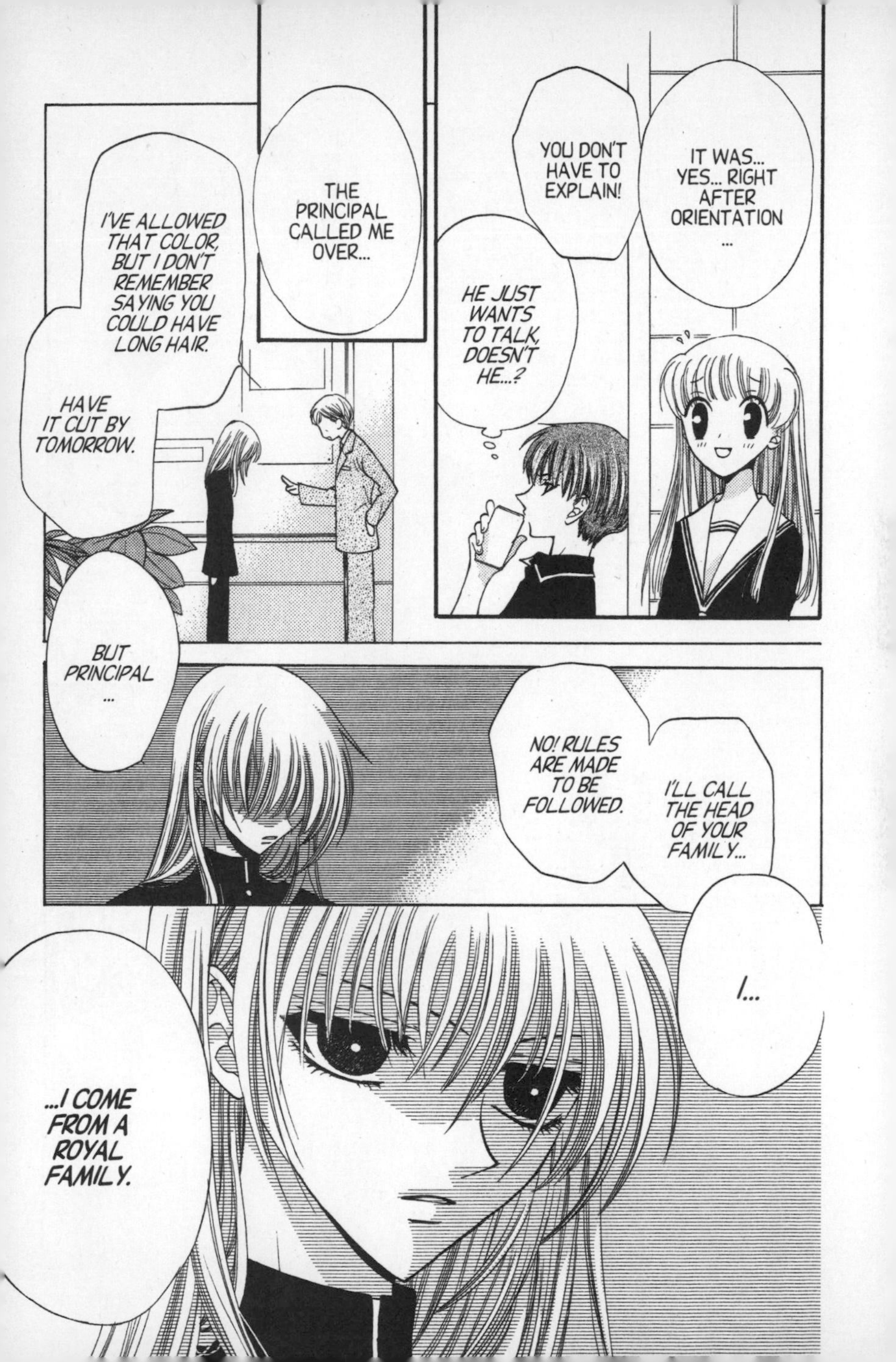
IT WAS... YES... RIGHT AFTER ORIENTATION ...
YOU DON'T HAVE TO EXPLAIN!
HE JUST WANTS TO TALK, DOESN'T HE...?
THE PRINCIPAL CALLED ME OVER...
I'VE ALLOWED THAT COLOR, BUT I DON'T REMEMBER SAYING YOU COULD HAVE LONG HAIR.
HAVE IT CUT BY TOMORROW.
BUT PRINCIPAL ...
NO! RULES ARE MADE TO BE FOLLOWED.
I'LL CALL THE HEAD OF YOUR FAMILY...
I...
...I COME FROM A ROYAL FAMILY.

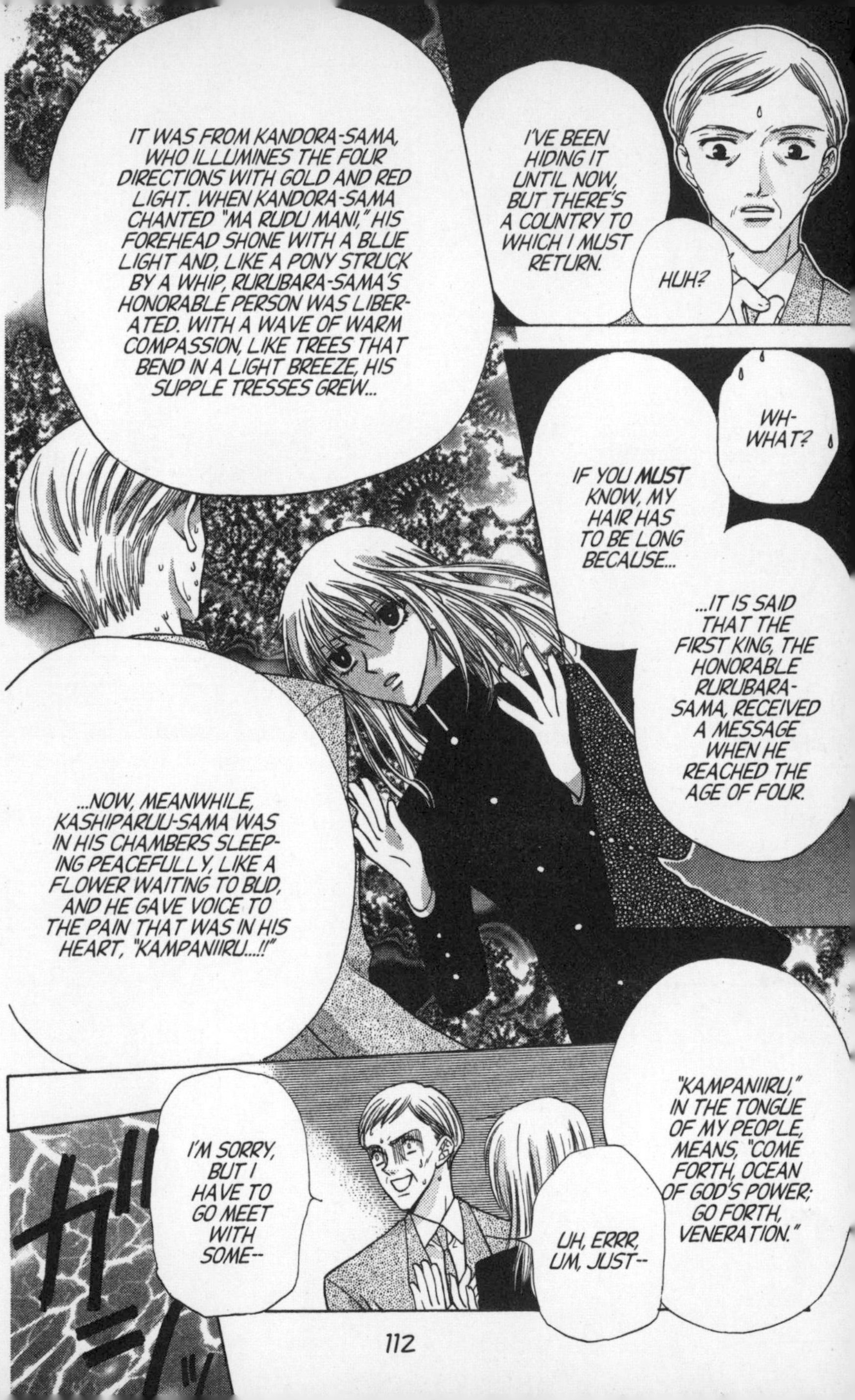
I'VE BEEN HIDING IT UNTIL NOW, BUT THERE'S A COUNTRY TO WHICH I MUST RETURN.
HUH?
WH- WHAT?
IF YOU MUST KNOW, MY HAIR HAS TO BE LONG BECAUSE...
...IT IS SAID THAT THE FIRST KING, THE HONORABLE RURUBARA-SAMA, RECEIVED A MESSAGE WHEN HE REACHED THE AGE OF FOUR.
IT WAS FROM KANDORA-SAMA, WHO ILLUMINES THE FOUR DIRECTIONS WITH GOLD AND RED LIGHT. WHEN KANDORA-SAMA CHANTED "MA RUDU MANI," HIS FOREHEAD SHONE WITH A BLUE LIGHT AND, LIKE A PONY STRUCK BY A WHIP, RURUBARA-SAMA'S HONORABLE PERSON WAS LIBER-ATED. WITH A WAVE OF WARM COMPASSION, LIKE TREES THAT BEND IN A LIGHT BREEZE, HIS SUPPLE TRESSES GREW...
...NOW, MEANWHILE, KASHIPARUU-SAMA WAS IN HIS CHAMBERS SLEEP-ING PEACEFULLY, LIKE A FLOWER WAITING TO BUD, AND HE GAVE VOICE TO THE PAIN THAT WAS IN HIS HEART, "KAMPANIIRU...!!"
"KAMPANIIRU," IN THE TONGUE OF MY PEOPLE, MEANS, "COME FORTH, OCEAN OF GOD'S POWER; GO FORTH, VENERATION."
UH, ERRR, UM, JUST--
I'M SORRY, BUT I HAVE TO GO MEET WITH SOME--

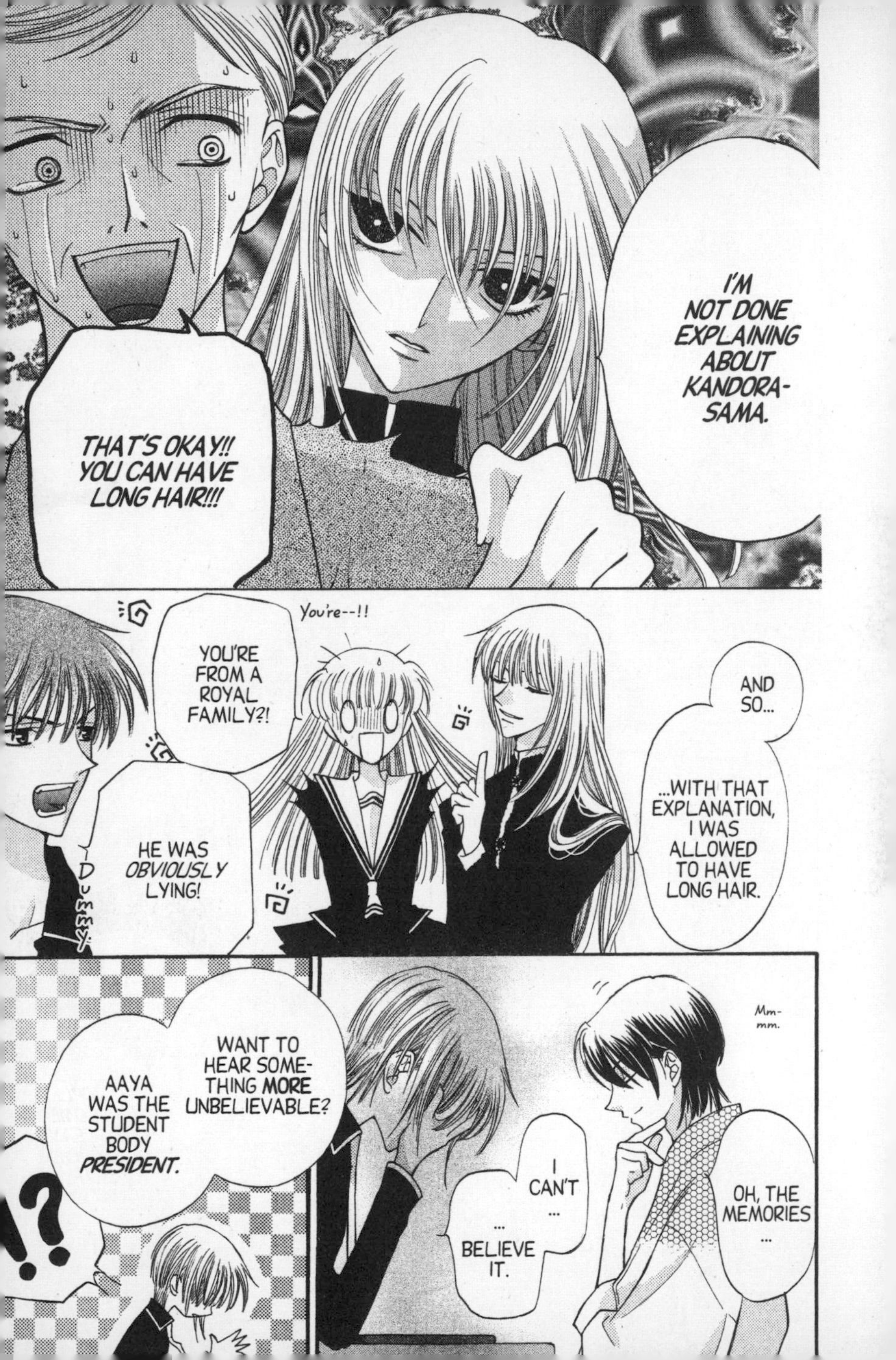
I'M NOT DONE EXPLAINING ABOUT KANDORA-SAMA.
THAT'S OKAY!! YOU CAN HAVE LONG HAIR!!!
AND SO...
...WITH THAT EXPLANATION, I WAS ALLOWED TO HAVE LONG HAIR.
You're--!!
YOU'RE FROM A ROYAL FAMILY?!
HE WAS OBVIOUSLY LYING!
Dummy.
Mm-mm.
OH, THE MEMORIES ...
I CAN'T ...
... BELIEVE IT.
WANT TO HEAR SOME-THING MORE UNBELIEVABLE?
AAYA WAS THE STUDENT BODY PRESIDENT.
!?

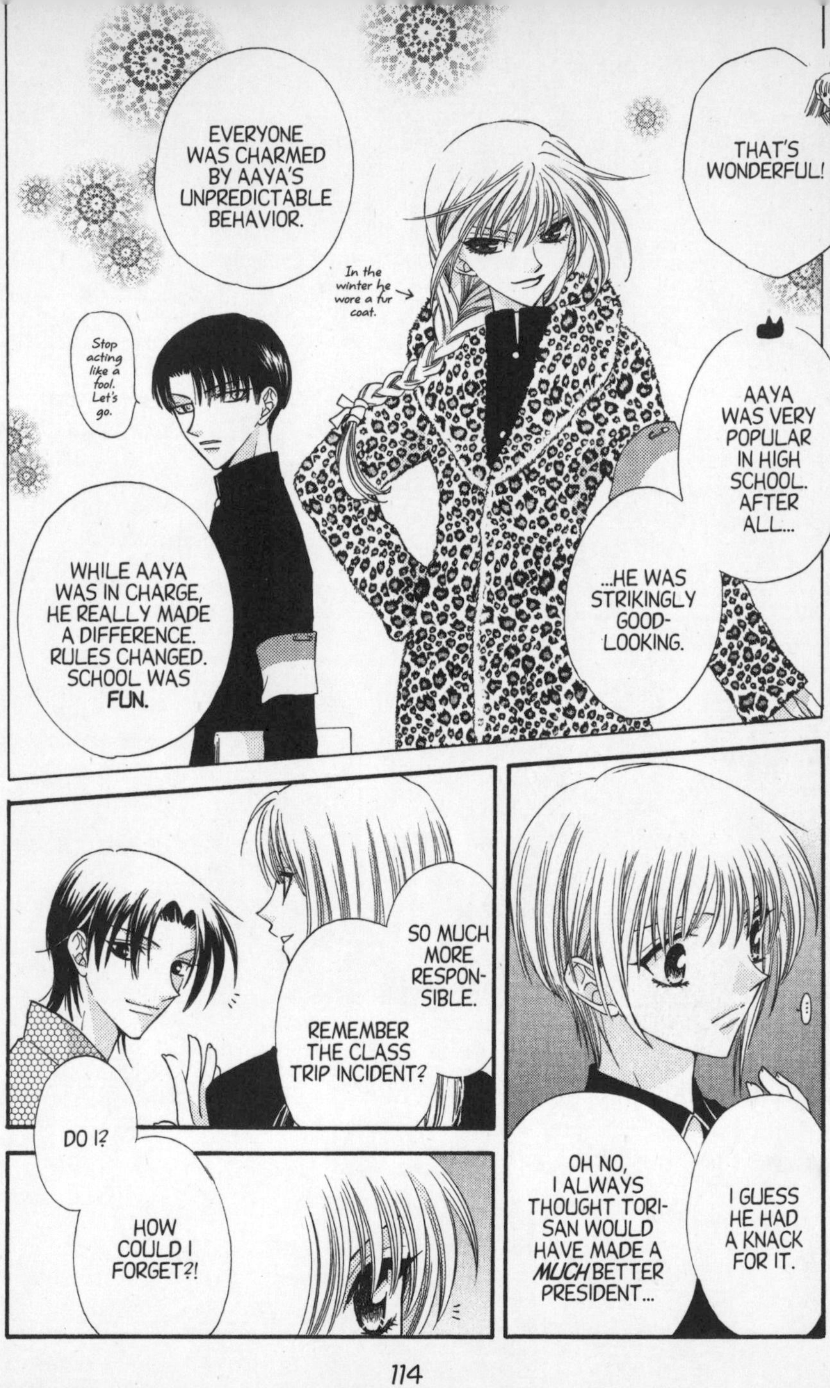

THAT'S WONDERFUL!
AAYA WAS VERY POPULAR IN HIGH SCHOOL. AFTER ALL...
...HE WAS STRIKINGLY GOOD-LOOKING.
EVERYONE WAS CHARMED BY AAYA'S UNPREDICTABLE BEHAVIOR.
In the winter he wore a fur coat.
Stop acting like a fool. Let's go.
WHILE AAYA WAS IN CHARGE, HE REALLY MADE A DIFFERENCE. RULES CHANGED. SCHOOL WAS FUN.
...
I GUESS HE HAD A KNACK FOR IT.
OH NO, I ALWAYS THOUGHT TORI-SAN WOULD HAVE MADE A MUCH BETTER PRESIDENT...
SO MUCH MORE RESPONSIBLE.
REMEMBER THE CLASS TRIP INCIDENT?
DO I?
HOW COULD I FORGET?!

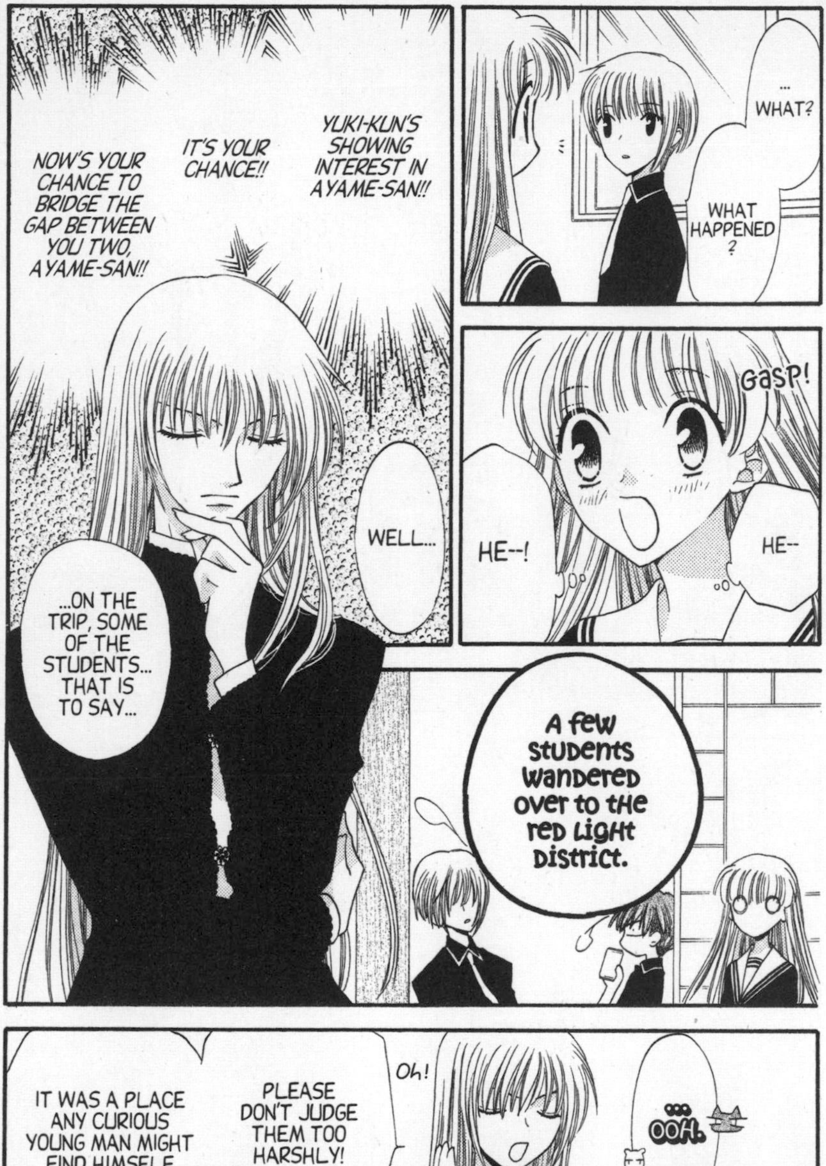

... WHAT?
WHAT HAPPENED ?
GASP!
HE--
HE--!
YUKI-KUN'S SHOWING INTEREST IN AYAME-SAN!!
IT'S YOUR CHANCE!!
NOW'S YOUR CHANCE TO BRIDGE THE GAP BETWEEN YOU TWO, AYAME-SAN!!
WELL...
...ON THE TRIP, SOME OF THE STUDENTS... THAT IS TO SAY...
A few students wandered over to the red light district.
...OOH.
Oh!
PLEASE DON'T JUDGE THEM TOO HARSHLY!
IT WAS A PLACE ANY CURIOUS YOUNG MAN MIGHT FIND HIMSELF WANDERING.

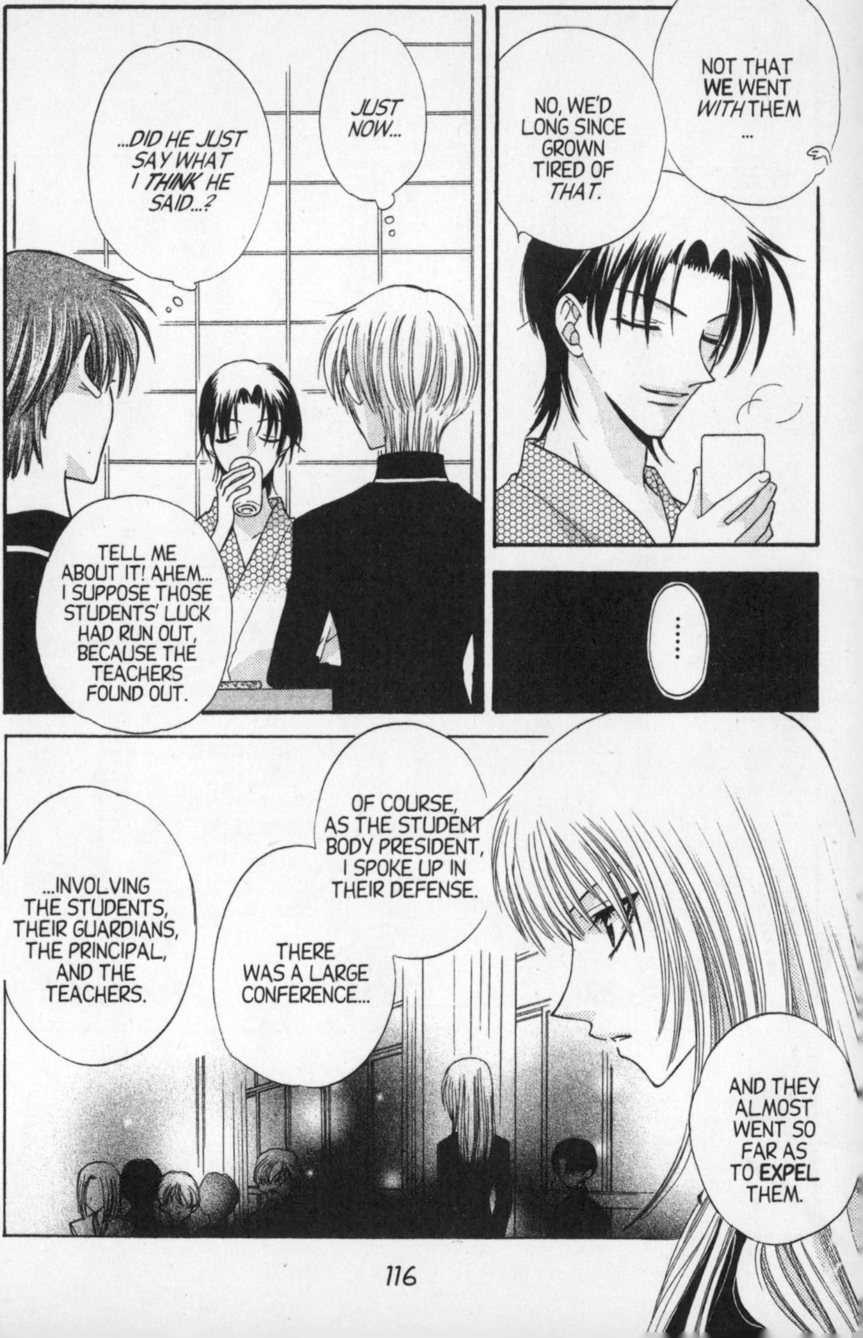
NOT THAT WE WENT WITH THEM ...
NO, WE'D LONG SINCE GROWN TIRED OF THAT.
……
JUST NOW...
...DID HE JUST SAY WHAT I THINK HE SAID...?
TELL ME ABOUT IT! AHEM... I SUPPOSE THOSE STUDENTS' LUCK HAD RUN OUT, BECAUSE THE TEACHERS FOUND OUT.
THERE WAS A LARGE CONFERENCE...
...INVOLVING THE STUDENTS, THEIR GUARDIANS, THE PRINCIPAL, AND THE TEACHERS.
OF COURSE, AS THE STUDENT BODY PRESIDENT, I SPOKE UP IN THEIR DEFENSE.
AND THEY ALMOST WENT SO FAR AS TO EXPEL THEM.

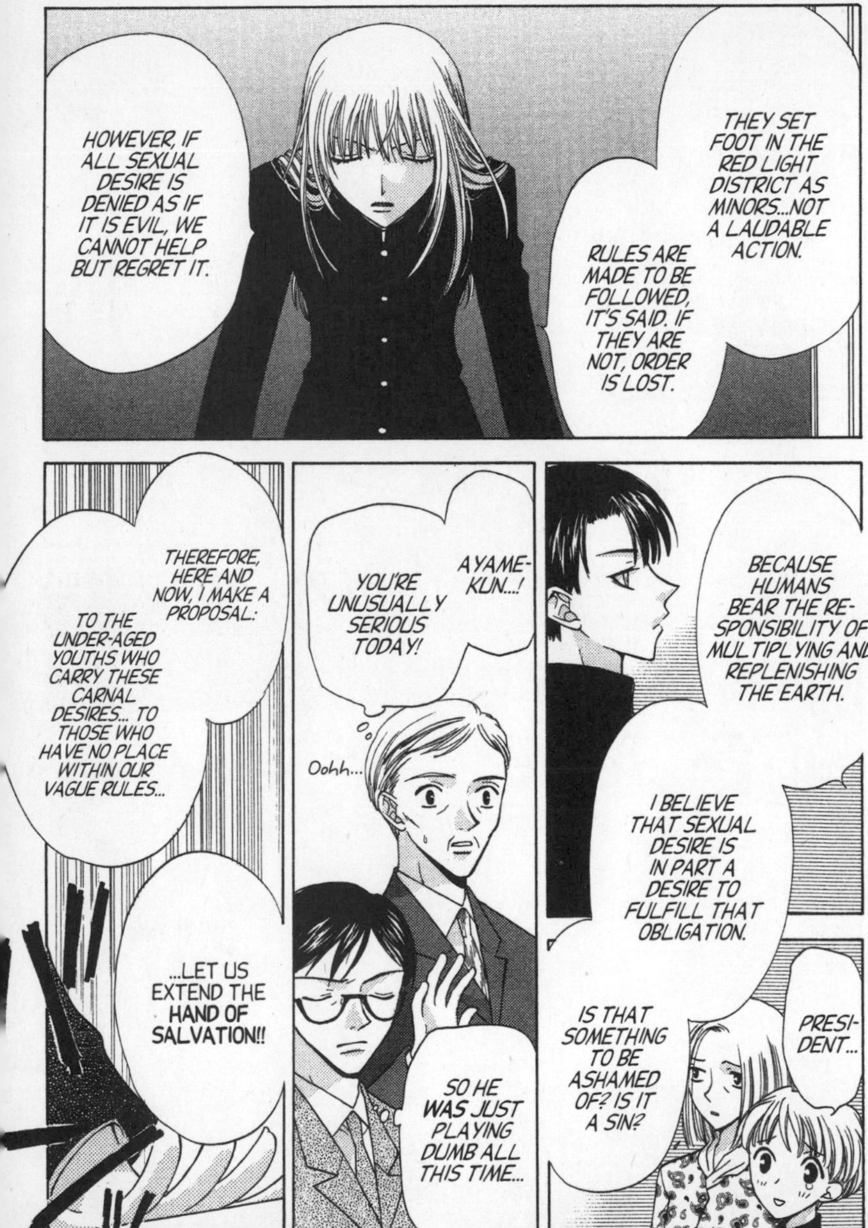
THEY SET FOOT IN THE RED LIGHT DISTRICT AS MINORS...NOT A LAUDABLE ACTION.
RULES ARE MADE TO BE FOLLOWED, IT'S SAID. IF THEY ARE NOT, ORDER IS LOST.
HOWEVER, IF ALL SEXUAL DESIRE IS DENIED AS IF IT IS EVIL, WE CANNOT HELP BUT REGRET IT.
BECAUSE HUMANS BEAR THE RE-SPONSIBILITY OF MULTIPLYING AND REPLENISHING THE EARTH.
I BELIEVE THAT SEXUAL DESIRE IS IN PART A DESIRE TO FULFILL THAT OBLIGATION.
PRESI-DENT...
IS THAT SOMETHING TO BE ASHAMED OF? IS IT A SIN?
AYAME-KUN...!
YOU'RE UNUSUALLY SERIOUS TODAY!
Oohh...
SO HE **WAS** JUST PLAYING DUMB ALL THIS TIME...
THEREFORE, HERE AND NOW, I MAKE A PROPOSAL:
TO THE UNDER-AGED YOUTHS WHO CARRY THESE CARNAL DESIRES... TO THOSE WHO HAVE NO PLACE WITHIN OUR VAGUE RULES...
...LET US EXTEND THE **HAND OF SALVATION!!**

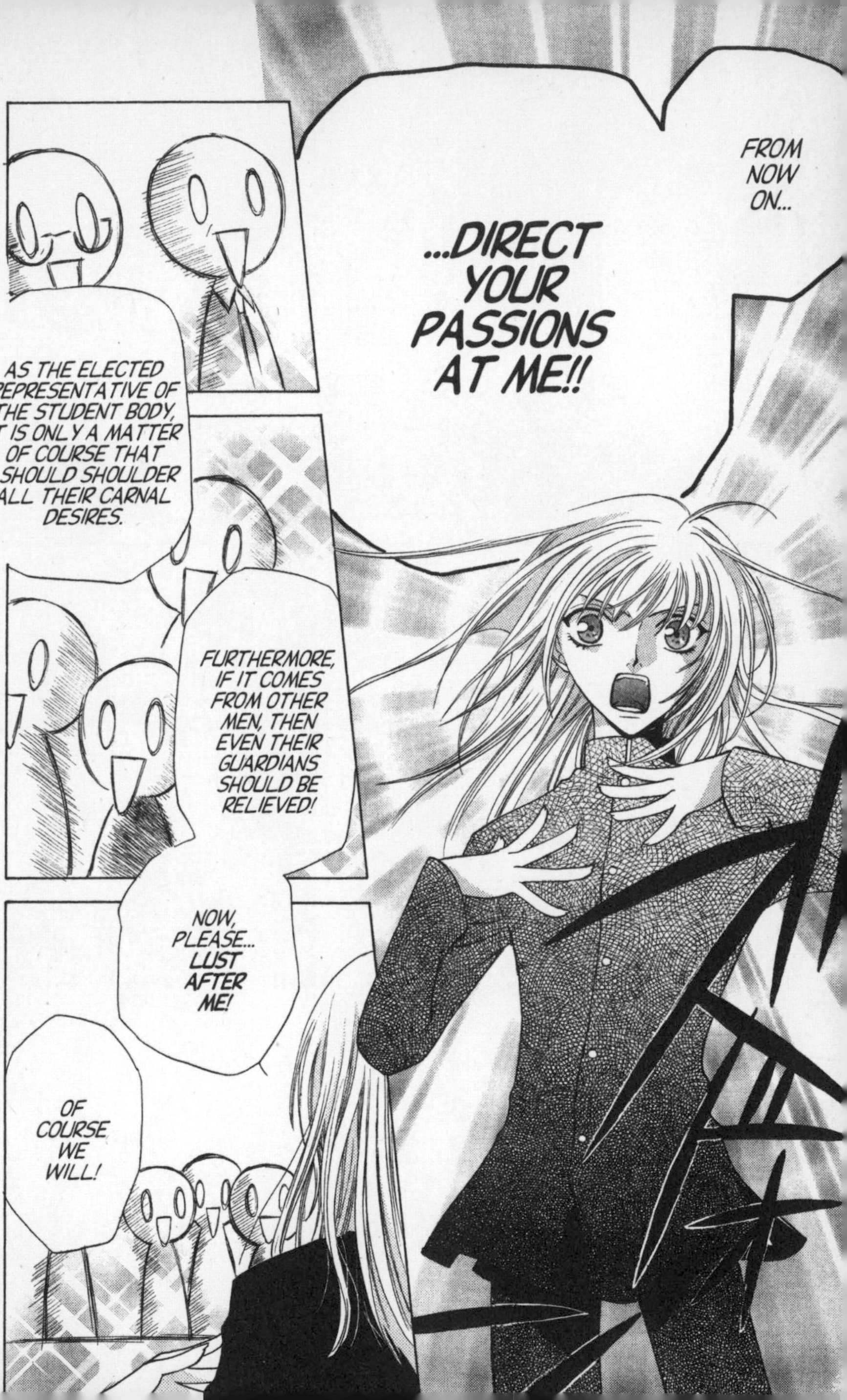
FROM NOW ON...
...DIRECT YOUR PASSIONS AT ME!!
AS THE ELECTED REPRESENTATIVE OF THE STUDENT BODY, IT IS ONLY A MATTER OF COURSE THAT I SHOULD SHOULDER ALL THEIR CARNAL DESIRES.
FURTHERMORE, IF IT COMES FROM OTHER MEN, THEN EVEN THEIR GUARDIANS SHOULD BE RELIEVED!
NOW, PLEASE... LUST AFTER ME!
OF COURSE WE WILL!

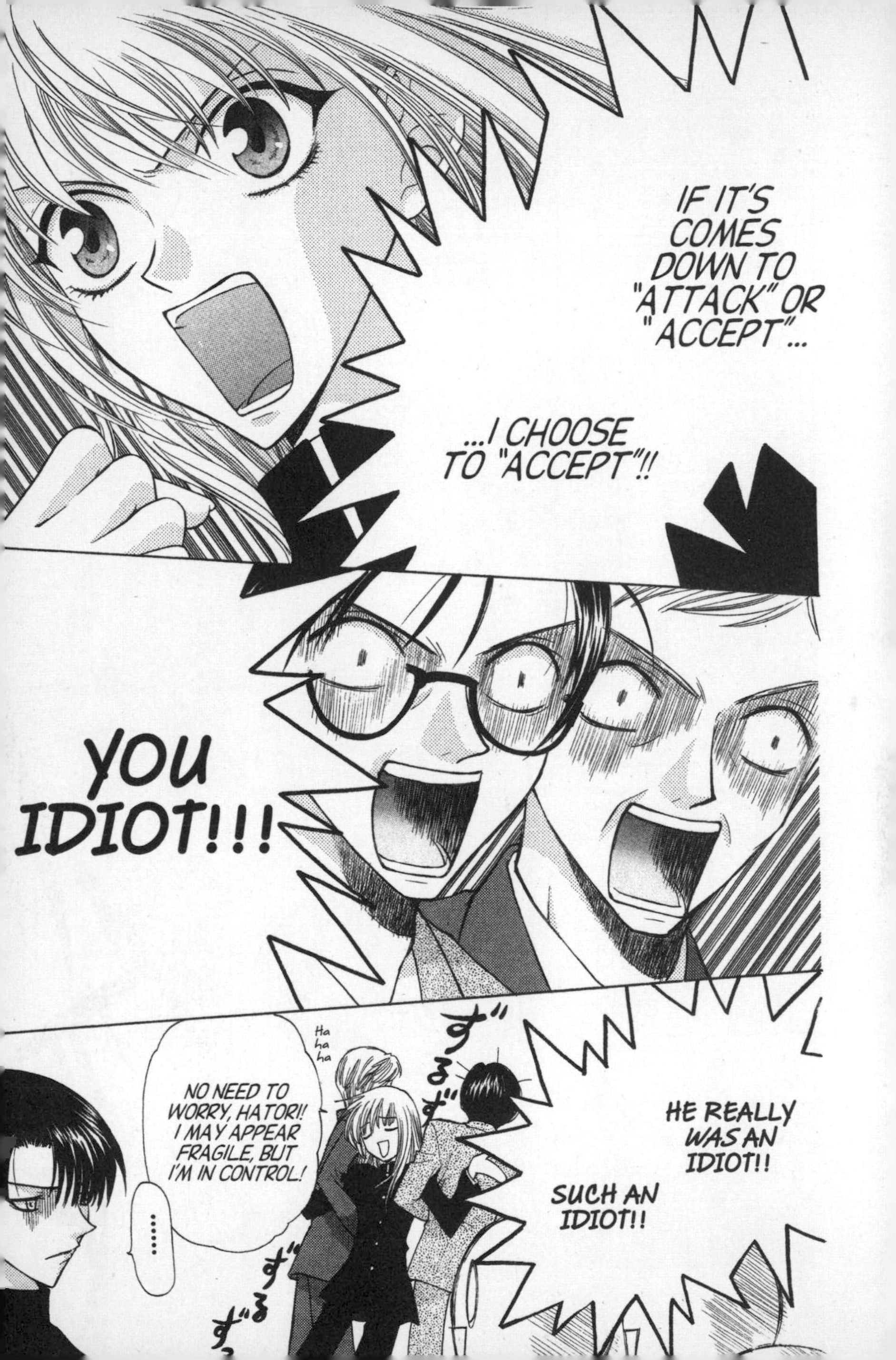
IF IT'S COMES DOWN TO "ATTACK" OR "ACCEPT"...
...I CHOOSE TO "ACCEPT"!!
YOU IDIOT!!!
HE REALLY WAS AN IDIOT!!
SUCH AN IDIOT!!
ずるずる
Ha ha ha
NO NEED TO WORRY, HATORI!! I MAY APPEAR FRAGILE, BUT I'M IN CONTROL!
......
ずるずる

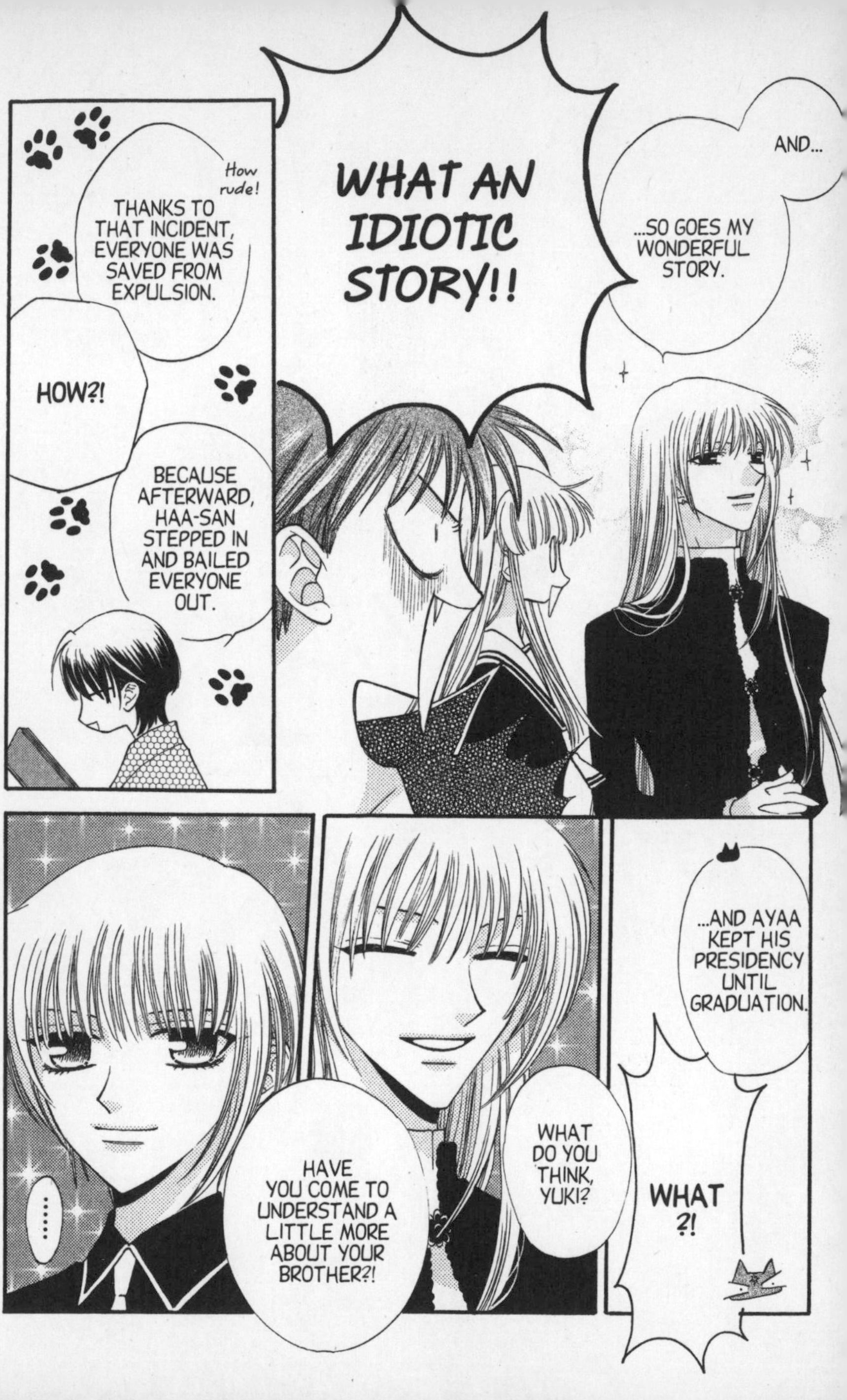
AND...
...SO GOES MY WONDERFUL STORY.
WHAT AN IDIOTIC STORY!!
How rude!
THANKS TO THAT INCIDENT, EVERYONE WAS SAVED FROM EXPULSION.
HOW?!
BECAUSE AFTERWARD, HAA-SAN STEPPED IN AND BAILED EVERYONE OUT.
...AND AYAA KEPT HIS PRESIDENCY UNTIL GRADUATION.
WHAT ?!
WHAT DO YOU THINK, YUKI?
HAVE YOU COME TO UNDERSTAND A LITTLE MORE ABOUT YOUR BROTHER?!
......

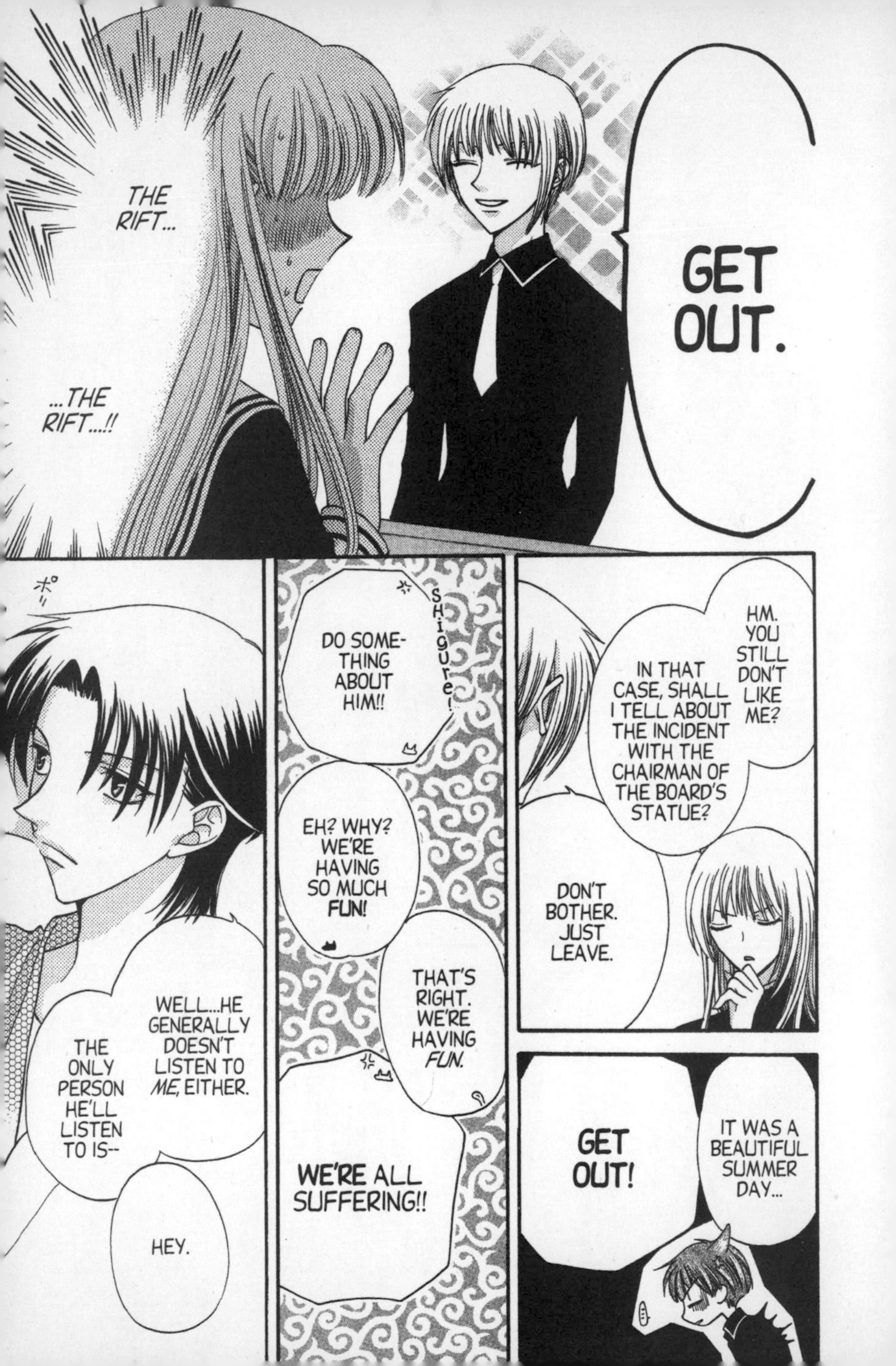
GET OUT.
THE RIFT...
...THE RIFT...!!
HM. YOU STILL DON'T LIKE ME?
IN THAT CASE, SHALL I TELL ABOUT THE INCIDENT WITH THE CHAIRMAN OF THE BOARD'S STATUE?
DON'T BOTHER. JUST LEAVE.
IT WAS A BEAUTIFUL SUMMER DAY...
GET OUT!
Shigure!
DO SOME-THING ABOUT HIM!!
EH? WHY? WE'RE HAVING SO MUCH FUN!
THAT'S RIGHT. WE'RE HAVING FUN.
WE'RE ALL SUFFERING!!
ポッ
WELL...HE GENERALLY DOESN'T LISTEN TO ME, EITHER.
THE ONLY PERSON HE'LL LISTEN TO IS--
HEY.

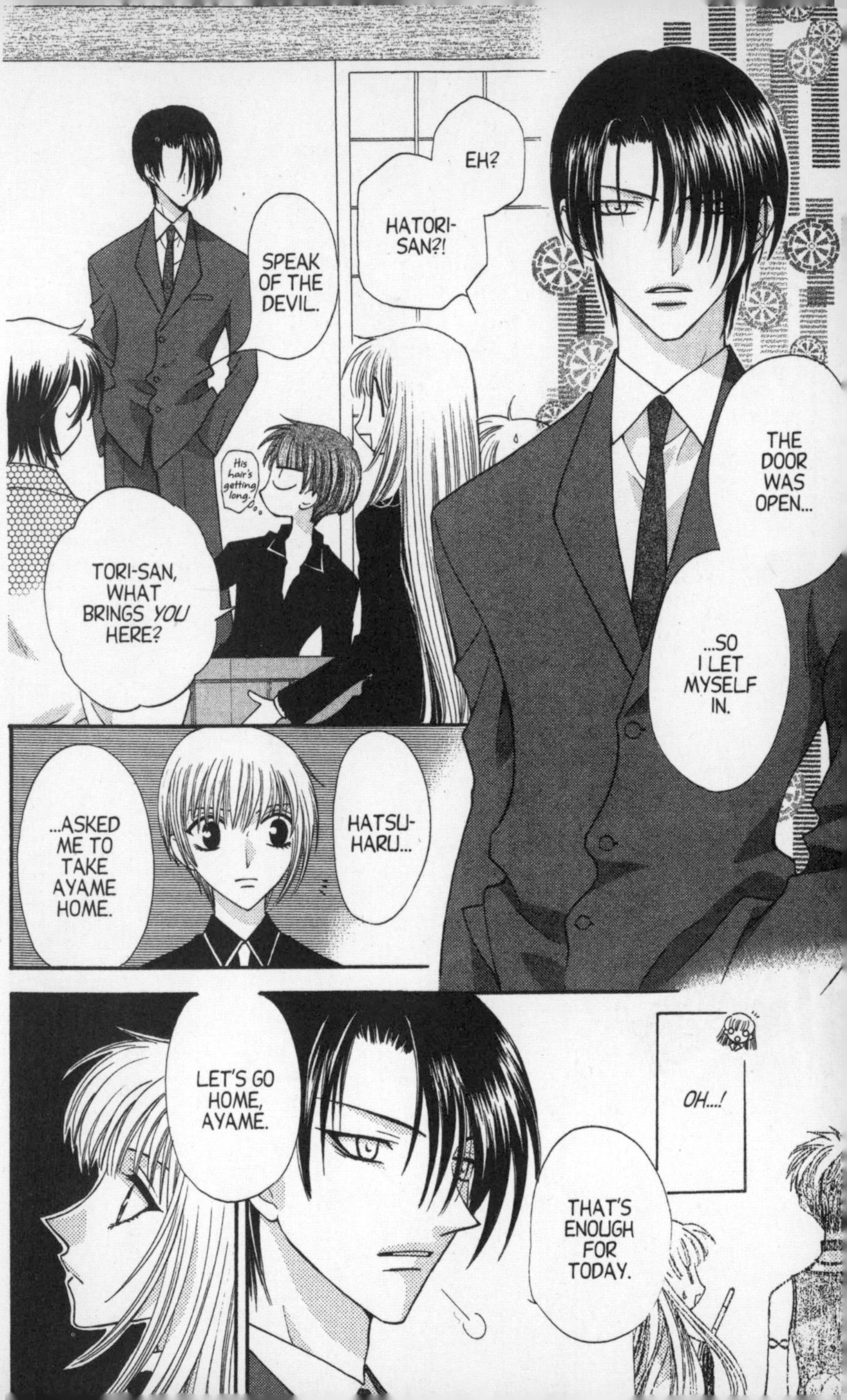
THE DOOR WAS OPEN...
...SO I LET MYSELF IN.
EH?
HATORI-SAN?!
SPEAK OF THE DEVIL.
His hair's getting long.
TORI-SAN, WHAT BRINGS *YOU* HERE?
HATSU-HARU...
...ASKED ME TO TAKE AYAME HOME.
OH...!
LET'S GO HOME, AYAME.
THAT'S ENOUGH FOR TODAY.

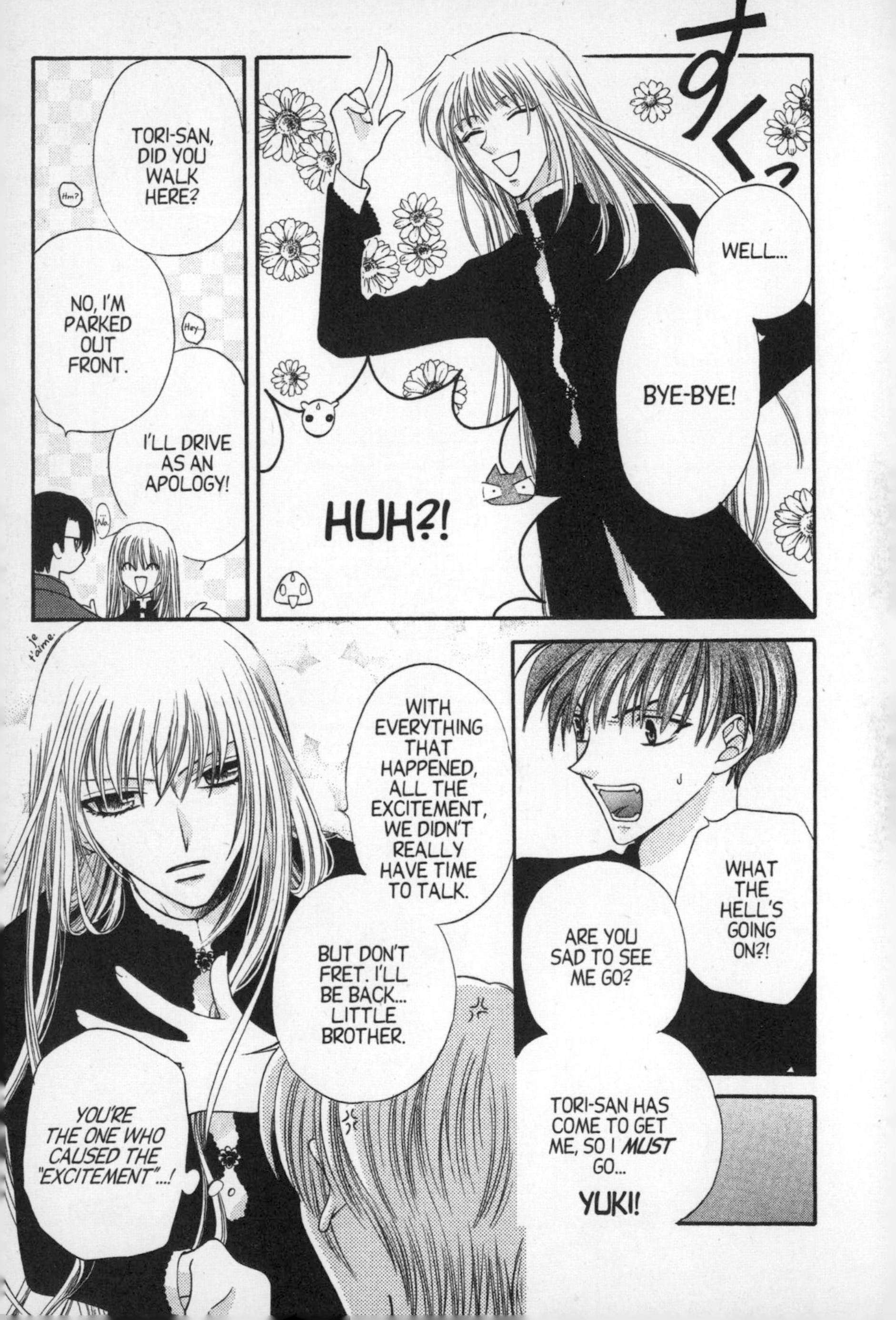
すくっ
WELL...
BYE-BYE!
HUH?!
TORI-SAN, DID YOU WALK HERE?
Hm?
NO, I'M PARKED OUT FRONT.
Hey...
I'LL DRIVE AS AN APOLOGY!
No.
WHAT THE HELL'S GOING ON?!
ARE YOU SAD TO SEE ME GO?
TORI-SAN HAS COME TO GET ME, SO I *MUST* GO...
YUKI!
je t'aime.
WITH EVERYTHING THAT HAPPENED, ALL THE EXCITEMENT, WE DIDN'T REALLY HAVE TIME TO TALK.
BUT DON'T FRET. I'LL BE BACK... LITTLE BROTHER.
YOU'RE THE ONE WHO CAUSED THE "EXCITEMENT"...!

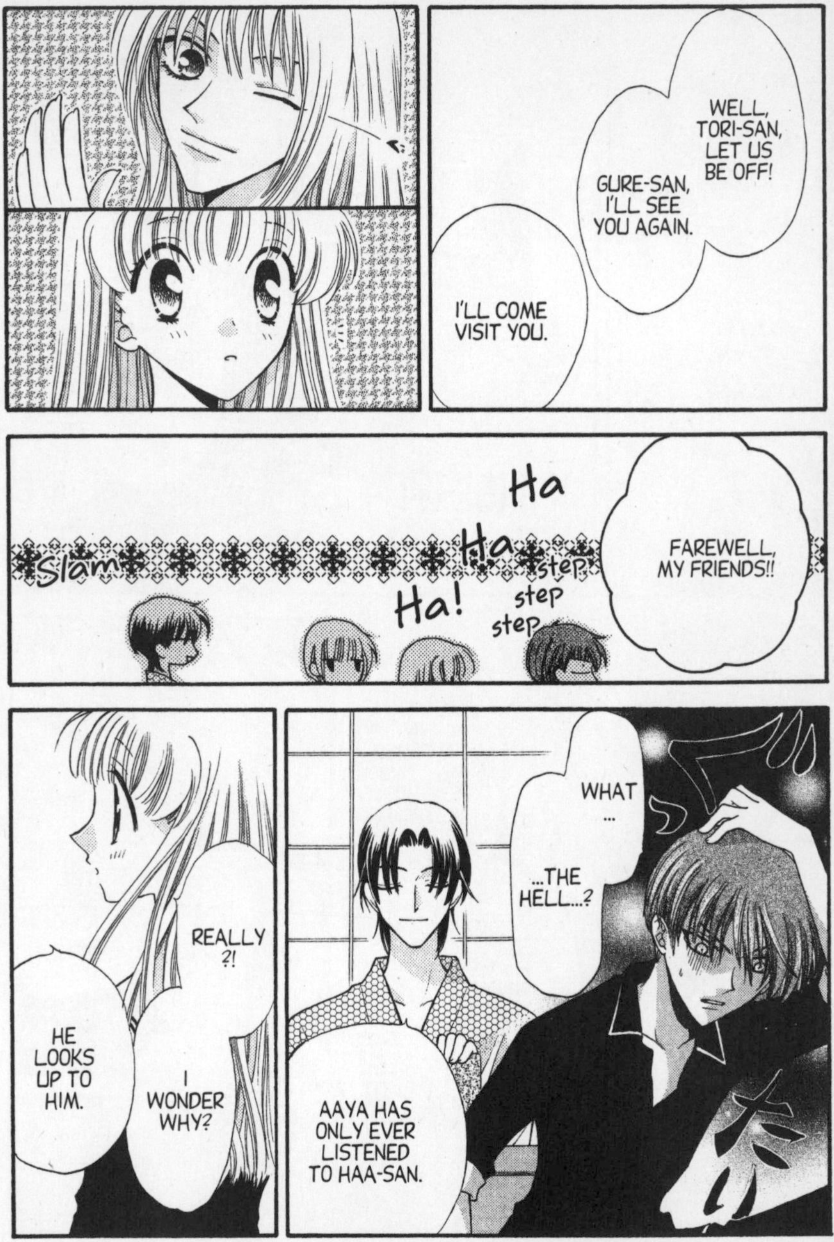
WELL, TORI-SAN, LET US BE OFF!
GURE-SAN, I'LL SEE YOU AGAIN.
I'LL COME VISIT YOU.
FAREWELL, MY FRIENDS!!
Ha
Ha
Ha!
step
step
step
Slam
WHAT ...
...THE HELL...?
AAYA HAS ONLY EVER LISTENED TO HAA-SAN.
REALLY ?!
I WONDER WHY?
HE LOOKS UP TO HIM.

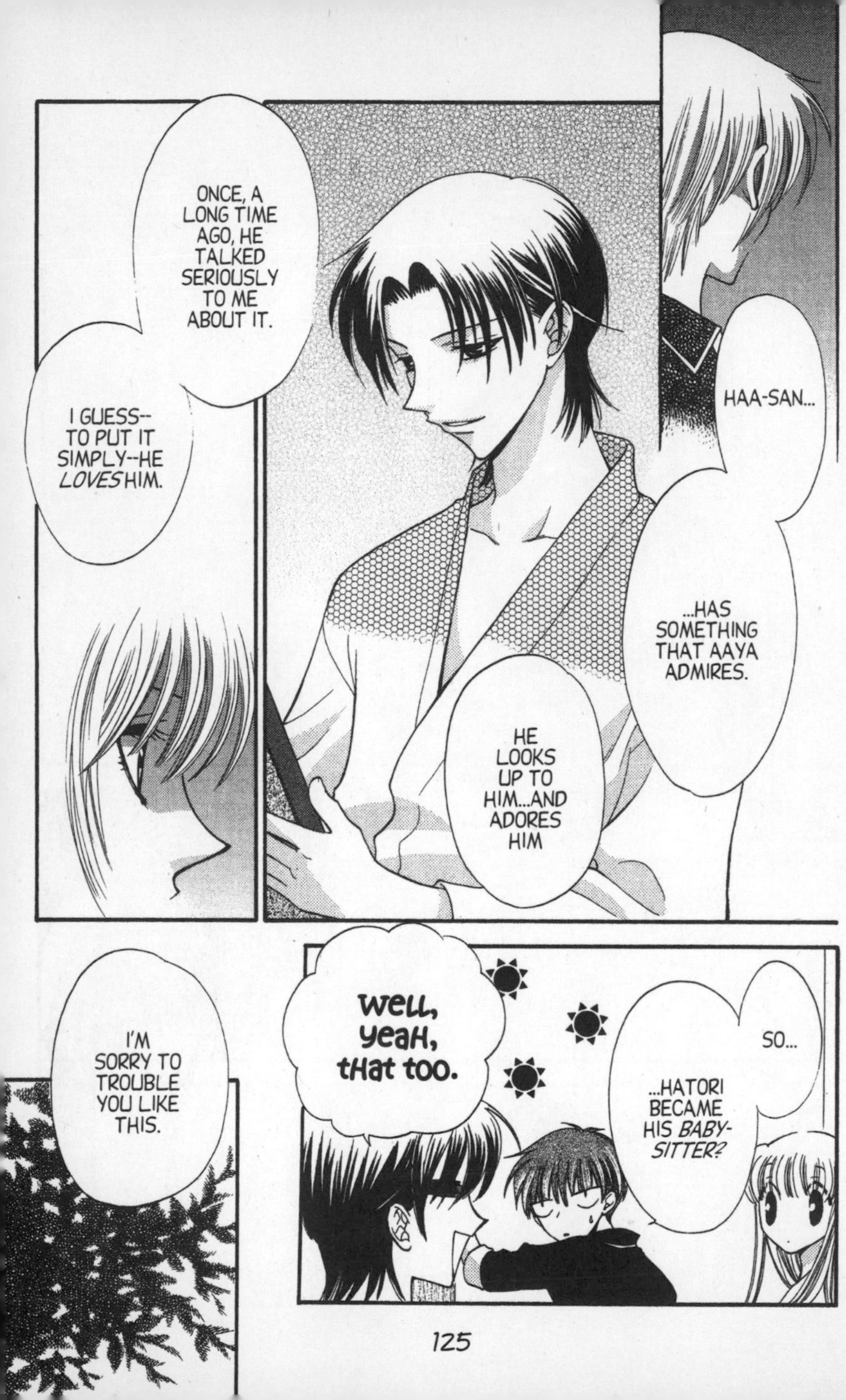
HAA-SAN...
...HAS SOMETHING THAT AAYA ADMIRES.
HE LOOKS UP TO HIM...AND ADORES HIM
ONCE, A LONG TIME AGO, HE TALKED SERIOUSLY TO ME ABOUT IT.
I GUESS--TO PUT IT SIMPLY--HE *LOVES* HIM.
SO...
...HATORI BECAME HIS *BABY-SITTER?*
Well, yeah, that too.
I'M SORRY TO TROUBLE YOU LIKE THIS.

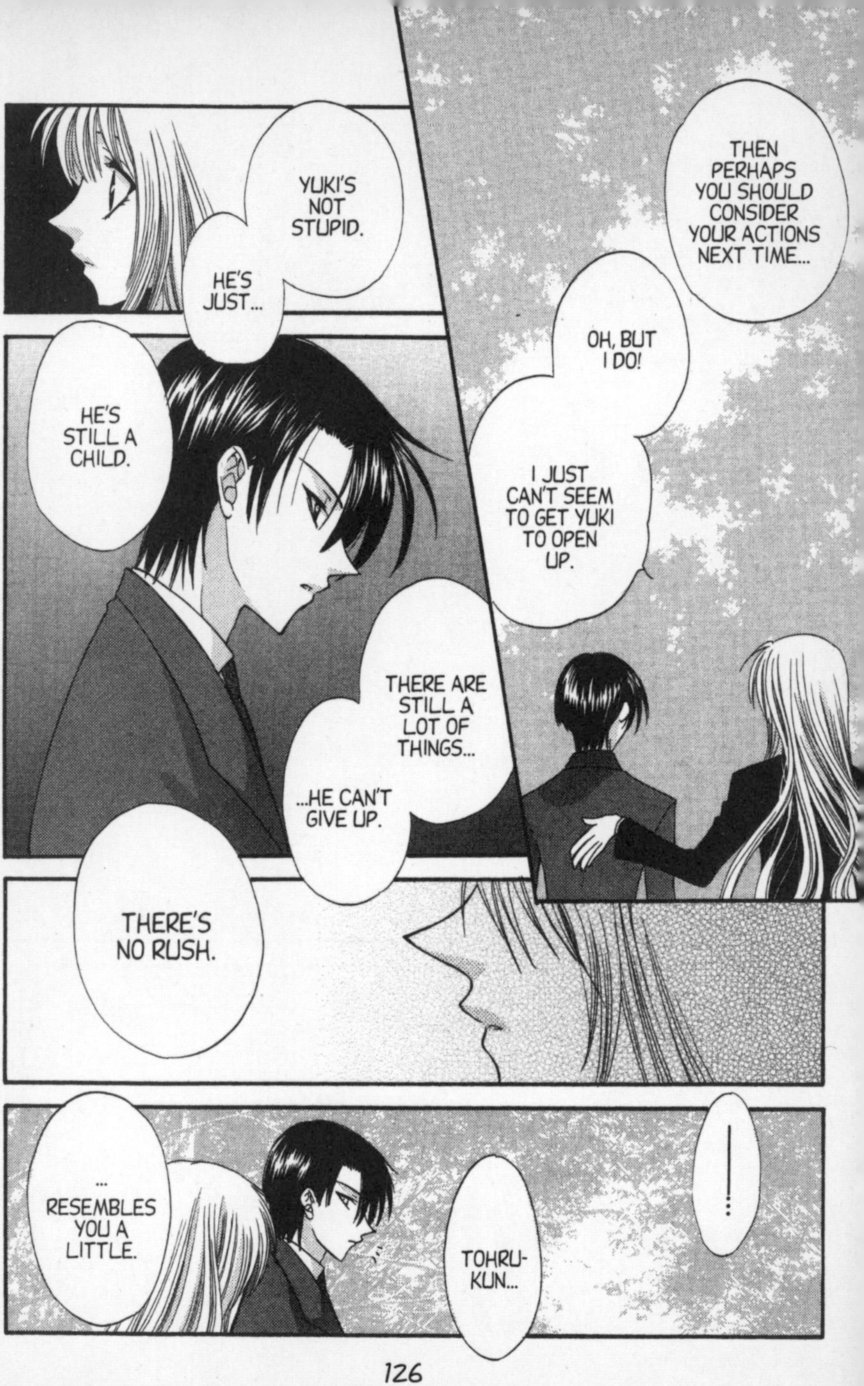
THEN PERHAPS YOU SHOULD CONSIDER YOUR ACTIONS NEXT TIME...
OH, BUT I DO!
I JUST CAN'T SEEM TO GET YUKI TO OPEN UP.
YUKI'S NOT STUPID.
HE'S JUST...
HE'S STILL A CHILD.
THERE ARE STILL A LOT OF THINGS...
...HE CAN'T GIVE UP.
THERE'S NO RUSH.
!
TOHRU-KUN...
... RESEMBLES YOU A LITTLE.

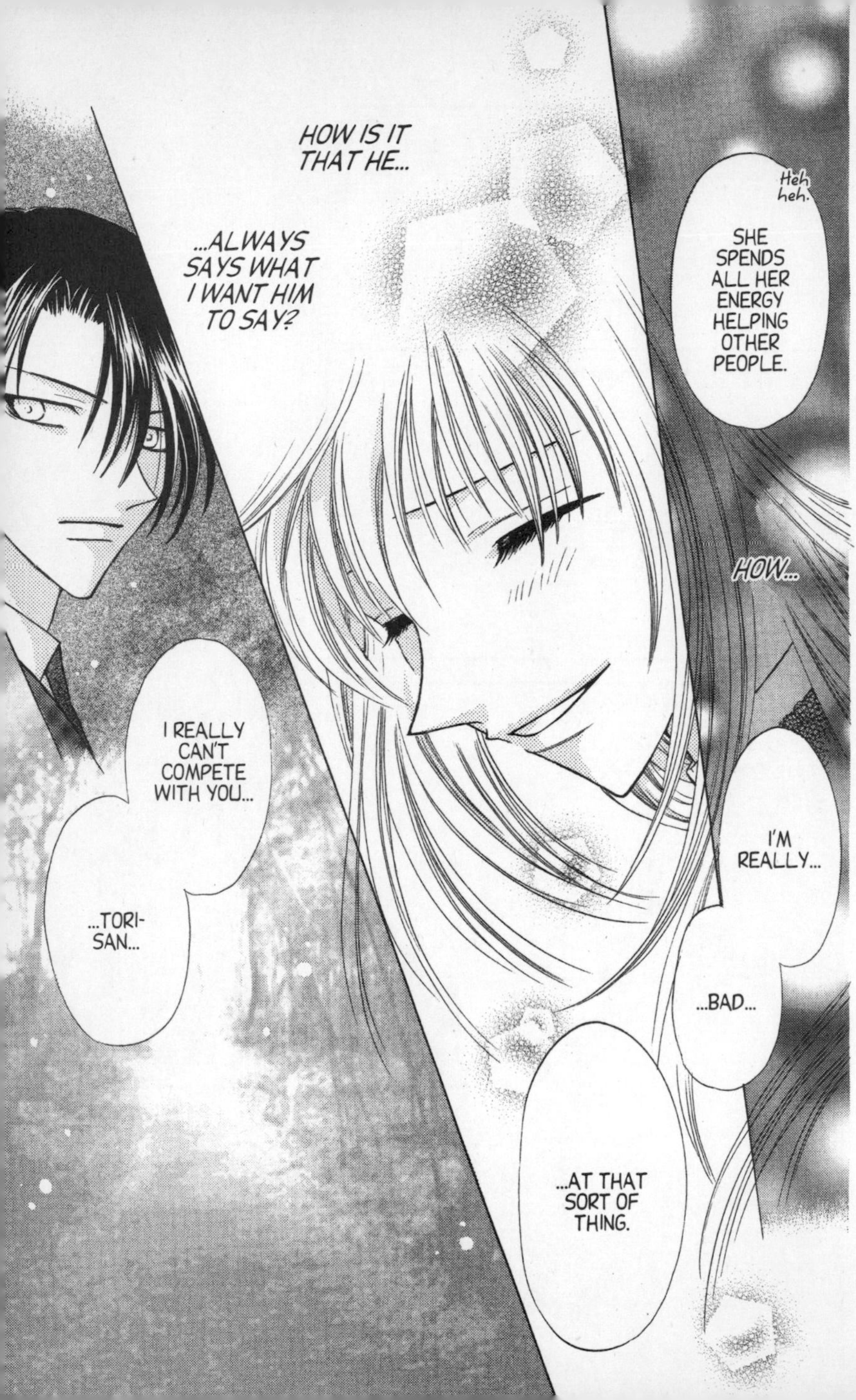
Heh heh.
SHE SPENDS ALL HER ENERGY HELPING OTHER PEOPLE.
HOW...
HOW IS IT THAT HE...
...ALWAYS SAYS WHAT I WANT HIM TO SAY?
I'M REALLY...
...BAD...
...AT THAT SORT OF THING.
I REALLY CAN'T COMPETE WITH YOU...
...TORI-SAN...

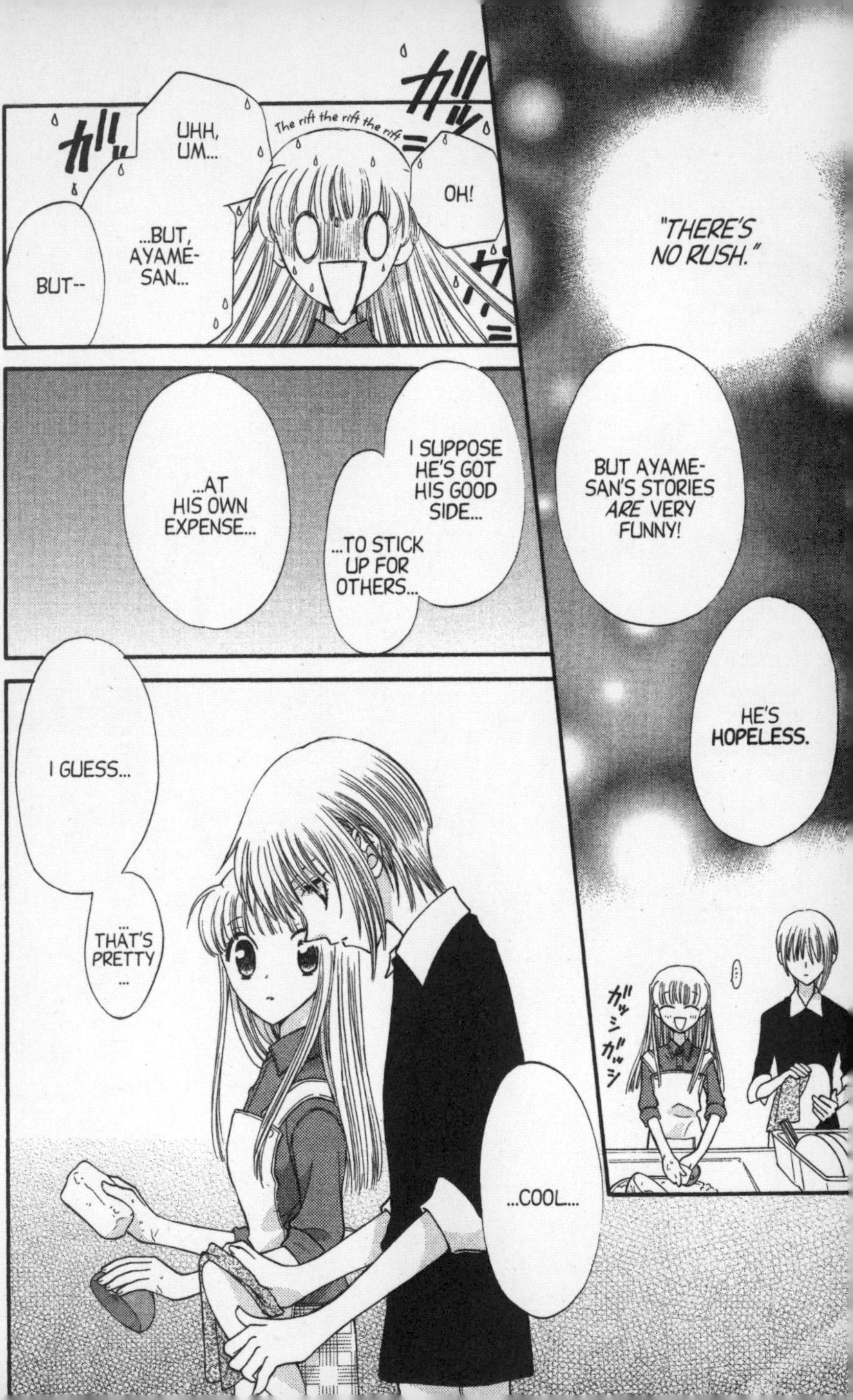
"THERE'S NO RUSH."
BUT AYAME-SAN'S STORIES *ARE* VERY FUNNY!
HE'S HOPELESS.
ガッシガッシ
OH!
The rift the rift the rift
UHH, UM...
...BUT, AYAME-SAN...
BUT--
I SUPPOSE HE'S GOT HIS GOOD SIDE...
...TO STICK UP FOR OTHERS...
...AT HIS OWN EXPENSE...
I GUESS...
...THAT'S PRETTY...
...COOL...

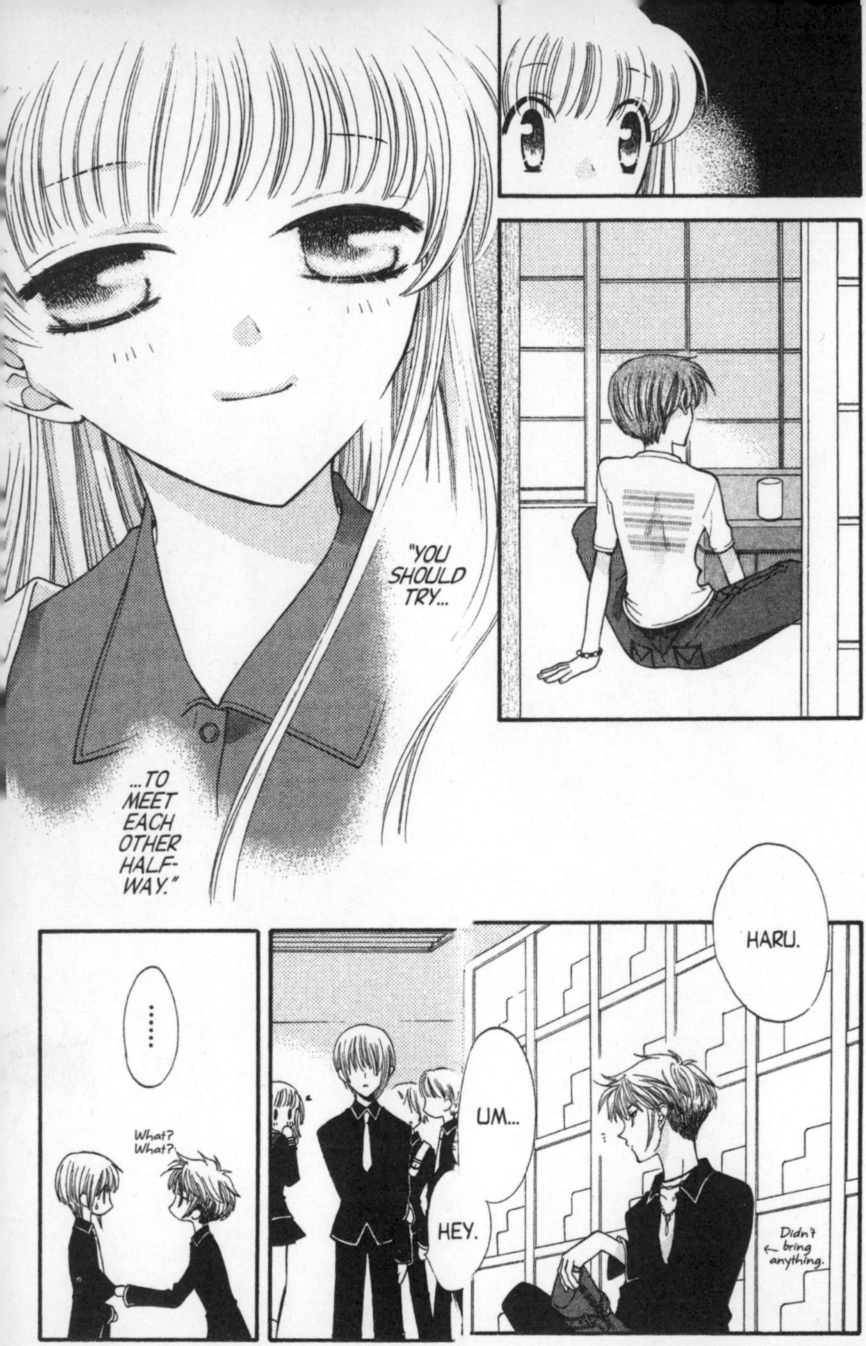
"YOU SHOULD TRY...
...TO MEET EACH OTHER HALF-WAY."
HARU.
Didn't bring anything.
UM...
HEY.
......
What? What?

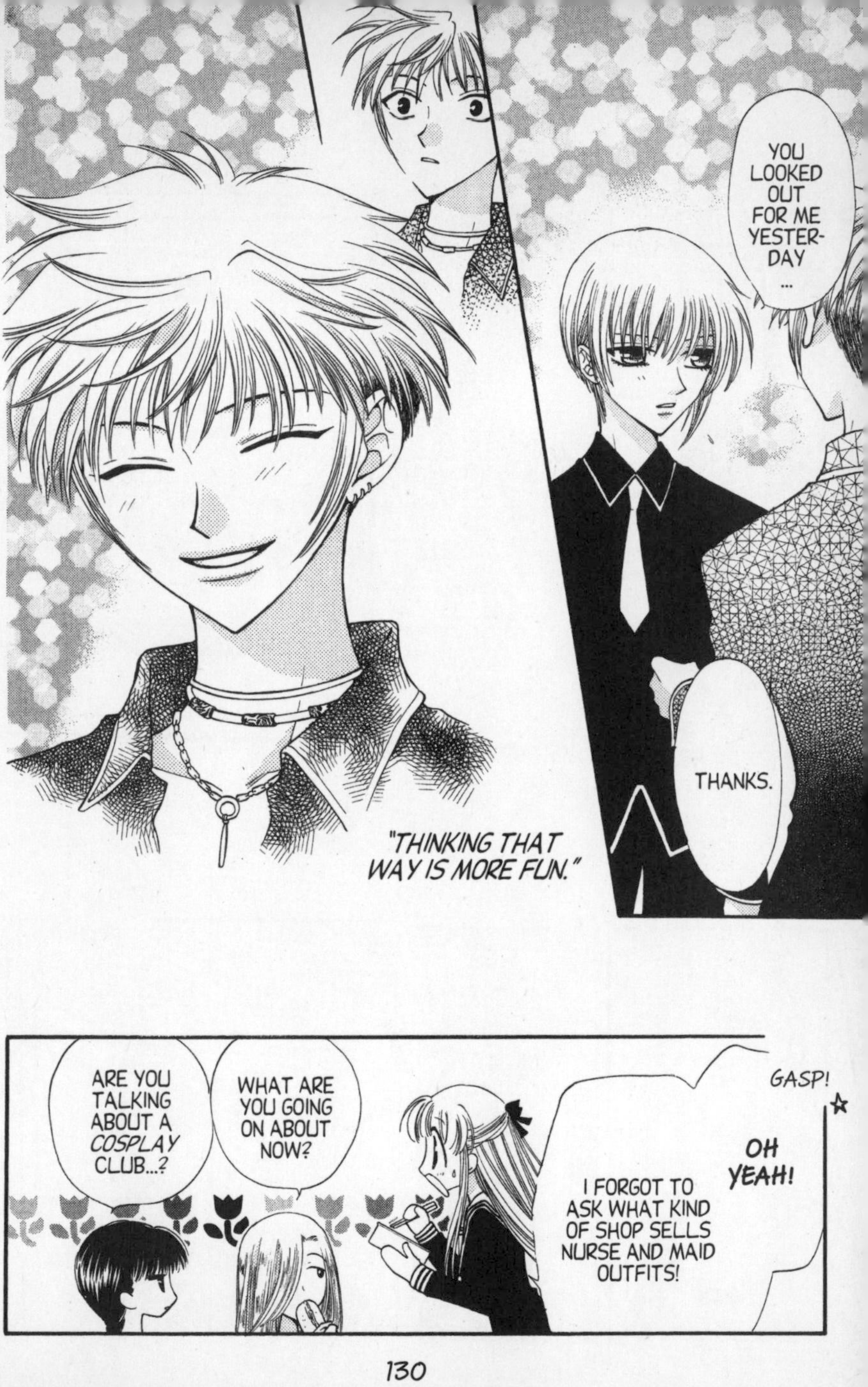
YOU LOOKED OUT FOR ME YESTER-DAY ...
THANKS.
"THINKING THAT WAY IS MORE FUN."
GASP!
OH YEAH!
I FORGOT TO ASK WHAT KIND OF SHOP SELLS NURSE AND MAID OUTFITS!
WHAT ARE YOU GOING ON ABOUT NOW?
ARE YOU TALKING ABOUT A *COSPLAY* CLUB...?

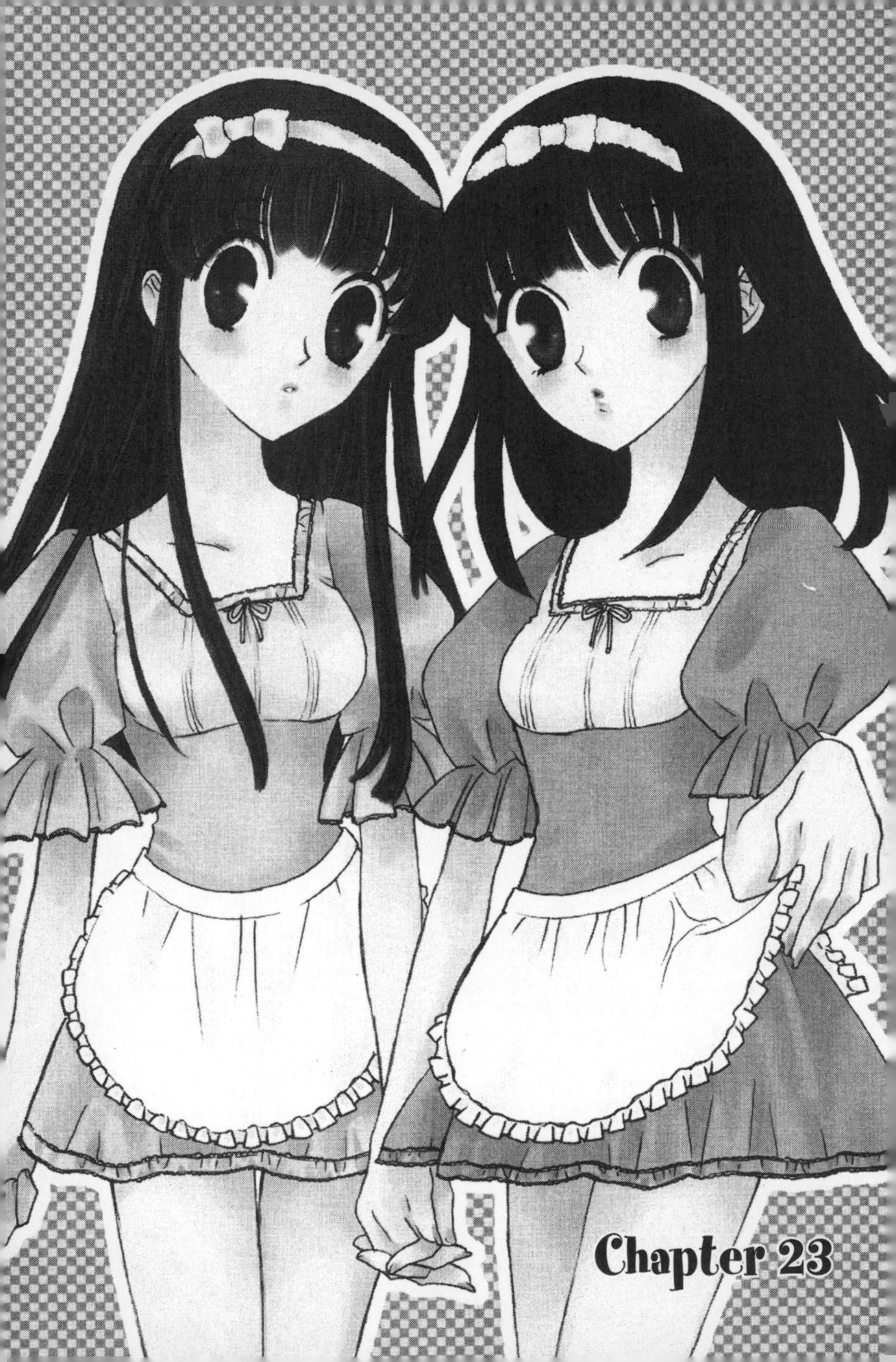
Chapter 23

THANK YOU!

NAN DESU YO, ONCE AGAIN!

Harada-sama, Araki-sama, mother, editor-sama ...and everyone who reads Furuba and supports me!

This has been Natsuki Takaya.

Next is Kagura, a flower. After that will be Momitchi, then Hatori--in the order they appeared in the series (that way, you clearly know their names and faces). I'll keep going through the members of the Zodiac one after another. Of course, even if I haven't gotten to them all, when it's time for Furuba to end, it will end. This is an unpleasant topic, but it can't be avoided.

132

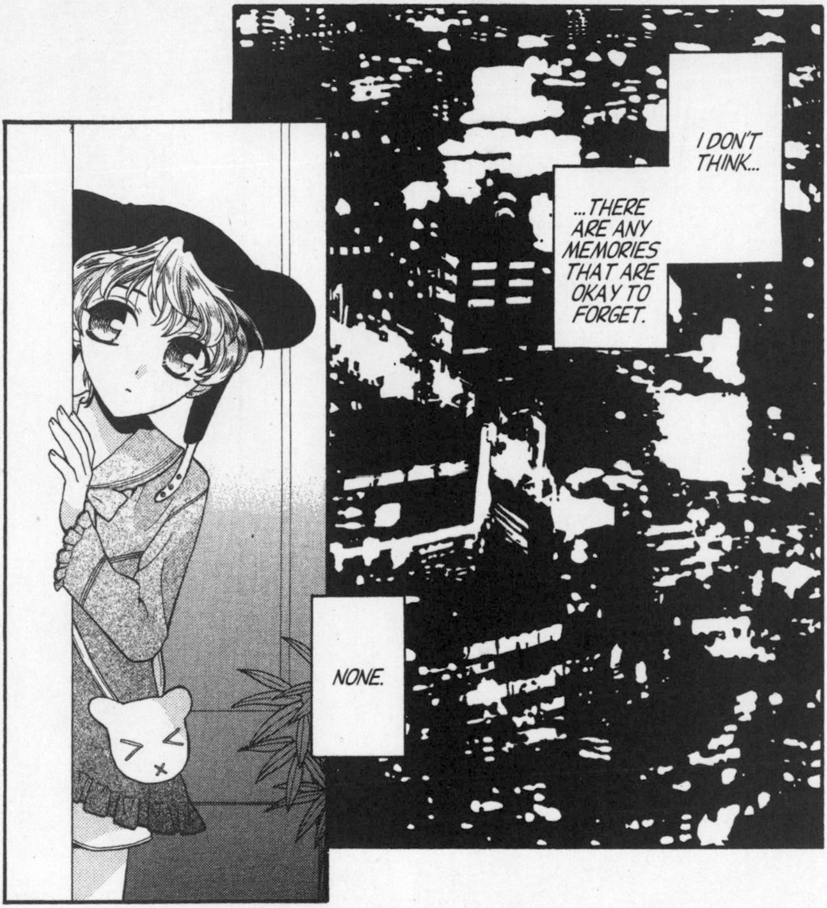
I DON'T THINK...
...THERE ARE ANY MEMORIES THAT ARE OKAY TO FORGET.
NONE.

ULTRA SPECIAL BLAH BLAH BLAH 5

They don't match at all! The chapter title page and the actual contents!! (I have no one to blame but myself.) Whether for good or ill, my mother is a big part of my life, so I can't think of Tohru or Momitchi as strangers. Well, they're not strangers! Each character that I create is an extension of myself. They're closer to me than if they were my children.

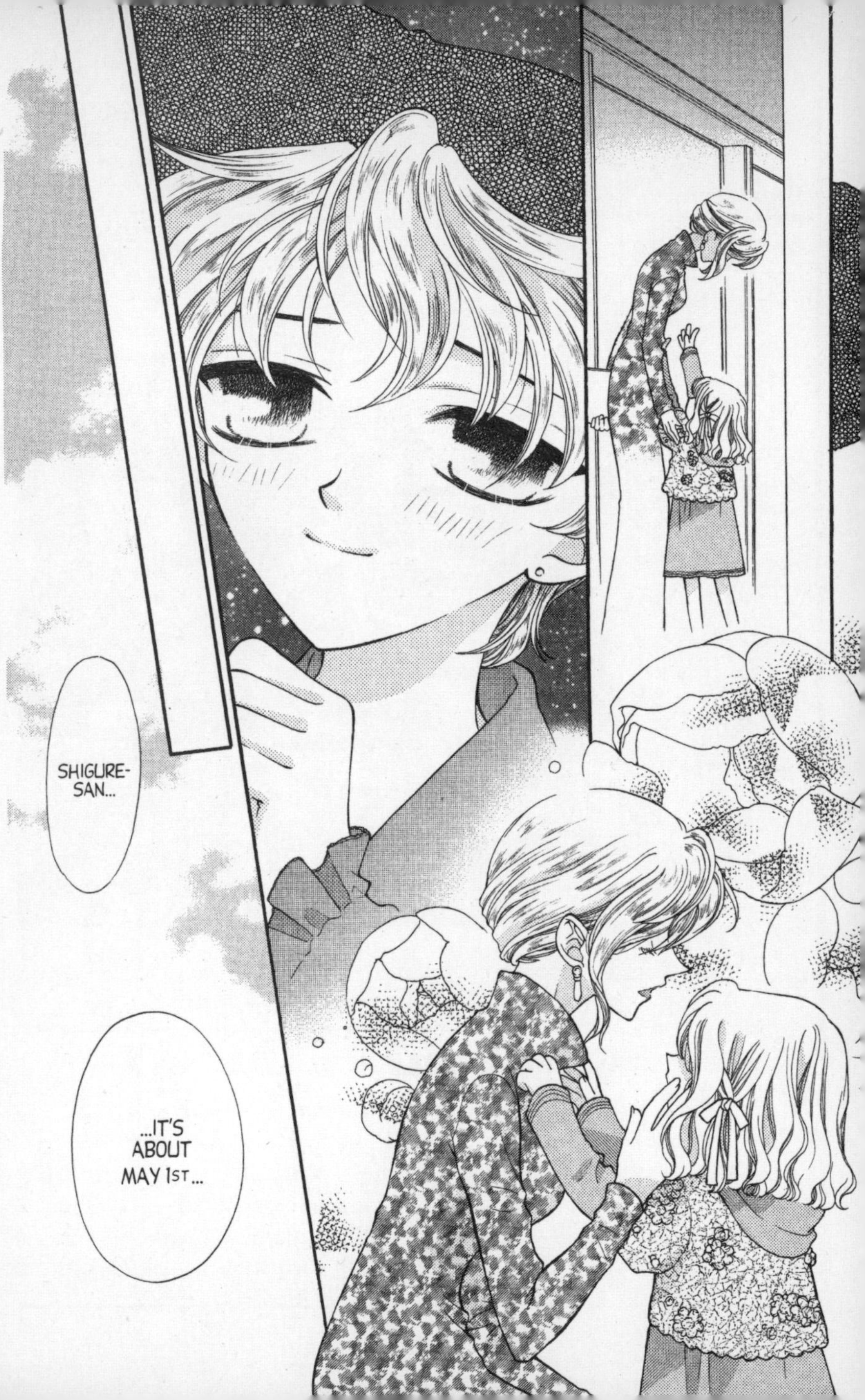
SHIGURE-SAN...
...IT'S ABOUT MAY 1ST...

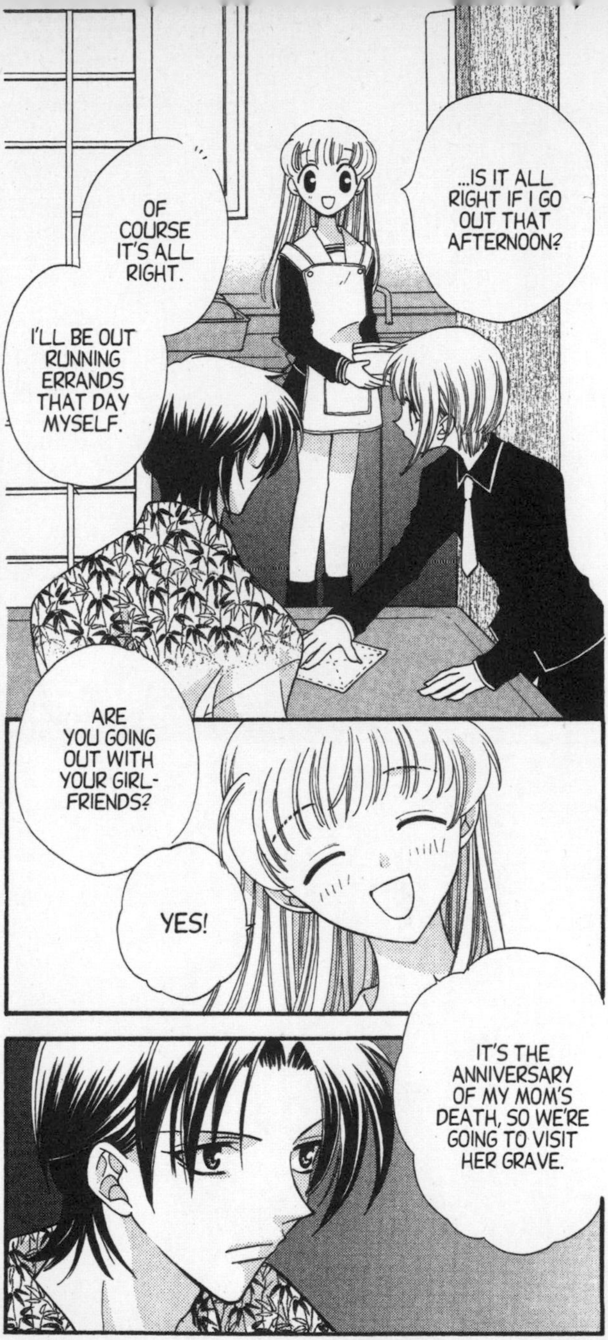
...IS IT ALL RIGHT IF I GO OUT THAT AFTERNOON?
OF COURSE IT'S ALL RIGHT.
I'LL BE OUT RUNNING ERRANDS THAT DAY MYSELF.
ARE YOU GOING OUT WITH YOUR GIRL-FRIENDS?
YES!
IT'S THE ANNIVERSARY OF MY MOM'S DEATH, SO WE'RE GOING TO VISIT HER GRAVE.

Fruits Basket 4 Part 5:

Marlow, from the RPG Kaeru Bibak, is adorable. I haven't seen the ending yet, but I'm really happy that the main character is female. In real life, I don't think I'd get along with Marlow, though. I mean, I think I'm the type of person Marlow hates! I always like the characters that wouldn't like me. Lately, I've been playing Chrono Cross. I wasn't interested before, but I saw the commercial in the game store and I thought, "I have to play it!!" I was caught in their trap. Completely! (ha ha!)

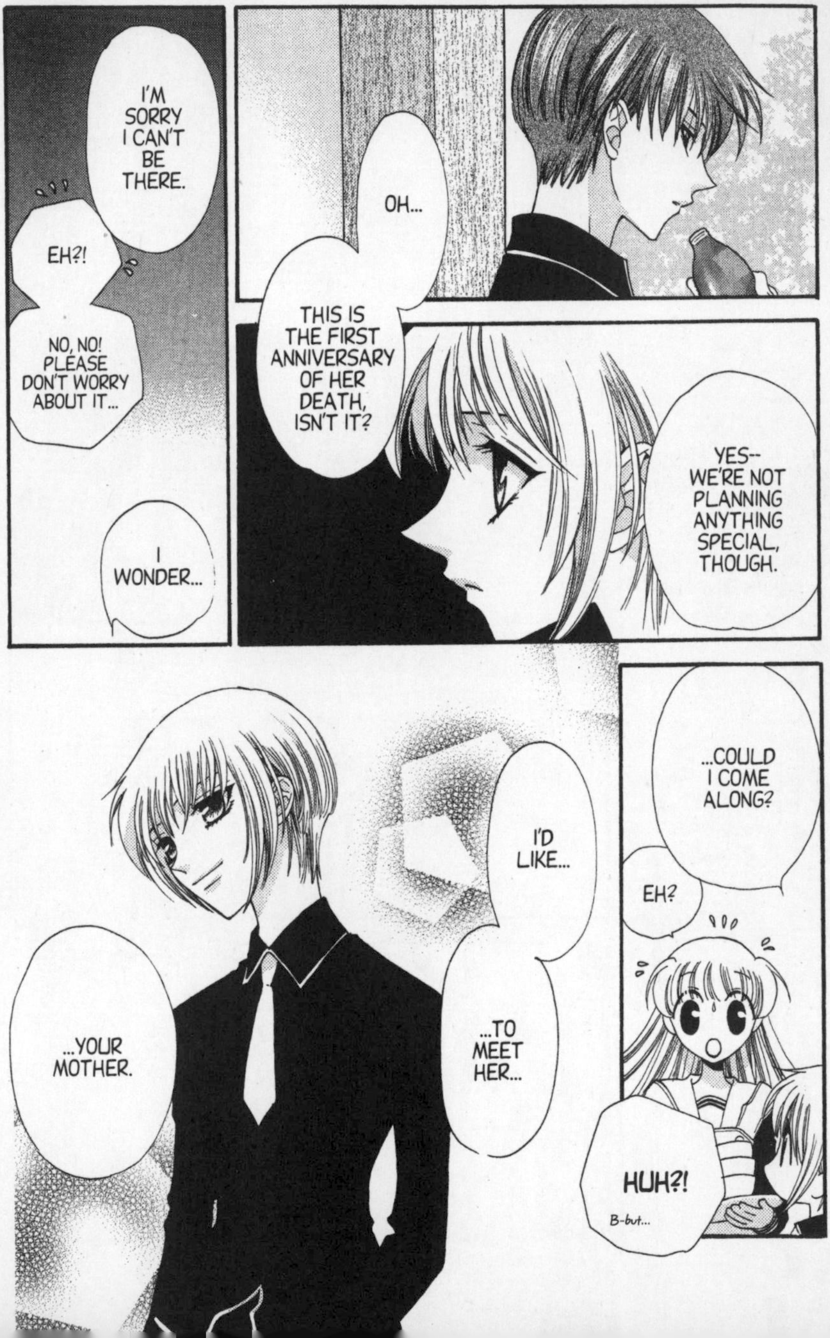
OH...
THIS IS THE FIRST ANNIVERSARY OF HER DEATH, ISN'T IT?
YES-- WE'RE NOT PLANNING ANYTHING SPECIAL, THOUGH.
I'M SORRY I CAN'T BE THERE.
EH?!
NO, NO! PLEASE DON'T WORRY ABOUT IT...
I WONDER...
...COULD I COME ALONG?
EH?
HUH?!
B-but...
I'D LIKE...
...TO MEET HER...
...YOUR MOTHER.

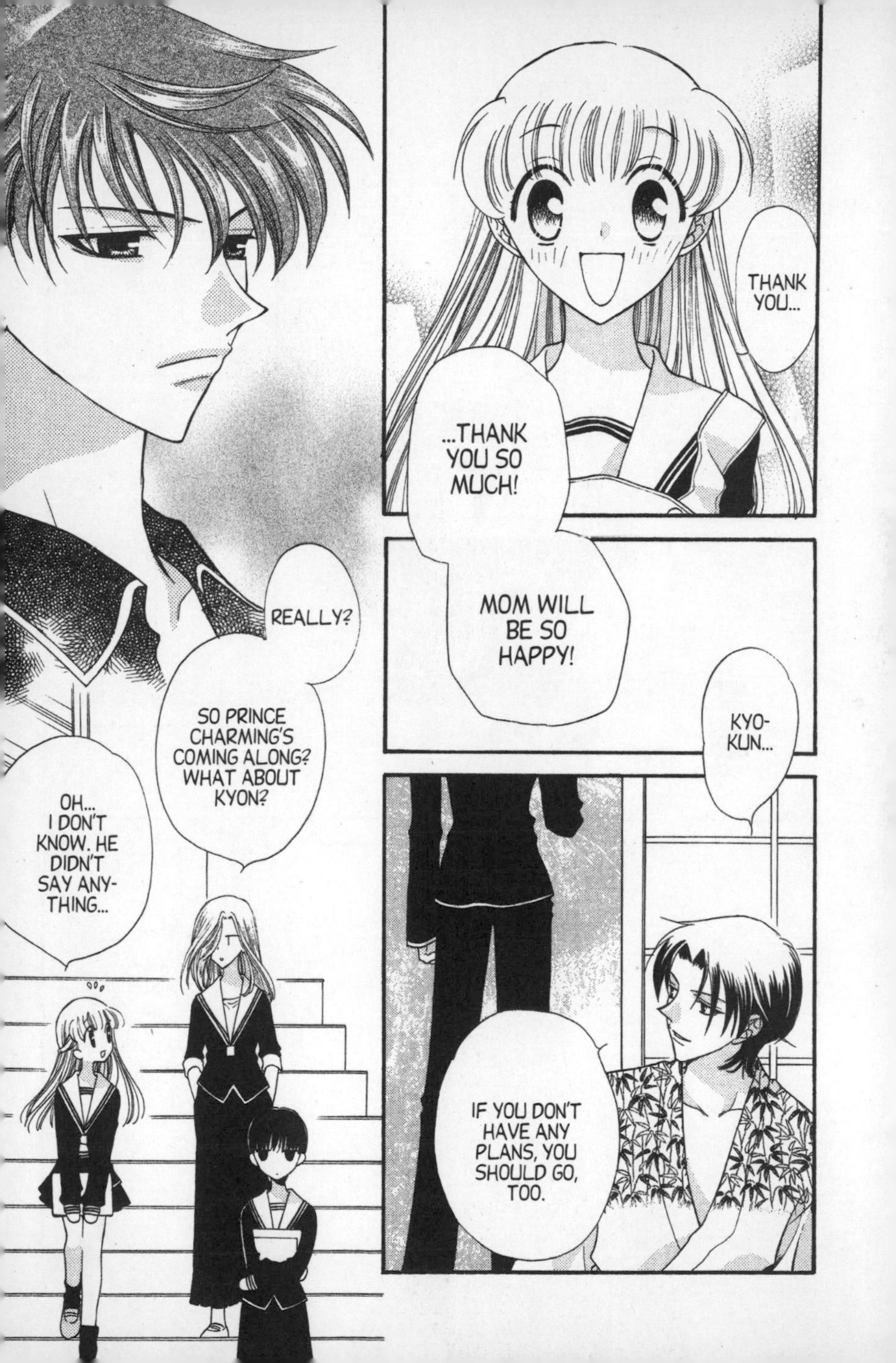
THANK YOU...
...THANK YOU SO MUCH!
MOM WILL BE SO HAPPY!
KYO-KUN...
IF YOU DON'T HAVE ANY PLANS, YOU SHOULD GO, TOO.
REALLY?
SO PRINCE CHARMING'S COMING ALONG? WHAT ABOUT KYON?
OH... I DON'T KNOW. HE DIDN'T SAY ANY-THING...

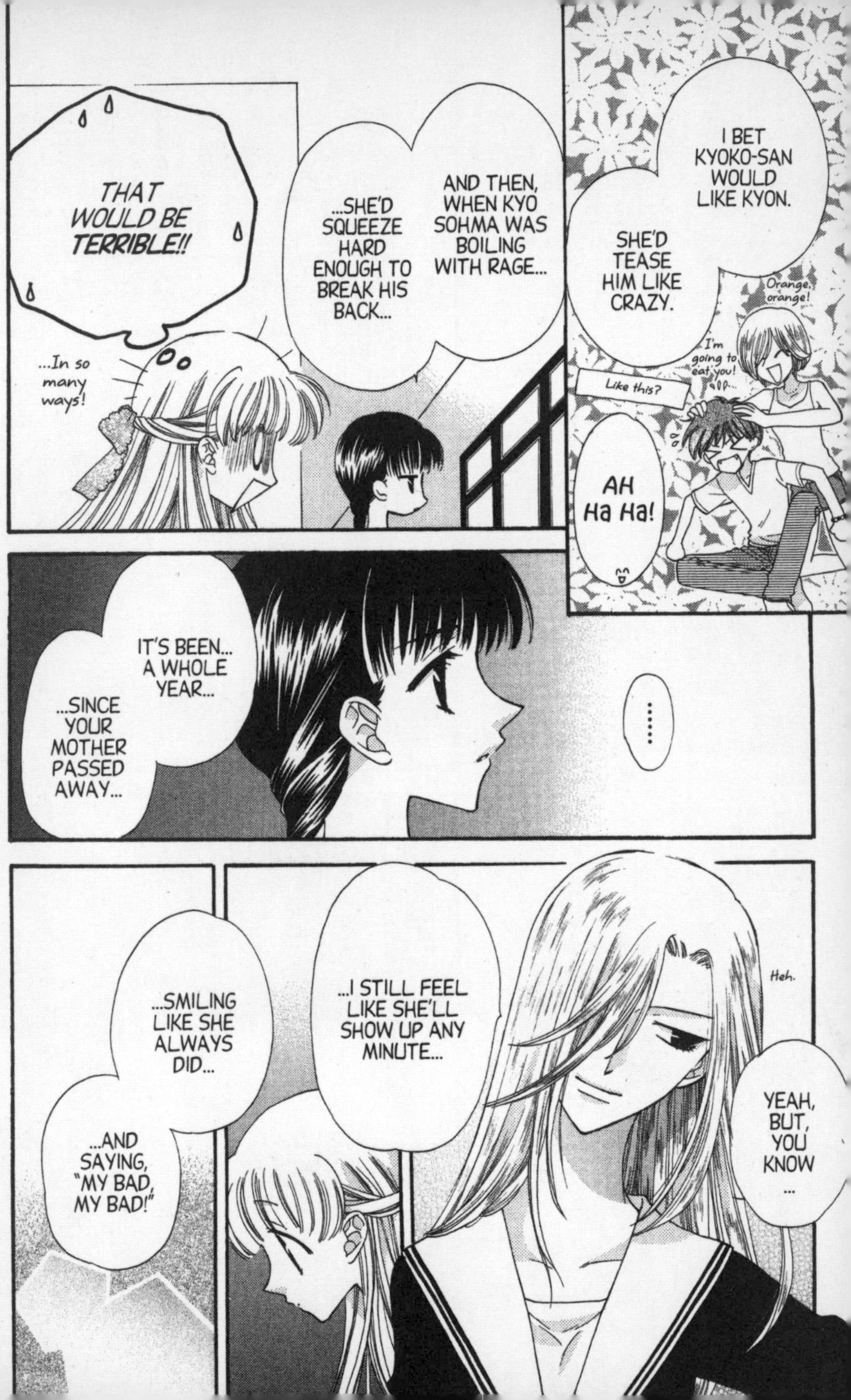
I BET KYOKO-SAN WOULD LIKE KYON.
SHE'D TEASE HIM LIKE CRAZY.
Orange, orange!
I'm going to eat you!
Like this?
AH Ha Ha!
AND THEN, WHEN KYO SOHMA WAS BOILING WITH RAGE...
...SHE'D SQUEEZE HARD ENOUGH TO BREAK HIS BACK...
THAT WOULD BE TERRIBLE!!
...In so many ways!
......
IT'S BEEN... A WHOLE YEAR...
...SINCE YOUR MOTHER PASSED AWAY...
Heh.
YEAH, BUT, YOU KNOW...
...I STILL FEEL LIKE SHE'LL SHOW UP ANY MINUTE...
...SMILING LIKE SHE ALWAYS DID...
...AND SAYING, "MY BAD, MY BAD!"

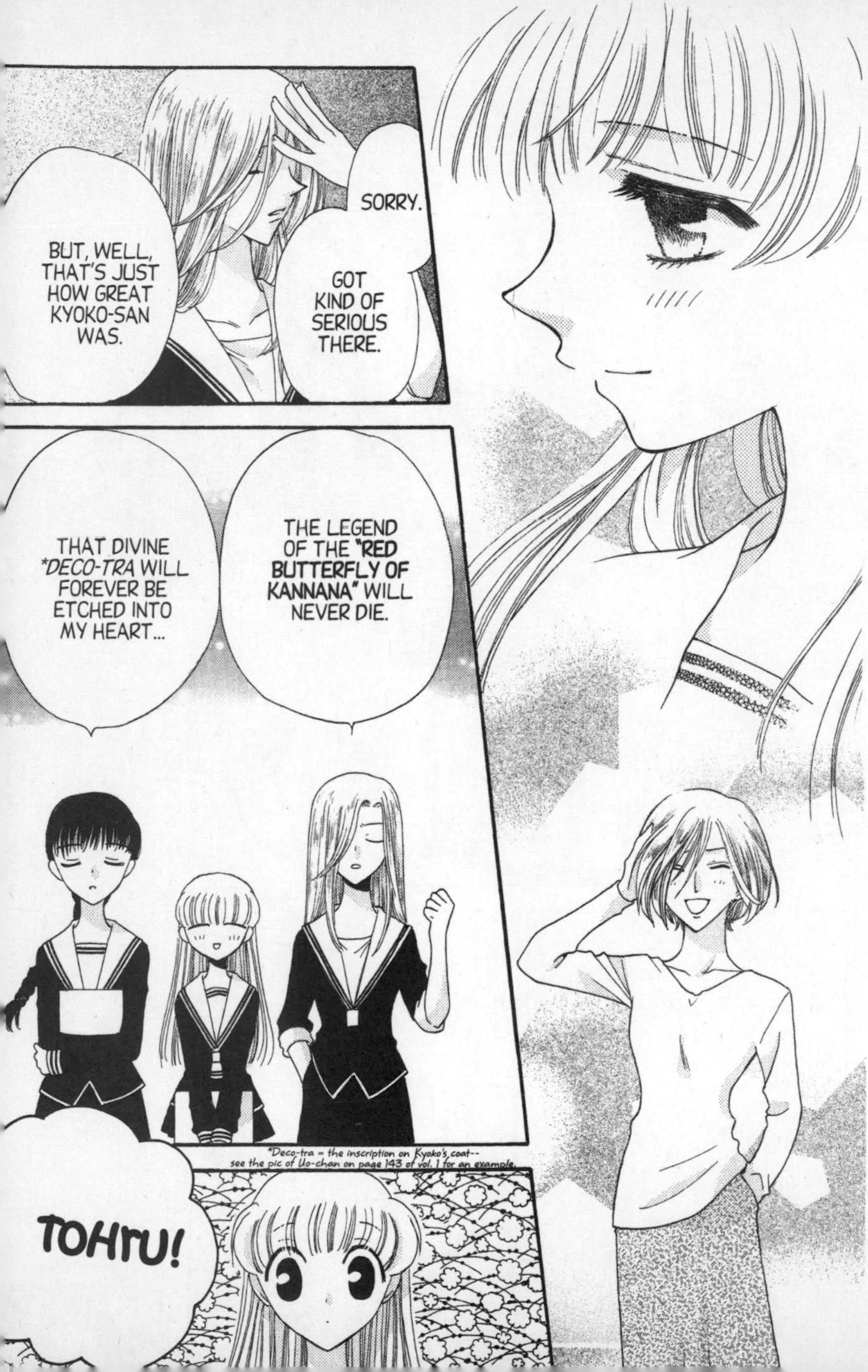
SORRY.
GOT KIND OF SERIOUS THERE.
BUT, WELL, THAT'S JUST HOW GREAT KYOKO-SAN WAS.
THE LEGEND OF THE "RED BUTTERFLY OF KANNANA" WILL NEVER DIE.
THAT DIVINE *DECO-TRA WILL FOREVER BE ETCHED INTO MY HEART...
TOHRU!

*Deco-tra = the inscription on Kyoko's coat-- see the pic of Uo-chan on page 143 of vol. 1 for an example.

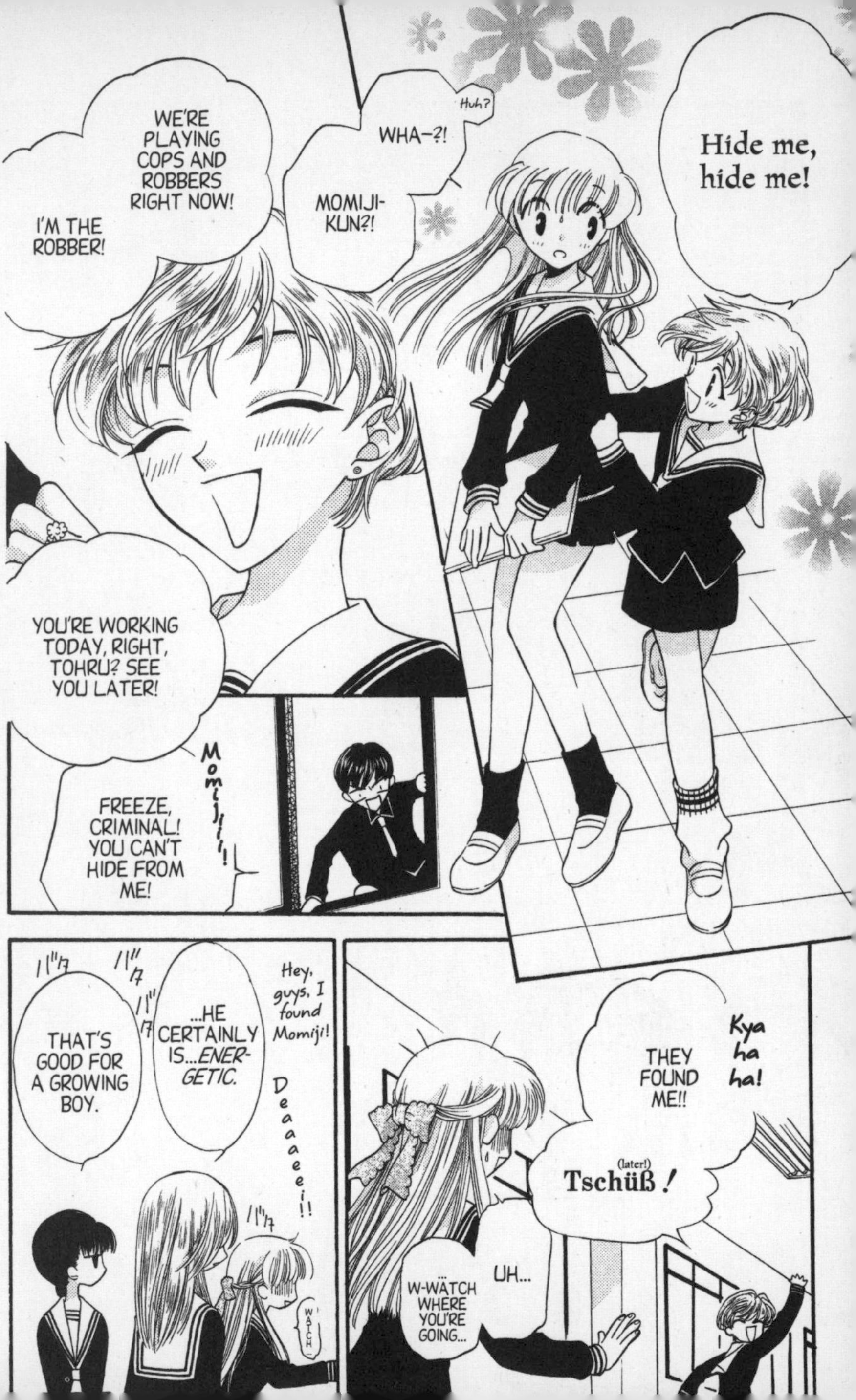
Hide me, hide me!
Huh?
WHA-?!
MOMIJI-KUN?!
WE'RE PLAYING COPS AND ROBBERS RIGHT NOW!
I'M THE ROBBER!
YOU'RE WORKING TODAY, RIGHT, TOHRU? SEE YOU LATER!
Momijiiii!
FREEZE, CRIMINAL! YOU CAN'T HIDE FROM ME!
Kya ha ha!
THEY FOUND ME!!
(later!) Tschüß!
UH...
W-WATCH WHERE YOU'RE GOING...
Hey, guys, I found Momiji!
Deaaaaeei!!
...HE CERTAINLY IS...ENERGETIC.
THAT'S GOOD FOR A GROWING BOY.
WATCH...

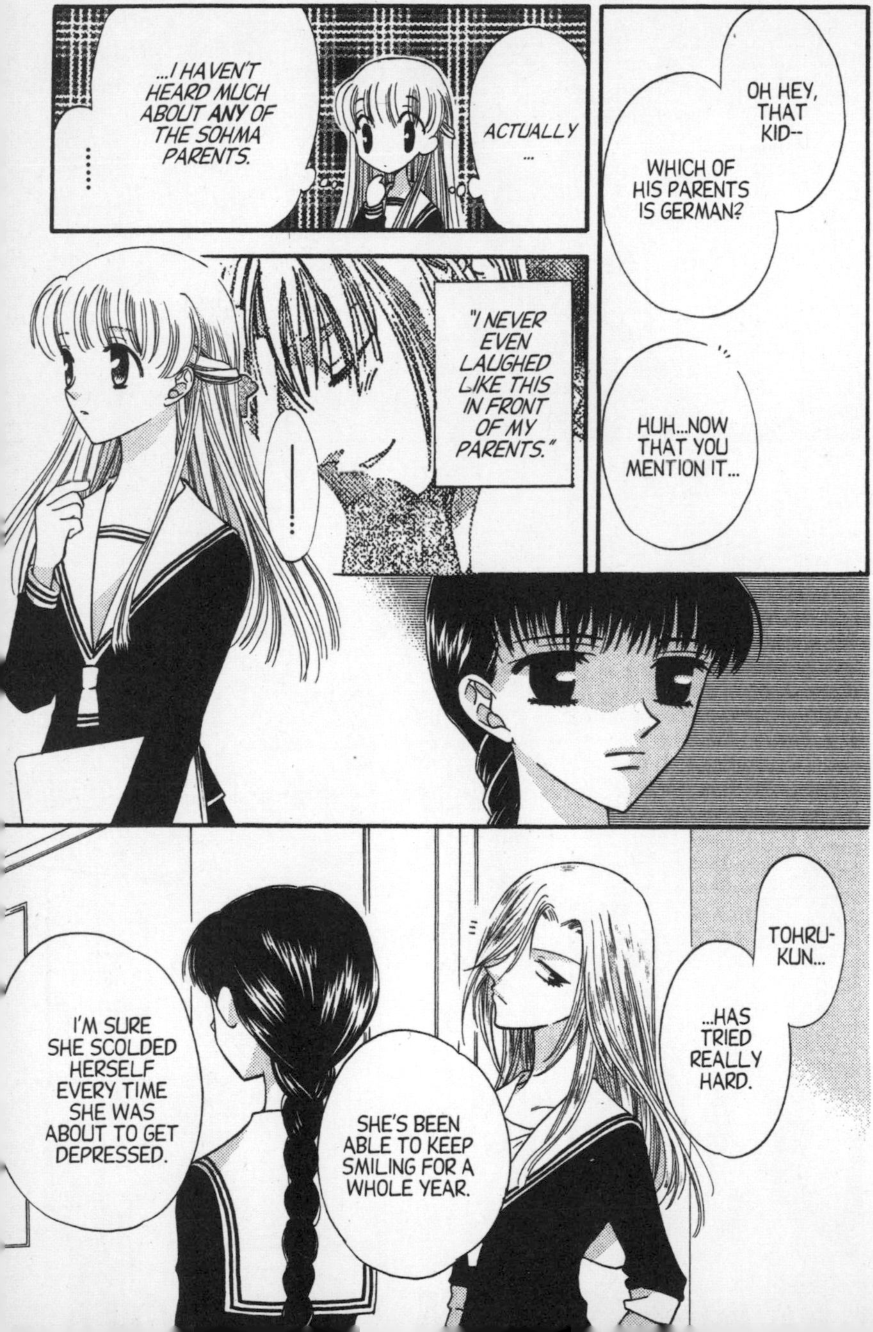
OH HEY, THAT KID--
WHICH OF HIS PARENTS IS GERMAN?
HUH...NOW THAT YOU MENTION IT...
ACTUALLY ...
...I HAVEN'T HEARD MUCH ABOUT ANY OF THE SOHMA PARENTS.
......
"I NEVER EVEN LAUGHED LIKE THIS IN FRONT OF MY PARENTS."
......
TOHRU-KUN...
...HAS TRIED REALLY HARD.
SHE'S BEEN ABLE TO KEEP SMILING FOR A WHOLE YEAR.
I'M SURE SHE SCOLDED HERSELF EVERY TIME SHE WAS ABOUT TO GET DEPRESSED.

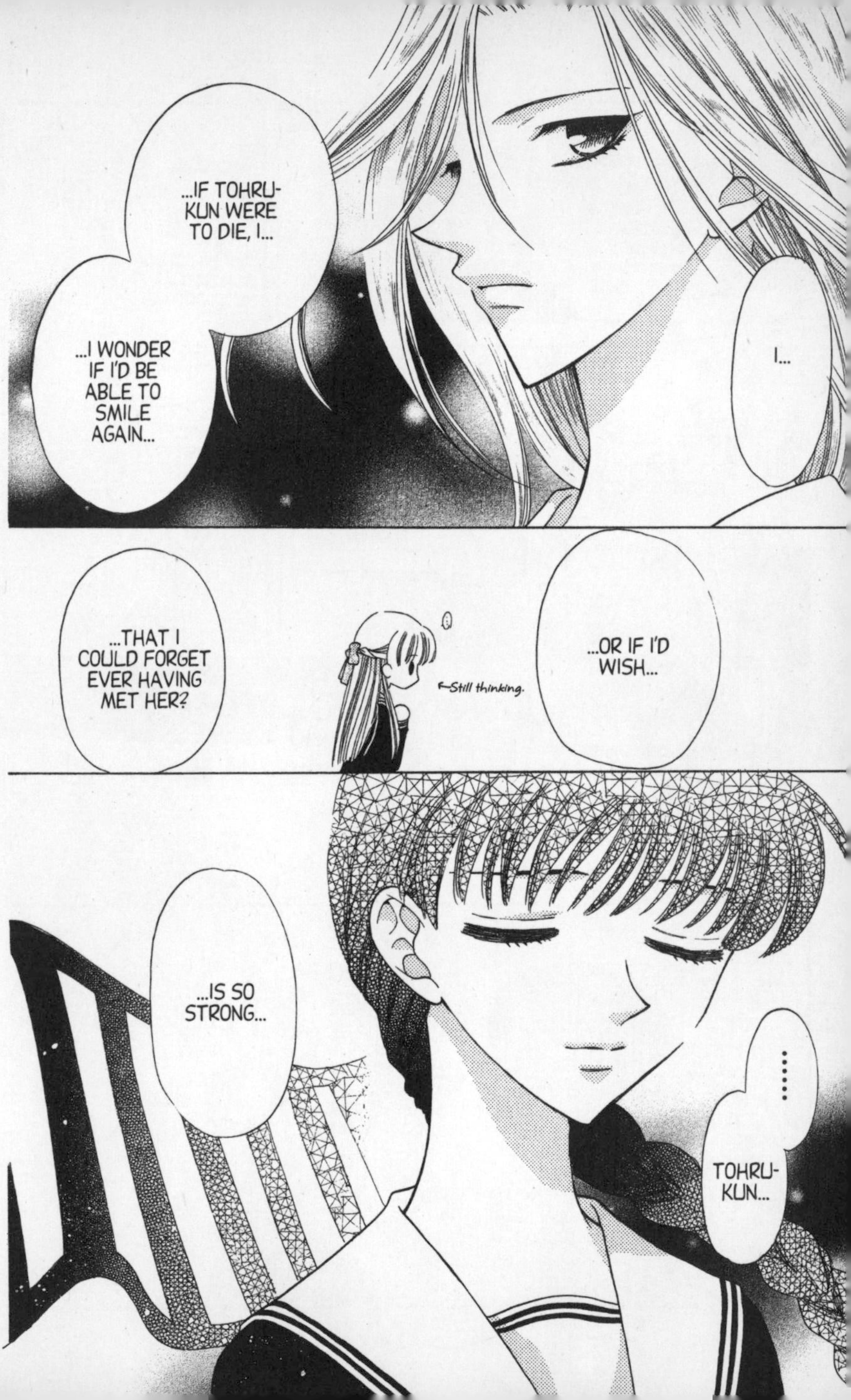
I...
...IF TOHRU-KUN WERE TO DIE, I...
...I WONDER IF I'D BE ABLE TO SMILE AGAIN...
...OR IF I'D WISH...
←Still thinking.
...THAT I COULD FORGET EVER HAVING MET HER?
......
TOHRU-KUN...
...IS SO STRONG...

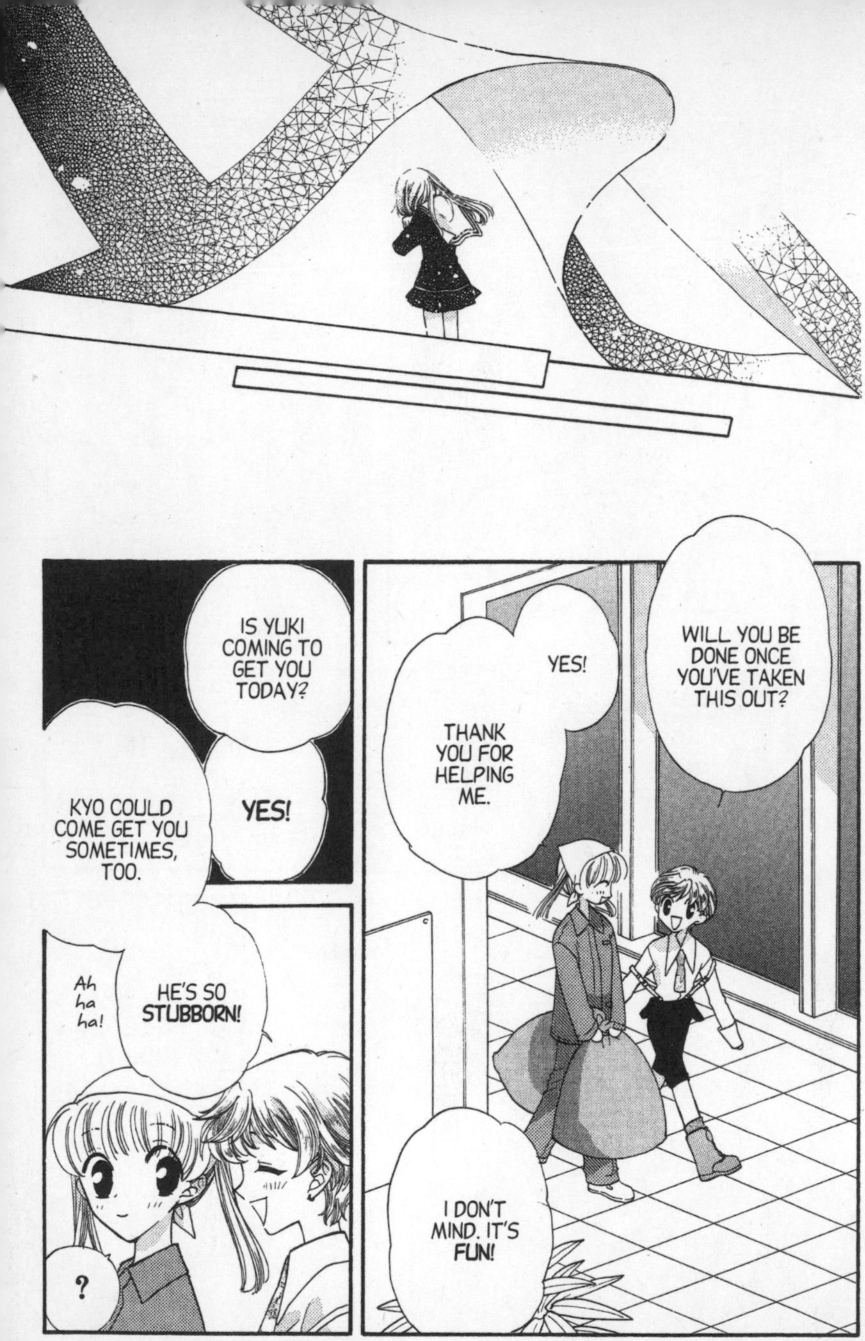
WILL YOU BE DONE ONCE YOU'VE TAKEN THIS OUT?
YES!
THANK YOU FOR HELPING ME.
I DON'T MIND. IT'S FUN!
IS YUKI COMING TO GET YOU TODAY?
YES!
KYO COULD COME GET YOU SOMETIMES, TOO.
HE'S SO STUBBORN!
Ah ha ha!
?

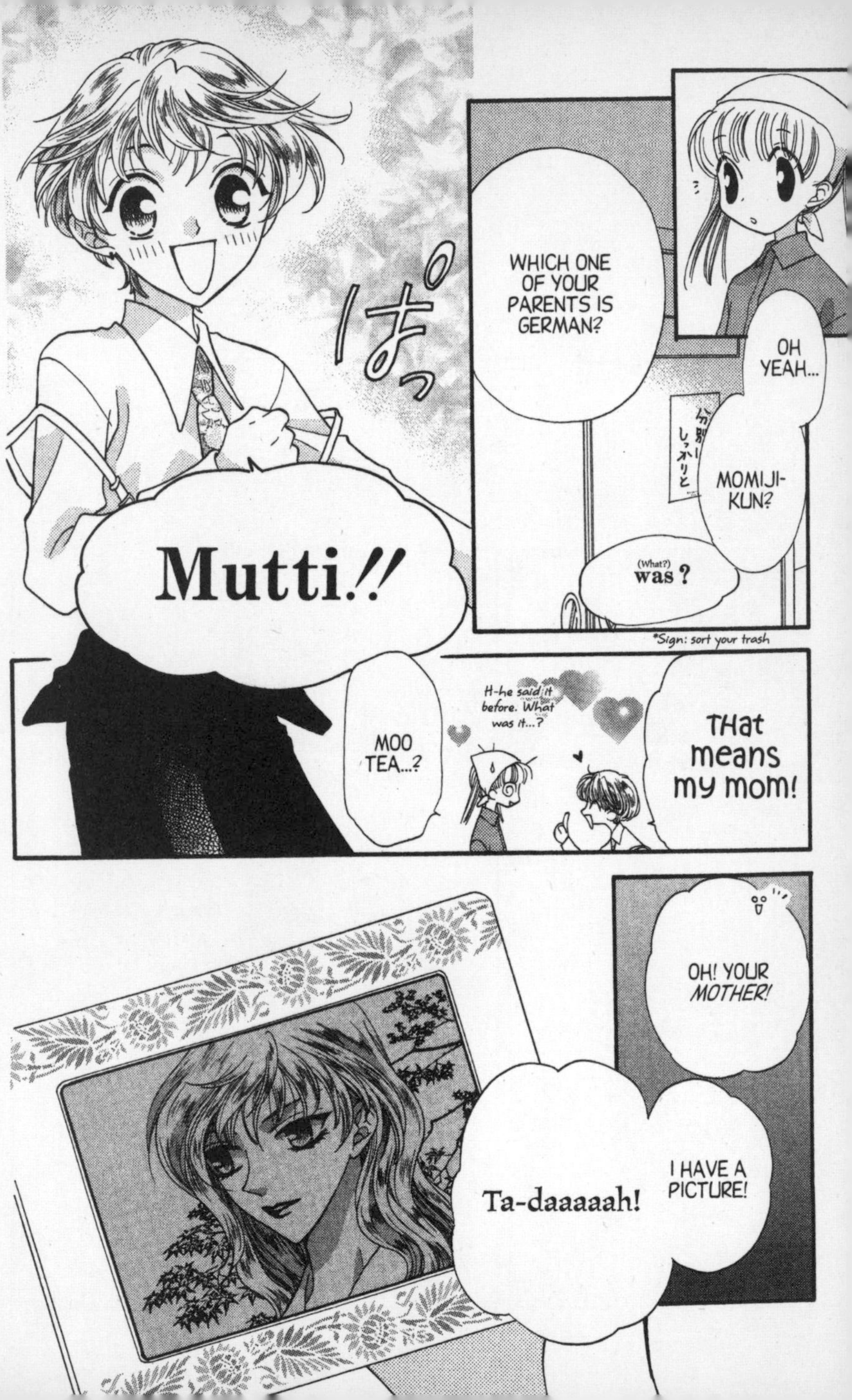
OH YEAH...
MOMIJI-KUN?
WHICH ONE OF YOUR PARENTS IS GERMAN?
分別し しっかりと
(What?) was ?
*Sign: sort your trash
ぱっ
Mutti!!
THAT means my mom!
H-he said it before. What was it...?
MOO TEA...?
OH! YOUR *MOTHER!*
I HAVE A PICTURE!
Ta-daaaaah!

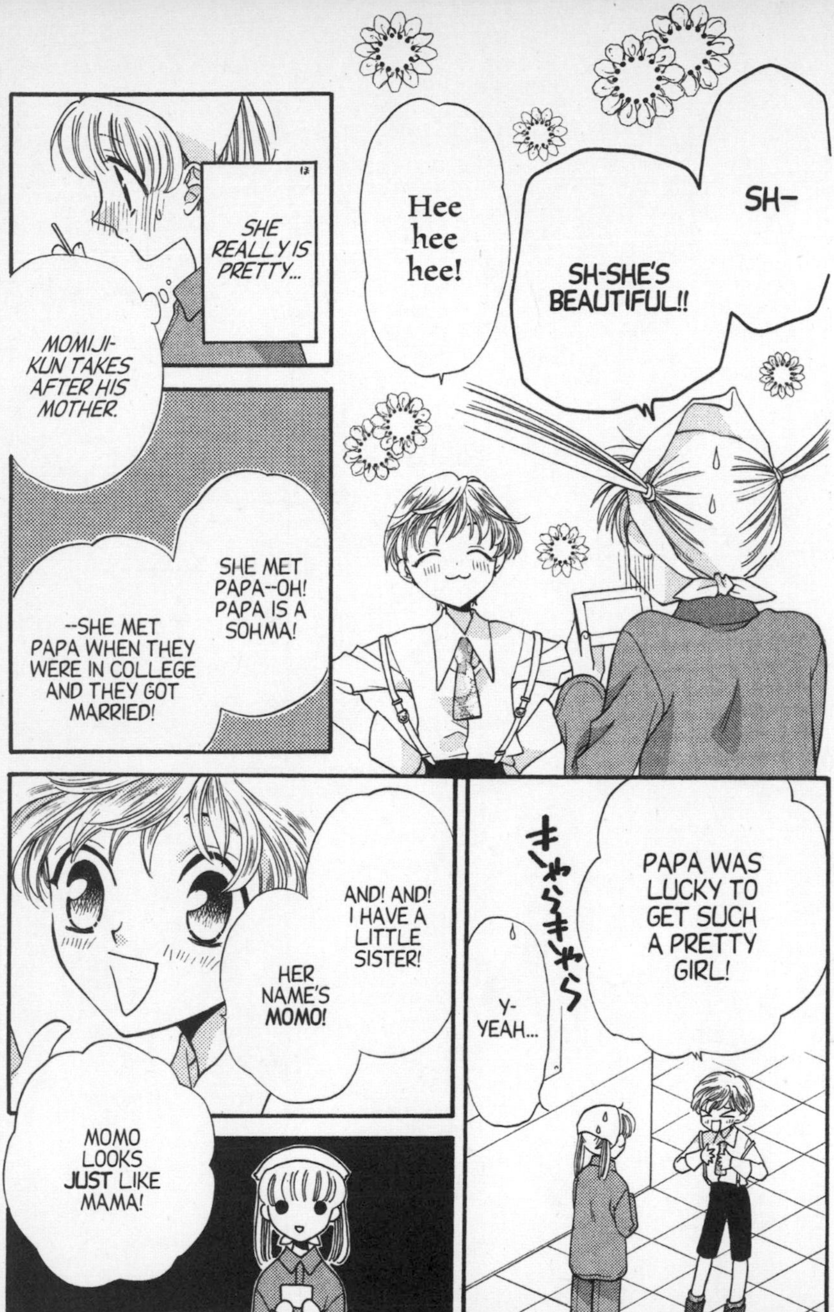
SH–
SH-SHE'S BEAUTIFUL!!
Hee hee hee!
SHE REALLY IS PRETTY...
MOMIJI-KUN TAKES AFTER HIS MOTHER.
SHE MET PAPA--OH! PAPA IS A SOHMA!
--SHE MET PAPA WHEN THEY WERE IN COLLEGE AND THEY GOT MARRIED!
PAPA WAS LUCKY TO GET SUCH A PRETTY GIRL!
きゃらきゃら
Y-YEAH...
AND! AND! I HAVE A LITTLE SISTER!
HER NAME'S MOMO!
MOMO LOOKS JUST LIKE MAMA!

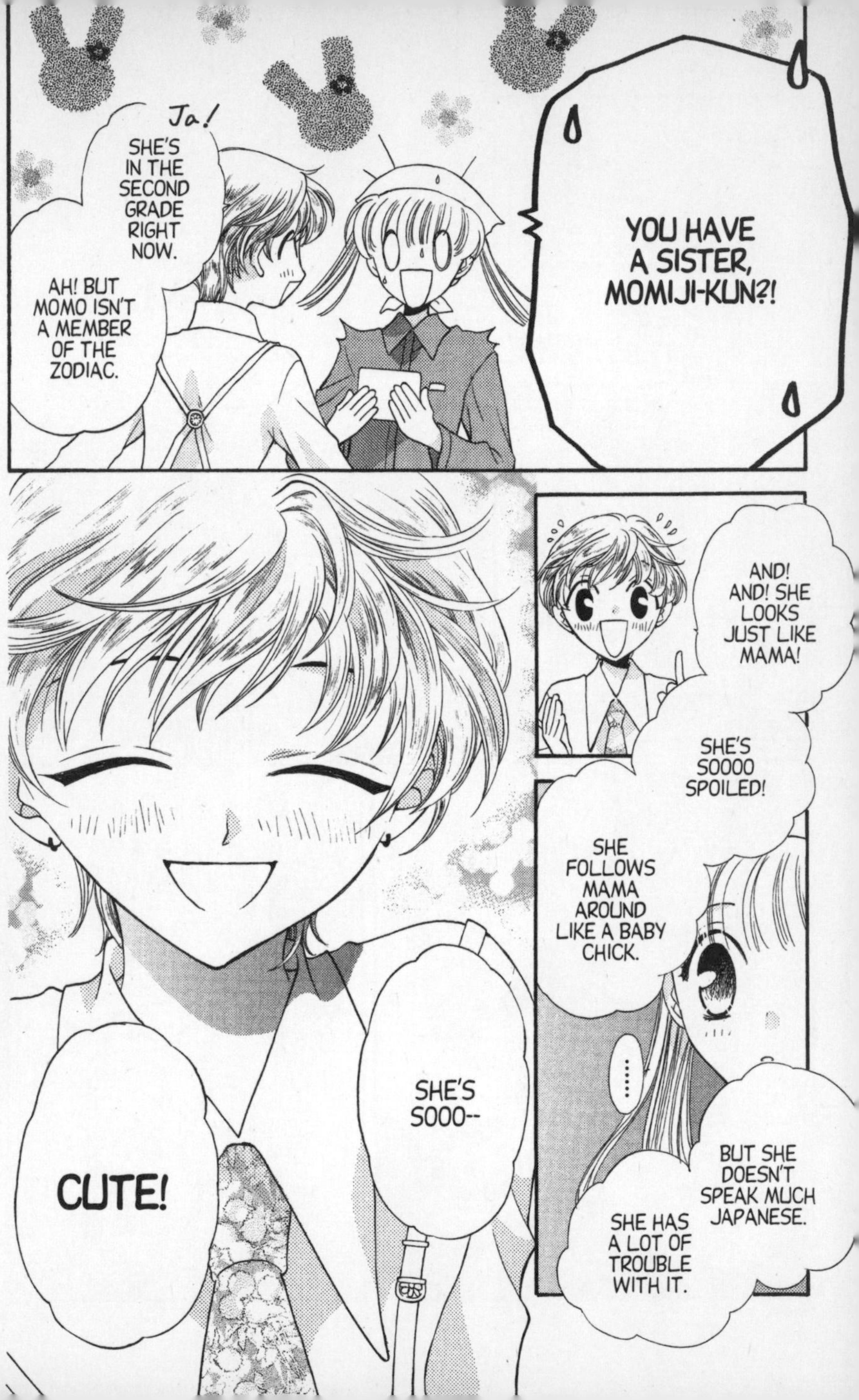
YOU HAVE A SISTER, MOMIJI-KUN?!
Ja!
SHE'S IN THE SECOND GRADE RIGHT NOW.
AH! BUT MOMO ISN'T A MEMBER OF THE ZODIAC.
AND! AND! SHE LOOKS JUST LIKE MAMA!
SHE'S SOOOO SPOILED!
SHE FOLLOWS MAMA AROUND LIKE A BABY CHICK.
......
BUT SHE DOESN'T SPEAK MUCH JAPANESE.
SHE HAS A LOT OF TROUBLE WITH IT.
SHE'S SOOO--
CUTE!

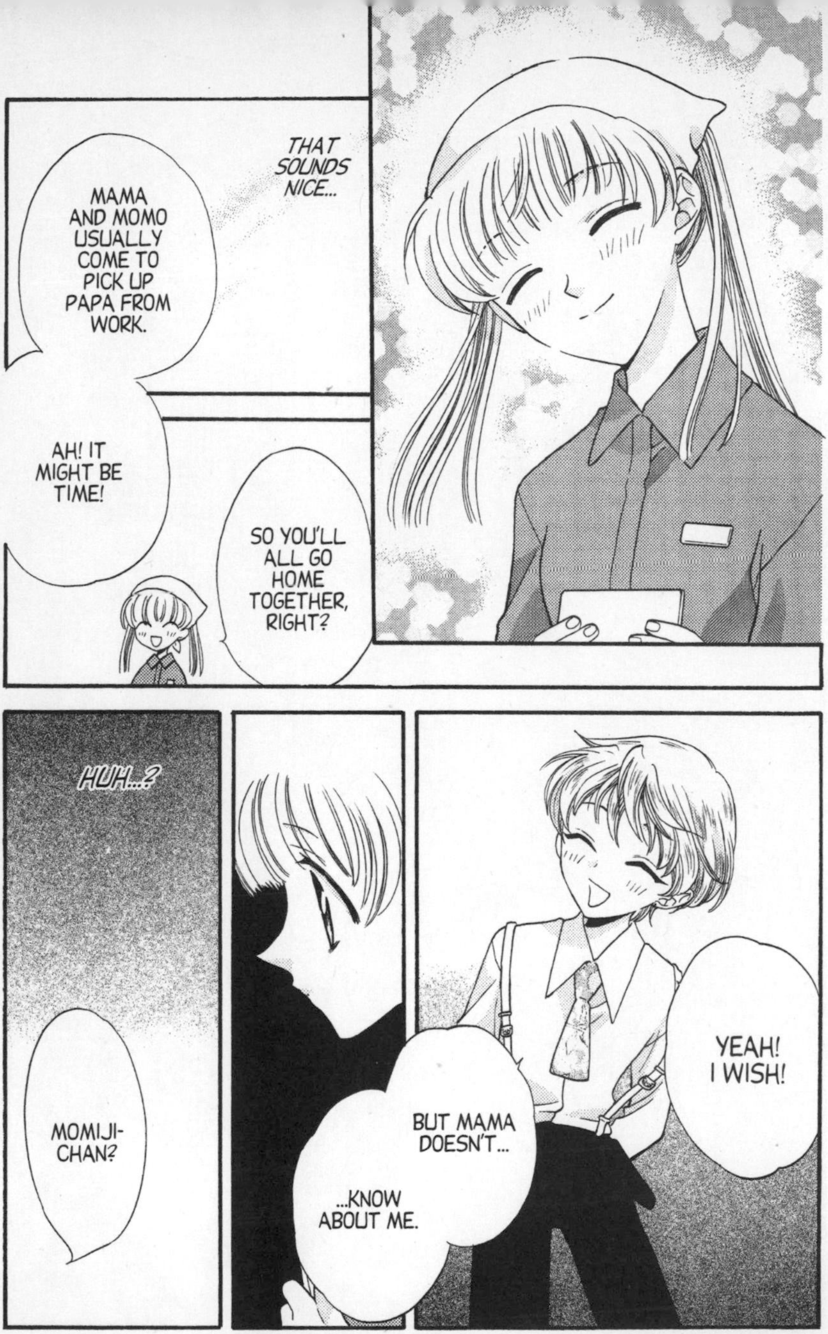

MAMA AND MOMO USUALLY COME TO PICK UP PAPA FROM WORK.
THAT SOUNDS NICE...
SO YOU'LL ALL GO HOME TOGETHER, RIGHT?
AH! IT MIGHT BE TIME!
YEAH! I WISH!
BUT MAMA DOESN'T...
...KNOW ABOUT ME.
HUH...?
MOMIJI-CHAN?

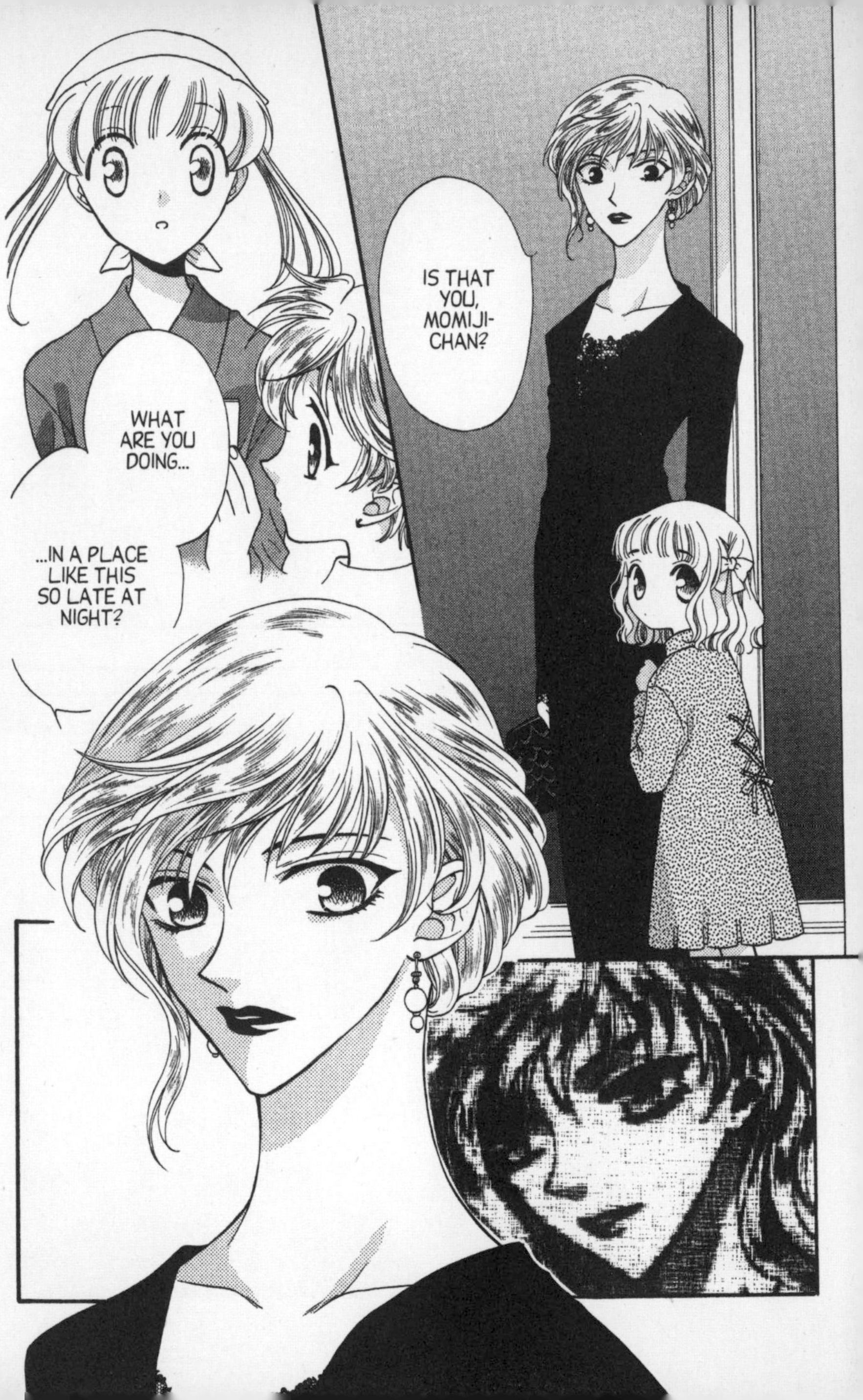
IS THAT YOU, MOMIJI-CHAN?
WHAT ARE YOU DOING...
...IN A PLACE LIKE THIS SO LATE AT NIGHT?

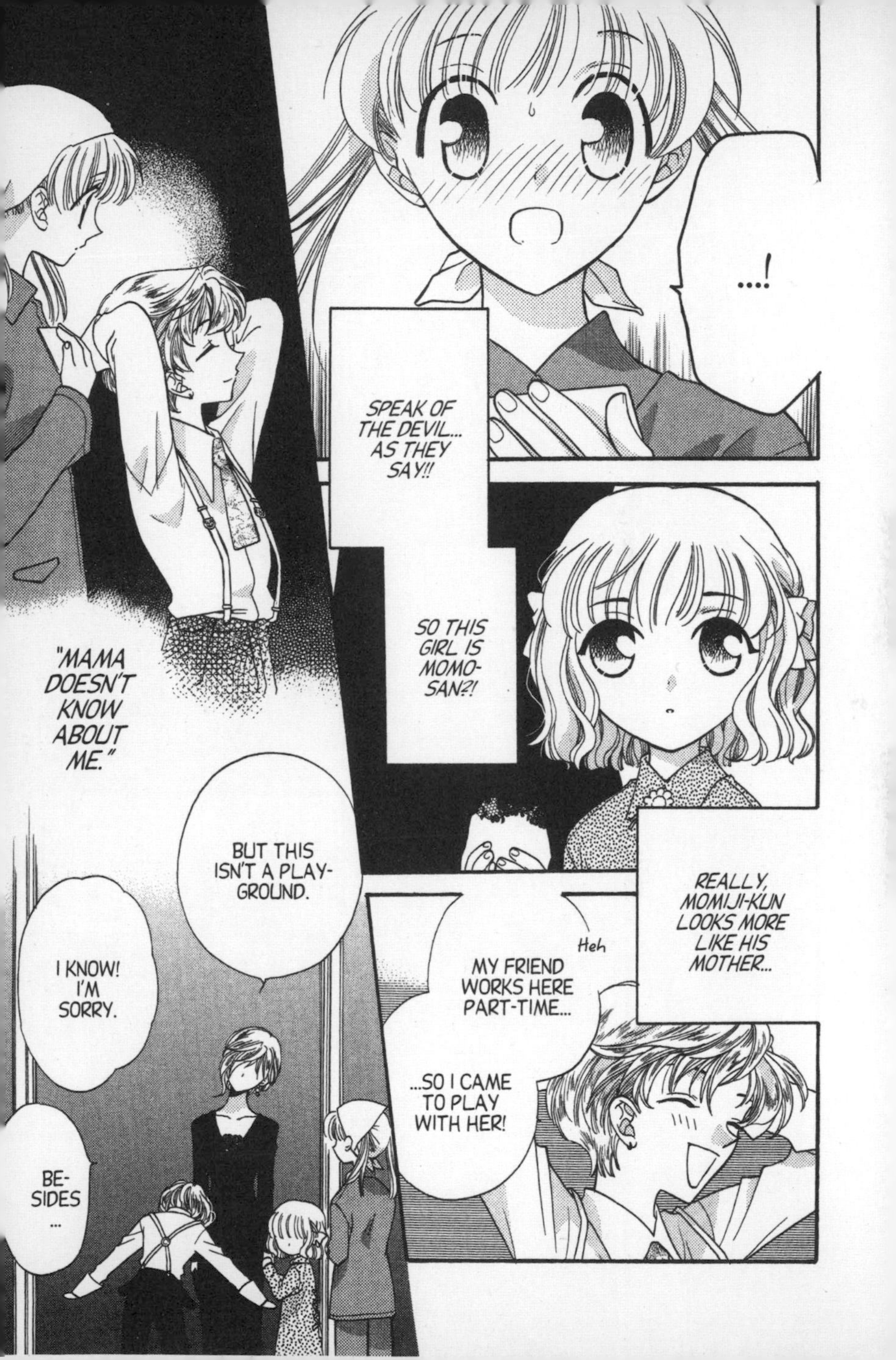
...!
SPEAK OF THE DEVIL... AS THEY SAY!!
SO THIS GIRL IS MOMO-SAN?!
REALLY, MOMIJI-KUN LOOKS MORE LIKE HIS MOTHER...
Heh
MY FRIEND WORKS HERE PART-TIME...
...SO I CAME TO PLAY WITH HER!
"MAMA DOESN'T KNOW ABOUT ME."
BUT THIS ISN'T A PLAY-GROUND.
I KNOW! I'M SORRY.
BE-SIDES ...

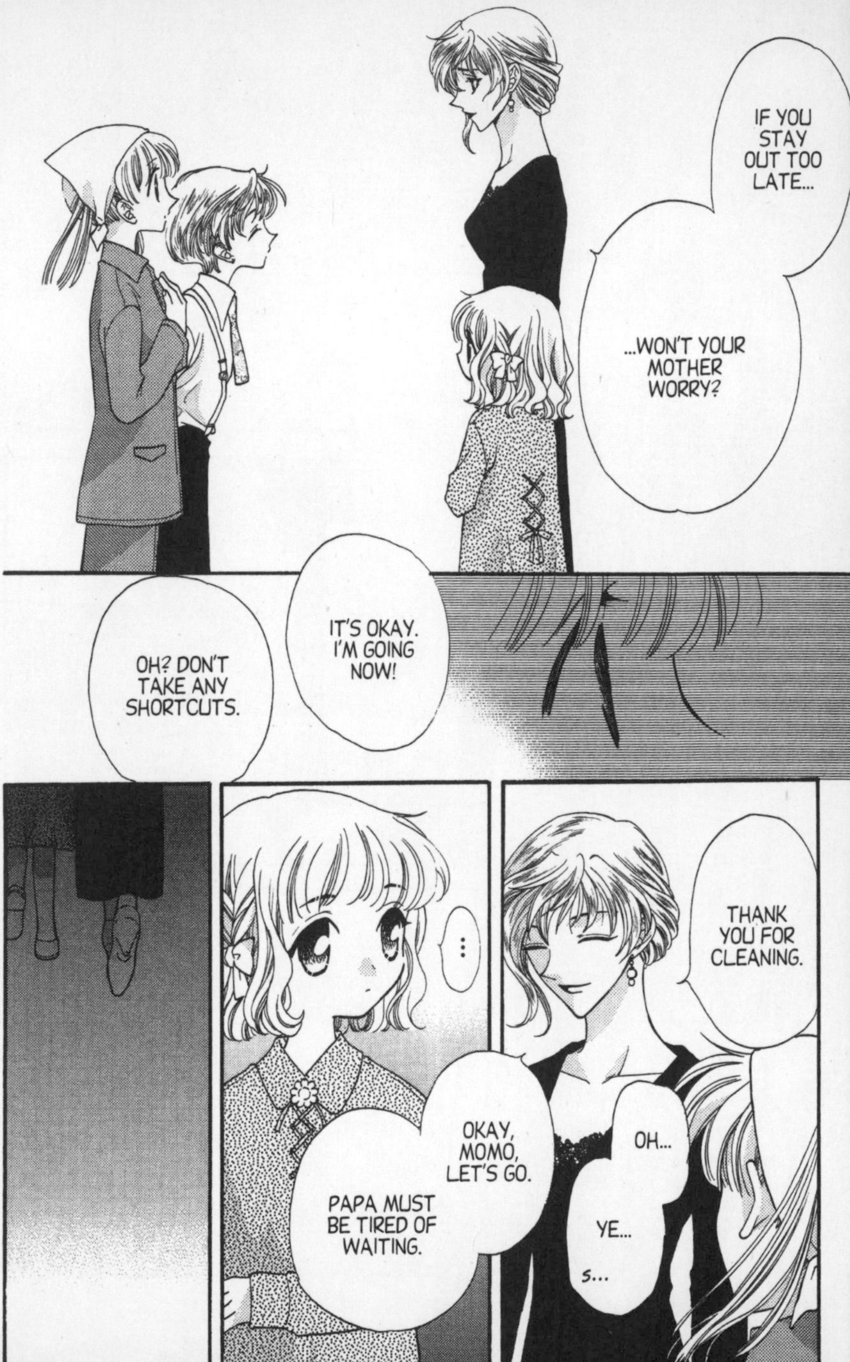
IF YOU STAY OUT TOO LATE...
...WON'T YOUR MOTHER WORRY?
IT'S OKAY. I'M GOING NOW!
OH? DON'T TAKE ANY SHORTCUTS.
THANK YOU FOR CLEANING.
OKAY, MOMO, LET'S GO.
PAPA MUST BE TIRED OF WAITING.
OH...
YE...
S...
...

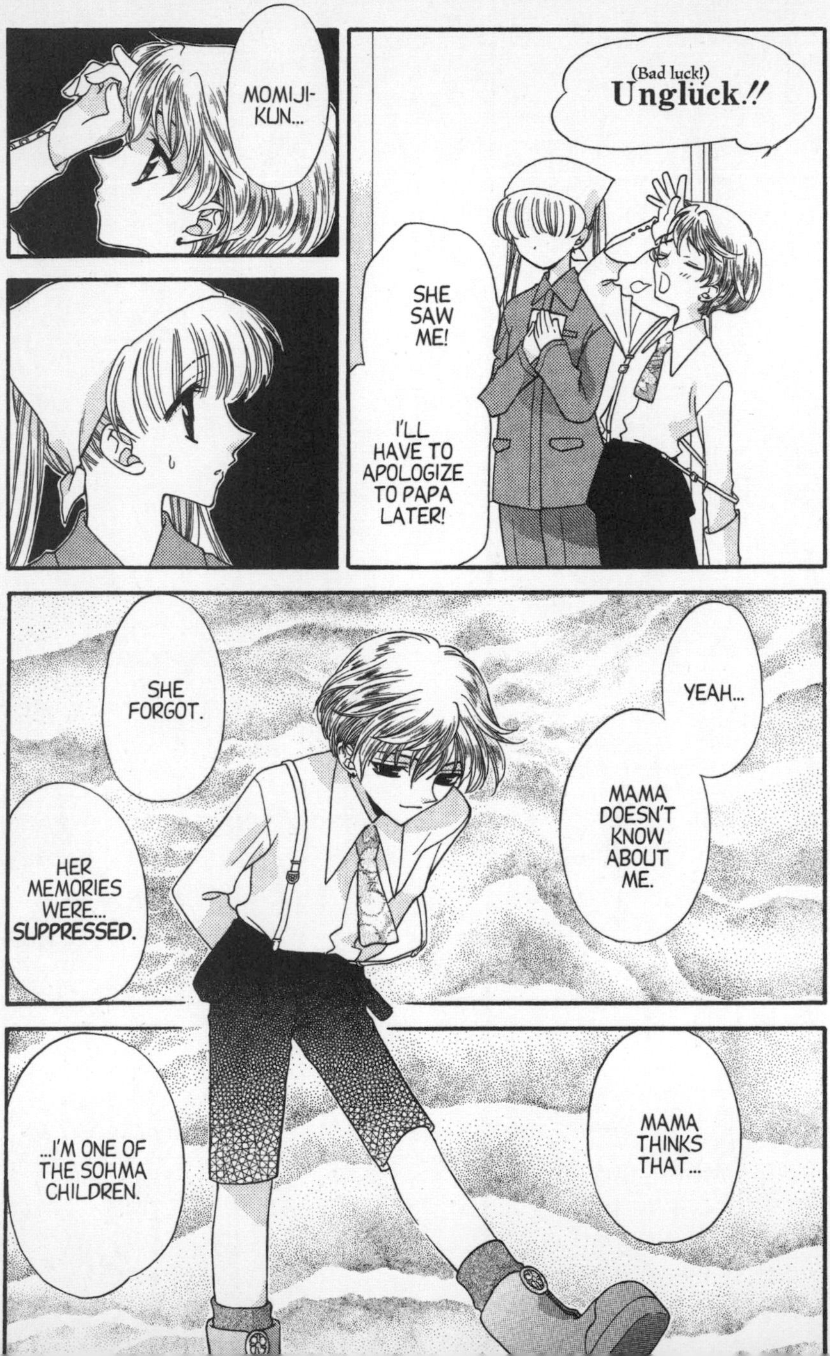
(Bad luck!)
Unglück!!
SHE SAW ME!
I'LL HAVE TO APOLOGIZE TO PAPA LATER!
MOMIJI-KUN...
YEAH...
MAMA DOESN'T KNOW ABOUT ME.
SHE FORGOT.
HER MEMORIES WERE... SUPPRESSED.
MAMA THINKS THAT...
...I'M ONE OF THE SOHMA CHILDREN.

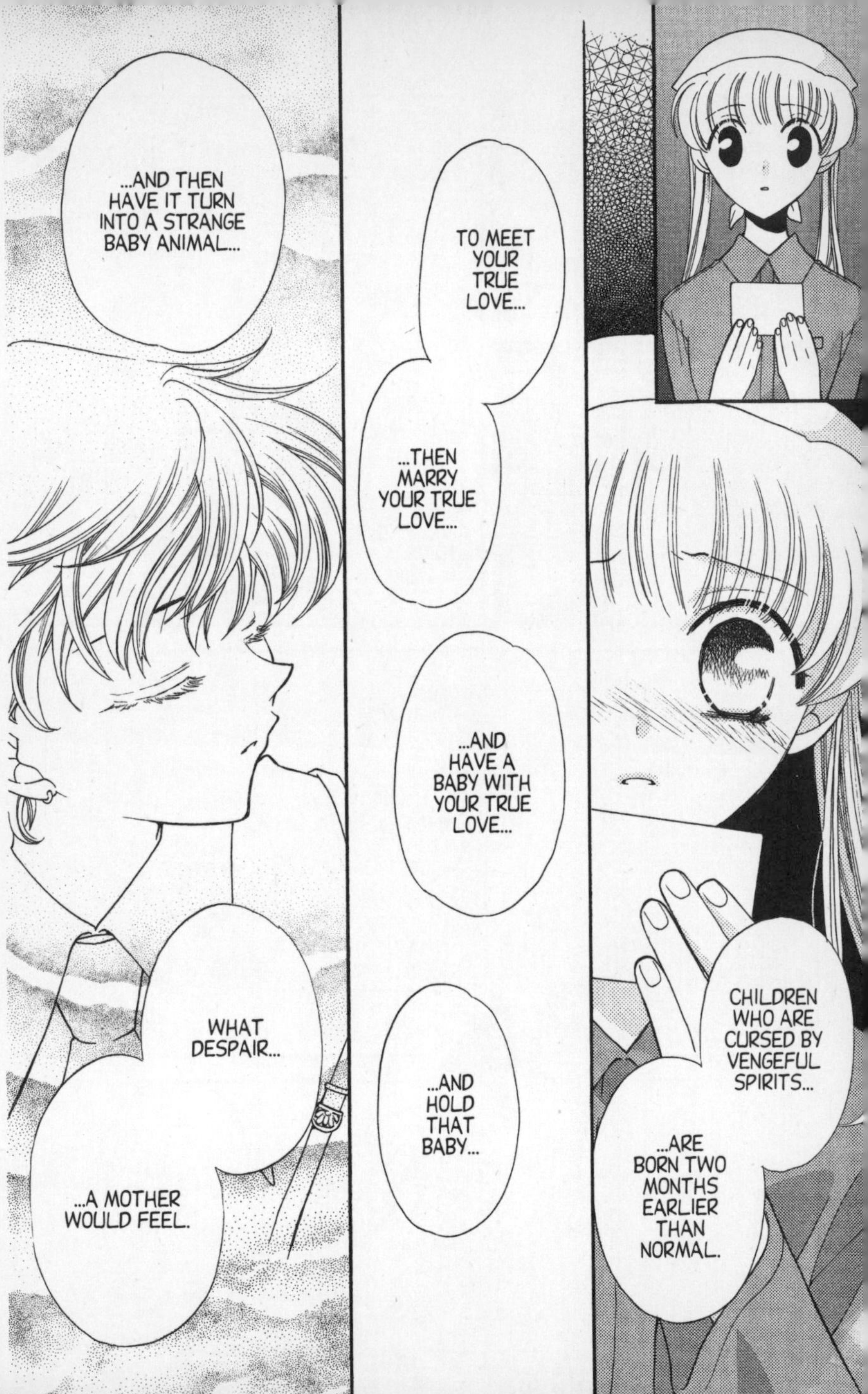
CHILDREN WHO ARE CURSED BY VENGEFUL SPIRITS...
...ARE BORN TWO MONTHS EARLIER THAN NORMAL.
TO MEET YOUR TRUE LOVE...
...THEN MARRY YOUR TRUE LOVE...
...AND HAVE A BABY WITH YOUR TRUE LOVE...
...AND HOLD THAT BABY...
...AND THEN HAVE IT TURN INTO A STRANGE BABY ANIMAL...
WHAT DESPAIR...
...A MOTHER WOULD FEEL.

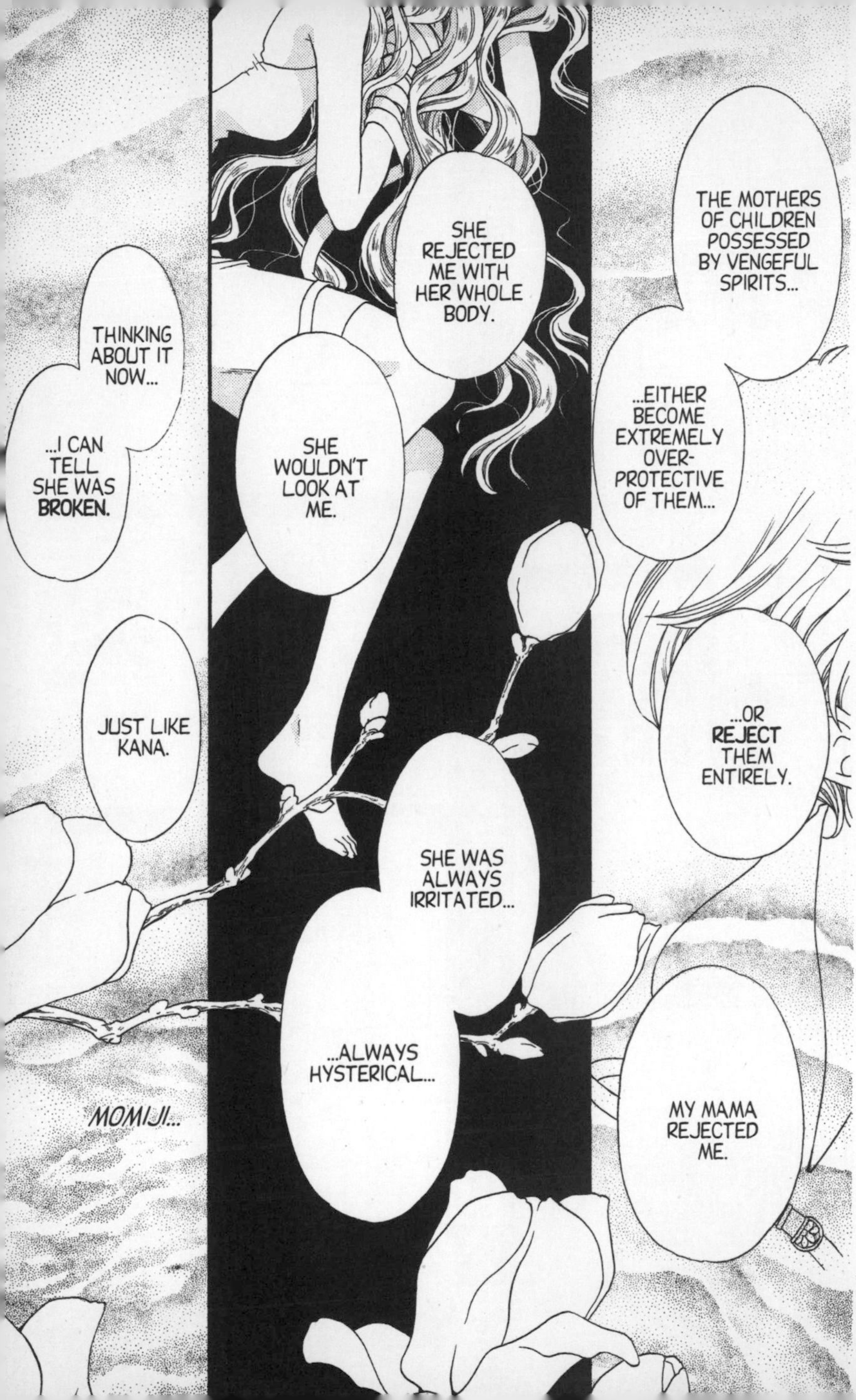
THE MOTHERS OF CHILDREN POSSESSED BY VENGEFUL SPIRITS...
...EITHER BECOME EXTREMELY OVER-PROTECTIVE OF THEM...
...OR REJECT THEM ENTIRELY.
MY MAMA REJECTED ME.
SHE REJECTED ME WITH HER WHOLE BODY.
SHE WOULDN'T LOOK AT ME.
SHE WAS ALWAYS IRRITATED...
...ALWAYS HYSTERICAL...
THINKING ABOUT IT NOW...
...I CAN TELL SHE WAS BROKEN.
JUST LIKE KANA.
MOMIJI...

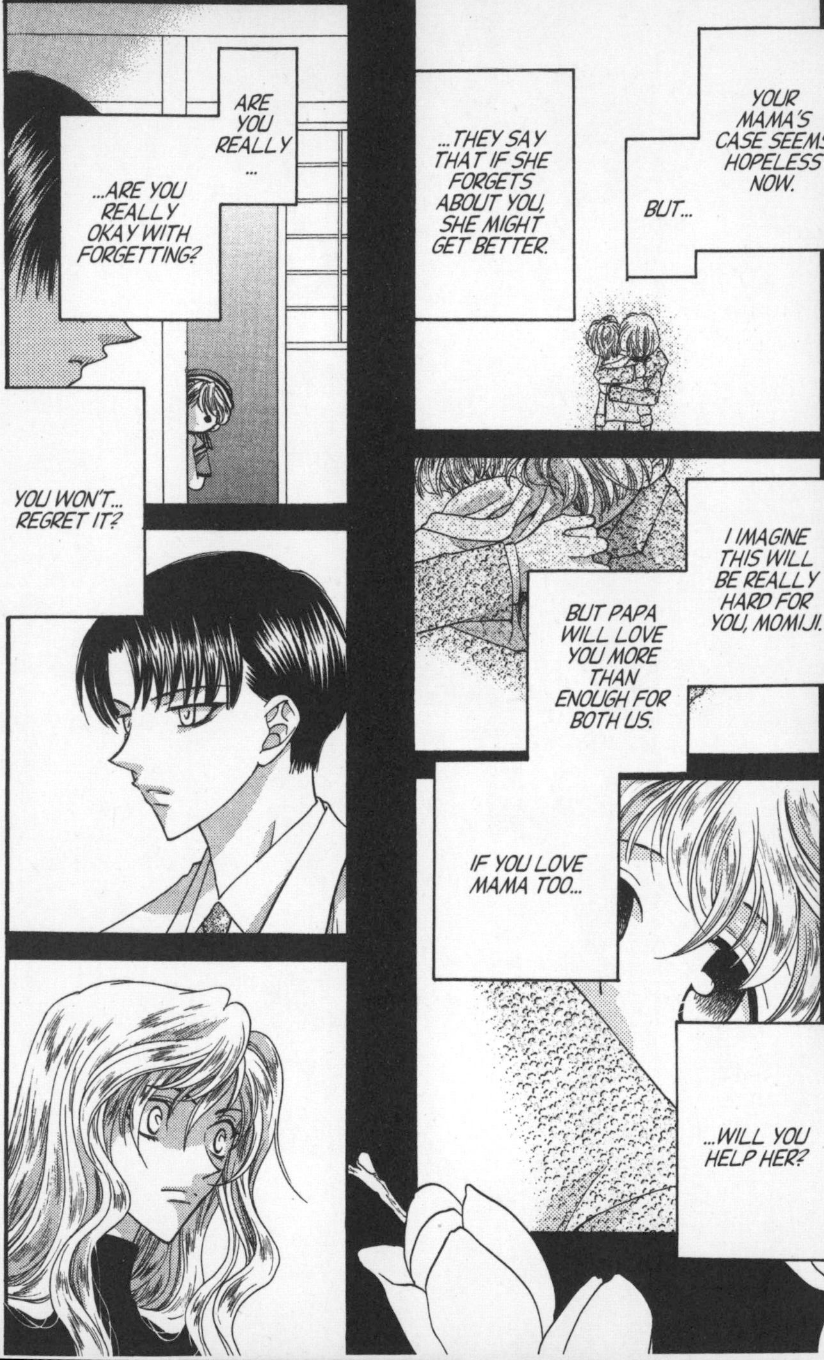
YOUR MAMA'S CASE SEEMS HOPELESS NOW.
BUT...
...THEY SAY THAT IF SHE FORGETS ABOUT YOU, SHE MIGHT GET BETTER.
I IMAGINE THIS WILL BE REALLY HARD FOR YOU, MOMIJI.
BUT PAPA WILL LOVE YOU MORE THAN ENOUGH FOR BOTH US.
IF YOU LOVE MAMA TOO...
...WILL YOU HELP HER?
ARE YOU REALLY ...
...ARE YOU REALLY OKAY WITH FORGETTING?
YOU WON'T... REGRET IT?

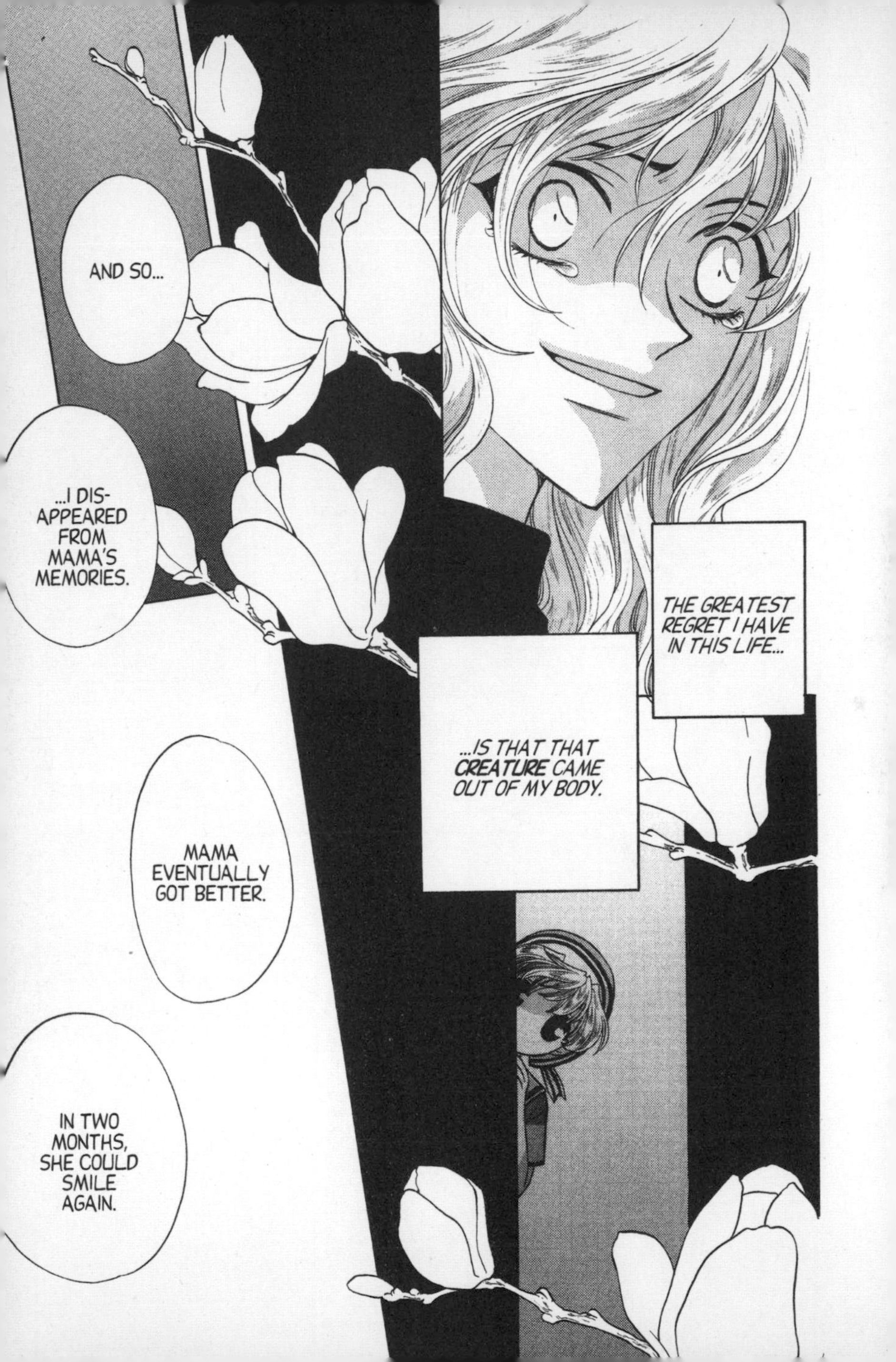
THE GREATEST REGRET I HAVE IN THIS LIFE...
...IS THAT THAT **CREATURE** CAME OUT OF MY BODY.
AND SO...
...I DIS-APPEARED FROM MAMA'S MEMORIES.
MAMA EVENTUALLY GOT BETTER.
IN TWO MONTHS, SHE COULD SMILE AGAIN.

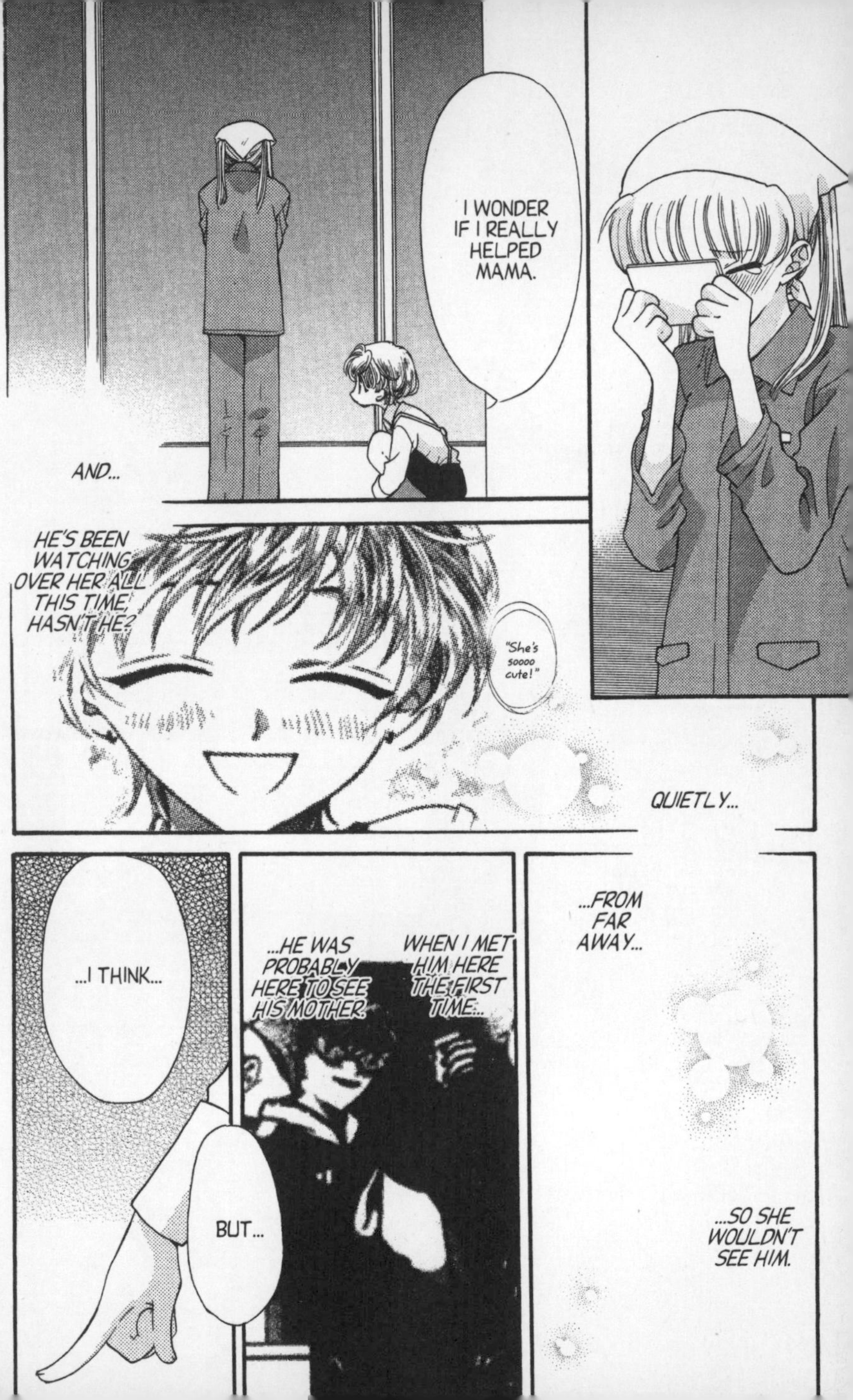
I WONDER IF I REALLY HELPED MAMA.
AND...
HE'S BEEN WATCHING OVER HER ALL THIS TIME, HASN'T HE?
"She's soooo cute!"
QUIETLY...
...FROM FAR AWAY...
...SO SHE WOULDN'T SEE HIM.
WHEN I MET HIM HERE THE FIRST TIME...
...HE WAS PROBABLY HERE TO SEE HIS MOTHER.
...I THINK...
BUT...

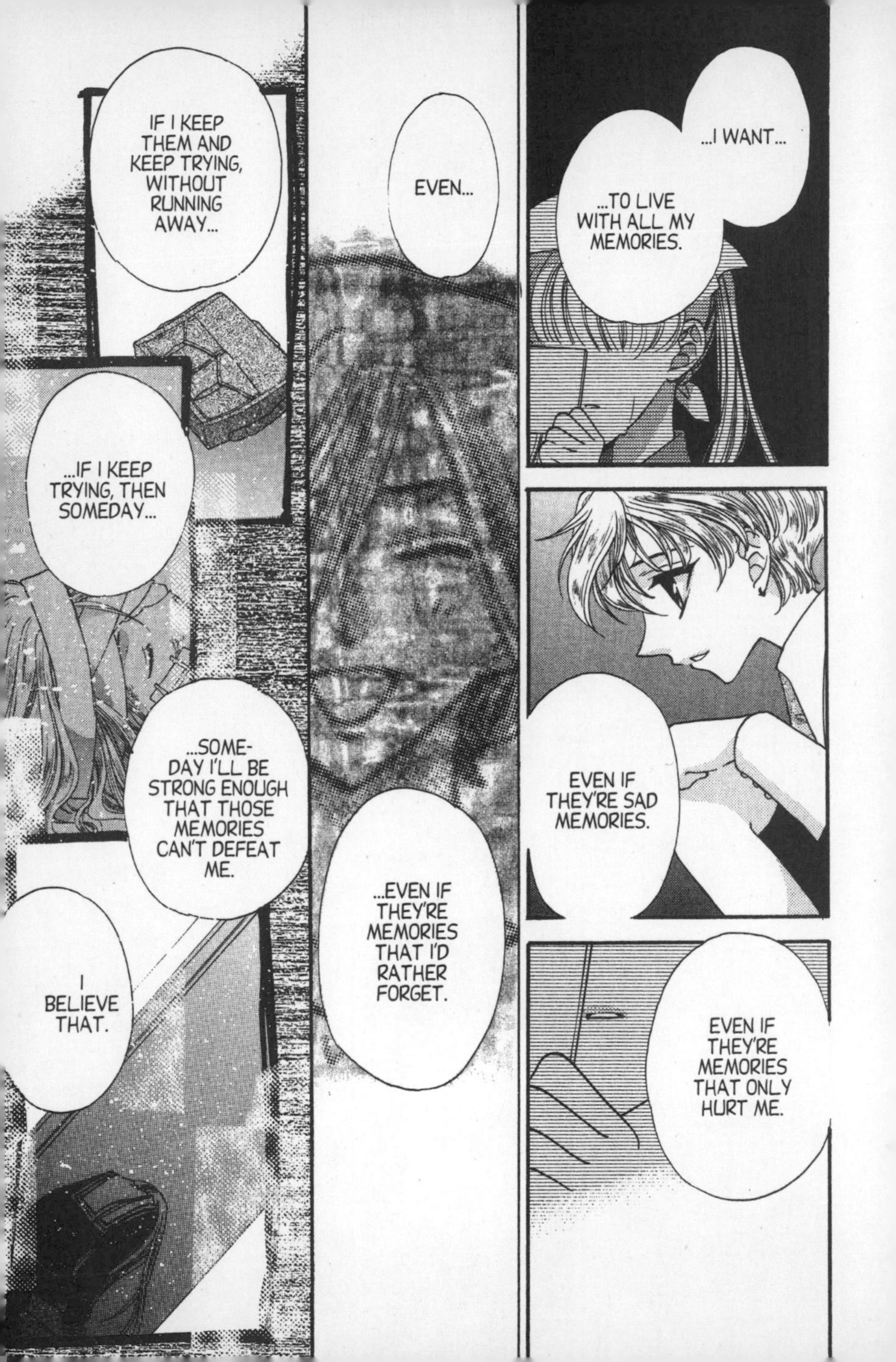
...I WANT...
...TO LIVE WITH ALL MY MEMORIES.
EVEN IF THEY'RE SAD MEMORIES.
EVEN IF THEY'RE MEMORIES THAT ONLY HURT ME.
EVEN...
...EVEN IF THEY'RE MEMORIES THAT I'D RATHER FORGET.
IF I KEEP THEM AND KEEP TRYING, WITHOUT RUNNING AWAY...
...IF I KEEP TRYING, THEN SOMEDAY...
...SOME-DAY I'LL BE STRONG ENOUGH THAT THOSE MEMORIES CAN'T DEFEAT ME.
I BELIEVE THAT.

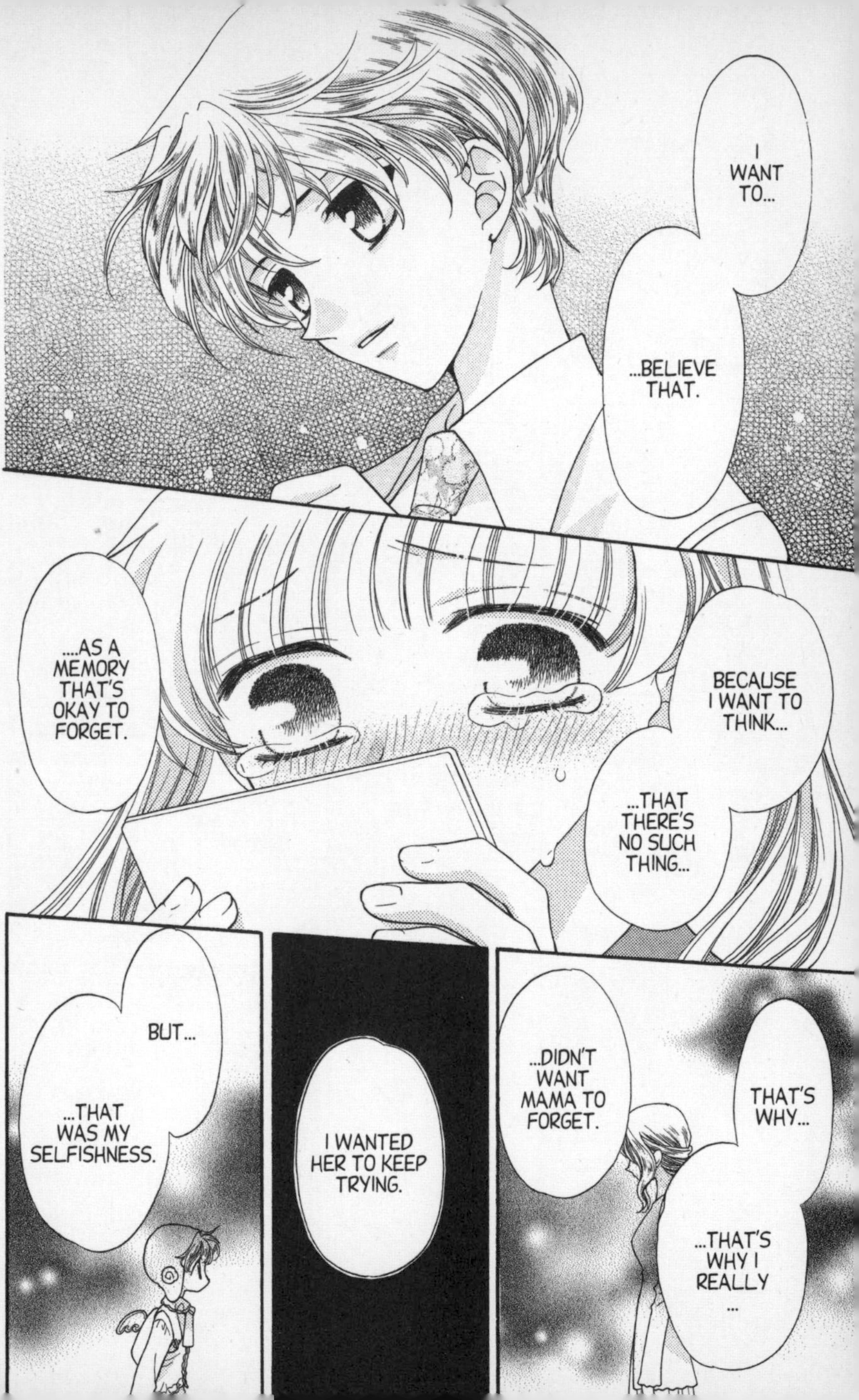
I WANT TO...
...BELIEVE THAT.
BECAUSE I WANT TO THINK...
...THAT THERE'S NO SUCH THING...
....AS A MEMORY THAT'S OKAY TO FORGET.
THAT'S WHY...
...THAT'S WHY I REALLY ...
...DIDN'T WANT MAMA TO FORGET.
I WANTED HER TO KEEP TRYING.
BUT...
...THAT WAS MY SELFISHNESS.

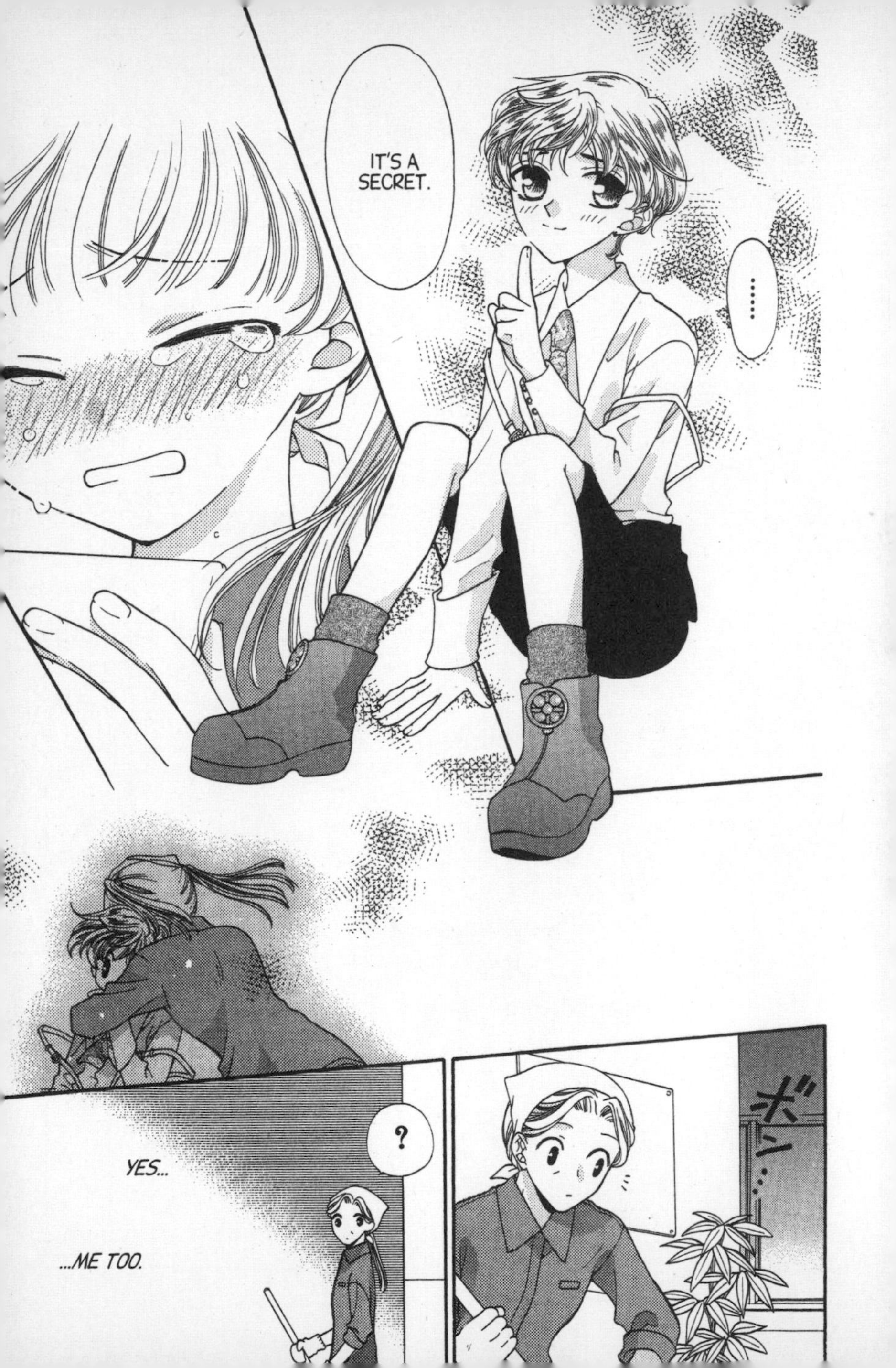
IT'S A SECRET.
......
ボン…
?
YES...
...ME TOO.

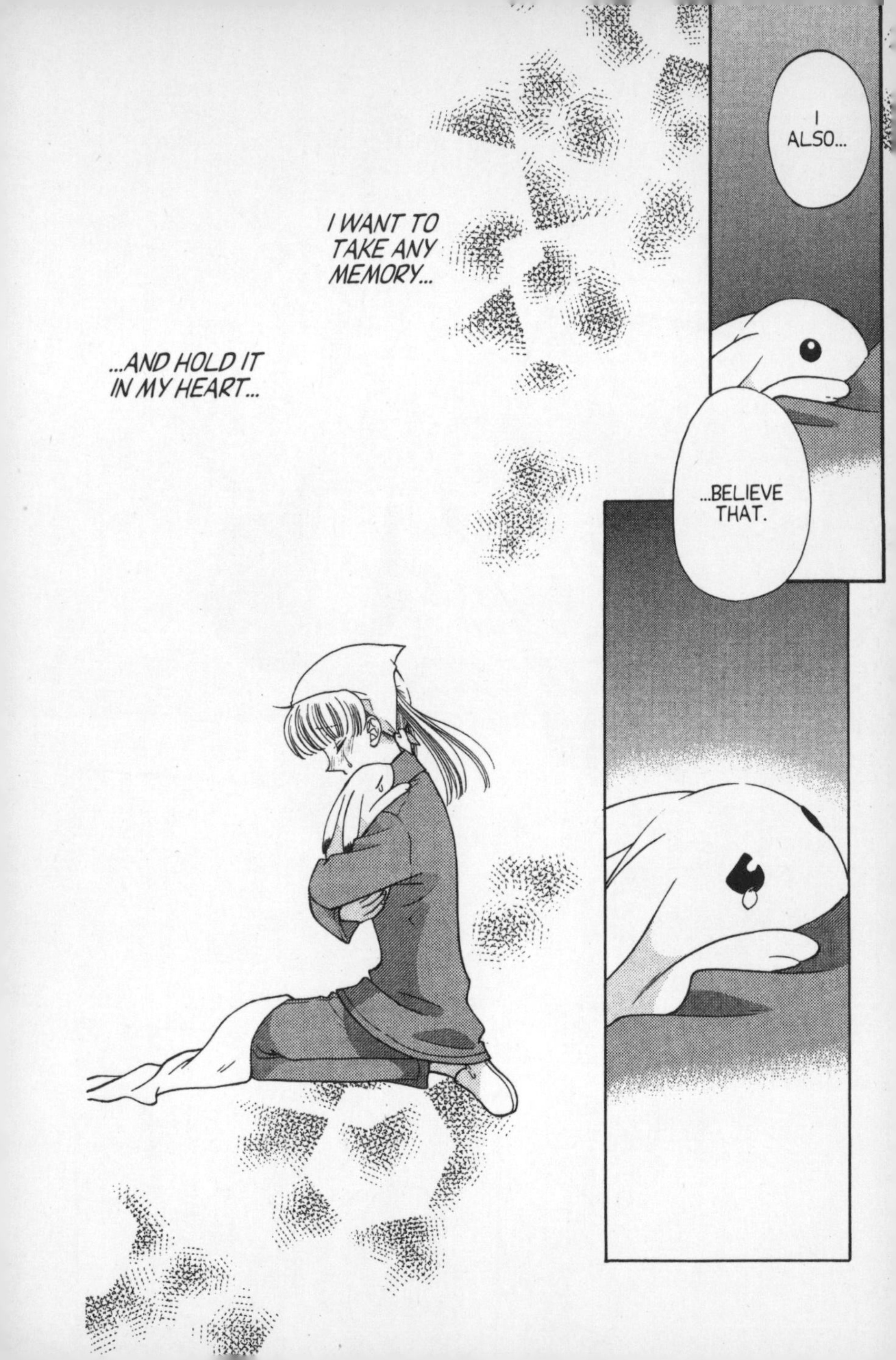
I ALSO...
...BELIEVE THAT.
I WANT TO TAKE ANY MEMORY...
...AND HOLD IT IN MY HEART...

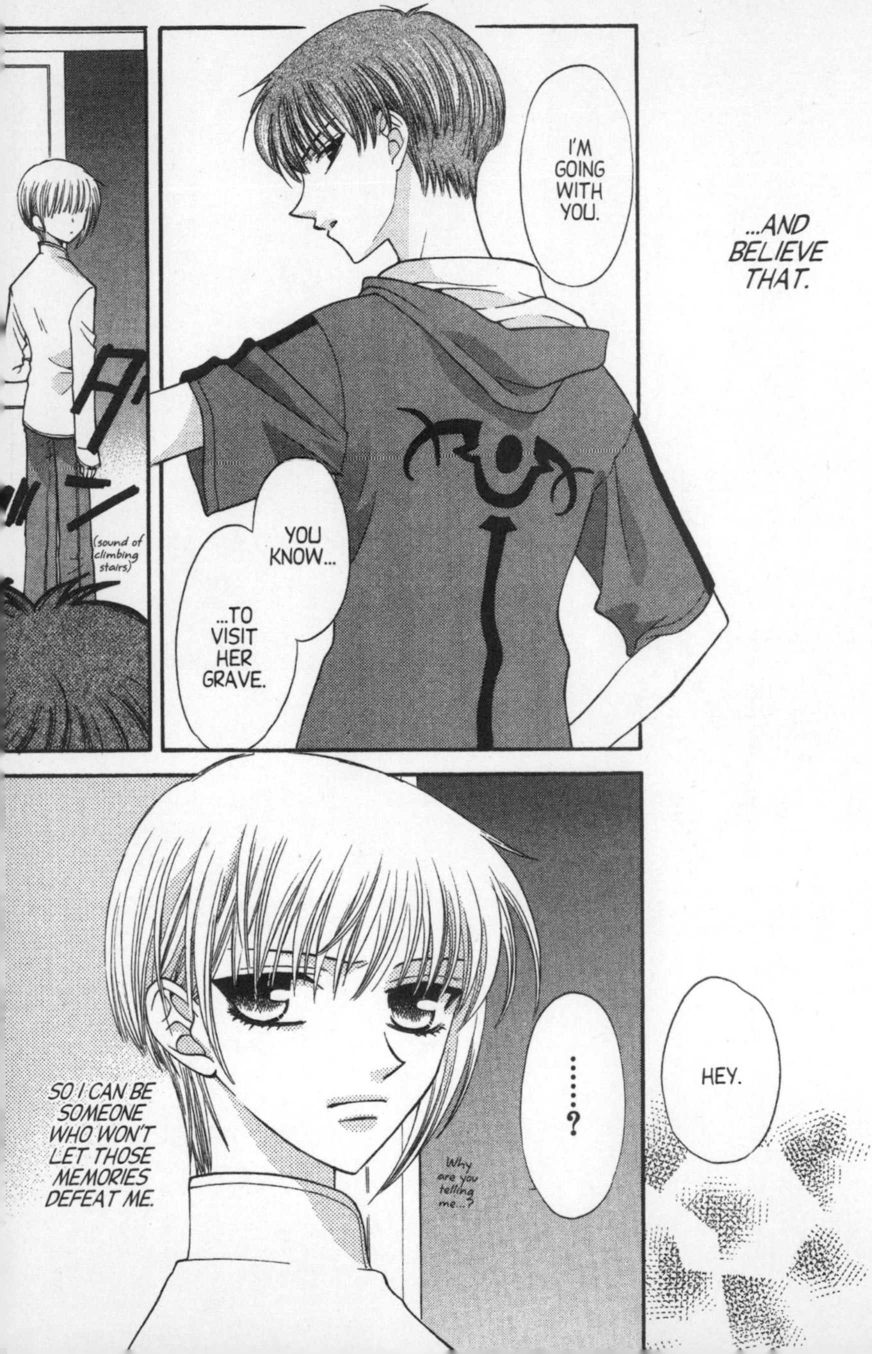
...AND BELIEVE THAT.
I'M GOING WITH YOU.
YOU KNOW...
...TO VISIT HER GRAVE.
(sound of climbing stairs)
HEY.
......?
Why are you telling me...?
SO I CAN BE SOMEONE WHO WON'T LET THOSE MEMORIES DEFEAT ME.

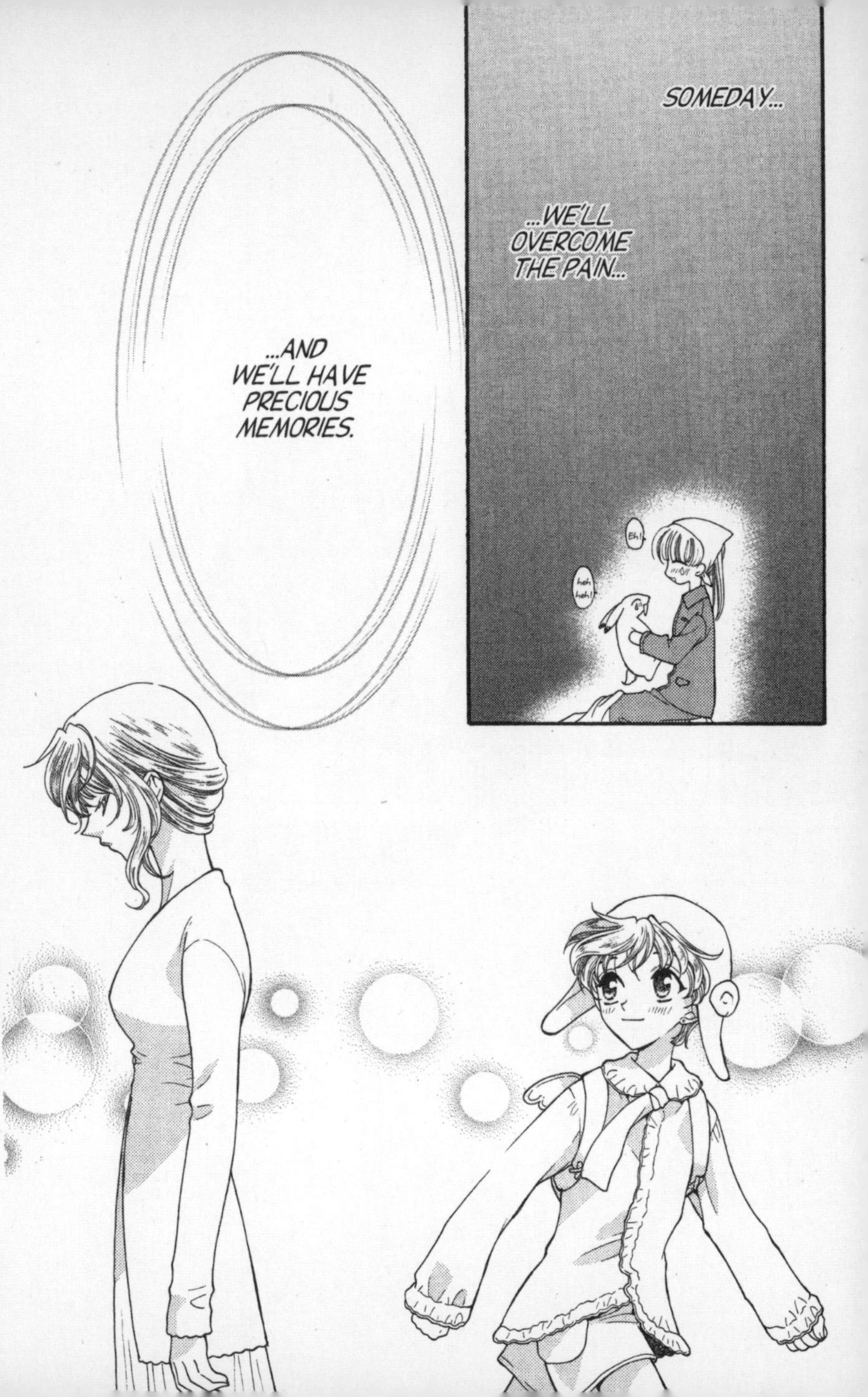
SOMEDAY...
...WE'LL OVERCOME THE PAIN...
Eh!
heh heh!
...AND WE'LL HAVE PRECIOUS MEMORIES.

Chapter 24

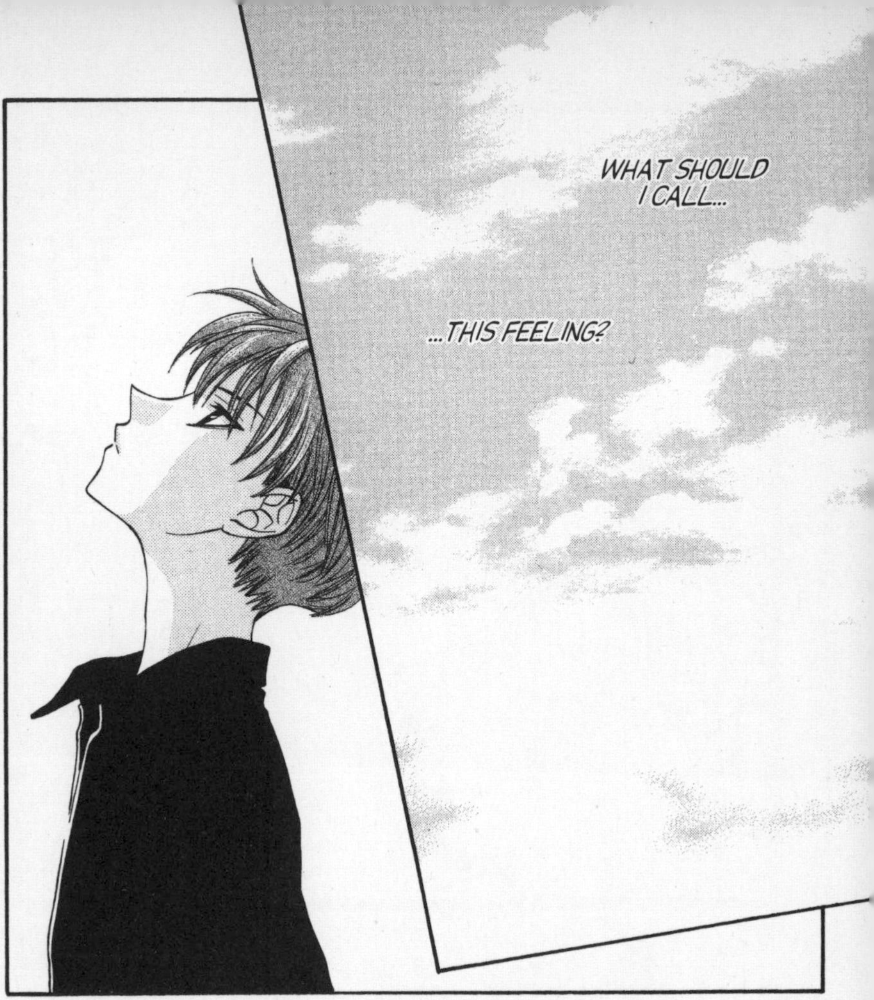
WHAT SHOULD I CALL...
...THIS FEELING?

ULTRA SPECIAL BLAH BLAH BLAH 6

This is where volume 4 ends!! This one's been really talky!! (But once again, I have no one to blame but myself.) But it's okay! (What is?) A lot of people told me they thought they should have kissed. Sorry, but I didn't want them to, and as the author, it's up to me...

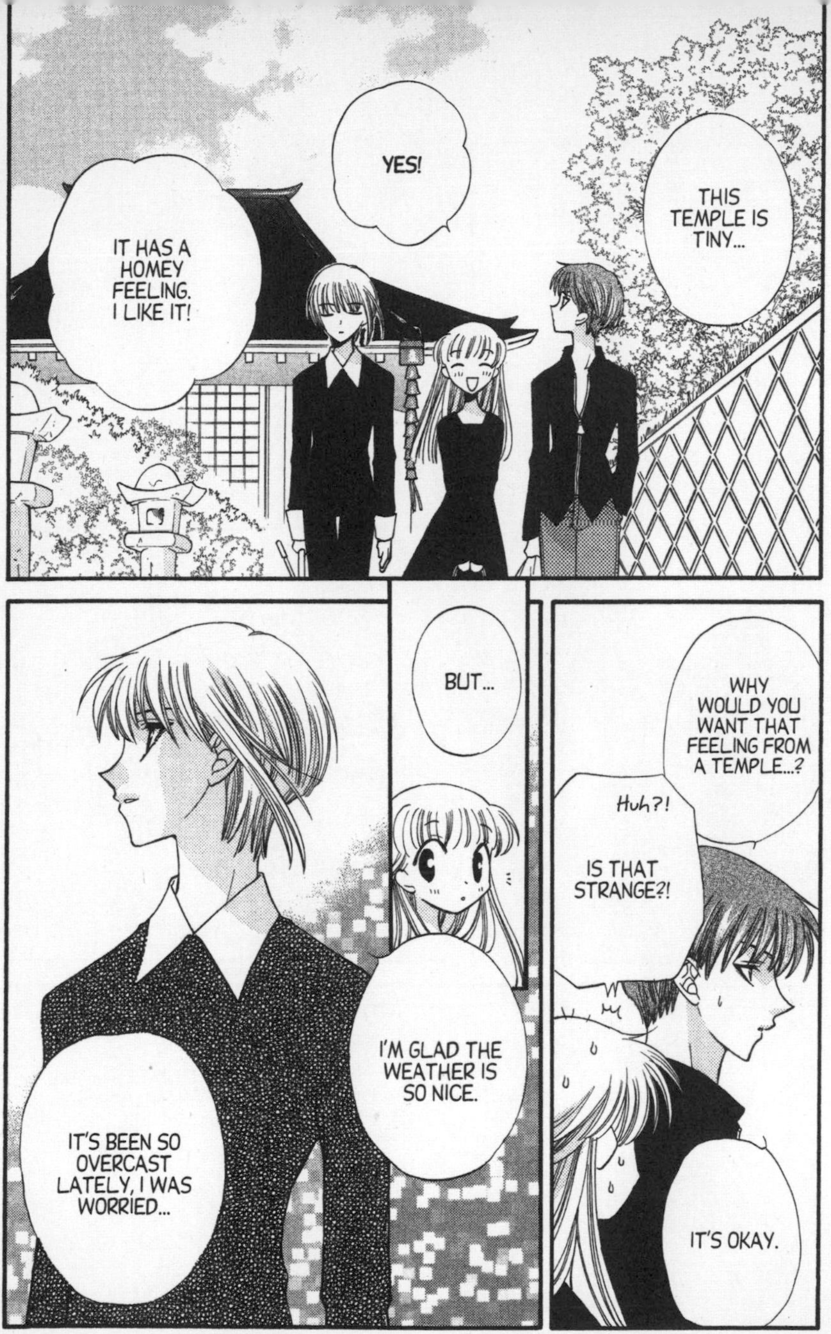
THIS TEMPLE IS TINY...
YES!
IT HAS A HOMEY FEELING. I LIKE IT!
WHY WOULD YOU WANT THAT FEELING FROM A TEMPLE...?
Huh?!
IS THAT STRANGE?!
IT'S OKAY.
BUT...
I'M GLAD THE WEATHER IS SO NICE.
IT'S BEEN SO OVERCAST LATELY, I WAS WORRIED...

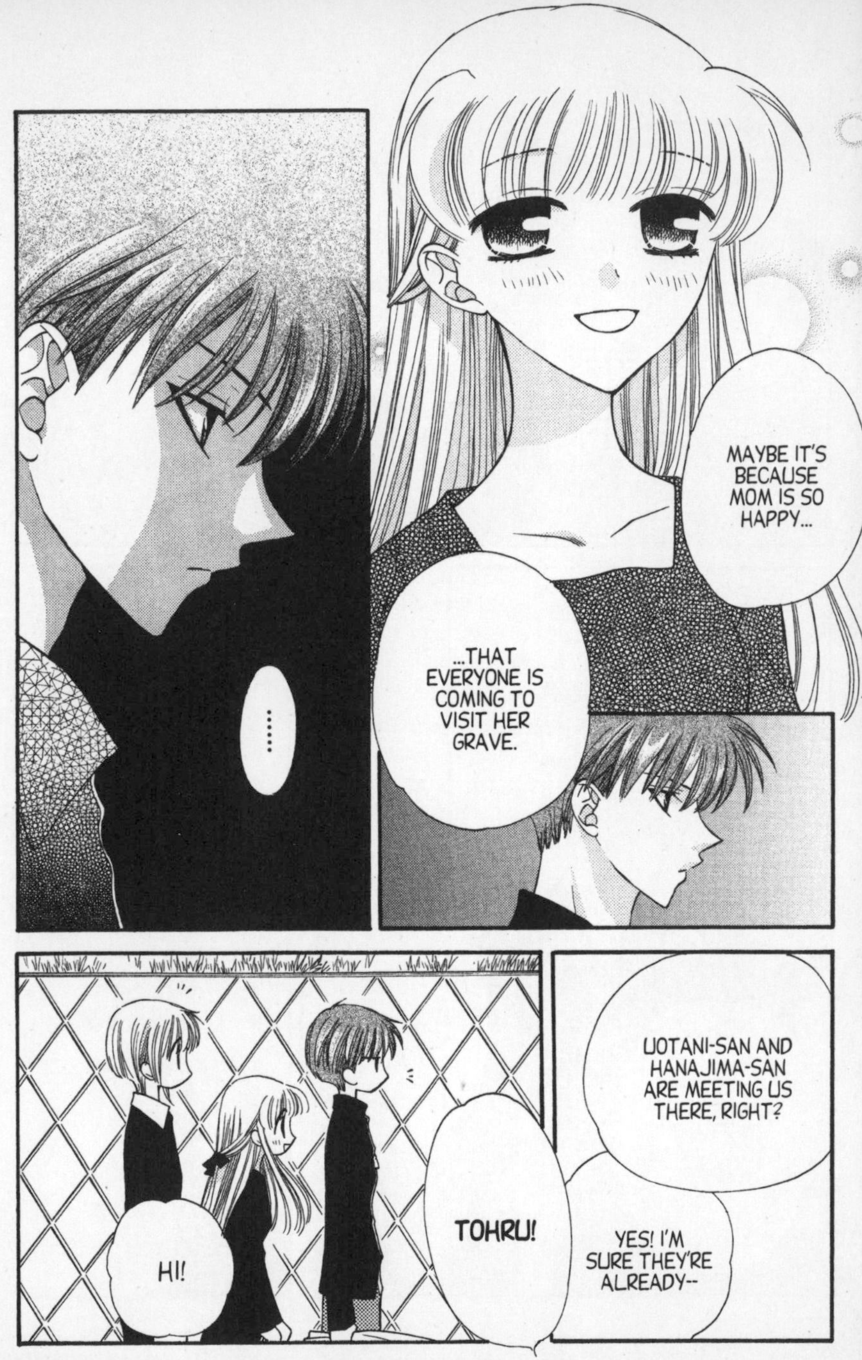
MAYBE IT'S BECAUSE MOM IS SO HAPPY...
...THAT EVERYONE IS COMING TO VISIT HER GRAVE.
......
UOTANI-SAN AND HANAJIMA-SAN ARE MEETING US THERE, RIGHT?
YES! I'M SURE THEY'RE ALREADY--
TOHRU!
HI!

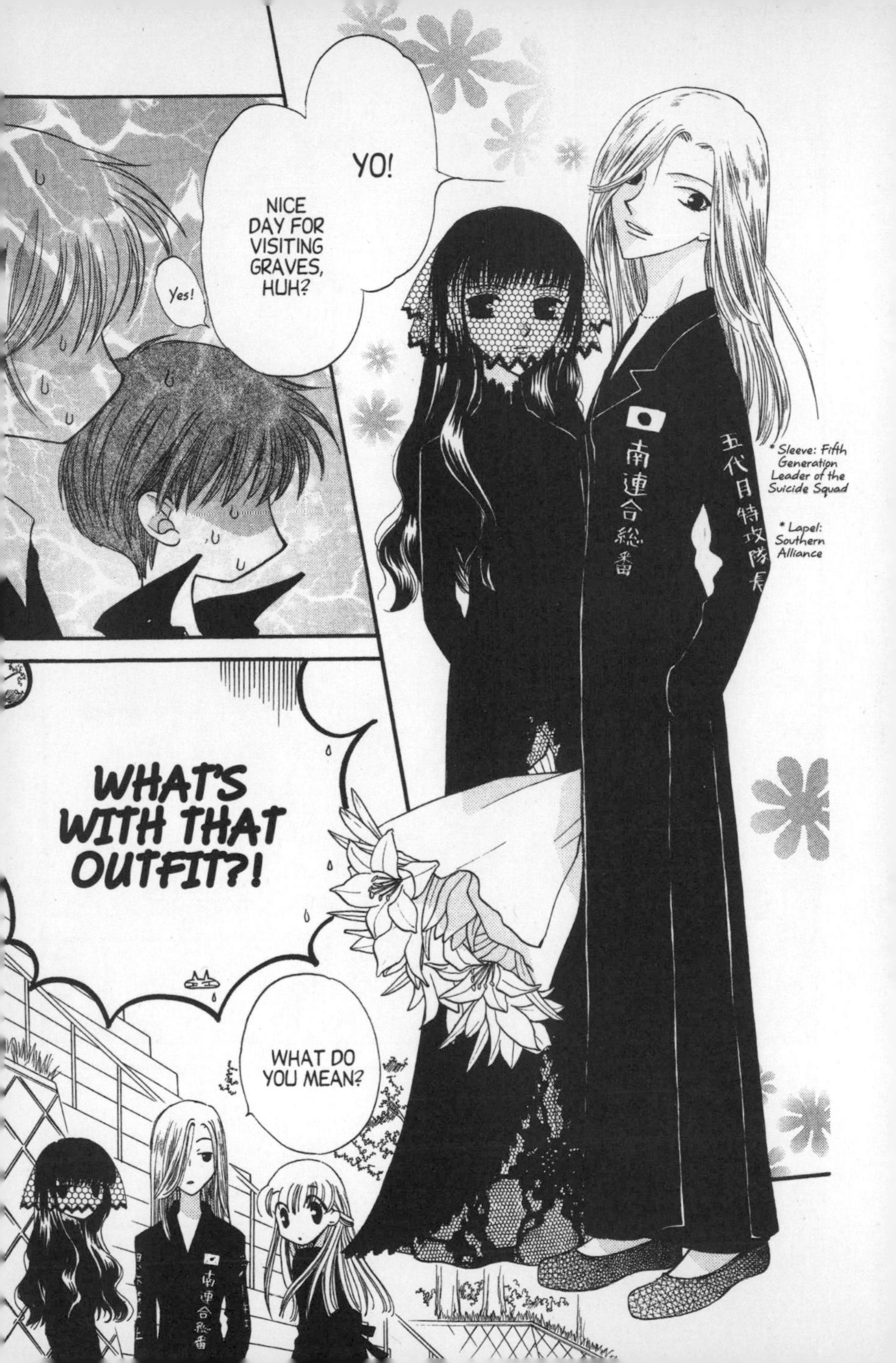
YO! NICE DAY FOR VISITING GRAVES, HUH?
南連合総番
五代目特攻隊長
* Sleeve: Fifth Generation Leader of the Suicide Squad
* Lapel: Southern Alliance
Yes!
WHAT'S WITH THAT OUTFIT?!
WHAT DO YOU MEAN?

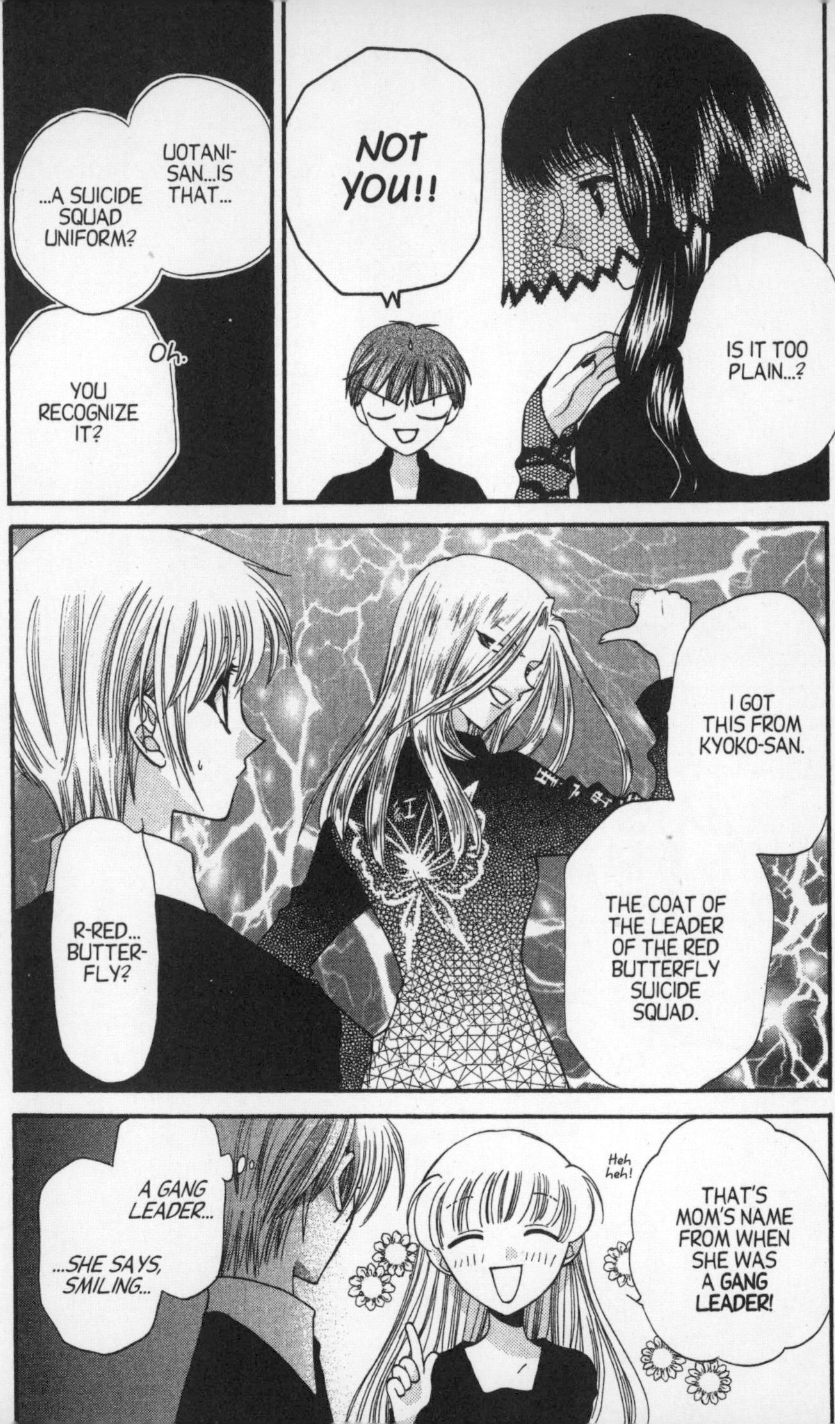
IS IT TOO PLAIN...?
NOT YOU!!
UOTANI-SAN...IS THAT...
...A SUICIDE SQUAD UNIFORM?
Oh.
YOU RECOGNIZE IT?
I GOT THIS FROM KYOKO-SAN.
THE COAT OF THE LEADER OF THE RED BUTTERFLY SUICIDE SQUAD.
R-RED... BUTTER-FLY?
Heh heh!
THAT'S MOM'S NAME FROM WHEN SHE WAS A GANG LEADER!
A GANG LEADER...
...SHE SAYS, SMILING...

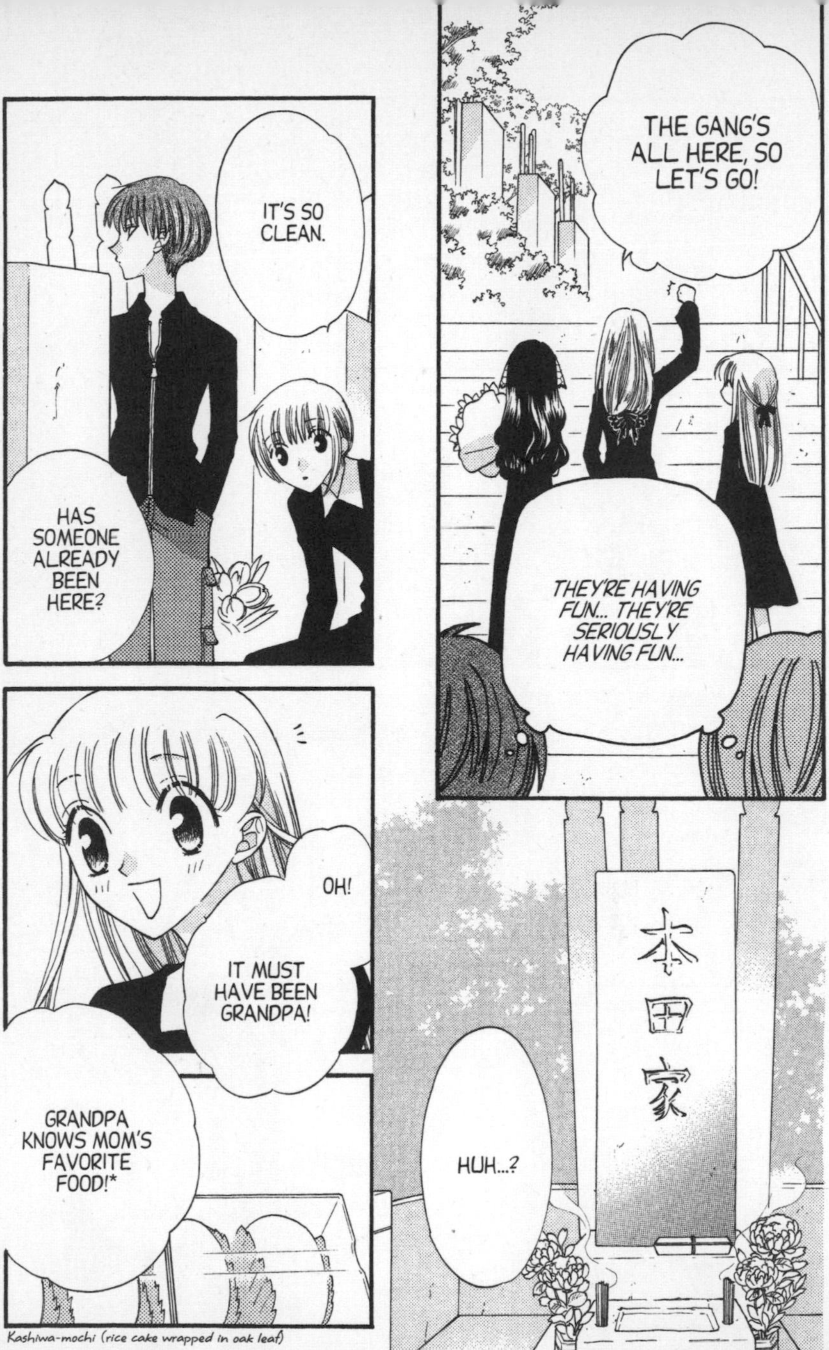
THE GANG'S ALL HERE, SO LET'S GO!
THEY'RE HAVING FUN... THEY'RE SERIOUSLY HAVING FUN...
IT'S SO CLEAN.
HAS SOMEONE ALREADY BEEN HERE?
本田家
HUH...?
HONDA FAMILY
OH!
IT MUST HAVE BEEN GRANDPA!
GRANDPA KNOWS MOM'S FAVORITE FOOD!*

Kashiwa-mochi (rice cake wrapped in oak leaf)

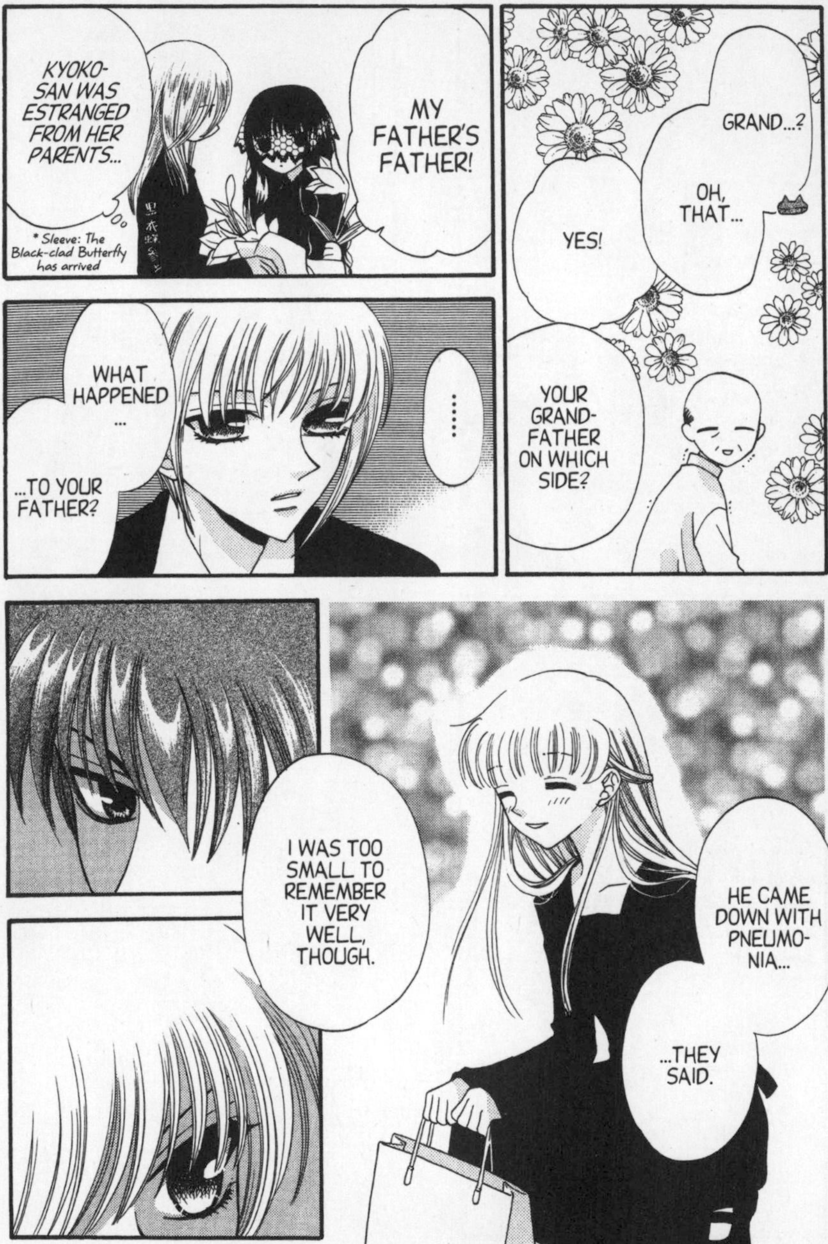
GRAND...?
OH, THAT...
YES!
YOUR GRAND-FATHER ON WHICH SIDE?
MY FATHER'S FATHER!
KYOKO-SAN WAS ESTRANGED FROM HER PARENTS...
* Sleeve: The Black-clad Butterfly has arrived
......
WHAT HAPPENED ...
...TO YOUR FATHER?
HE CAME DOWN WITH PNEUMO-NIA...
...THEY SAID.
I WAS TOO SMALL TO REMEMBER IT VERY WELL, THOUGH.

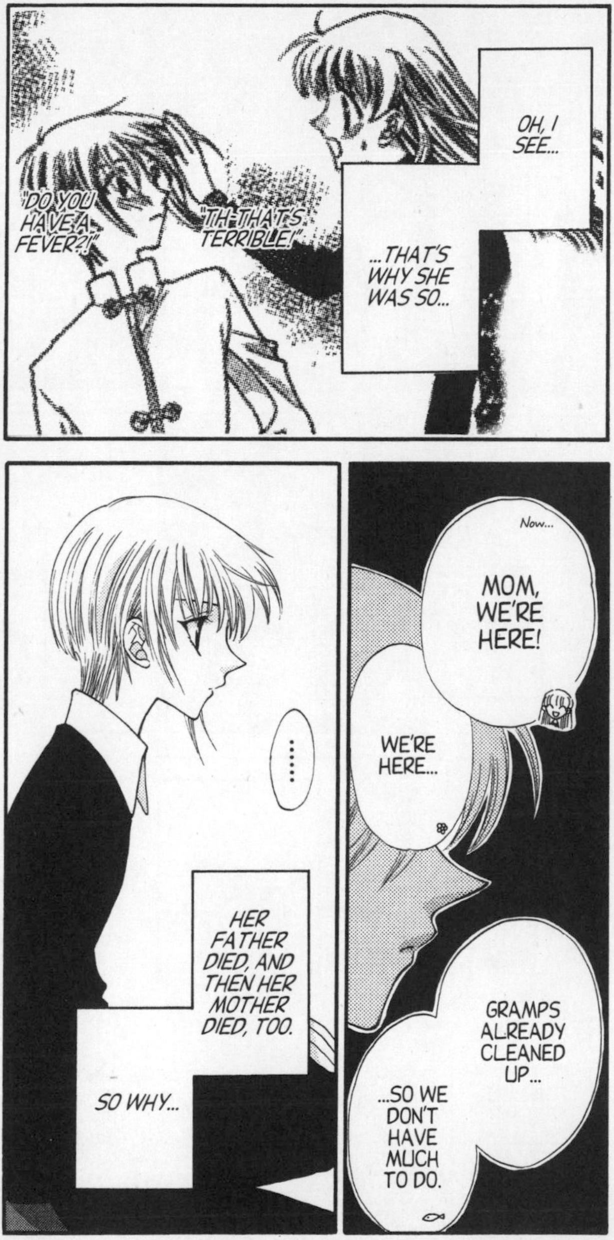
OH, I SEE...
...THAT'S WHY SHE WAS SO...
"TH-THAT'S TERRIBLE!"
"DO YOU HAVE A FEVER?!"
Now...
MOM, WE'RE HERE!
WE'RE HERE...
GRAMPS ALREADY CLEANED UP...
...SO WE DON'T HAVE MUCH TO DO.
......
HER FATHER DIED, AND THEN HER MOTHER DIED, TOO.
SO WHY...

Fruits Basket 4 Part 6:

I started crying when I saw the opening. I thought, "How very, very sad!" And "Oh, poor Serge. I want to protect him." That's proof that I'm totally hooked! He's like Cloud. (But it's worse for Cloud.) Square really does always have good music. I played Chrono Trigger on Su-Fami [Super Nintendo], so the music brought back a lot of memories. Oh, but I cried. It's so sad! I'm also playing Tokimeki Memorial [a popular romance sim]. I'm getting called Takaya-kun. And while I'm doing all this, I'm waiting for Sakura [Taisen] to come out...

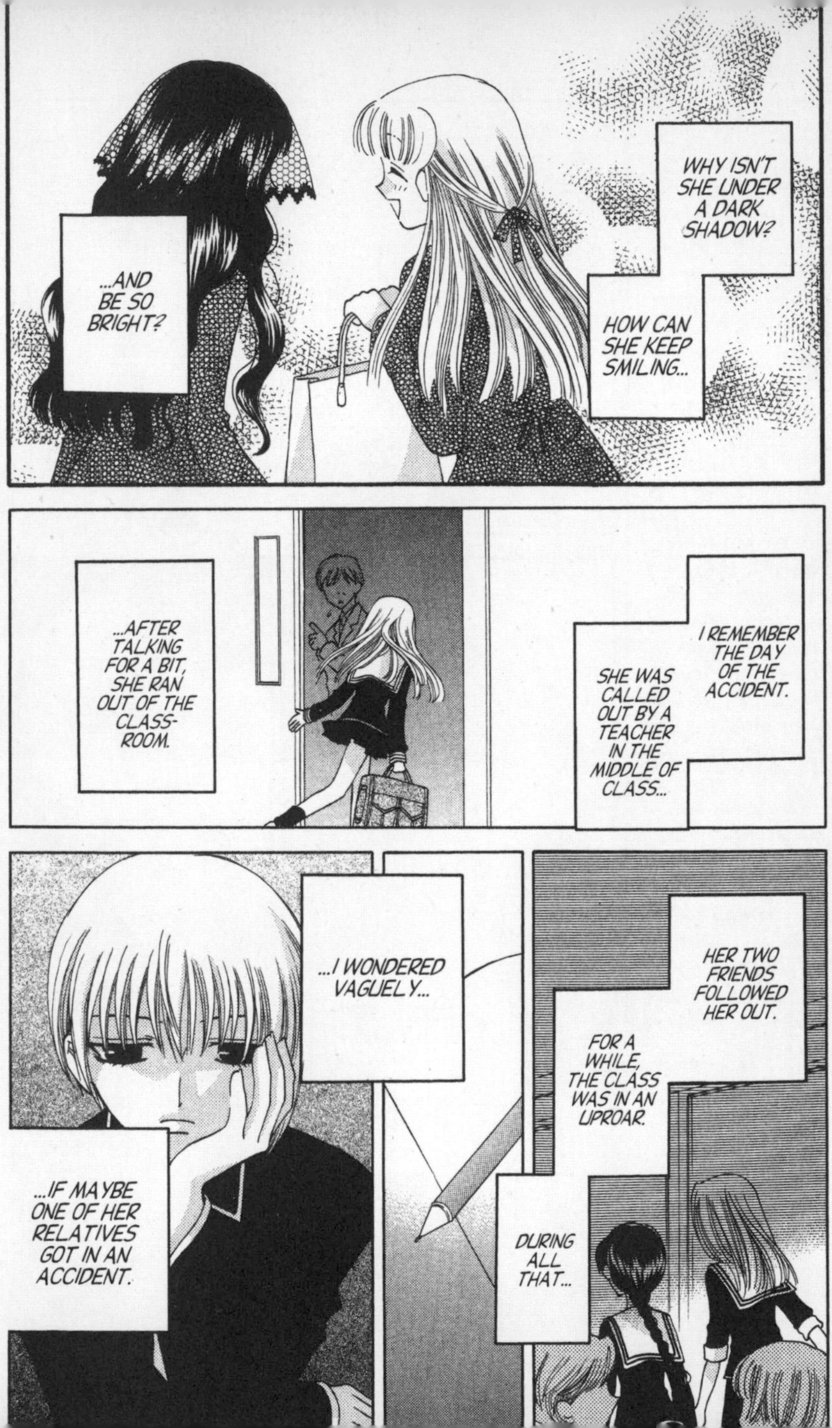
WHY ISN'T SHE UNDER A DARK SHADOW?
HOW CAN SHE KEEP SMILING...
...AND BE SO BRIGHT?
I REMEMBER THE DAY OF THE ACCIDENT.
SHE WAS CALLED OUT BY A TEACHER IN THE MIDDLE OF CLASS...
...AFTER TALKING FOR A BIT, SHE RAN OUT OF THE CLASS-ROOM.
HER TWO FRIENDS FOLLOWED HER OUT.
FOR A WHILE, THE CLASS WAS IN AN UPROAR.
DURING ALL THAT...
...I WONDERED VAGUELY...
...IF MAYBE ONE OF HER RELATIVES GOT IN AN ACCIDENT.

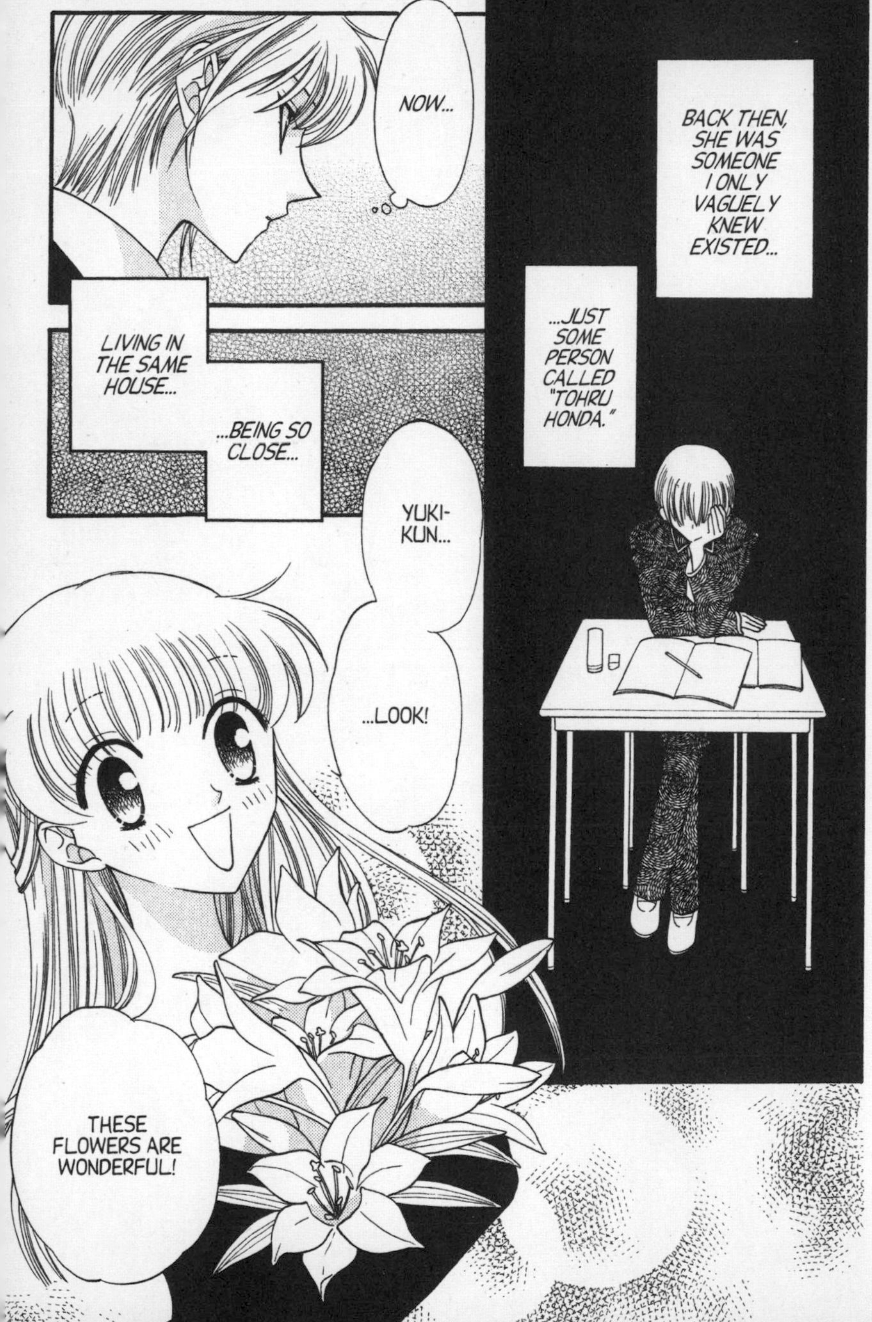
BACK THEN, SHE WAS SOMEONE I ONLY VAGUELY KNEW EXISTED...
...JUST SOME PERSON CALLED "TOHRU HONDA."
NOW...
LIVING IN THE SAME HOUSE...
...BEING SO CLOSE...
YUKI-KUN...
...LOOK!
THESE FLOWERS ARE WONDERFUL!

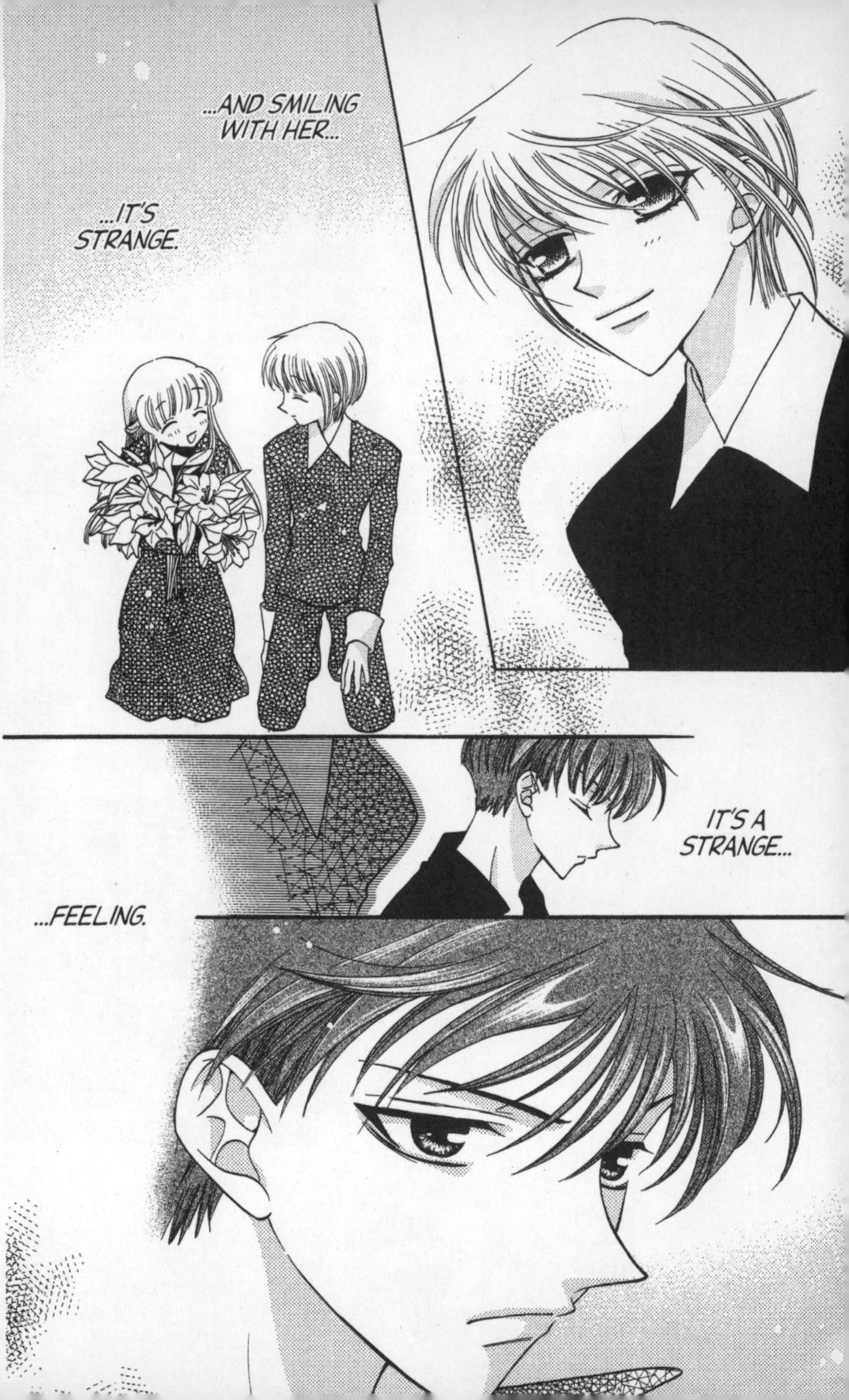
...AND SMILING WITH HER...
...IT'S STRANGE.
IT'S A STRANGE...
...FEELING.

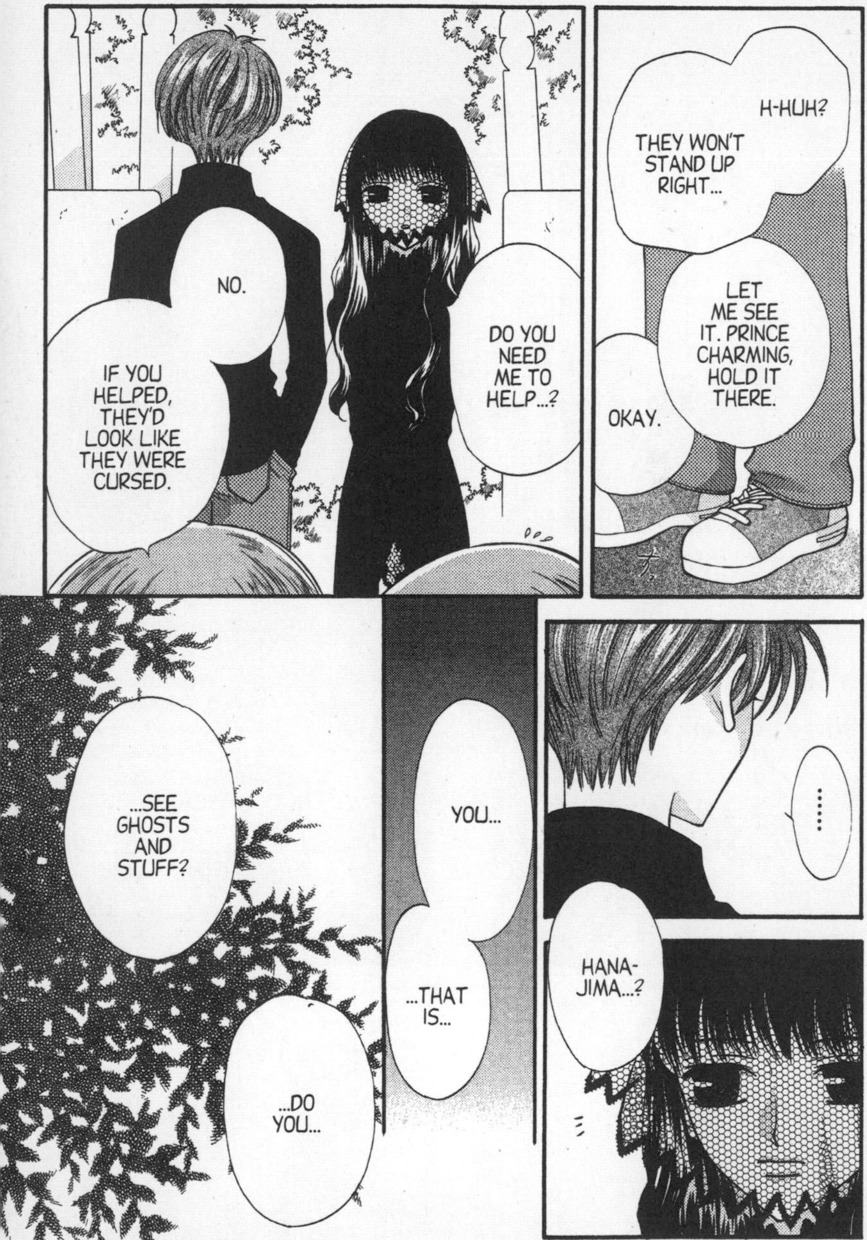
H-HUH?
THEY WON'T STAND UP RIGHT...
LET ME SEE IT. PRINCE CHARMING, HOLD IT THERE.
OKAY.
DO YOU NEED ME TO HELP...?
NO.
IF YOU HELPED, THEY'D LOOK LIKE THEY WERE CURSED.
......
HANA-JIMA...?
YOU...
...THAT IS...
...DO YOU...
...SEE GHOSTS AND STUFF?

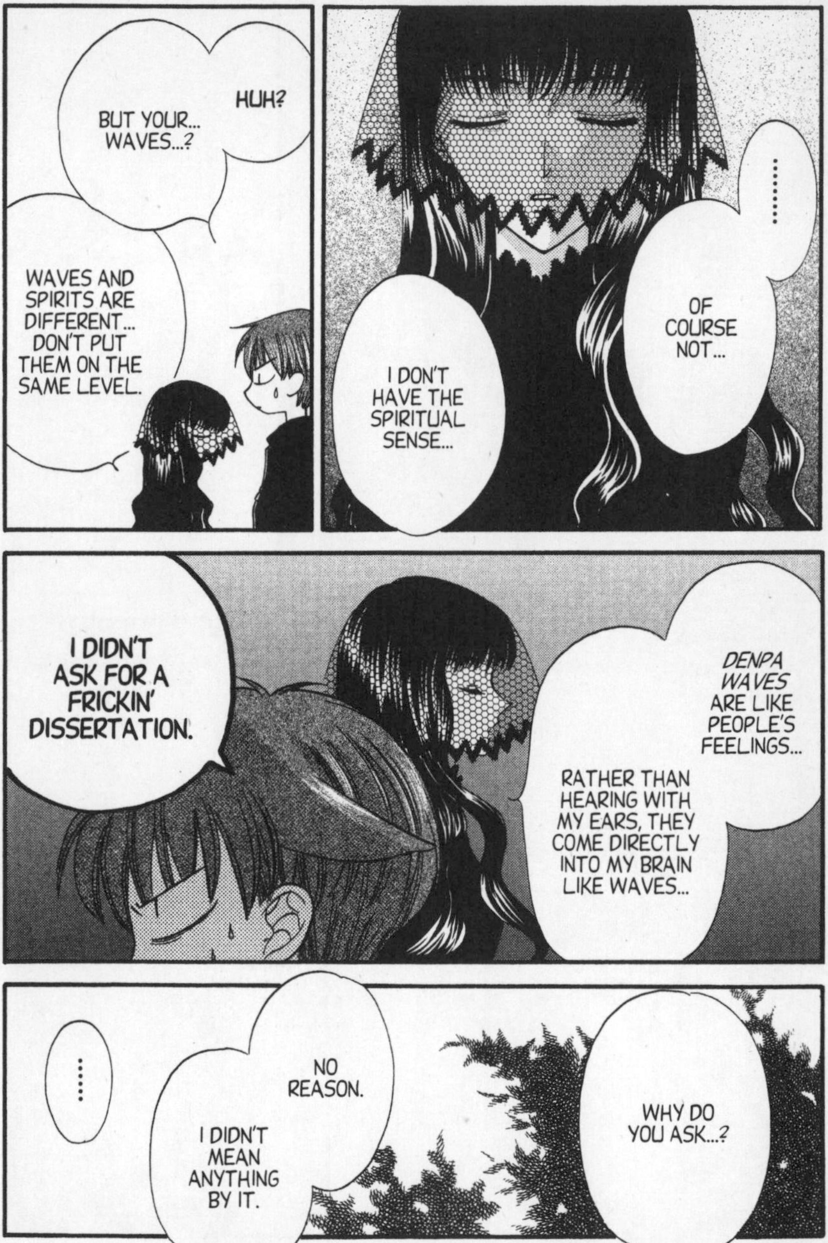

……
OF COURSE NOT...
I DON'T HAVE THE SPIRITUAL SENSE...
HUH?
BUT YOUR... WAVES...?
WAVES AND SPIRITS ARE DIFFERENT... DON'T PUT THEM ON THE SAME LEVEL.
DENPA WAVES ARE LIKE PEOPLE'S FEELINGS...
RATHER THAN HEARING WITH MY EARS, THEY COME DIRECTLY INTO MY BRAIN LIKE WAVES...
I DIDN'T ASK FOR A FRICKIN' DISSERTATION.
WHY DO YOU ASK...?
NO REASON.
I DIDN'T MEAN ANYTHING BY IT.
……

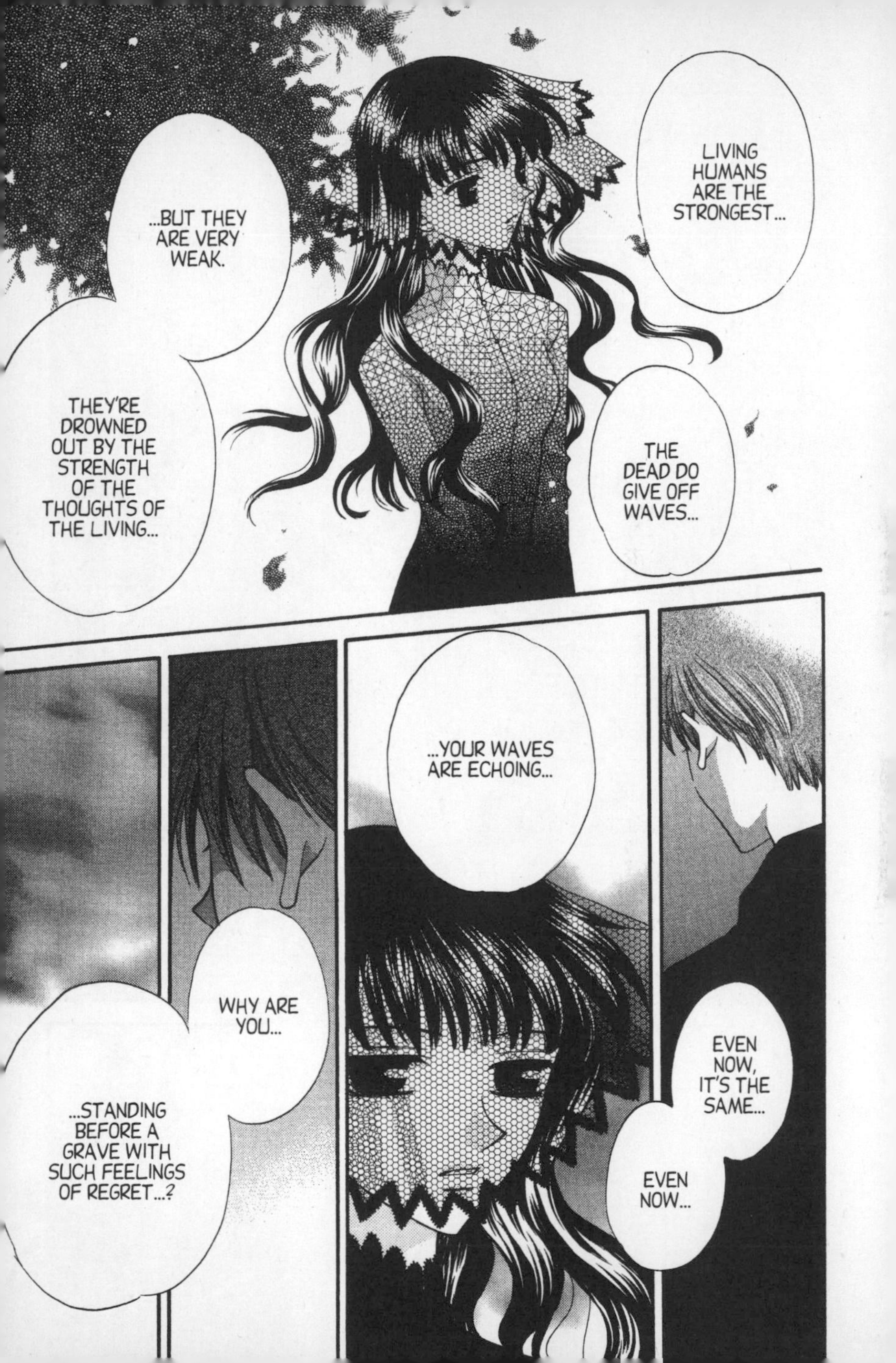
LIVING HUMANS ARE THE STRONGEST...
THE DEAD DO GIVE OFF WAVES...
...BUT THEY ARE VERY WEAK.
THEY'RE DROWNED OUT BY THE STRENGTH OF THE THOUGHTS OF THE LIVING...
...YOUR WAVES ARE ECHOING...
EVEN NOW, IT'S THE SAME...
EVEN NOW...
WHY ARE YOU...
...STANDING BEFORE A GRAVE WITH SUCH FEELINGS OF REGRET...?

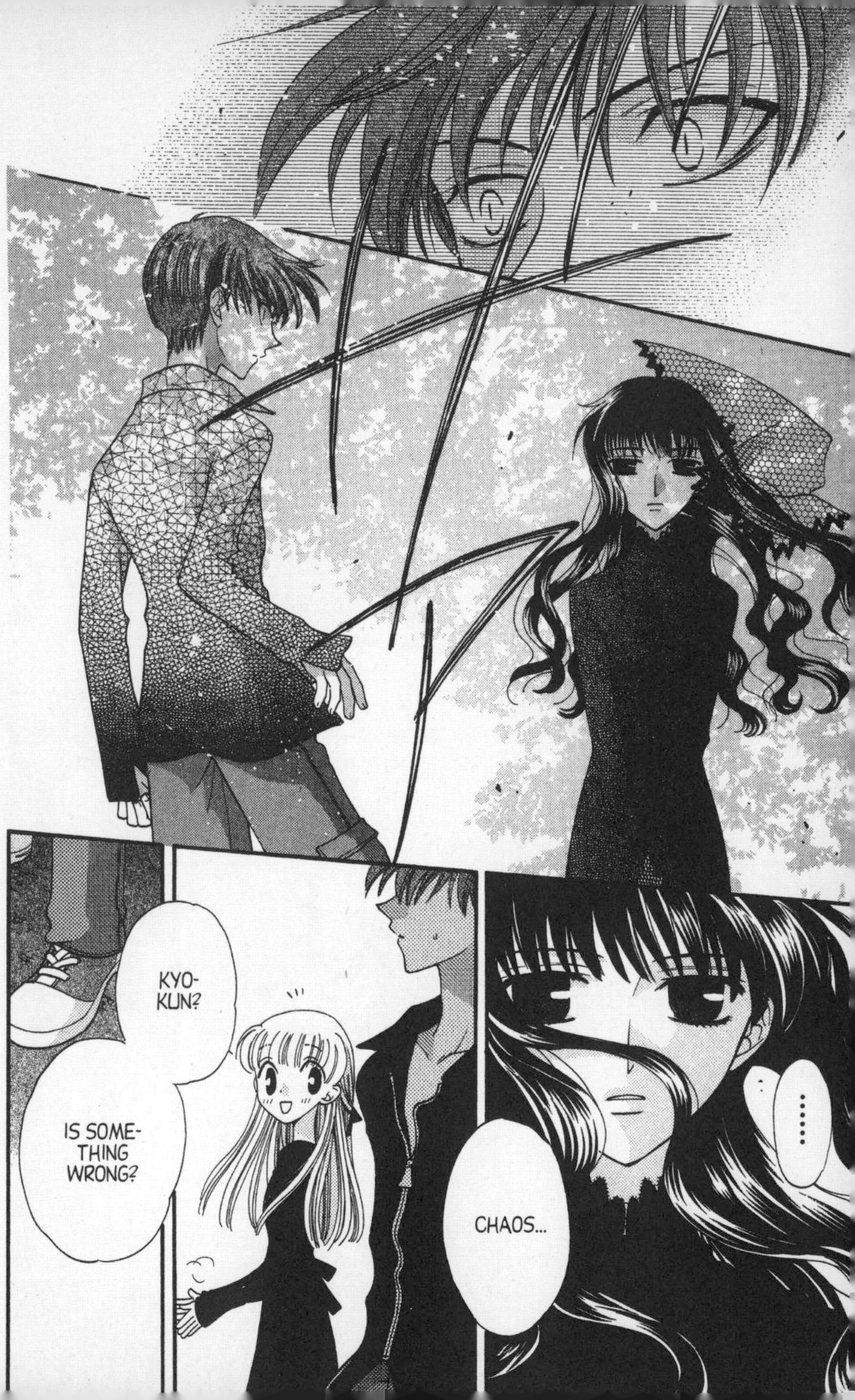

......
CHAOS...
KYO-KUN?
IS SOMETHING WRONG?

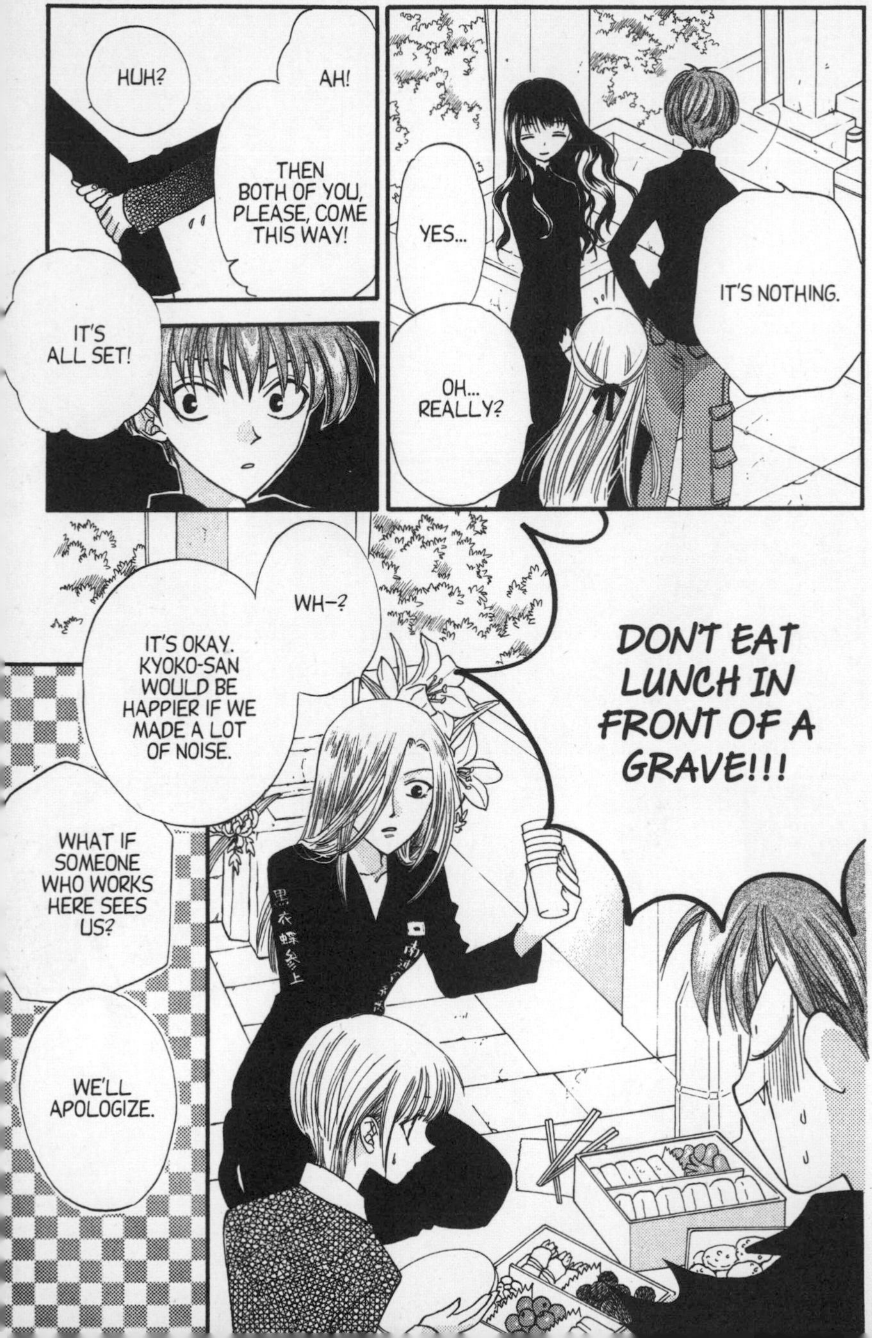
IT'S NOTHING.
YES...
OH... REALLY?
AH!
THEN BOTH OF YOU, PLEASE, COME THIS WAY!
HUH?
IT'S ALL SET!
DON'T EAT LUNCH IN FRONT OF A GRAVE!!!
WH-?
IT'S OKAY. KYOKO-SAN WOULD BE HAPPIER IF WE MADE A LOT OF NOISE.
WHAT IF SOMEONE WHO WORKS HERE SEES US?
WE'LL APOLOGIZE.

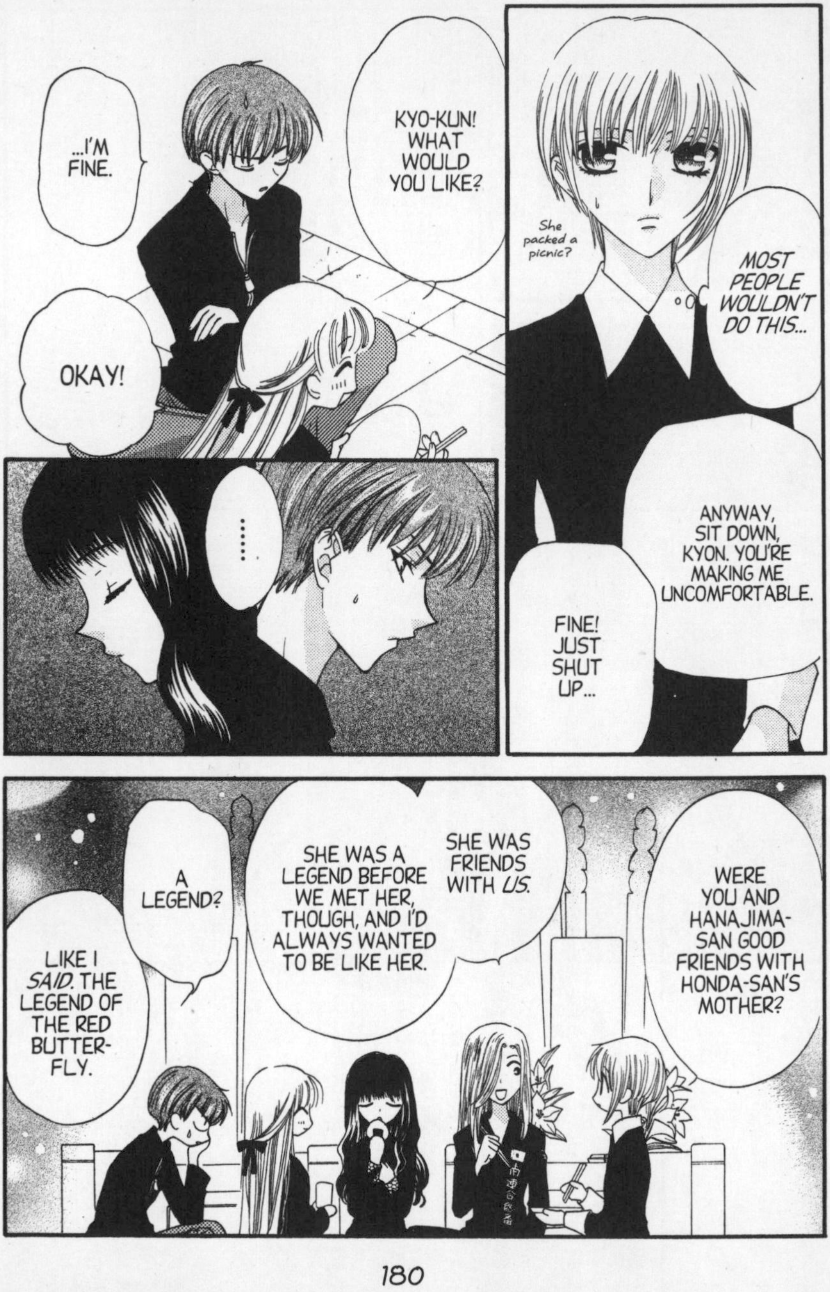
She packed a picnic?
MOST PEOPLE WOULDN'T DO THIS...
ANYWAY, SIT DOWN, KYON. YOU'RE MAKING ME UNCOMFORTABLE.
FINE! JUST SHUT UP...
KYO-KUN! WHAT WOULD YOU LIKE?
...I'M FINE.
OKAY!
......
WERE YOU AND HANAJIMA-SAN GOOD FRIENDS WITH HONDA-SAN'S MOTHER?
SHE WAS FRIENDS WITH *US*.
SHE WAS A LEGEND BEFORE WE MET HER, THOUGH, AND I'D ALWAYS WANTED TO BE LIKE HER.
A LEGEND?
LIKE I *SAID*. THE LEGEND OF THE RED BUTTERFLY.

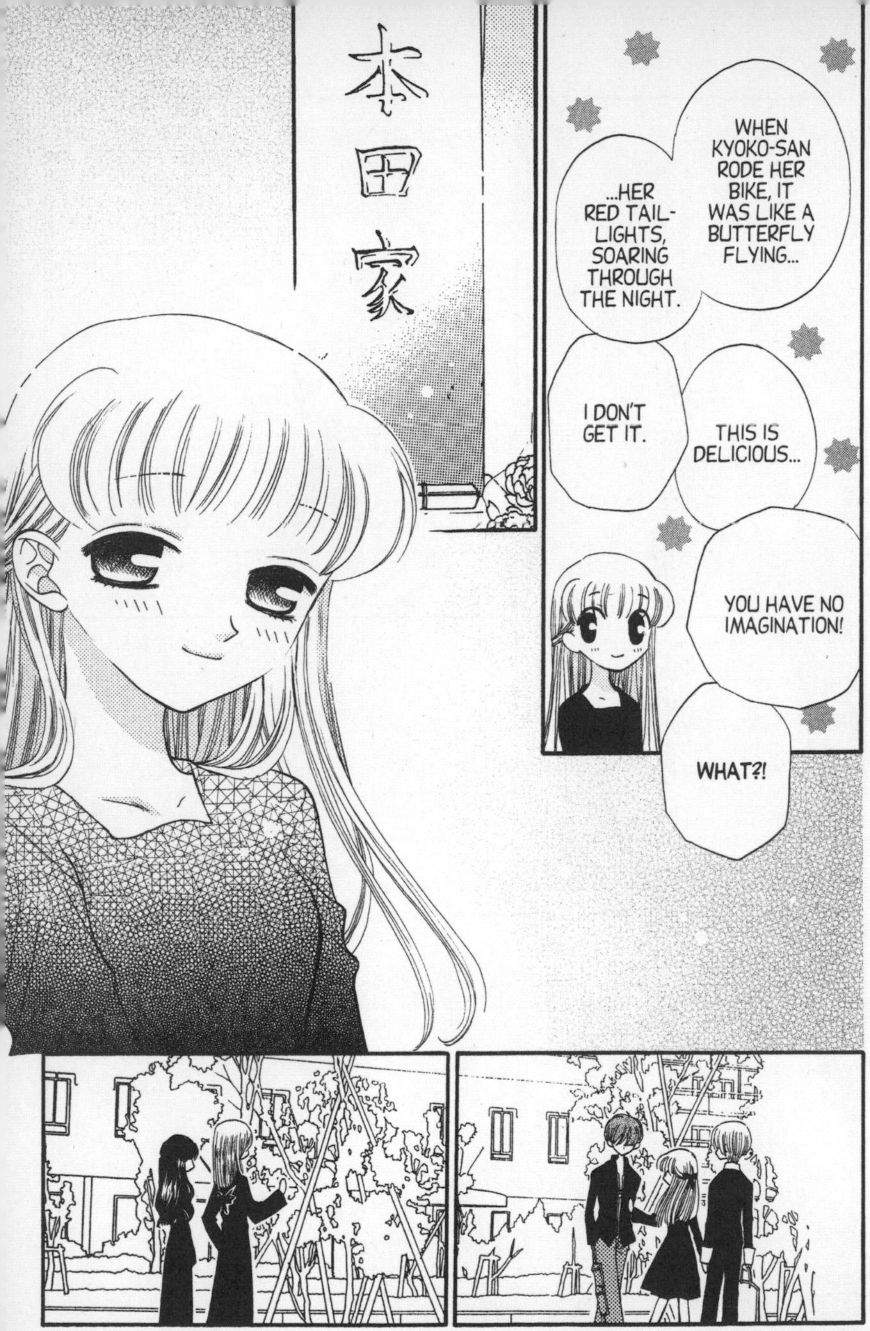
WHEN KYOKO-SAN RODE HER BIKE, IT WAS LIKE A BUTTERFLY FLYING...
...HER RED TAIL-LIGHTS, SOARING THROUGH THE NIGHT.
THIS IS DELICIOUS...
I DON'T GET IT.
YOU HAVE NO IMAGINATION!
WHAT?!
本田家

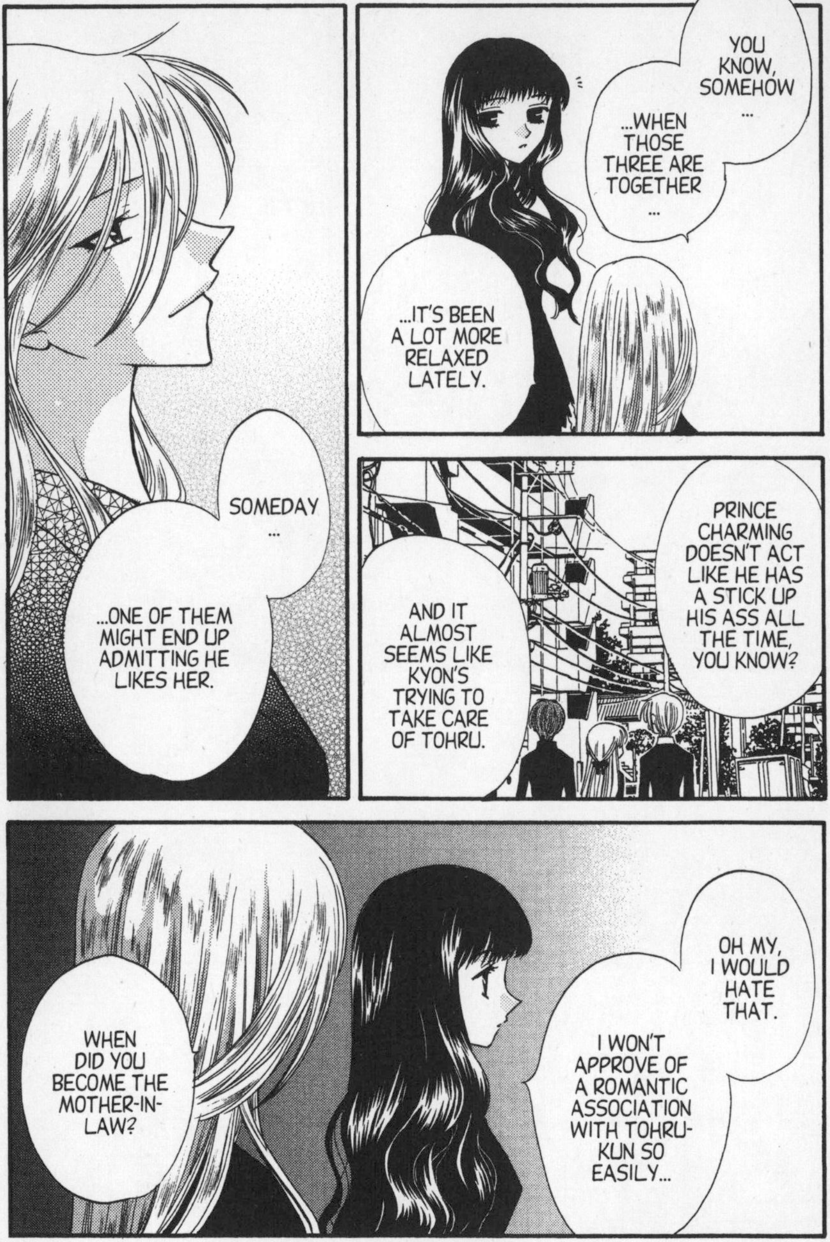
YOU KNOW, SOMEHOW...
...WHEN THOSE THREE ARE TOGETHER...
...IT'S BEEN A LOT MORE RELAXED LATELY.
PRINCE CHARMING DOESN'T ACT LIKE HE HAS A STICK UP HIS ASS ALL THE TIME, YOU KNOW?
AND IT ALMOST SEEMS LIKE KYON'S TRYING TO TAKE CARE OF TOHRU.
SOMEDAY...
...ONE OF THEM MIGHT END UP ADMITTING HE LIKES HER.
OH MY, I WOULD HATE THAT.
I WON'T APPROVE OF A ROMANTIC ASSOCIATION WITH TOHRU-KUN SO EASILY...
WHEN DID YOU BECOME THE MOTHER-IN-LAW?

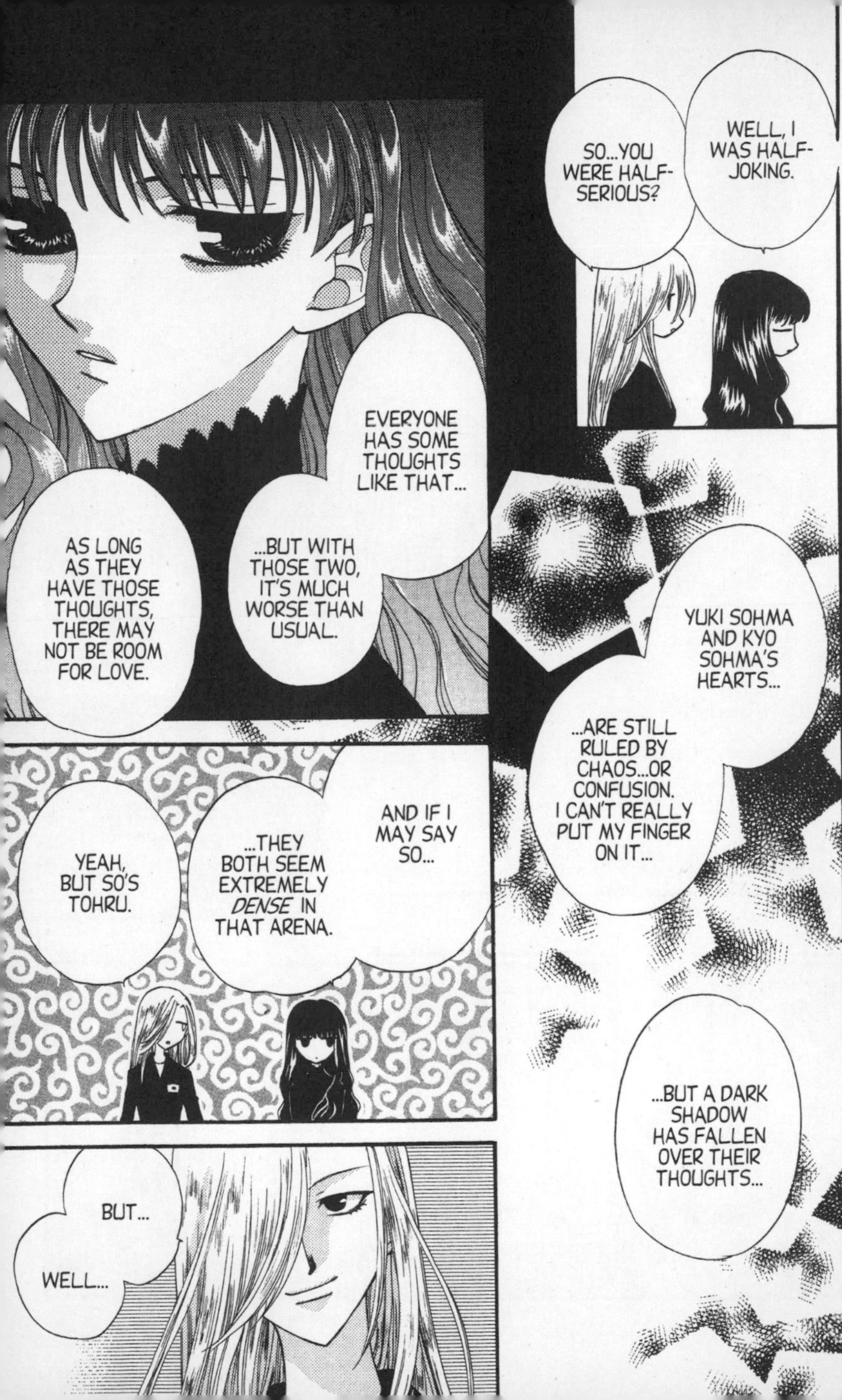
WELL, I WAS HALF-JOKING.
SO...YOU WERE HALF-SERIOUS?
YUKI SOHMA AND KYO SOHMA'S HEARTS...
...ARE STILL RULED BY CHAOS...OR CONFUSION. I CAN'T REALLY PUT MY FINGER ON IT...
...BUT A DARK SHADOW HAS FALLEN OVER THEIR THOUGHTS...
EVERYONE HAS SOME THOUGHTS LIKE THAT...
...BUT WITH THOSE TWO, IT'S MUCH WORSE THAN USUAL.
AS LONG AS THEY HAVE THOSE THOUGHTS, THERE MAY NOT BE ROOM FOR LOVE.
AND IF I MAY SAY SO...
...THEY BOTH SEEM EXTREMELY *DENSE* IN THAT ARENA.
YEAH, BUT SO'S TOHRU.
BUT...
WELL...

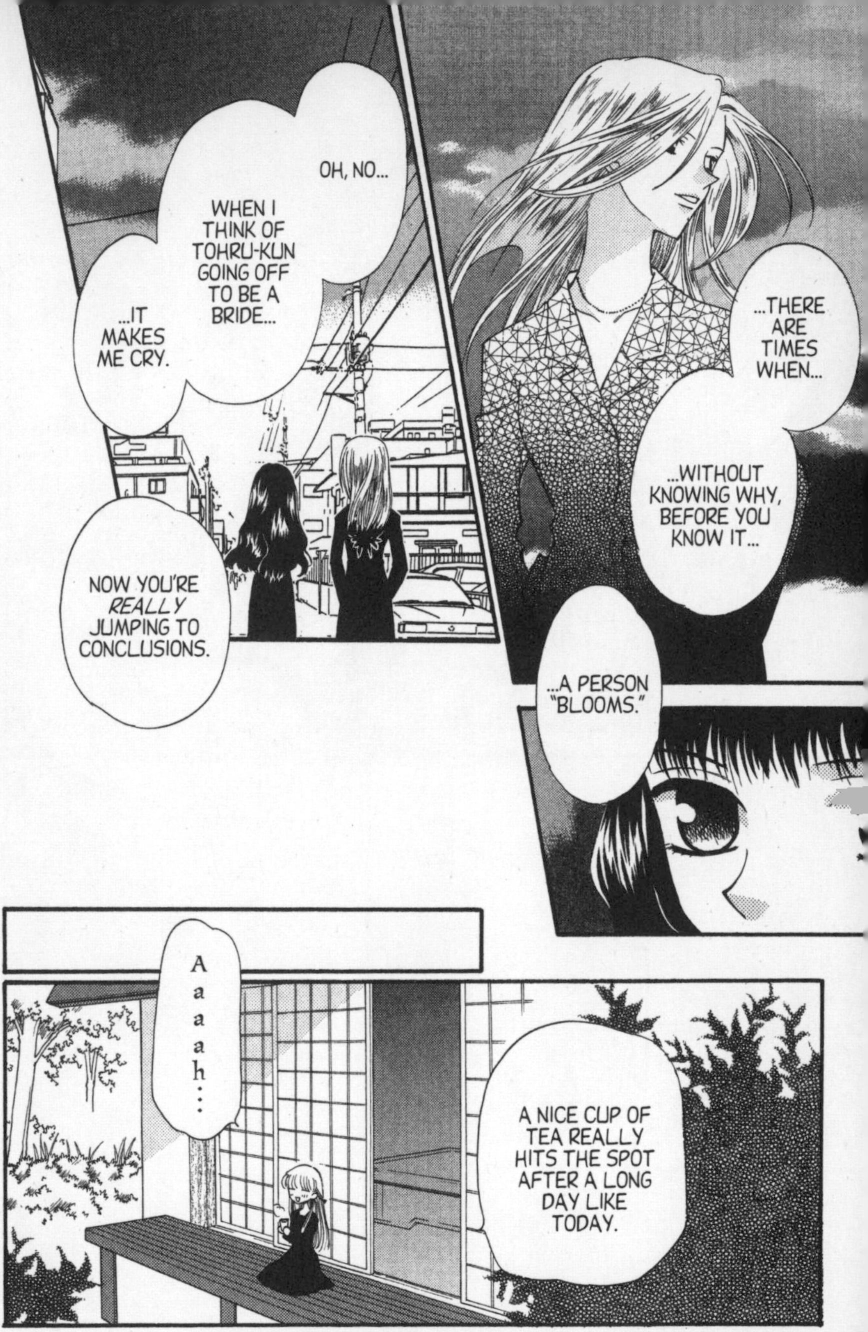
...THERE ARE TIMES WHEN...
...WITHOUT KNOWING WHY, BEFORE YOU KNOW IT...
...A PERSON "BLOOMS."
OH, NO...
WHEN I THINK OF TOHRU-KUN GOING OFF TO BE A BRIDE...
...IT MAKES ME CRY.
NOW YOU'RE *REALLY* JUMPING TO CONCLUSIONS.
Aaaah...
A NICE CUP OF TEA REALLY HITS THE SPOT AFTER A LONG DAY LIKE TODAY.

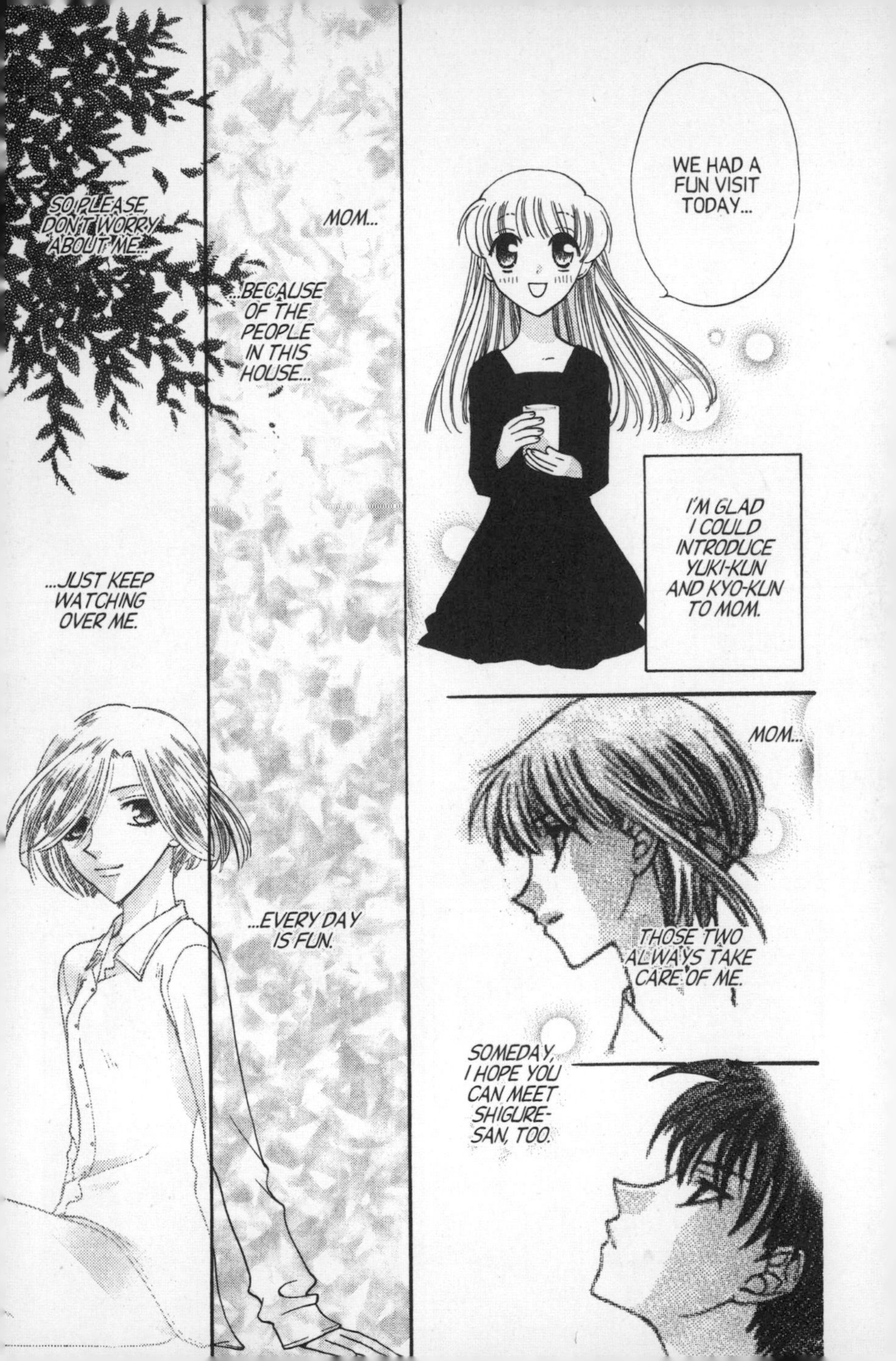
WE HAD A FUN VISIT TODAY...
I'M GLAD I COULD INTRODUCE YUKI-KUN AND KYO-KUN TO MOM.
MOM...
THOSE TWO ALWAYS TAKE CARE OF ME.
SOMEDAY, I HOPE YOU CAN MEET SHIGURE-SAN, TOO.
MOM...
...BECAUSE OF THE PEOPLE IN THIS HOUSE...
...EVERY DAY IS FUN.
SO PLEASE, DON'T WORRY ABOUT ME...
...JUST KEEP WATCHING OVER ME.

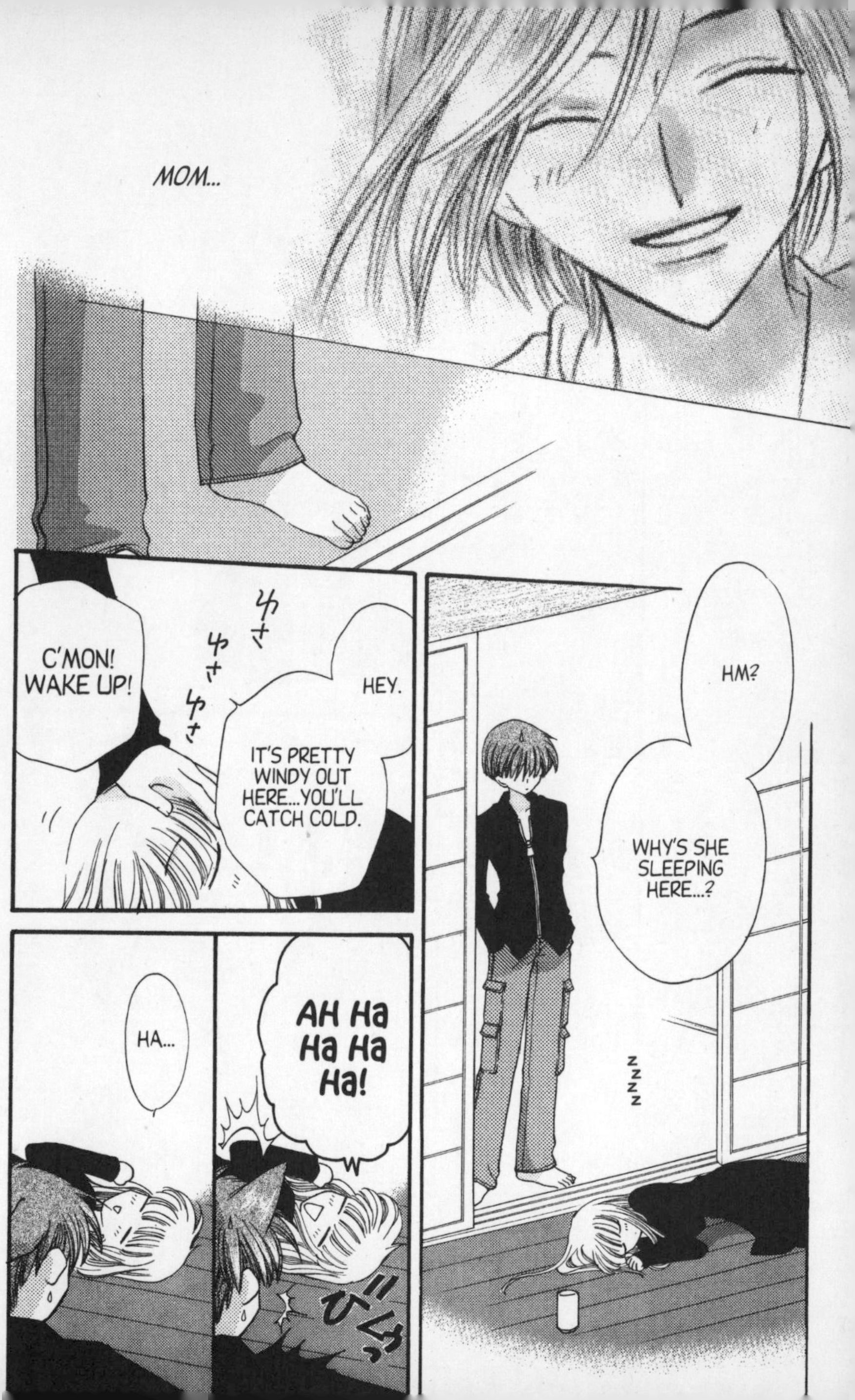
MOM...
HM?
WHY'S SHE SLEEPING HERE...?
ZZZZ
HEY.
IT'S PRETTY WINDY OUT HERE...YOU'LL CATCH COLD.
ゆさ ゆさ ゆさ
C'MON! WAKE UP!
AH Ha Ha Ha Ha!
ひくっ
HA...

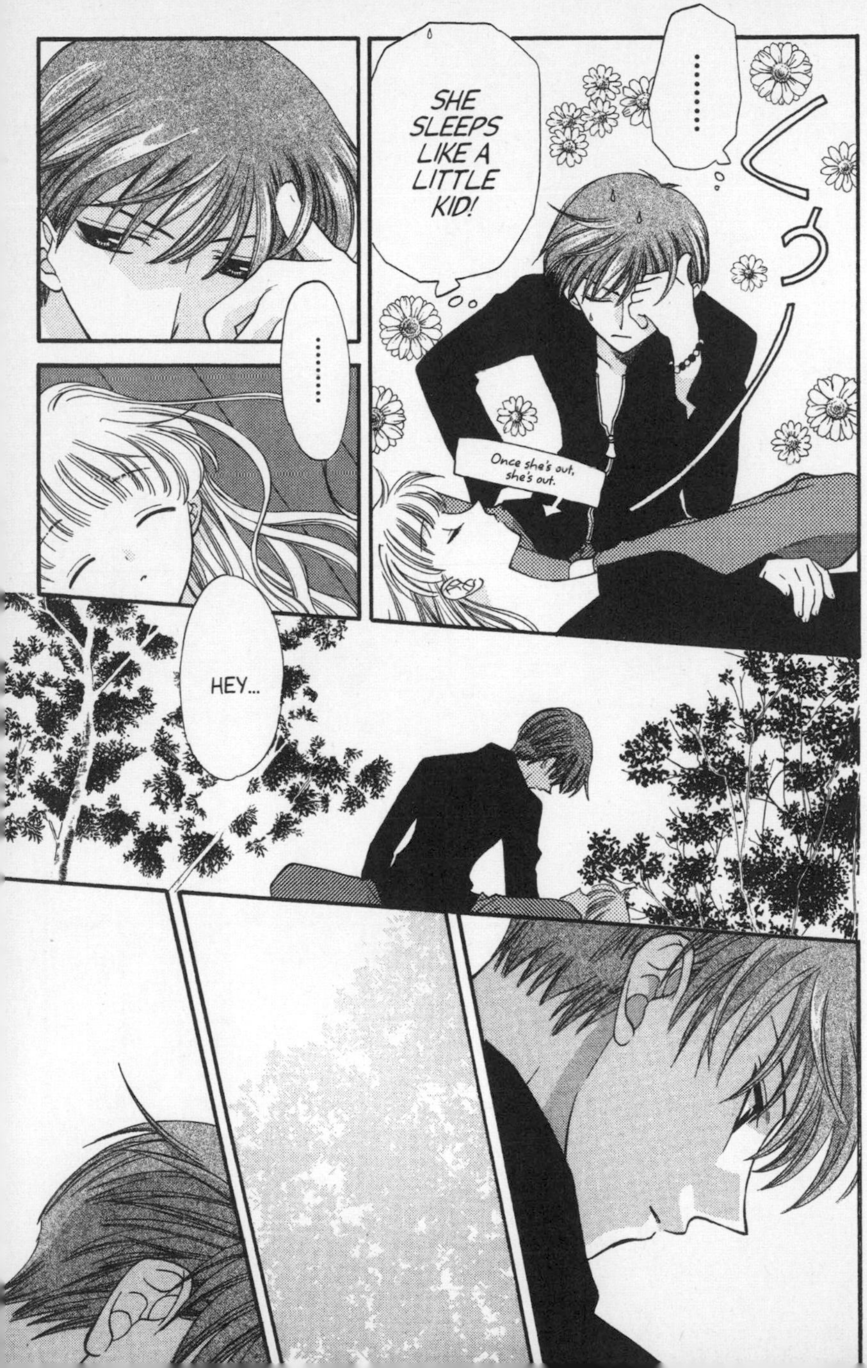
......
SHE SLEEPS LIKE A LITTLE KID!
くぅ
Once she's out, she's out.
......
HEY...

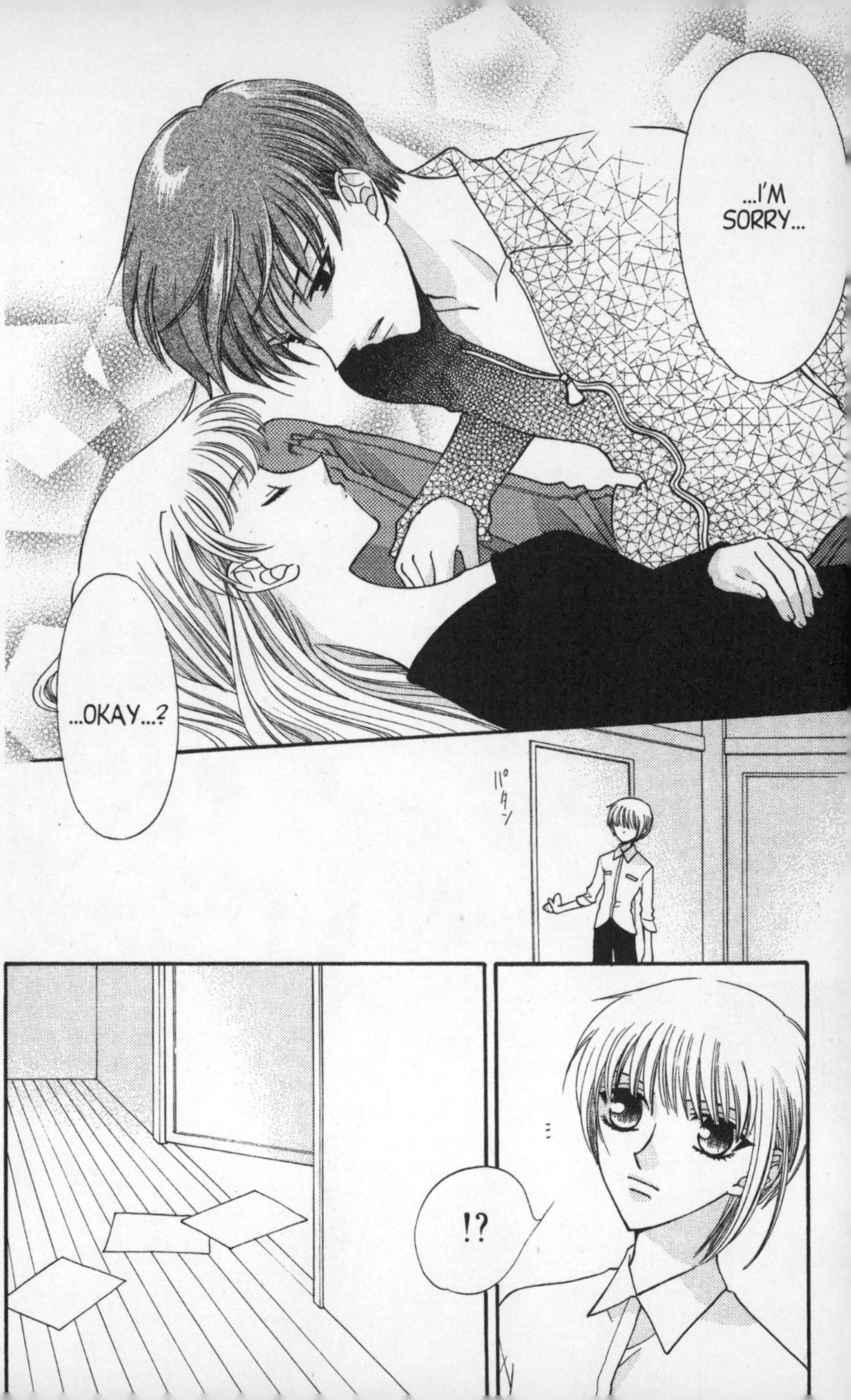
...I'M SORRY...
...OKAY...?
パタン
!?

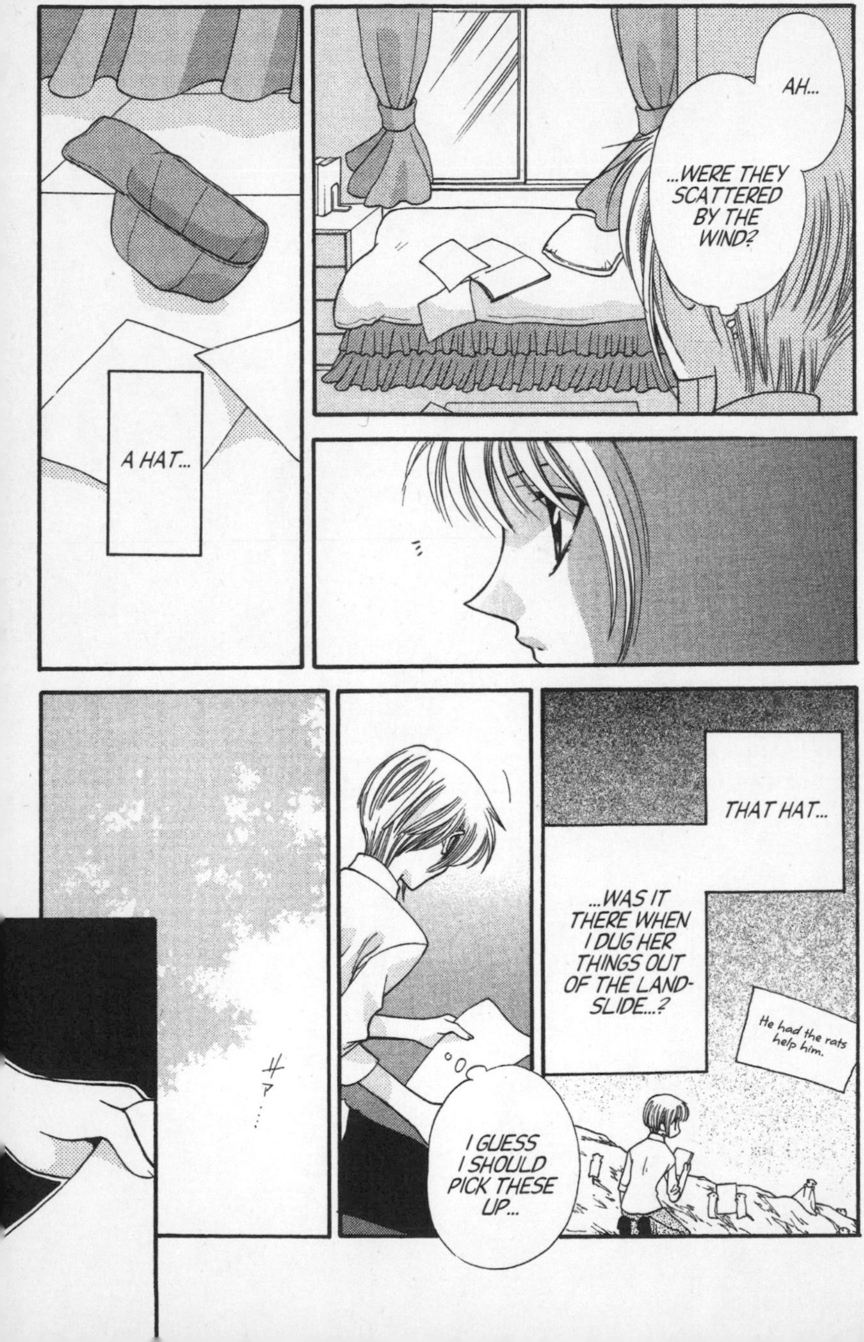
AH...
...WERE THEY SCATTERED BY THE WIND?
A HAT...
THAT HAT...
...WAS IT THERE WHEN I DUG HER THINGS OUT OF THE LAND-SLIDE...?
He had the rats help him.
I GUESS I SHOULD PICK THESE UP...

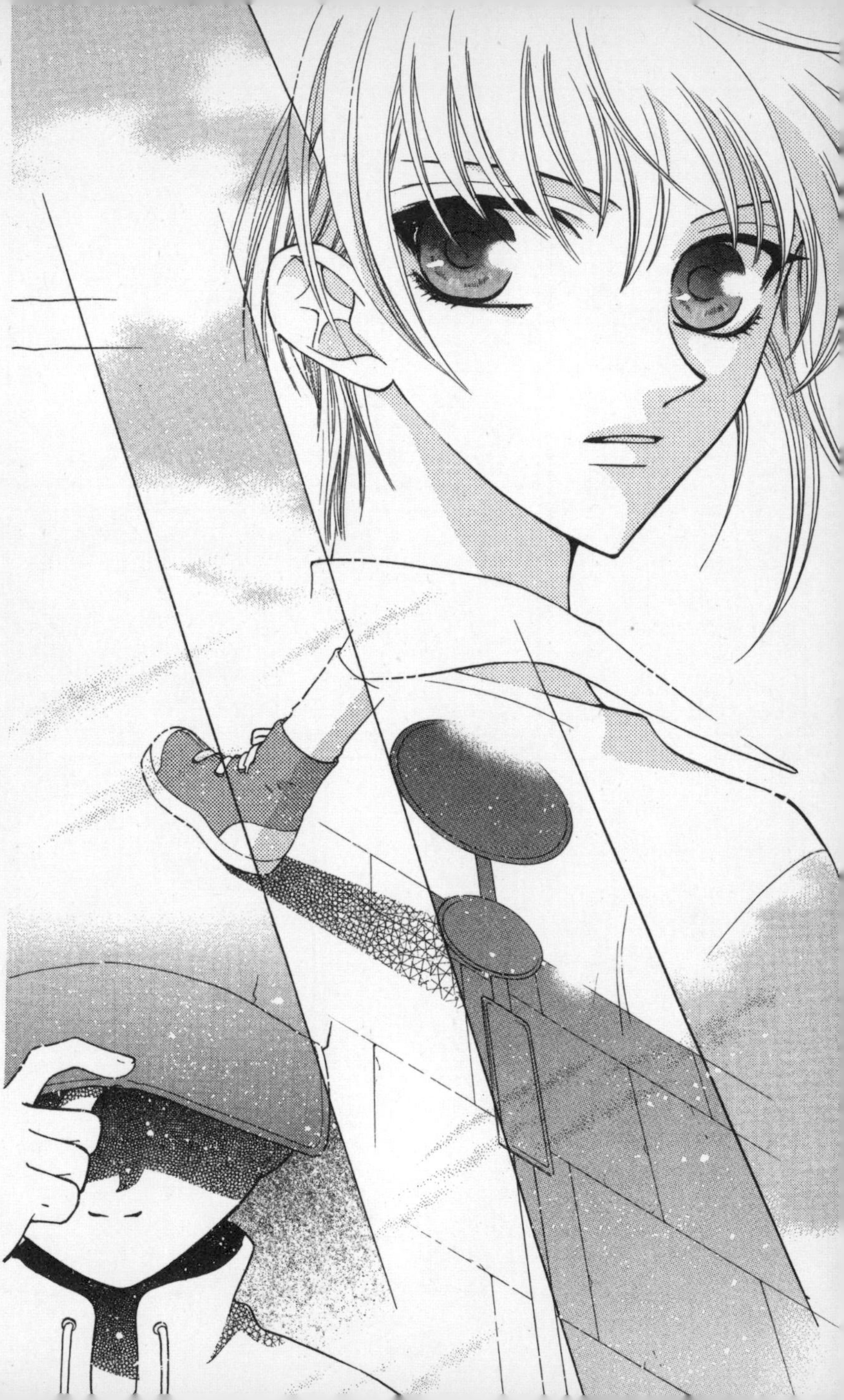

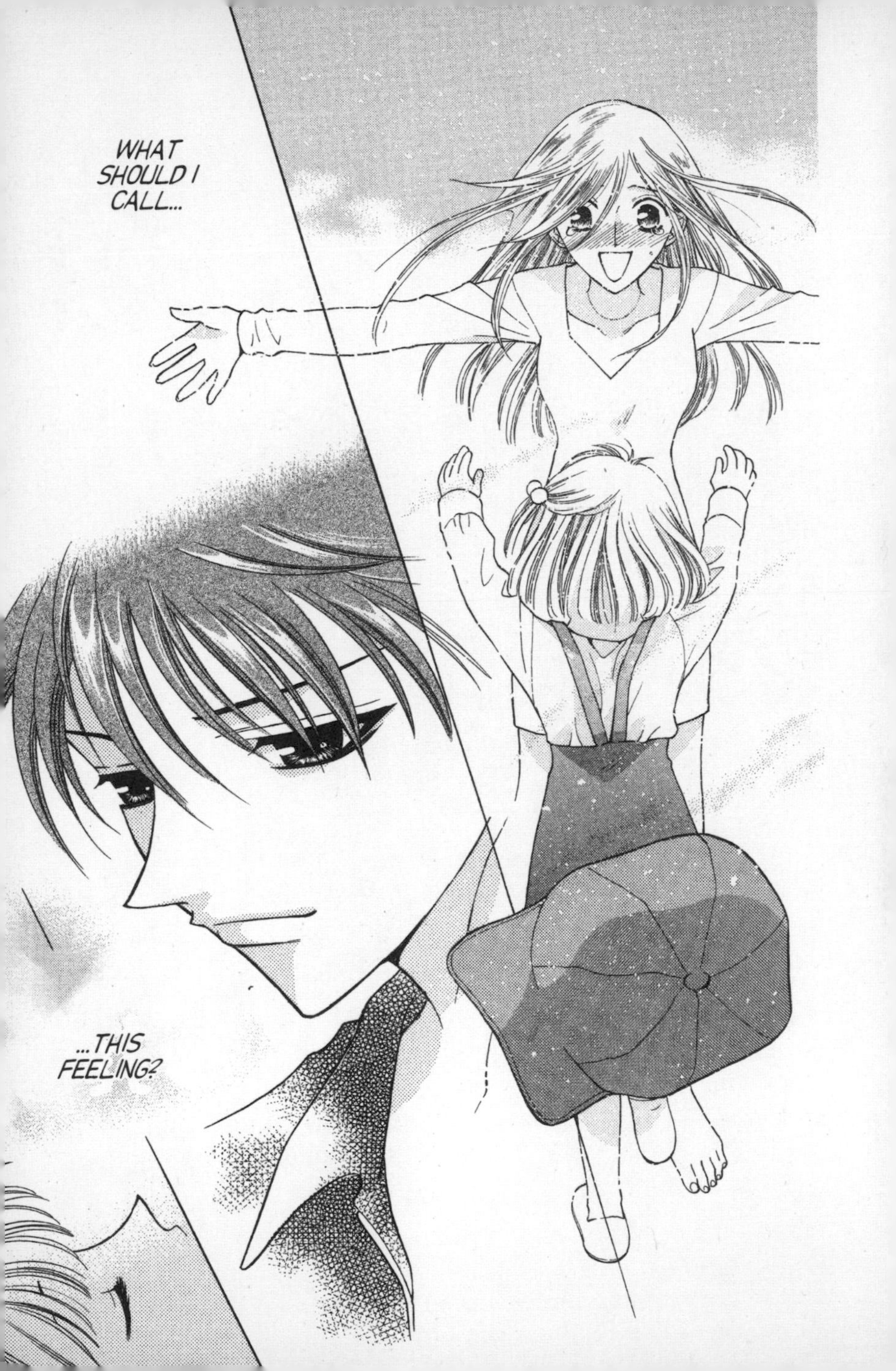
WHAT SHOULD I CALL...
...THIS FEELING?

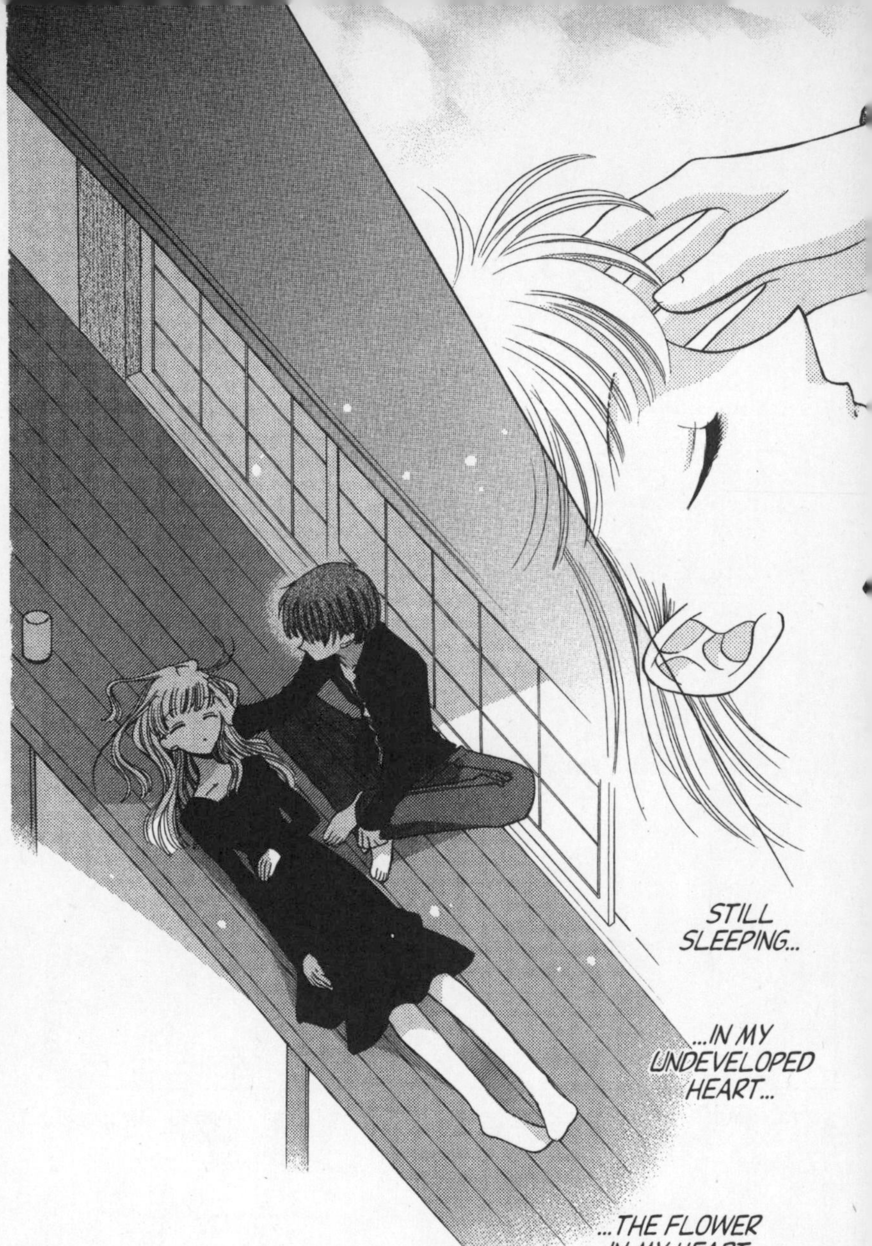
STILL SLEEPING...
...IN MY UNDEVELOPED HEART...
...THE FLOWER IN MY HEART.

To be continued in volume 4...

BONUS CHAPTER

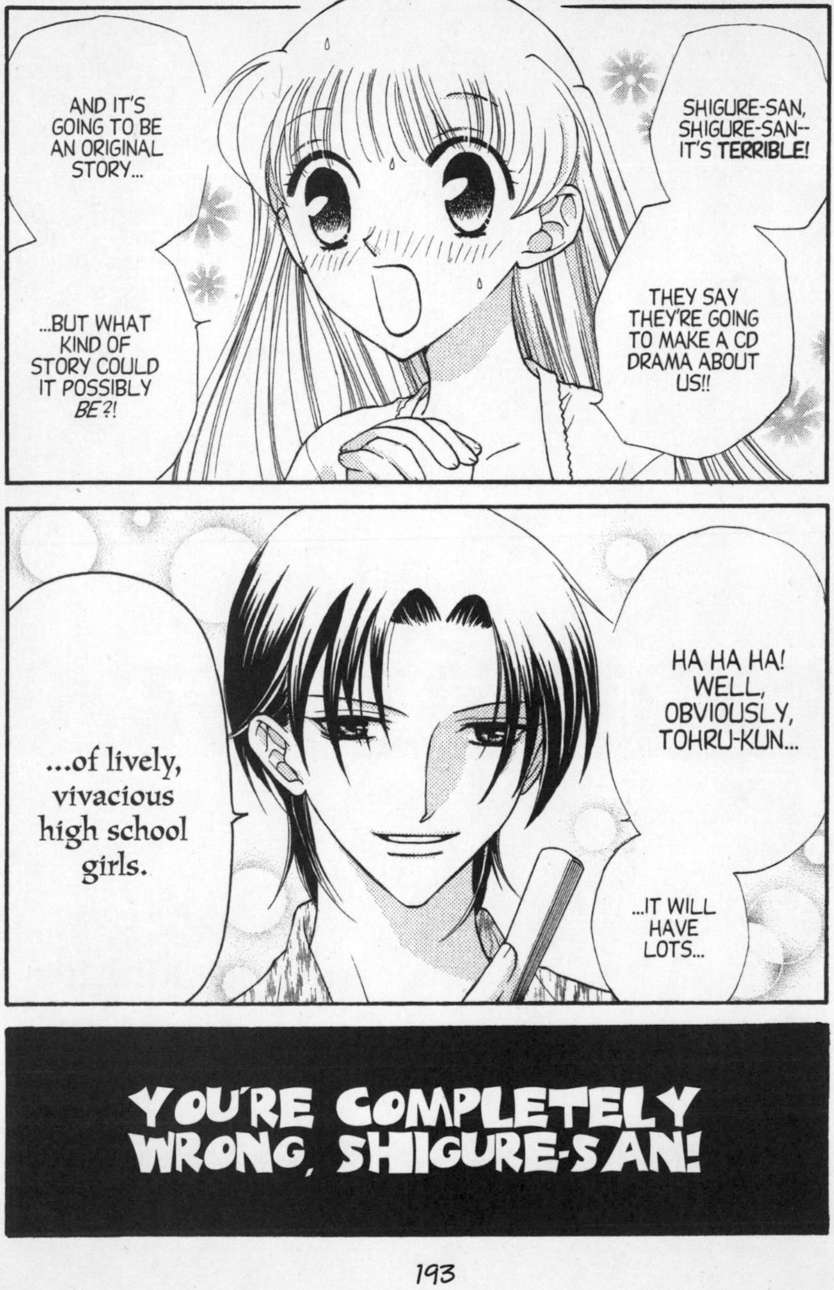
SHIGURE-SAN, SHIGURE-SAN-- IT'S **TERRIBLE!**
THEY SAY THEY'RE GOING TO MAKE A CD DRAMA ABOUT US!!
AND IT'S GOING TO BE AN ORIGINAL STORY...
...BUT WHAT KIND OF STORY COULD IT POSSIBLY *BE*?!
HA HA HA! WELL, OBVIOUSLY, TOHRU-KUN...
...IT WILL HAVE LOTS...
...of lively, vivacious high school girls.

YOU'RE COMPLETELY WRONG, SHIGURE-SAN!

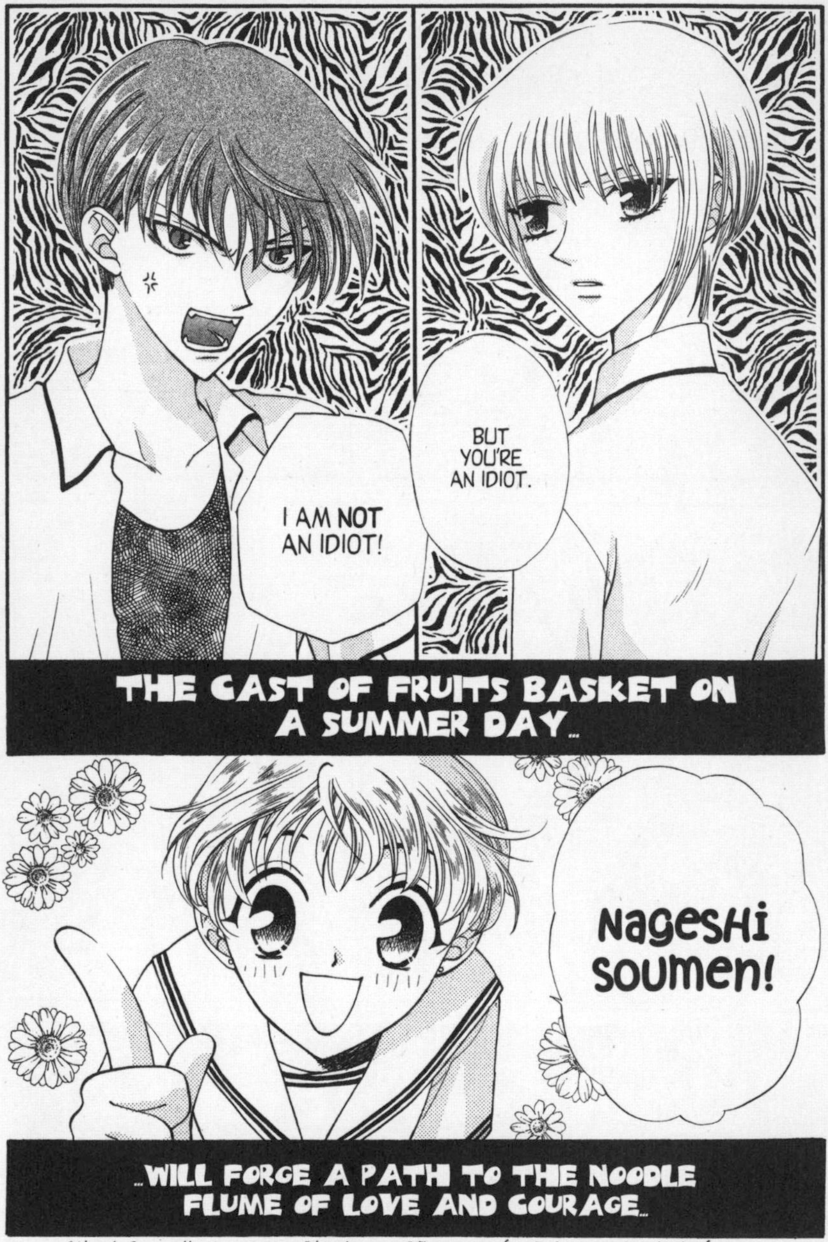
BUT YOU'RE AN IDIOT.
I AM NOT AN IDIOT!
THE CAST OF FRUITS BASKET ON A SUMMER DAY...
NAGESHI SOUMEN!
...WILL FORGE A PATH TO THE NOODLE FLUME OF LOVE AND COURAGE...

* Nageshi Soumen: Momiji means to say "Nagashi soumen." This is a type of noodle that is served in a bamboo flume. As the noodles flow down the flume, diners pick them out with chopsticks.

...AND DISAPPOINTMENT!

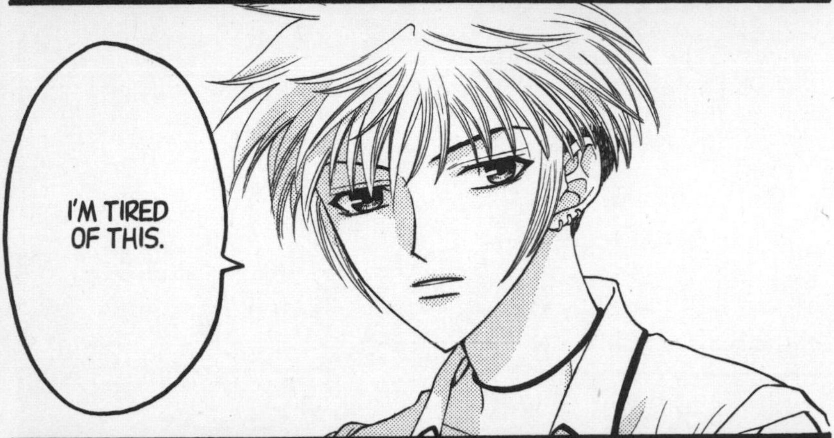
I'M TIRED OF THIS.

WELL, IT WILL BE...AND IT WON'T BE!

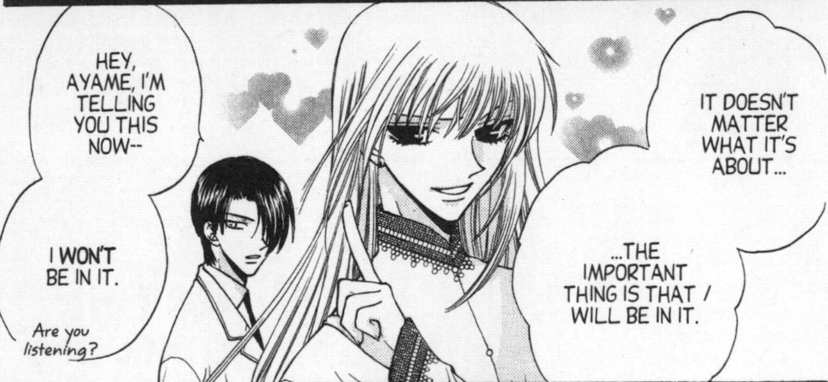
IT DOESN'T MATTER WHAT IT'S ABOUT...
...THE IMPORTANT THING IS THAT *I* WILL BE IN IT.
HEY, AYAME, I'M TELLING YOU THIS NOW--
I WON'T BE IN IT.
Are you listening?

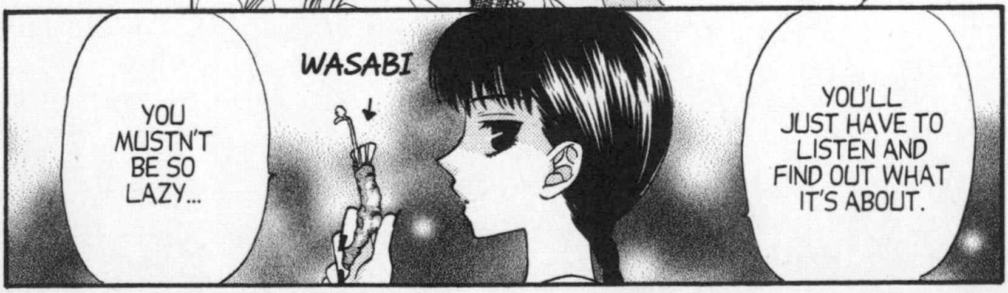
YOU'LL JUST HAVE TO LISTEN AND FIND OUT WHAT IT'S ABOUT.
WASABI
YOU MUSTN'T BE SO LAZY...

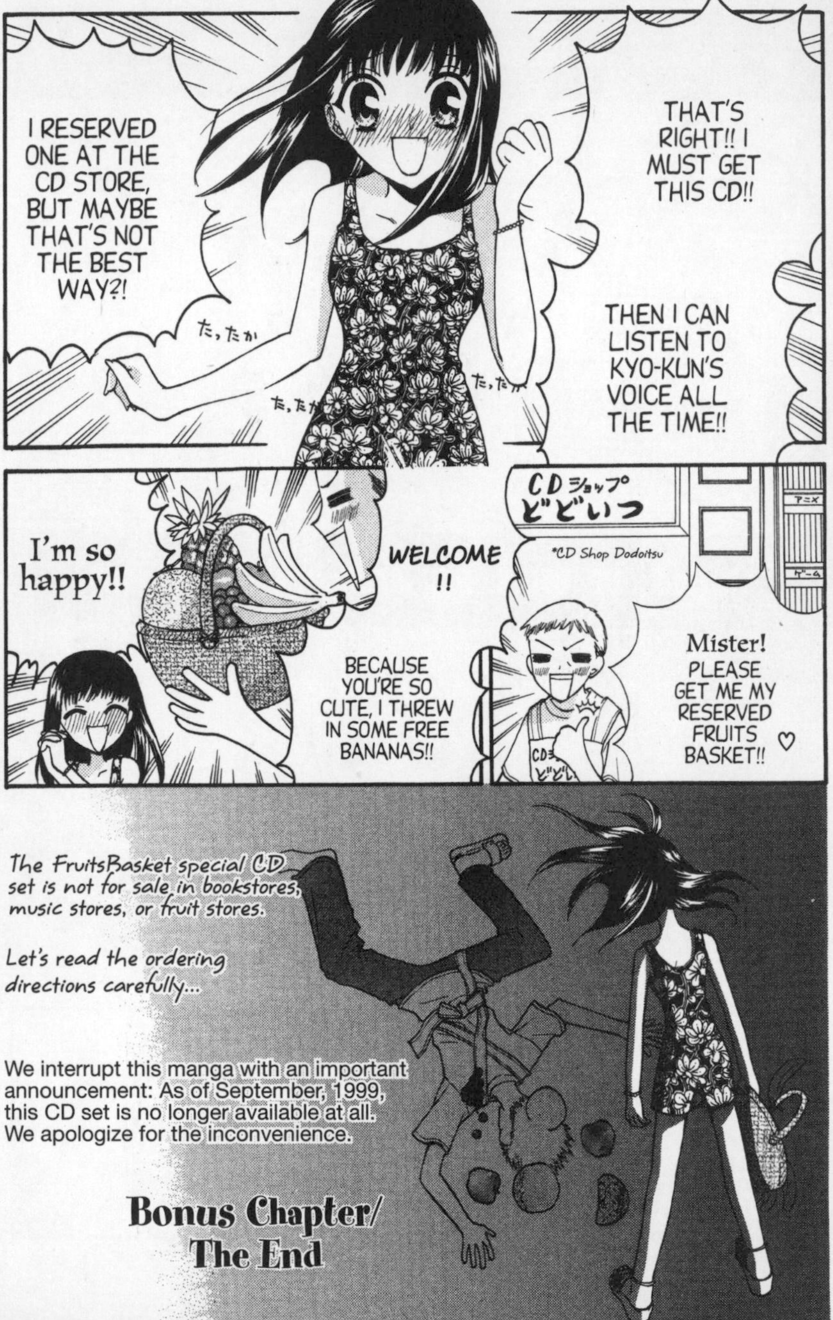
THAT'S RIGHT!! I MUST GET THIS CD!!
THEN I CAN LISTEN TO KYO-KUN'S VOICE ALL THE TIME!!
I RESERVED ONE AT THE CD STORE, BUT MAYBE THAT'S NOT THE BEST WAY?!
たったか
たったか
たったか
CDショップ どどいつ
*CD Shop Dodoitsu
アニメ
ゲーム
Mister! PLEASE GET ME MY RESERVED FRUITS BASKET!! ♡
WELCOME !!
BECAUSE YOU'RE SO CUTE, I THREW IN SOME FREE BANANAS!!
I'm so happy!!
The FruitsBasket special CD set is not for sale in bookstores, music stores, or fruit stores.
Let's read the ordering directions carefully...
We interrupt this manga with an important announcement: As of September, 1999, this CD set is no longer available at all. We apologize for the inconvenience.
Bonus Chapter/ The End

Next time in...

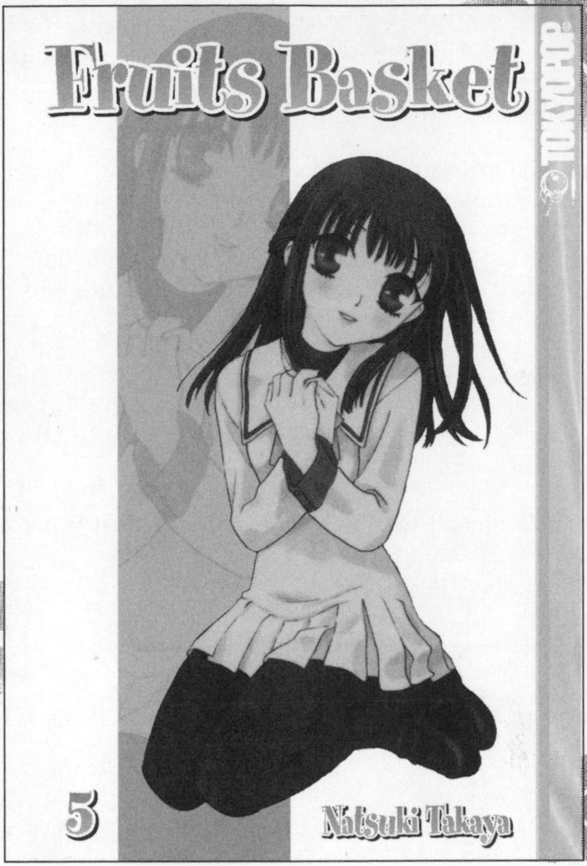
Fruits Basket
TOKYOPOP
5
Natsuki Takaya

Enter the Tiger...

The Sohma household takes to the lake for a vacation at their summer-house. However, the peaceful silence is deafening, as Yuki and Kyo are once again not on speaking terms. Will Tohru's klutzy kindness get the dueling duo back to their old cat-and-mouse antics once again?

Fruits Basket Volume 5
Available October 2004

Interview with Takaya-sensei
Part 2

About Takaya-sensei's Hobbies

9) What kind of music and musical artists do you like?
Lately I've been listening to a lot of video game music. Songs, too. I like Nematsu-san and Hikaruda-san's music. I like how the video game music perfectly matches the world in the game. That's wonderful, but when I listen to the battle music it makes me want to fight, so sometimes I do and that gets me in trouble (ha ha!).

10) What movies and TV shows do you like?
These are old movies but…*Field of Dreams* and *Laputa: Castle in the Sky.* I don't watch much TV. Sometimes I think I should watch, but…It just gets in the way, like when I need to be working on my manga.

11) You often talk about video games in your freetalks. What type of games do you like?
I pretty much like any type of game, but I'm never very good at action ones.

Character sketches for Tsubasa o Motsumono

Character sketches for Gen`eimusou`

12) Do you have a favorite game to recommend?
I like so many that it's hard to name just one. I'd recommend the *Sakura Taisen* series—that's really fun.

13) What do you think makes a good game?
I like it when games do stuff manga can't. Just like how there's stuff you can only do in manga, there are things you can only do in video games. I think games where you really feel it's a "game" are best.

14) Are there any game characters you really like?
I really love cute and strong girls with a bit of a dark side. I have more trouble finding male characters I like.

15) Do you work on your webpage "Chotto Ippuku"(A Short Break) by yourself?
Yes, I do it myself. That's why it's never updated…
[editor's note: Her website is no longer active.]

16) What was the hardest part about making a webpage?
Hmm… Well, it was tough when I first started because I had nobody I could discuss things with. Those were rough times, but now I have a lot of friends who can help me out.

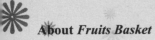

About *Fruits Basket*

17) When and how did you come up with *Fruits Basket*?
I was slowly working on it in my mind as I was finishing up my last series, *Tsubasa wo motsu mono* (*Those with Wings*). But all the final details didn't come together until after "*Boku ga utauto anata ga warau kara*," (*Because When I Sing You Smile*) a one-shot I did before *Furuba* started. I kept thinking there wasn't enough time, but it all came to me inside my head. Tohru just appeared and said "Hello!" The rest came together pretty easily after that.

18) Were there any other title possibilities besides *Fruits Basket*?
There kind of were... Though I'm happy I chose *Fruits Basket*, it's easy to say and remember.

19) Why did you choose the Zodiac animals as a motif?
Basically, I like them a lot and assumed everyone else would, too. Japanese culture is captivating, right?

20) What's the most important thing when creating the plot or doing the rough sketches?
The pacing and dialog, and of course whether it's fun to read. You can't forget what's at the heart of making a reader laugh or cry.

21) In the works you do, the story and tone are often different, but they seem to share an underlying theme. What's your theme?
I'm happy to hear that, thank you very much. As long as I'm creating it, I don't think the underlying theme will ever change. (Actually, if it changed, then there would be no point...) But I don't think the theme needs to be put into *words*. It's something that the reader experiences for themselves. At least, that's my company line, but sometimes I think I'd like to be able to express it in words. (ha ha!)

Read the rest of the interview with Takaya-sensei in Volume 5!

Year of the Dog: Letting the Dogs Out

Dog

Years*: 1934, 1946, 1958, 1970, 1982, 1994, 2006, 2018, 2030
Positive Qualities: Honest, faithful, generous, studious, energetic
Negative Qualities: Quiet, cynical, stubborn, eccentric, pessimistic
Suitable Jobs: Writer, teacher, activist, politician, secret agent
Compatible With: Horse, Snake, Monkey, Boar
Must Avoid: Rooster, Ox, Sheep
Ruling Hours: 7 PM to 9 PM
Season: Fall
Ruling Month: October
Sign Direction: West-Northwest
Fixed Element: Metal
Corresponding Western Sign: Libra

Like Shigure, other Dogs are gifted with the ability to see people for who they really are. As, such, Dogs make for excellent advice-givers, as they can so easily see another's shortcomings and quickly point them out in a sensitive, objective and non-hurtful way.

Though Dogs are often cold emotionally and seem distant when in a crowd, they are actually very warm-hearted and love to make friends. Interestingly enough, friendships are often long-lasting, because Dogs always love to listen to others and the friends can never seem to get enough of a Dog's keen advice. Fittingly, a relationship with a Dog is much like the bond between a canine and its master—monogamous and loyal to the end.

Celebrity Dogs:
Alec Baldwin
Kirsten Dunst
Jennifer Lopez
Carrie Anne Moss
Uma Thurman
Snoopy

Possessing the best traits humanity has to offer, Dogs are natural-born leaders and inspire confidence in others. They seldom lose their temper when antagonized, but when they do, it is a surefire way to clear the air around them. These flare-ups can turn hardened rivals into allies as the harsh words being said are never used to air out the other person's dirty laundry or stab them in the back; it is simply a way toward a meeting of minds. Compromise also factors heavily into the Dogs' everyday life and personal dealings with people, as it often leads to much-needed respect and success in their chosen career. Though money is of little value to Dogs, they are never at a loss for finding ways to rake it in when they truly need it.

* Note: If you were born in January or early February, then chances are you are probably the animal of the preceding year. The only way to know for certain is to know on which day Chinese New Year's was held. Example: 1982 actually began on January 25, so anyone born from January 1 to January 24 is actually a Rooster.

Fans Basket

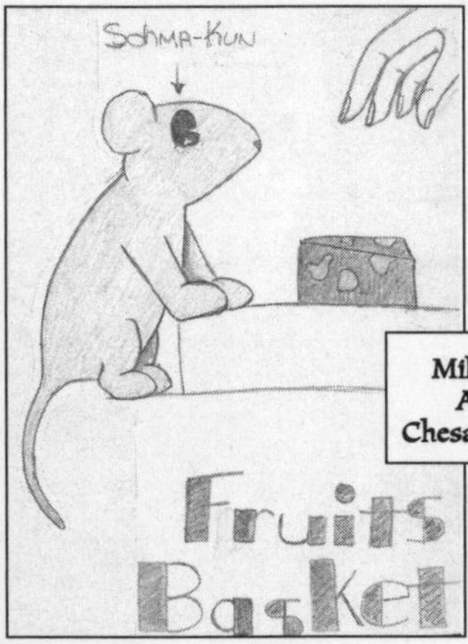
SOHMA-KUN
Fruits
Basket

Millicent P.
Age 18
Chesapeake, VA

Your Rat-Yuki is SOOO adorable! If only he weren't so freaked out by confinement in small rooms, I'd love to keep him as a pet! (Sorry, Sohma-kun...I can't help myself)

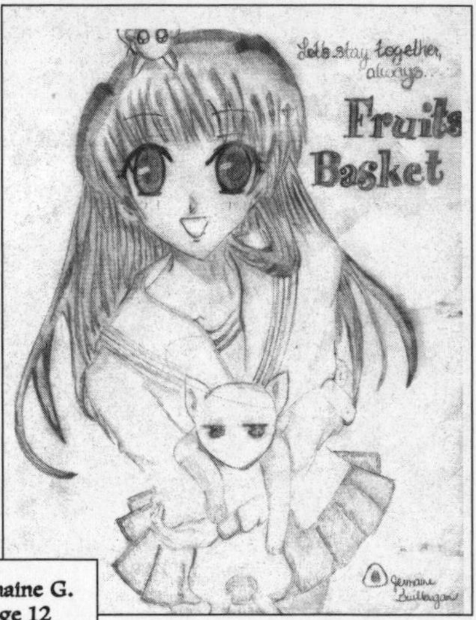
Let's stay together, always.
Fruits
Basket

Jermaine G.
Age 12
Sanford, NC

Kawaii desu ne! Cute, isn't it?!

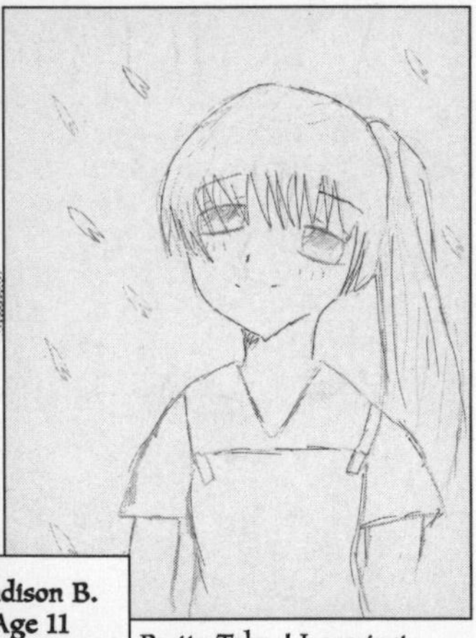

Madison B.
Age 11
Lansing, MI

Pretty Tohru! I can just imagine her enjoying a nice breeze after a day in the garden...

Rachael J.
Age 15
Clermont, FL

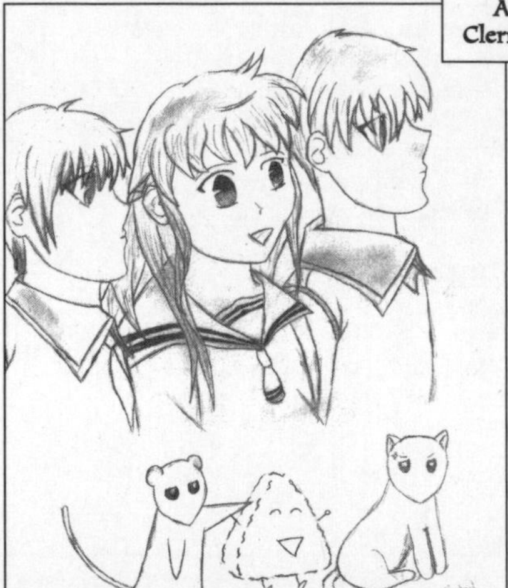

Three students boldly entering their second year... Nice work, Rachael!

Do you want to share your love for *Fruits Basket* with fans around the world? "Fans Basket" is taking submissions of fan art, poetry, cosplay photos, or any other Furuba fun you'd like to share!

How to submit:

1) Send your work via regular mail (NOT e-mail) to:

"Fans Basket"
c/o TOKYOPOP
5900 Wilshire Blvd.
Suite 2000
Los Angeles, CA 90036

2) All work should be in black-and-white and no larger than 8.5" x 11". (And try not to fold it too many times!)

3) Anything you send will not be returned. If you want to keep your original, it's fine to send us a copy.

4) Please include your full name, age, city and state for us to print with your work. If you'd rather us use a pen name, please include that, too.

5) IMPORTANT: If you're under the age of 18, you must have your parent's permission in order for us to print your work. Any submissions without a signed note of parental consent cannot be used.

6) For full details, please check out our website: http://www.tokyopop.com/aboutus/fanart.php

Disclaimer: Anything you send to us becomes the exclusive property of TOKYOPOP Inc. and, as we said before, will not be returned to you. We will have the right to print, reproduce, distribute, or modify the artwork for use in future volumes of Fruits Basket or on the web royalty-free.

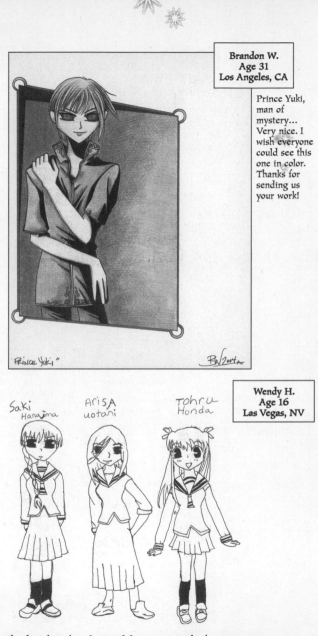

Brandon W.
Age 31
Los Angeles, CA

"PRINCE YUKI"

Prince Yuki, man of mystery... Very nice. I wish everyone could see this one in color. Thanks for sending us your work!

Wendy H.
Age 16
Las Vegas, NV

Saki Hanajima
ArisA uotani
Tohru Honda

The three best friends. You did an amazing job of capturing the nuances of everyone's clothing—and this was before we printed Takaya-sensei's fashion notes in volume 3!

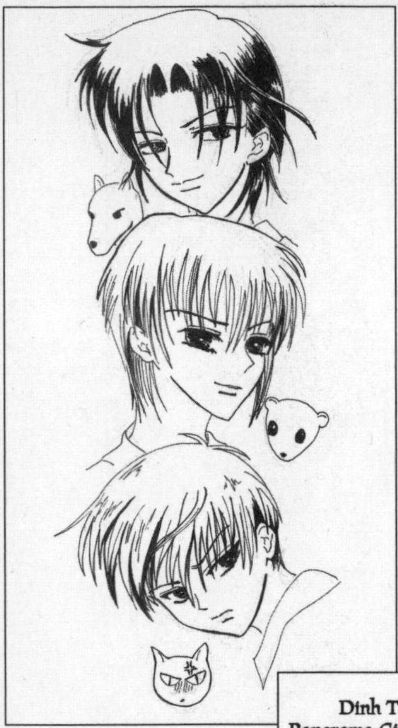

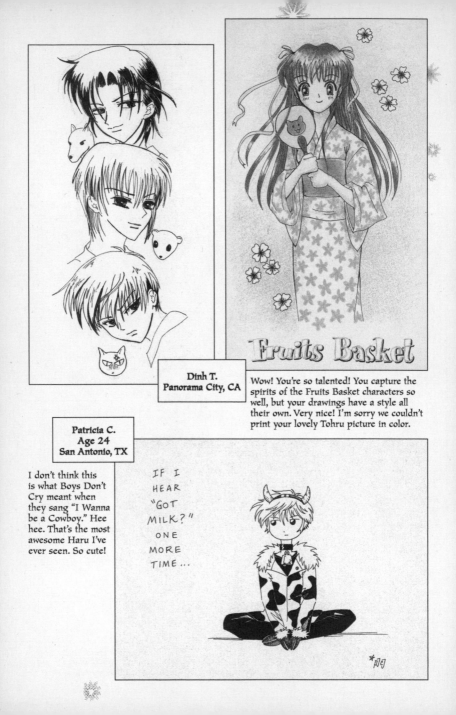

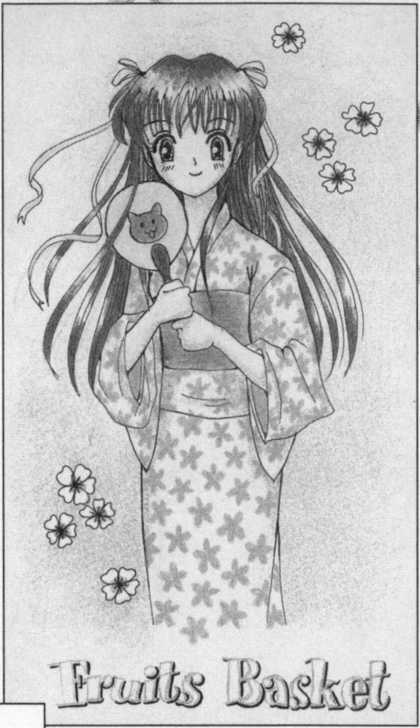
Fruits Basket

Dinh T.
Panorama City, CA

Wow! You're so talented! You capture the spirits of the Fruits Basket characters so well, but your drawings have a style all their own. Very nice! I'm sorry we couldn't print your lovely Tohru picture in color.

Patricia C.
Age 24
San Antonio, TX

I don't think this is what Boys Don't Cry meant when they sang "I Wanna be a Cowboy." Hee hee. That's the most awesome Haru I've ever seen. So cute!

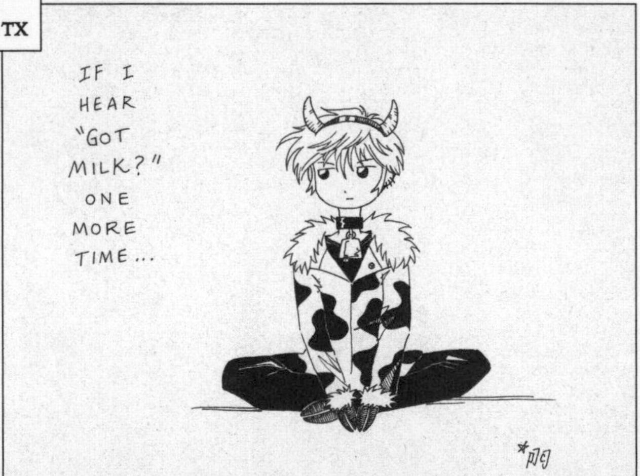
IF I HEAR "GOT MILK?" ONE MORE TIME...

Dear TOKYOPOP,
My name is Jenny and I'm so happy that you guys translate *Fruits Basket*. I totally love this series. I have all the DVDs and manga books 1 and 2. Anyhoo, the reason that I'm writing is I have a question that's been bothering me forever. Why is it that Hatori, the "dragon" sign, turns into a "seahorse"? I've watched the anime over and over and read the manga over and over but still can't figure it out. Also, who are the chicken and horse signs? They weren't in the anime, so I was wondering if the manga will have them. And what sign is Akito? Why is he sick all the time? Can't wait for the answers and for more *Fruits Basket* to come out!

Fellow Anime lover,
Jenny W.
Santa Clarita, CA

Thanks for the kind words, Jenny! You ask a lot of good questions (and not as weird as the ones Takaya-sensei answers back on page 10). I'll see what I can do to help.
1) In Japan, one of the names for a seahorse translates literally to "baby dragon." This is how Hatori refers to himself. Japanese dragons are traditionally associated with the sea, so the bizarre seahorse became associated with the mythical creatures.
2) It's too early to say who the chicken and the horse signs might be, but yes, they do show up in the manga. The anime covers the first 8 volumes of manga, but as of now, the manga is up to 14 volumes in Japan!
3) What's Akito's deal? Well, Takaya-sensei would be really mad if we gave that away. Akito is a deep well of secrets, and he'll continue to be a central part of Fruits Basket until it ends!
To everyone else with burning questions, send them this way and we'll try and answer them.

-Editor

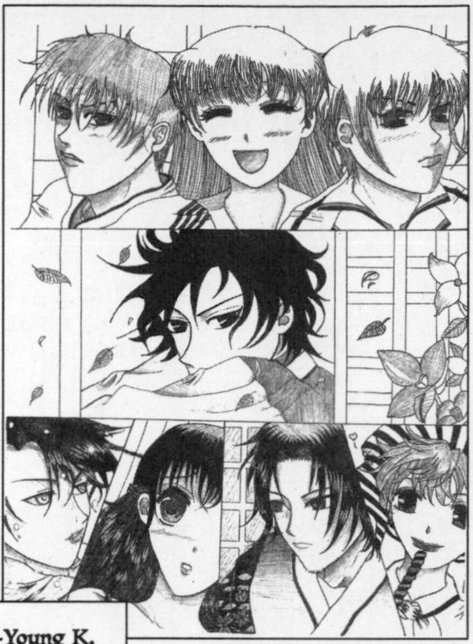

Na-Young K.
Age 15
Sprout Spring, VA

The gang's all here. And who should be at the center of it all but dearest Akito... I like the way you captured Kagura and Shigure's serious side.

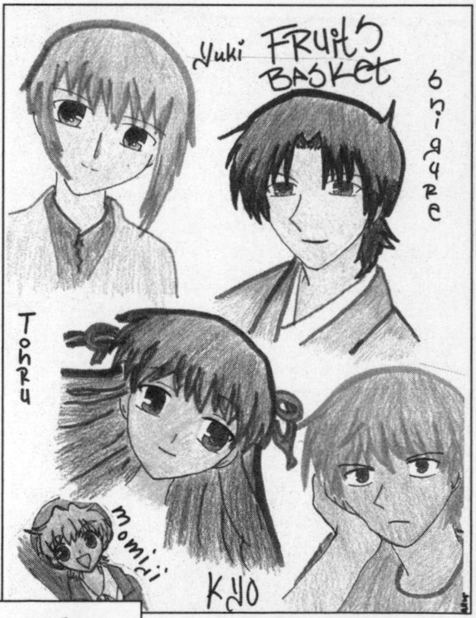
Yuki
FRUitS BASKet
Shigure
Tohru
Momiji
Kyo

Ariadne R.
Age. 14
Daly City, CA

Shigure and his flatmates... and Momiji, too! Yuki looks especially sweet. Thanks, Ariadne!

SOUND EFFECT INDEX

THE FOLLOWING IS A LIST OF THE SOUND EFFECTS USED IN FRUITS BASKET. EACH SOUND IS LABELED BY PAGE AND PANEL NUMBER, SEPARATED BY A PERIOD. THE FIRST DESCRIPTION IS THE PHONETIC READING OF THE JAPANESE, AND IS FOLLOWED BY THE EQUIVALENT ENGLISH SOUND OR A DESCRIPTION.

79.3	patan: shut
81.3	bon: poof
81.5	hira: flutter
81.6	shuu: rustle
81.7	sura: slide
86.1	ban x 2: slap
86.4	guii: grab
95.2a	ha!: gasp
95.2b	jii: stare
96.2	zuun: slump
99.2	zuri: slide
100.1	don doka gashan: crash bang pow
103.2	gyuu: squeeze
103.3	gaba: stumble
112.5	gashii: grab
117.5	ban!: slam
118.1	zudoon: (fanfare)
119.3	zuru x 3: drag
121.5	pori x 2: scratch
123.1	suku: stand
124.5	gutari: confused
129.1	gashi x 2: scrub
129.2	gashi x 3: scrub
140.5	bata x 4: pitter patter
144.3	pa!: shine
159.4	bon: poof
161.3	dan x 2: clack
186.4	wasa x 3: rub
186.5	bikuu: twitch
187.1	kuu: snore
188.2	patan: shut
189.6	saa: rustle
196.1	ta ta ka x 3: dash
16.4	pon: pat
16.5	zuoooo: (creepy aura)
17.3	pekka: perky
19.2	goh: slam
24.1	bah: block
28.3	gyoh: shock
28.5	gah: grab
29.2	bun x 3: shake
31.1	kira x 4: sparkle
32.1	kira x 3: sparkle
33.4	zuru x 3: drag
33.5	patan: shut

KIRA KIRA

キラ キラ

THE "SOUND" OF SPARKLING, USED FOR LITERAL SPARKLING AND FOR GLAMOR SHOTS. IN SHOUJO MANGA, SPARKLES ARE A COMMON ACCESSORY TO BISHOUNEN--ESPECIALLY WHEN THEY'RE SHOWN DRESSED IN A GIRLS' UNIFORM LIKE YUKI!

33.6	kii: creak
35.2	goh: slam
35.4	pachi: (wake up)
35.5	mukuri: rise
36.1	gakkuu: slump
36.2	kiin koon: (school bells)
75.1	ha!: gasp
75.5	zah: rush
77.1	su: shuffle
77.2	don: ta-da!
77.5	gui: squeeze

Add more "Fruits" to your Basket! Collect them all!

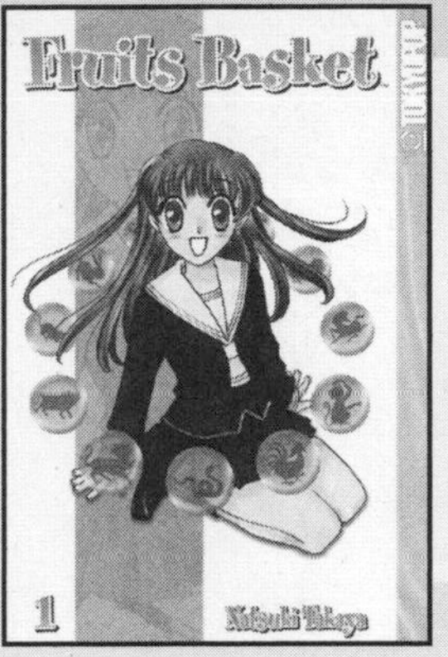

Fruits Basket
1

Volume 1

Tohru Honda was an orphan with no place to go until the mysterious Sohma family offered her a place to call home. Now her ordinary high school life is turned upside-down as she's introduced to the Sohma's world of magical curses and family secrets. Discover for yourself the Secret of the Zodiac in the first volume of *Fruits Basket*!

Volume 2

Ever since Tohru Honda discovered the Zodiac secret of the Sohma clan, her eyes have been opened to a world of magic and wonder. But with such a great secret comes great responsibility. When her best friends Hana-chan and Uo-chan come to the Sohma house for a sleepover, Tohru has her work cut out for her keeping the "Cat" in the bag and the "Dog" on a leash.

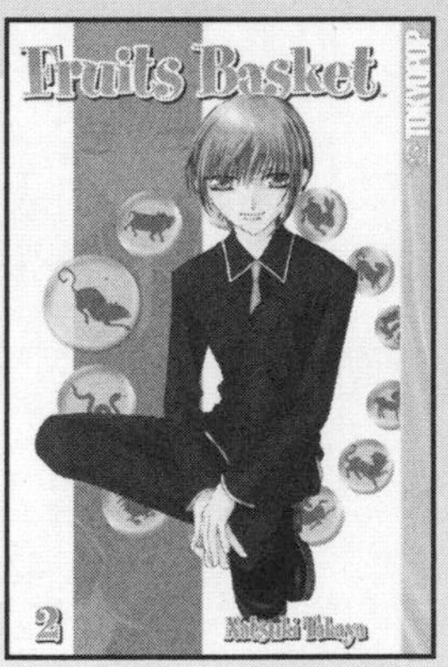

Fruits Basket
2

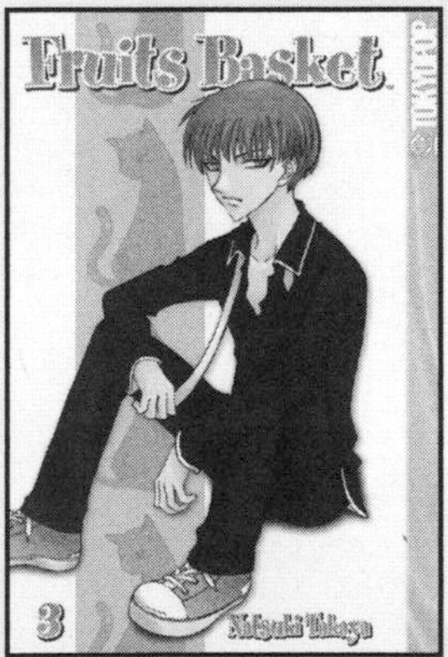

Fruits Basket
3

Volume 3

It's Valentine's Day and you know what that means--lots of chocolates for the cutest boys at school! In this case, it's a pretty close tie between hot-headed Kyo Sohma and Yuki "prince charming" Sohma. Of course the kind-hearted Tohru, guest of the Sohma family, has chocolates for everyone! But when White Day comes around, what will the Sohma family give back? How about a trip to the family hot springs?! Also, a new member of the Zodiac shows up at school to lay the "MOO"ves on Kyo.

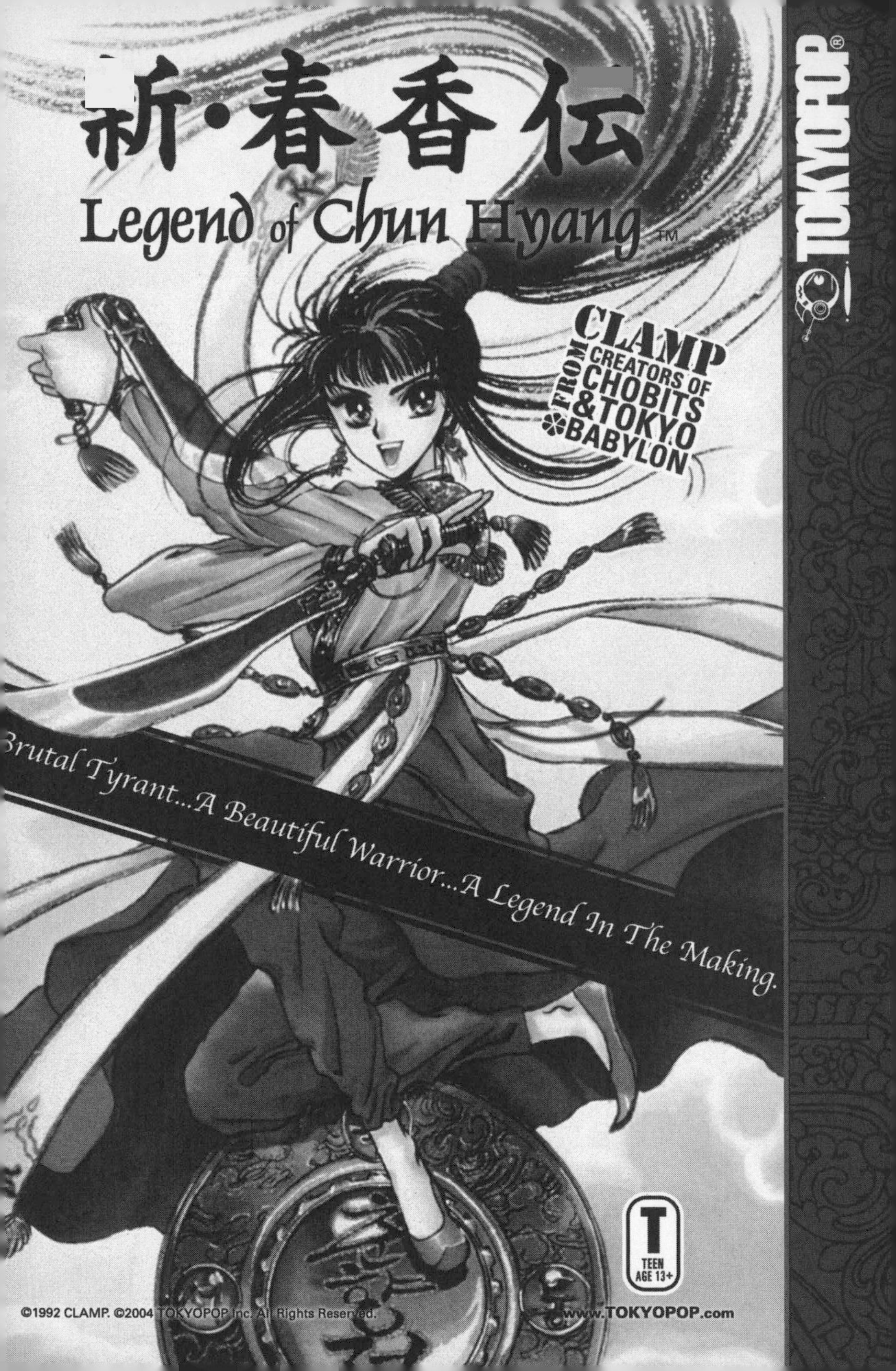
新・春香伝
Legend of Chun Hyang™
FROM CLAMP
CREATORS OF CHOBITS & TOKYO BABYLON
Brutal Tyrant...A Beautiful Warrior...A Legend In The Making.
T
TEEN AGE 13+
TOKYOPOP®
©1992 CLAMP. ©2004 TOKYOPOP Inc. All Rights Reserved.
www.TOKYOPOP.com

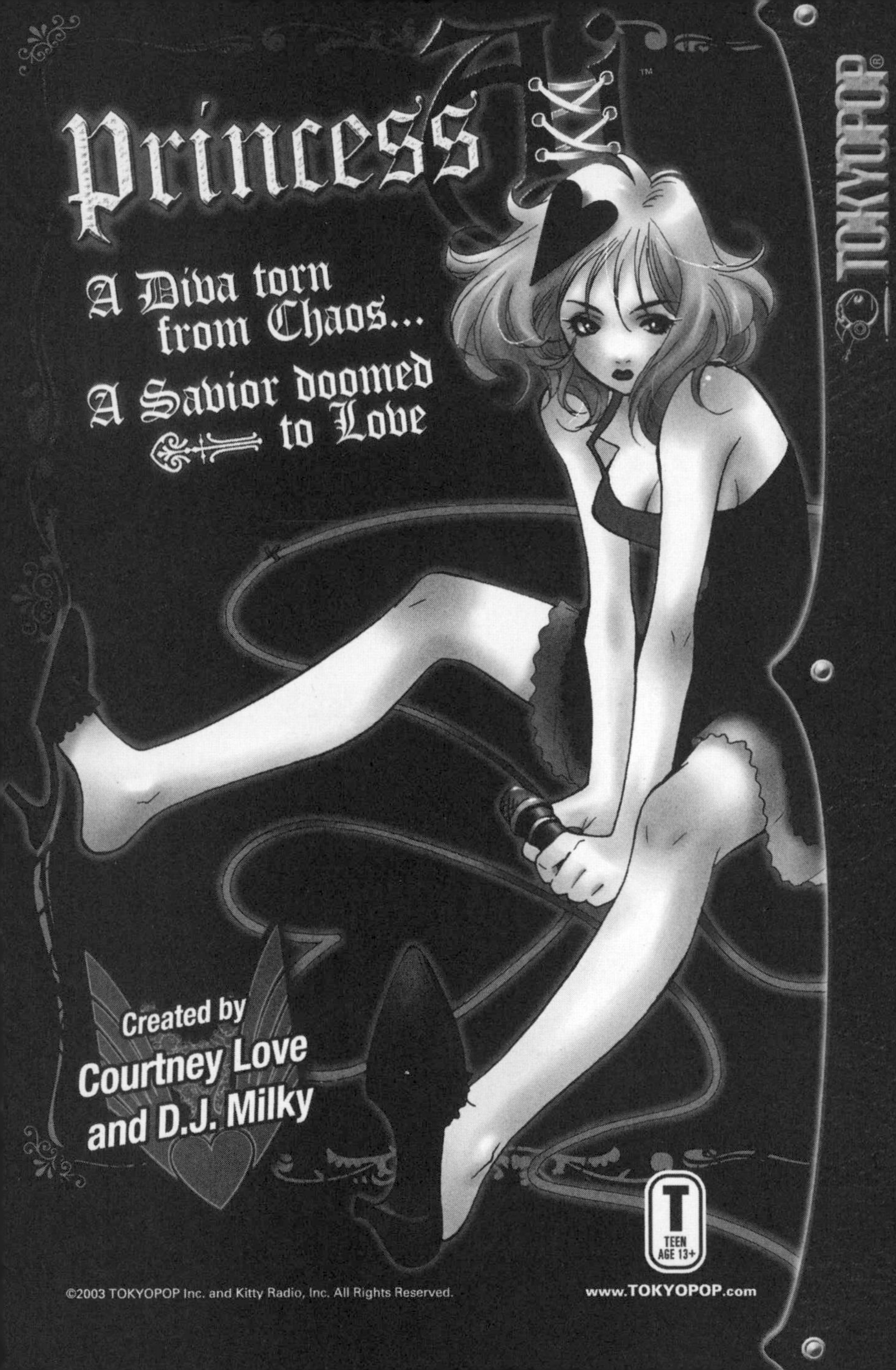
Princess Ai™
A Diva torn from Chaos...
A Savior doomed to Love
Created by
Courtney Love
and D.J. Milky
TOKYOPOP®
T
TEEN
AGE 13+
©2003 TOKYOPOP Inc. and Kitty Radio, Inc. All Rights Reserved.
www.TOKYOPOP.com

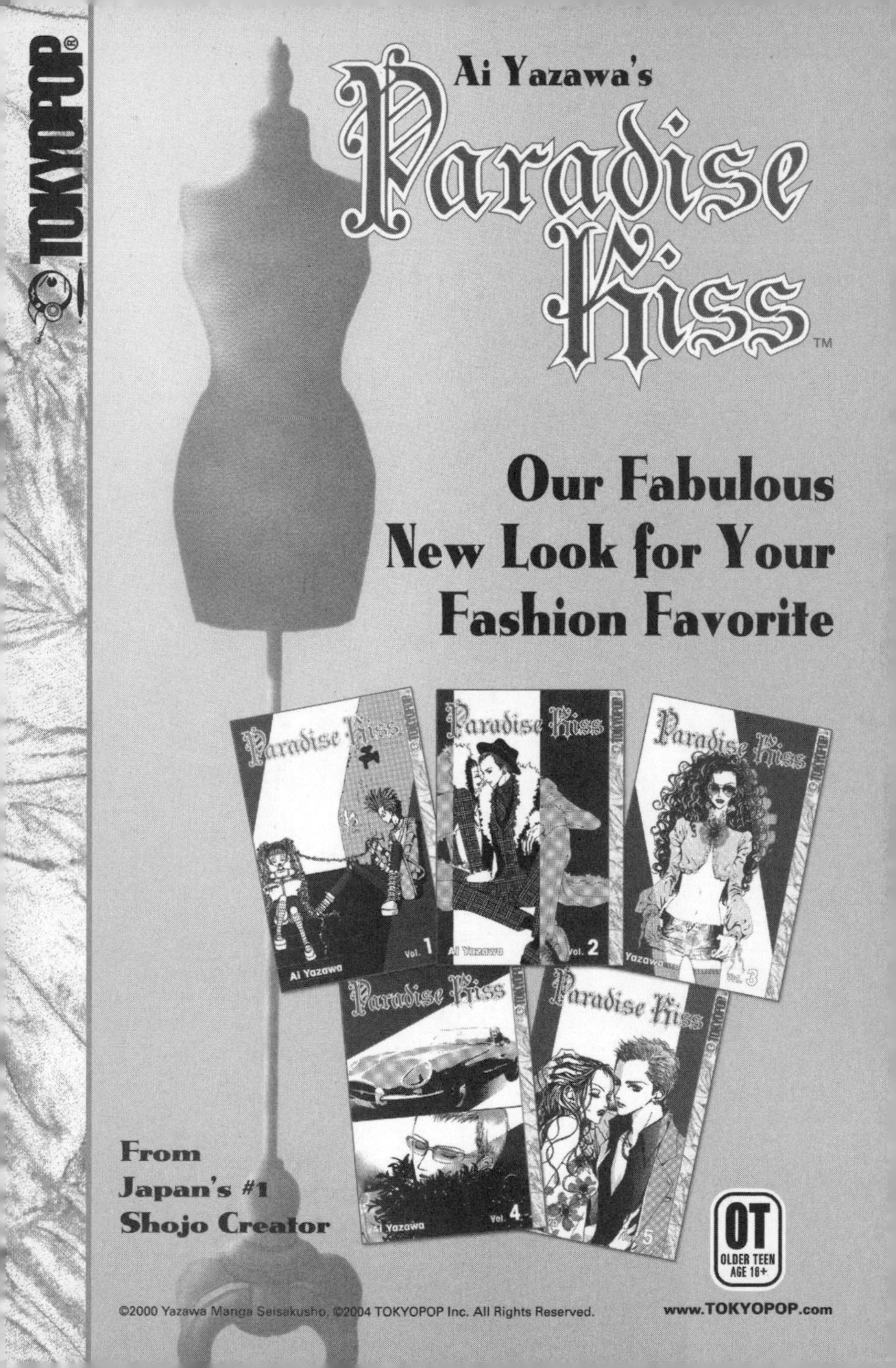
TOKYOPOP®
Ai Yazawa's
Paradise Kiss™
Our Fabulous New Look for Your Fashion Favorite
Paradise Kiss Vol. 1 Ai Yazawa
Paradise Kiss Ai Yazawa Vol. 2
Paradise Kiss Yazawa Vol. 3
Paradise Kiss Ai Yazawa Vol. 4
Paradise Kiss 5
From Japan's #1 Shojo Creator
OT OLDER TEEN AGE 16+
©2000 Yazawa Manga Seisakusho. ©2004 TOKYOPOP Inc. All Rights Reserved.
www.TOKYOPOP.com

The One I Love

watashi no suki na hito

FROM CLAMP
CREATORS OF
CHOBITS
& TOKYO
BABYLON

breathtaking stories of love and romance

T
TEEN
AGE 13+

www.TOKYOPOP.com

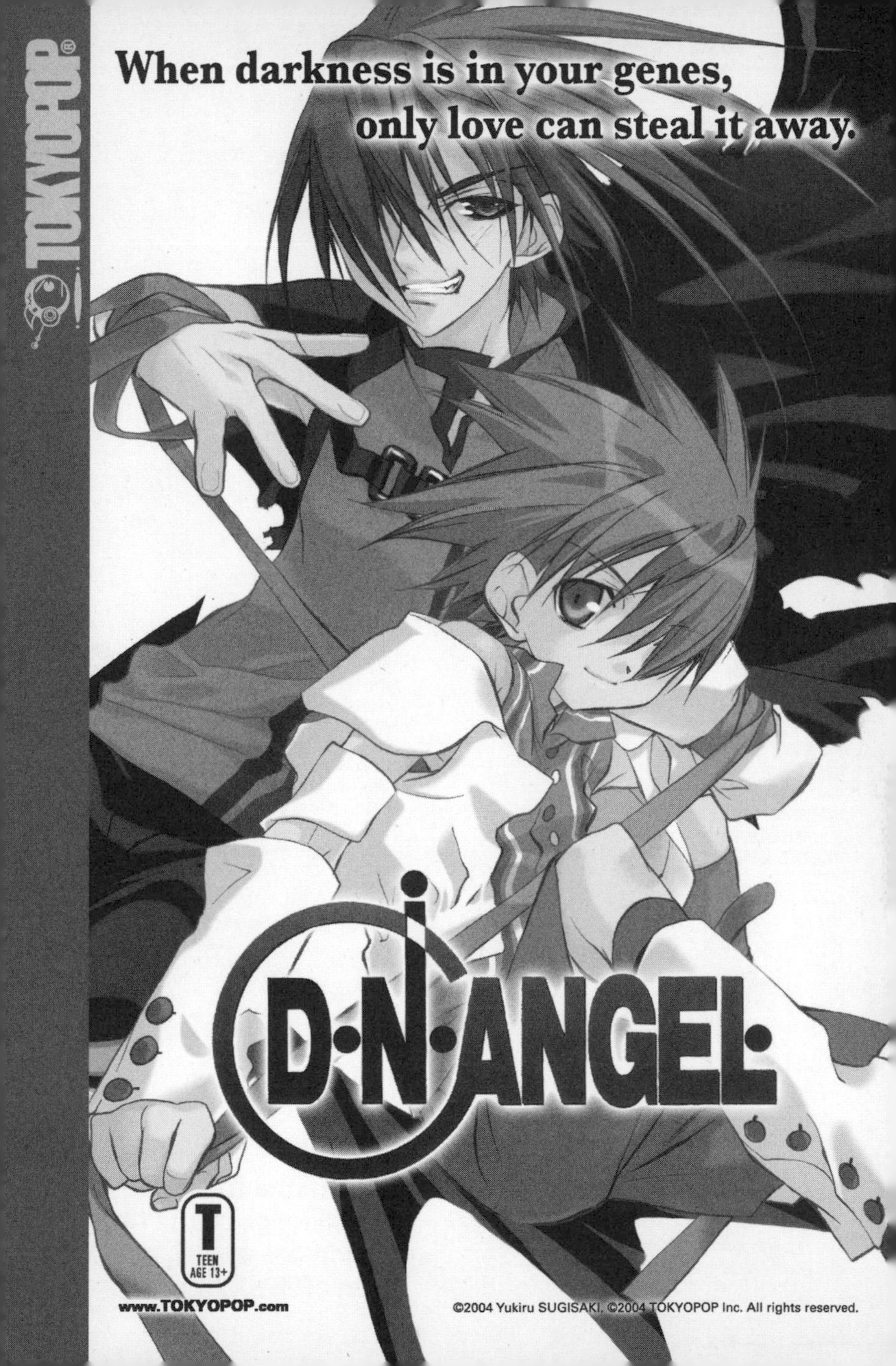
TOKYOPOP
When darkness is in your genes,
only love can steal it away.
D•N•ANGEL
T
TEEN
AGE 13+
www.TOKYOPOP.com
©2004 Yukiru SUGISAKI. ©2004 TOKYOPOP Inc. All rights reserved.

ALSO AVAILABLE FROM TOKYOPOP®

ALSO AVAILABLE FROM ❦TOKYOPOP®

MANGA

.HACK//LEGEND OF THE TWILIGHT
@LARGE
ABENOBASHI: MAGICAL SHOPPING ARCADE
A.I. LOVE YOU
AI YORI AOSHI
ANGELIC LAYER
ARM OF KANNON
BABY BIRTH
BATTLE ROYALE
BATTLE VIXENS
BRAIN POWERED
BRIGADOON
B'TX
CANDIDATE FOR GODDESS, THE
CARDCAPTOR SAKURA
CARDCAPTOR SAKURA - MASTER OF THE CLOW
CHOBITS
CHRONICLES OF THE CURSED SWORD
CLAMP SCHOOL DETECTIVES
CLOVER
COMIC PARTY
CONFIDENTIAL CONFESSIONS
CORRECTOR YUI
COWBOY BEBOP
COWBOY BEBOP: SHOOTING STAR
CRAZY LOVE STORY
CRESCENT MOON
CROSS
CULDCEPT
CYBORG 009
D•N•ANGEL
DEMON DIARY
DEMON ORORON, THE
DEUS VITAE
DIABOLO
DIGIMON
DIGIMON TAMERS
DIGIMON ZERO TWO
DOLL
DRAGON HUNTER
DRAGON KNIGHTS
DRAGON VOICE
DREAM SAGA
DUKLYON: CLAMP SCHOOL DEFENDERS
EERIE QUEERIE!
ERICA SAKURAZAWA: COLLECTED WORKS
ET CETERA
ETERNITY
EVIL'S RETURN
FAERIES' LANDING
FAKE
FLCL
FLOWER OF THE DEEP SLEEP
FORBIDDEN DANCE
FRUITS BASKET
G GUNDAM

GATEKEEPERS
GETBACKERS
GIRL GOT GAME
GIRLS' EDUCATIONAL CHARTER
GRAVITATION
GTO
GUNDAM BLUE DESTINY
GUNDAM SEED ASTRAY
GUNDAM WING
GUNDAM WING: BATTLEFIELD OF PACIFISTS
GUNDAM WING: ENDLESS WALTZ
GUNDAM WING: THE LAST OUTPOST (G-UNIT)
GUYS' GUIDE TO GIRLS
HANDS OFF!
HAPPY MANIA
HARLEM BEAT
I.N.V.U.
IMMORTAL RAIN
INITIAL D
INSTANT TEEN: JUST ADD NUTS
ISLAND
JING: KING OF BANDITS
JING: KING OF BANDITS - TWILIGHT TALES
JULINE
KARE KANO
KILL ME, KISS ME
KINDAICHI CASE FILES, THE
KING OF HELL
KODOCHA: SANA'S STAGE
LAMENT OF THE LAMB
LEGAL DRUG
LEGEND OF CHUN HYANG, THE
LES BIJOUX
LOVE HINA
LUPIN III
LUPIN III: WORLD'S MOST WANTED
MAGIC KNIGHT RAYEARTH I
MAGIC KNIGHT RAYEARTH II
MAHOROMATIC: AUTOMATIC MAIDEN
MAN OF MANY FACES
MARMALADE BOY
MARS
MARS: HORSE WITH NO NAME
MINK
MIRACLE GIRLS
MIYUKI-CHAN IN WONDERLAND
MODEL
MY LOVE
NECK AND NECK
ONE
ONE I LOVE, THE
PARADISE KISS
PARASYTE
PASSION FRUIT
PEACH GIRL
PEACH GIRL: CHANGE OF HEART
PET SHOP OF HORRORS
PITA-TEN

05.11.04T

STOP!

This is the back of the book.
You wouldn't want to spoil a great ending!

This book is printed "manga-style," in the authentic Japanese right-to-left format. Since none of the artwork has been flipped or altered, readers get to experience the story just as the creator intended. You've been asking for it, so TOKYOPOP® delivered: authentic, hot-off-the-press, and far more fun!

DIRECTIONS

If this is your first time reading manga-style, here's a quick guide to help you understand how it works.

It's easy... just start in the top right panel and follow the numbers. Have fun, and look for more 100% authentic manga from TOKYOPOP®!

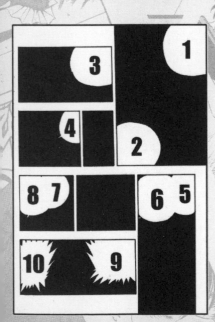